HUNTINGTON LIBRARY PUBLICATIONS

MAP SHOWING THE LOCATION OF THE CALIFORNIA MISSIONS, REPRODUCED
FROM A PAINTING AT MISSION SAN CARLOS, CARMEL.

FRANCISCAN
MISSIONARIES

IN
HISPANIC
CALIFORNIA
1769-1848

A BIOGRAPHICAL DICTIONARY

BY MAYNARD GEIGER, O.F.M.

THE HUNTINGTON LIBRARY · SAN MARINO

1969

*The publication of this volume has been assisted by the
James Irvine Foundation Publication Fund of the Huntington Library.*

CONTENTS

◄§ FOREWORD §►

THIS PRESENTATION of succinct biographies of the 142 Franciscan missionaries who evangelized California between the years 1769 and 1848 is the result of labors begun a quarter of a century ago. Pioneers in California history such as Hubert Howe Bancroft and Zephyrin Engelhardt, O.F.M., indeed, did much significant work in this particular field. The very scattered and often incomplete data concerning the Seraphic Foreign Legion needed, however, to be brought together in one handy reference volume. And subsequently the author was able to gather additional material with correctional value in Spain, Mexico, Rome, and in the United States.

Though every effort was made to obtain the basic data on each friar, the effort was not always successful. If one were to wait until perfection were attained, a biographical dictionary would perhaps never be written. Nor would anyone be served by an attitude so idealistic. Hence this work is neither complete nor final. Rather it should be considered a starting point of assembly and initial correction of existing biographical data.

The data is missing on some of the missionaries and can never be obtained because of the loss or destruction of certain necessary documents. In other instances there has been little of interest recorded about several of the friars either because of the short term of their service or because they did not participate in any prominent events or movements or because their activities did not emerge above ordinary, routine service. Finally, in the case of those friars who left California after their missionary service and who continued to minister in Mexico or Spain, it is most difficult to obtain biographical material. This is especially true if the colleges or provinces did not keep complete dossiers on their activity or if the biographical data was scattered through revolution, war, or secularization of religious institutions. Both in Spain and in Mexico particularly, in consequence of such events, the friars were forced to live outside the religious community.

The sources of biographical data on an individual friar are often widely scattered and must at times be rather painstakingly pieced together. Only one of the friars was the subject of an extensive biography in colonial times, namely Junípero Serra, in the *Relación histórica* by Francisco Palóu. Only one friar, Antonio Peyrí, left a short autobiography in his own hand.

Concise biographies of many other friars, together with appraisals of their talents and abilities, were written by the commissary prefects, Vicente Francisco de Sarría and Mariano Payeras, in 1817 and 1820 respectively, but only for the missionaries then actually under their jurisdiction. Consisting of two lengthy documents, the originals, which are in the Santa Barbara Mission Archives, were drawn up as a result of a request made by Fray Juan Buenaventura Bestard, O.F.M., commissary general of the Indies, resident at Madrid, May 6, 1816. These two documents will be frequently cited in the biographies to follow because of their importance. In many cases short biographies of those who died in California are to be found in the burial registers of the missions where the missionaries were buried.

The official registers of the provinces or colleges where the friars entered the Franciscan order or in which they died at times furnish additional material. But many registers no longer exist. The *reseñas*, too, or official documents of the Spanish government, prepared when the friars left Spain for service in the American missions, also help to round out necessary details. The lists of missionaries serving the California missions were sent by the president to the governor each year. These are retained in the Santa Barbara Mission Archives. The "Libro de Decretos" of San Fernando College, the official record of the college's activity with regard to its personnel, now in the Archivo General de la Nación, Mexico City, has material on the California missionaries not obtainable elsewhere. The registers of the individual missions are especially rich sources of information on the missionaries administering them. These show a day-to-day record of their activity and give the proximate dates of their arrival and departure at a mission. If all these categories of sources were complete, we could have at least a rounded-out, even if sometimes brief, account of each missionary. However, in no one category are all documents available. Still, surprisingly much has been preserved.

The widely scattered sources of biographical information on the missionaries are found principally in the Archivo de Indias, Seville; the archival centers of the various Franciscan provinces and bishoprics of Spain; the Archivo General de la Nación, the

Biblioteca Nacional, and the Biblioteca del Museo Nacional, all in Mexico City; the remains of the archives of the former colleges and provinces of Mexico; and documents in private collections; the Archives of the Propagation of the Faith in Rome; and in California, the Santa Barbara Mission Archives, the Archives of the Archdiocese of San Francisco, the Bancroft Library, Berkeley, and the mission registers scattered in the dioceses to which the several missions belong.

In 1904, Father Zephyrin Engelhardt, O.F.M., visited the California missions and a few other centers where the early registers were kept. The assiduous historian personally examined each register of baptism, marriage, and burial, noting the first and last signatures of each missionary who served a mission, thus computing the length of service of each one at a particular mission. Also he noted the signatures of visiting or temporary missionaries. This was basic and tedious work, as this writer, who made a similar study of the Santa Barbara and Carmel registers, can testify.

Finally, we have in many cases descriptions of the missionaries from the pens of visitors to the missions — such notable persons as George Vancouver, Alfred Robinson, Auguste Duhaut-Cilly, Eugène Duflot de Mofras, Sir George Simpson, and others — as well as pen pictures from contemporary residents such as Angustias de la Guerra y Ord, Eulalia Pérez, Mariano Vallejo, and less well-known soldiers and civilians. Not everything that has been said concerning a missionary can be used in connection with a work such as this. Some items are of only minor importance. Other statements are not well substantiated. The purpose here is to offer a unified essay on each missionary, outlining the chronology of his life, the areas of his activity, the principal contributions resulting from his labors, the physical, spiritual, intellectual, and social description and appraisal of his person, all in a relatively balanced manner.

The conversion of the Indian tribes of California was committed to the apostolic colleges of San Fernando, Mexico City; Our Lady of Guadalupe, Zacatecas; and Santa Cruz, Querétaro. Of these colleges by far the most important was San Fernando. It sent a total of 127 missionaries into Upper California between 1769 and 1833. Zacatecas sent 11 men from 1833 on. Querétaro sent 4 into the Yuma field in 1780. San Fernando College founded the twenty-one missions along the coast from San Diego to Sonoma between 1769 and 1823. The Zacatecans took over the administration of the missions from Soledad to Sonoma in 1833. Querétaro founded the two missions of Purísima Concepción at Fort Yuma and San Pedro y San Pablo de Bicuñer along the Colorado in 1780. These two were destroyed and their four missionaries killed in the uprising of July 1781. They were not refounded in colonial times.

Through the course of seventy-nine years these 142 missionaries spent 2,269 man years, each averaging 16 years of service, to bring into the Christian fold and into the ambient of Hispanic civilization nearly one hundred thousand aborigines, while they also attended to the spiritual needs of the conquering Spaniards and Mexicans in presidios, pueblos, and ranches. Most of the missionaries were born in Spain, the next significant number coming from Mexico. Those of the college of Querétaro were all Spaniards. All of the Zacatecans who labored in California, save one, were natives of Mexico. Most of the Fernandinos were Spaniards, except for a few Mexicans and a few from the Caribbean area.

At this writing, the exact place of origin of ten of the friars of San Fernando College has not been determined. The Spanish origin of the other friars is as follows: the Franciscan province of Cantabria led with thirty. Next came Catalonia with twenty-two. The province of Majorca gave sixteen, followed by that of Aragon with fourteen. Burgos and Estremadura (San Miguel) each gave seven. Galicia sent five; Old Castile (Concepción), five; Andalusia (Los Angeles), four; Castile, four; and Valencia, one. The province of Santa Elena in Cuba provided four. The province of the Holy Gospel, Mexico City, gave one; the province of the Holy Cross (Caribbean area), also one. All of these friars, from whosoever they came originally, first entered San Fernando College and through its auspices were sent to the mission field. Some few were "sons of San Fernando," born in Spain or elsewhere, but who initially became Franciscans at the college itself.

Of the 127 Fernandinos who came to California as missionaries, 58 died at their missions, the rest returning to their college. There they remained either until their deaths or returned to the provinces of origin in Spain or joined other colleges or provinces in Mexico. Two of the Fernandinos were murdered by the Indians. Of the 11 Zacatecans who came to California, 7 returned to Mexico. Two died in California before 1850, and 2 lived on deep into the American period.

The Spanish Franciscans who came to the colleges were obliged by law to serve for at least ten years since their expenses were paid from the royal exchequer. Only Tomás Esténaga did not travel at royal expense. Some of those who entered the colleges never became Indian missionaries but rather home missionaries. About the middle of the eighteenth century the time computation for service began with the departure from Spain.

Not all who became missionaries found their work congenial, nor were all able to meet the physical hardships or psychological impact inherent in their vocation. A surprising number suffered ill health in California and had to return to Mexico for this reason alone, sometimes before the expiration of the term of service. A lesser number succumbed to mental afflictions.

A few died prematurely. Fifty-seven spent less than ten years at the missions, thirty-six labored in them from ten to twenty years; twenty-two served from twenty to thirty years; twenty-two more from thirty to forty years; while five served for forty years or more. The majority served beyond the requirement of the law. Julián López died of consumption after a few months. Ramón Abella served for forty-four years.

As in all other departments of life, there were shadows in the relatively small group of this corps of 142 missionaries. By far the greater number persevered with fidelity to their vows of priesthood and Franciscan life. At the top we find the leaders, men of talent, ability, and eminent virtue, who accomplished great things against overwhelming odds, six of whom sacrificed their lives, while most were in a dangerously exposed condition. The preponderance might be classed as men of ordinary ability, zeal, learning, and virtue. They were good and faithful workers. Only one Spaniard, toward the close of the mission period, bears the proven stigma of immorality; two became alcoholics, one of whom attempted suicide. Two became miscreant in behavior, who evidently needed psychiatric treatment as well as paternal correction. The range of character and personal characteristics was wide and diversified.

The Zacatecans as a class were inferior to the Fernandinos, considering the fewness of their number. Four of the eleven had reputations for immorality and other unclerical behavior. Three others had reputations for great probity, even saintliness. All four Quere-tarans early in life won a martyr's crown.

It was this corps of soldiers of the cross who two hundred years ago effected the first triumphs of religion and civilization in what is now the golden state of California. Even the least of them deserves an honorable mention for endeavor if not for accomplishment. California was destined to grow and prosper until it became the most populous and one of the richest states of the American Union. Never would its condition be as primitive, as rugged, or as difficult as it was in the beginning. Soldier and missionary alike referred to California in colonial days as "this last corner of the earth." To many it seemed exile. What was accomplished here with the material at hand and at a disadvantageous distance from civilization could only be accomplished by men who made sacrifices and who were dedicated. All were pioneers who bore the burden and the heat of the day as well as the solitude of night. A number were outstanding. Many were merely successful. All tried and a few were failures. Each one deserves the niche in history he earned. *Memoria eorum manet in aeternum.*

As to the presentation of the matter, the author has deemed it fitting to be as condensed as possible. A parade of interminable footnotes was eschewed to lessen the bulk of the book. Lengthy citations from manuscript and printed material are acknowledged, while a generous bibliography indicates the principal fonts of information. The frequent abbreviation SBMA signifies the Santa Barbara Mission Archives.

The author, of course, has not been able to verify all allegations of earlier writers with regard to the probity or characteristics of certain missionaries. Often he cites merely what has been written, not necessarily agreeing with the opinion stated. Visitors to missions, especially, may have been favorably impressed or unfavorably disposed in sizing up the characters of the friars whom they met, may not have stayed long enough to form a rounded-out evaluation, and in some cases were not actual witnesses of what they record, depending rather on hearsay or rumor concerning past events. In certain instances the author has been able to rehabilitate the reputation of certain friars who were maligned; while, on the other hand, he has added more damaging material than heretofore offered concerning those whose reputations were unworthy of their calling. Where statements were made without proof or reference, the matter, so to speak, was thrown out of court. What is gratuitously asserted may be gratuitously denied. The purpose here has been to introduce the known facts even though resolution of all questions in connection with some individuals has not been possible.

Now let us call the roll of famous men that were our fathers long ago . . . . Here were men that had power and bore rule, men that excelled in strength or in the wisdom that dowered them . . . . Here were men that had skill to devise melodies, to make songs and set them down in writing . . . . Here were men noble of aim, that dwelt peacefully in their homes. They were the glories of their race, the ornament of their times . . . . These were men of tender conscience; their deeds of charity will never be forgotten . . . . Their bodies rest in peace; their name lasts on, age after age. Their wisdom is yet a legend among the people; wherever faithful men assemble, their story is told.

— ECCLESIASTES

Their civilization, such as it is, their agriculture and the astonishing multiplication of herds of all classes, their small industry and knowledge, although imperfect, of the arts, the commerce which this combination of circumstances has allowed . . . the reduction of many thousands of gentiles who have been converted from savage wandering vagabonds into established families and useful workers in agriculture and the arts, and into men capable of social relationships — all this is owing exclusively to the missionaries . . . . A weak population had no protection other than the missionaries. In these it saw and still sees today its fathers and protectors. It is they who have educated it from infancy to most advanced age, inculcating with the affability appropriate to their calling the principles of the religion which we profess. It is they who have formed their customs and guided their consciences. From them they have received and are receiving protection in their undertakings, succor in their necessities, remedy for the infirmities which afflict them, consolation in their troubles, and counsel in their doubts and anxieties. Such a population . . . must of necessity . . . have become deeply attached to men from whom it received so much, who were the only ones it has found interested in its welfare. This is the reason for the prestige and influence which the missionaries enjoy in that country.

— CARLOS ANTONIO CARRILLO, *Exposition . . . of the Pious Fund*

ABELLA, JOSÉ RAMÓN (1764-1842)

Fray José Ramón Abella was born at Monforte, archdiocese of Zaragosa, Spain, May 28, 1764, entered the Franciscan order at the friary of Nuestra Señora de Jesús, Zaragosa, March 6, 1784, and pronounced his vows on March 7, the following year. Ordained a priest, September 20, 1788, he subsequently held the offices of preacher and confessor. When Abella left Spain for the Indies, he was vicar of the friary of San Antonio at Mora in the Franciscan province of Aragón. At Cádiz, awaiting embarcation, September 9, 1794, the friar was declared (according to passport records) to be thirty years of age, of regular height, with dark hair and eyes, large temples, thick lips, with a scar on his chin, and having a smoothly shaven face.

With twenty-two companions, Abella sailed from Cádiz aboard the *Santiago de España,* May 8, 1795, under the commissary, Manuel Arévalo. Disembarking at Vera Cruz, Mexico, June 26, the same year, he traveled on to Mexico City, where he entered San Fernando College. As a volunteer for the California missions, Abella with seven companions sailed from San Blas on the *Concepción* and arrived at Santa Barbara, California, May 8, 1798. Abella's first assignment under the administration of President Fermín Francisco de Lasuén was to Mission San Francisco, where he arrived in July. He served there and at the presidio until sometime after April 22, 1819.

When Abella arrived at San Francisco, the mission had been in existence for twenty-two years. During his missionary career there, between the end of 1798 and the end of 1818, the number of baptisms rose from 1,975 to 5,797. After Abella had written a report to Governor Pablo Solá on January 29, 1817, on the causes of Indian diseases and mortality at his mission, it was decided to found an *asistencia* at San Rafael in the warmer climate north of the Golden Gate. This was done on December 14, that same year, with Abella in attendance. Later, this *asistencia* became a full-fledged mission. On November 11, 1814, Abella signed the ethnological report on the customs and beliefs of the San Francisco Indians, requested by the government, and, though written in the hand of his companion Juan Sainz de Lucio, it may well have been the composition of Abella himself, the senior missionary and the longest in residence.

San Francisco, as a port of call, gave Abella an opportunity to entertain such famous guests as Nikolai Petrovich Rezánov and his Russian party in 1806, Otto von Kotzebue in 1816, and Camille de Roquefeuil in 1817.

From this same port Abella set out on two explorations into the interior in 1811 and 1817. On October 15, 1811, the friar with Buenaventura Fortuny of Mission San Jose, under Sergeant José Sánchez and fifty-five personnel, departed in launches to reconnoiter the lower reaches of the Sacramento and San Joaquin rivers. On this occasion the friars named the two points separating San Francisco and San Pablo bays, San Pedro and San Pablo. After exploring San Pablo Bay, the party sailed through Suisun Bay and Carquinez Strait and entered successively both the San Joaquin and Sacramento rivers. The first was named San Juan Capistrano, the second, San Francisco. Masses were said at several places, and baptisms were administered to the dying and aged. The explorers came into contact with the Indians of from fifteen to twenty rancherias. Abella kept a diary of the exploration — the deepest penetration into the interior of California by water up to that date. The party returned to San Francisco on October 30.

Again on May 13, 1817, Abella with Fray Narciso Durán of Mission San Jose, under Lieutenant Luís Argüello, set out from San Francisco in launches and explored the Sacramento River (applying to the river and the confluent San Joaquin their modern names) for a distance of about forty leagues, reaching the area between present-day Clarksburg and Freeport. On this occasion Durán kept a diary of the expedition. Masses were said for the first time along the banks of the Sacramento on Ascension Day, May 15, and on the following Sunday. The party returned to San Francisco on May 26.

Abella's second tour of duty in California was at Mission San Carlos, Carmel, where he remained from 1819 to 1833. California's second mission, founded by Junípero Serra on June 3, 1770, was just short of being half a century old. During Abella's years of administration there, the resident Indian population dwindled from 397 to 185. Abella surrendered the mission to his Zacatecan successor, Fray Rafael Moreno, who with Governor José Figueroa and other Mexican missionaries had arrived at Monterey, January 15, 1833, to take over the northern missions. While at Carmel, Abella, like his predecessors, also attended to the spiritual needs of the *gente de razón* at Monterey.

When, after 1821, Mexico became independent of Spain, Abella declined to take the oath to uphold the constitution of 1824 but promised to continue to serve in matters spiritual and temporal with fidelity corresponding to his priestly office. Governor José María Echeandía recommended that Abella be given his passport in 1829. However, because of the need for missionaries in California and the government's inability to replace them, this proposal was not acted upon.

Abella, in a state of ill health, was assigned to Mission San Luis Obispo in July 1834, where he remained until November 1841, taking care of Mission San Miguel also from December 1840 until July 1841. At San Luis Obispo, Abella, ill and in impoverished surroundings,

4

witnessed the decline of the mission consequent to its secularization. The distasteful presence there of Angel Ramírez, an ex-Mercedarian friar from Mexico now a government official who lived in open immorality, added to the dreariness of the local situation. Abella tried to bring the ex-friar back to higher standards of living but was unsuccessful.

When Faxon Dean Atherton, a young man from New England, visited San Luis Obispo on business on June 27, 1836, he met Abella and described the encounter in his diary:

> The Padre whose name is Ramon is without exception the most dirty brutish looking person I ever met with. His hands are so covered with a crust of dirt that I question whether a sharp knife would cut through it without their being first soaked some hours in water. His nostrils and the corners of his mouth are filled with snuff which he is continually taking and by continually rubbing his eyes with his dirty hands they have become inflamed and are complete running sores. And I should suppose that his dress has never been changed since it was first put on some years since.[1]

It might be added here that Abella had complained of eye trouble as early as 1800, according to a statement of Lasuén.

Eugène Duflot de Mofras, who visited Abella in 1841, gave a different view of Abella:

> In the Mission building, which is now in ruin, we found, reduced to a state of greatest want, the oldest Spanish Franciscan of California, the Rev. Fr. Ramón Abella, an Aragonese .... The Mission has suffered such devastations that the poor friar was bedded on an ox-hide, and used the horn of an ox as a drinking cup, and for nourishment had only some strips of meat dried in the sun. The venerable Father distributes the little that is sent to him among some Indian children, who with their parents occupy the tumble-down houses that surround the Mission. Several kind-hearted persons, and the Rev. Fr. Presidente Durán himself, have offered a home and comfort to Fr. Abella, but he always declines and says that he wants to die at his post .... He bears without murmuring his old age and the privations and humiliations which poverty entails.[2]

Beneath the crust there was still a golden heart.

In 1841, Abella was transferred to Mission Purisima. He was described as in his dotage, though Engelhardt, citing a letter of the missionary of the period, questions the applicability of the epithet. To prepare himself for death, Abella went to Mission Santa Ines where, after receiving the sacraments devoutly, he died on May 24, 1842. He was buried by Fray José Joaquín Jimeno at that mission on the Epistle side of the sanctuary about two varas from the wall.

At the time of his death, Abella was the senior Fernandino missionary in California and the last survivor of those who had come before 1800. He had spent forty-four years in California, the longest record of service of any missionary in the province. He had seen the missions at the height of their prosperity and had witnessed their secularization and ruin. He was four days short of seventy-eight years when he died and had spent fifty-eight years in the Franciscan order.

In the course of his California ministry Abella had firsthand acquaintance with most of the missions between Santa Barbara and San Rafael. While stationed at San Francisco, he ministered at times at San Carlos, San Jose, and Santa Clara; when in residence at San Carlos, he officiated at San Juan Bautista, San Antonio, San Miguel, and San Luis Obispo. From the latter mission he ministered at San Antonio, San Miguel, and Purisima.

Both Friars Vicente Francisco de Sarría and Mariano Payeras, under whom he served, left biographical sketches of Abella in 1817 and 1820 respectively. Sarría declared that the friar administered Mission San Francisco with great fidelity, that he possessed a sincere and religious character, was experienced with the Indians, and was solicitous and patient in his labors. He ventured to say that Abella was one of the best missionaries in the entire territory. Payeras wrote that Abella's merit was great, that he had full aptitude for missionary work among the *gente de razón* and the Indians, and that he was a fit subject for one or other office of honor in the Franciscan order.

General Mariano Vallejo, speaking at the San Francisco Centennial in 1876, recalled the friars he had known, and among those "worthy ministers of God and indefatigable apostles" he mentioned Abella. Mrs. W. E. McKee, daughter of Estevan Munrás, who had known Abella at Monterey, told Engelhardt in 1907: "Padre Abella on Sundays used to come to Monterey on horseback with a little Indian boy from the Mission to celebrate holy Mass.... There was no house for the priest near the church at Monterey, wherefore Father Abella and his attendant would take meals at our house.... Father Abella would have his sleeve pocket full of apples for the children."[3]

[1] Doyce B. Nunis, Jr., ed. *The California Diary of Faxon Dean Atherton 1836-1839* (San Francisco, 1964), p. 22.

[2] Engelhardt, *Mission San Luis Obispo*, pp. 141-142.

[3] Engelhardt, *Mission San Carlos Borromeo*, p. 174.

ALTIMIRA, JOSÉ (1787-1860?)

Fray José Altimira was born at Barcelona, Catalonia, Spain, in 1787 and there joined the Franciscan order and was ordained to the priesthood. He sailed from Cádiz shortly after June 14, 1819, on *El Relámpago*, being thirty-two years old. After entering San Fernando College, Mexico City, he set out with Friars Francisco González de Ibarra, Tomás Esténaga, and Blas Ordaz for California, arriving at Monterey early in August 1820. There the commissary prefect, Mariano Payeras, chose him as secretary for an official visitation he was to make. Altimira with Payeras signed the official registers at Santa Clara on September 19 and at San Francisco, September 28. In his biographical sketches composed in 1820, Payeras wrote of Altimira: "His actions will reveal his merits; for this he lacks neither talent nor still less application."

Altimira's first assignment was to Mission San Francisco, where the registers indicate that he baptized between October 3, 1820, and July 25, 1823. The cold climate and unhealthful conditions prevailing at Mission San Francisco were recognized facts. For those reasons Mission San Rafael had been founded on December 14, 1817, first, indeed, only as an *asistencia* to San Francisco. A site still farther north appealed to Altimira. He broached the subject of founding a mission there to Payeras and to the Mexican commissioner, Agustín Fernández de San Vicente, during their northern visit in October 1822. At a later date, Altimira contended that Payeras had approved his plan and had authorized him to put it into effect. On March 22, 1823, he drew up a memorandum on the project, presented it to the legislature at Monterey, which in Bancroft's opinion, was done at the instigation of Governor Luís Antonio Argüello. The assembly approved the plan on April 9. It provided for the evacuation of Missions San Francisco and San Rafael and the removal of the Indians to Sonoma.

Altimira's appeal to the legislature was not only unprecedented, it was without legal basis. Before Mexican independence, missions had been founded only after permission had been granted by San Fernando College and the approval of the viceroy had been obtained. Vicente Francisco de Sarría, successor to Payeras as commissary prefect, contended that the arrangements between Altimira and the legislature had no binding effect in law until they had been approved by the federal authorities in Mexico. Fray Juan Amorós, Altimira's superior at San Francisco, sent a protest to Argüello. The latter forwarded the pertinent documents to Mexico.

Altimira wrote to Fray José Señán, the mission president residing at San Buenaventura, informing him of what he intended to do but, without waiting for an answer, proceeded with his plans. On June 25, 1823, he set out with a military escort under *Alférez* José Antonio Sánchez and a civilian deputy for an exploratory trip through the northern country. The party passed through present-day San Rafael, Petaluma, Sonoma, Napa, and the Suisun Valley, according to Sánchez' and Altimira's diaries of the reconnaissance, and the site of Sonoma was considered the best place for the mission. On July 4 the missionary set up the cross and said Mass; thus was the new mission, San Francisco de Asís, founded. The expedition returned to San Francisco on July 16.

Señán was amazed at "the summary and illegal" procedures of the

7

assembly as well as at the audacity of Altimira. Close to death at the time, Señán wrote to Sarría at Monterey declaring that he was not adverse to the transfer but condemned the manner in which it was done. Sarría, after consulting with Estevan Tapis and Narciso Durán, wrote to Altimira reprobating his action.

Before this letter arrived, Argüello had asked Altimira why the transfer of missions had not been made and advised the latter not to wait for the permission of his superiors. Argüello sent letters to Señán, to Amorós, and to the San Francisco presidio commander to the same effect. Altimira thereupon set out with Lieutenant Ignacio Martínez, August 12, 1823, for San Rafael, where he made out an inventory and then returned to San Francisco. On the twenty-third, he set out with an escort for Sonoma, where he arrived two days later, and began the work of constructing a granary, irrigation ditch, corral, and other structures. On August 31 Sarría's letter of reprobation arrived.

According to Bancroft, Altimira became furious, and Engelhardt states that Altimira's letter to Argüello justifies the use of that expression. "I wish to know whether the diputación has any authority in this province, and if these men [his superiors] can overthrow Your Honor's wise provision. I came here to convert gentiles and to establish new missions. If I cannot do it here, where as we all agree is the best spot in California for the purpose, I will leave the country."[1] Altimira's conceit, self-will, and audacity were exposed in his words and his actions.

Argüello backed the young missionary. Sarría, in a letter to Argüello, September 5, 1823, elaborated on the eleven reasons why the founding of the mission was wrong. Argüello's answer dwelt on the fact that the missionaries had made no progress in converting the northern Indians in fifty years. The secular power intended at least to see that the temporal conquest of the area take place.

As a result a compromise was effected. The newly founded mission was allowed to remain, and Altimira was acknowledged as its minister. But he was to be the associate of the missionary at San Rafael. Neither San Rafael nor San Francisco was vacated. The mission at Sonoma, new San Francisco de Asís, was renamed San Francisco Solano to avoid confusion. By April 4, 1824, a new mission church, 105 by 24 feet, constructed of boards, had been completed and dedicated.

Altimira complained to the governor that some of his fellow missionaries, particularly Durán of Mission San Jose, had not furnished him with all the necessary aid. He stated, moreover, that too much liberty had been allowed the Indians in permitting them to choose their abode and that a show of military might would be of help. To this Sarría reported that Indians were running away from Sonoma because they did not like Altimira's ways.

Still the mission continued to develop. Altimira established Rancho Santa Eulalia near Suisun. At the end of 1824, there were 602 Christianized Indians at the mission, the majority of whom had come from Missions San Francisco, San Jose, and San Rafael. Altimira's last baptism at Sonoma occurred on August 3, 1826, his successor being Buenaventura Fortuny of Mission San Jose. Before leaving Sonoma, however, Altimira saw his mission settlement burned by a band of Indians. With some faithful neophytes he retreated to San Rafael.

On June 30, 1826, Altimira declined to take the oath upholding the Mexican constitution of October 4, 1824, maintaining that the oath would contravene "the higher law of God."

Altimira's name appears in the Baptismal Register of Mission San Carlos between December 14, 1826, and February 17, 1827. Finally, he was stationed at Mission San Buenaventura until January 20, 1828. At the latter mission, when he heard of the Mexican decree of December 20, 1827, that all Spaniards would be expelled from the country, he again took the situation into his own hands. Not waiting to be ejected by force, he journeyed to Santa Barbara and from there, with Fray Antonio Ripoll, obtained passage on the American brig, *The Harbinger,* under the command of Captain Joseph Steele. The two friars left Santa Barbara stealthfully on January 23, 1828, under the very nose of Governor José María Echeandía who happened to be there at the time. He notified the federal authorities who in turn communicated the news to San Fernando College where nothing was known of the flight. Ripoll had served his ten years in California as the law required, Altimira about seven.

Before leaving Santa Barbara, January 23, Altimira addressed a letter to his friend and recent convert, George Coleman, announcing his intended flight. He left the keys of the mission with Fray Antonio Jayme of Santa Barbara and asked Coleman to watch over the mission until a new missionary could be assigned.

The flight of the two padres caused a sensation and gave rise to rumors and gossip. Altimira, particularly, was accused of taking money with him which had belonged to the mission. An investigation was held at Santa Barbara, February 1, 1828. Nothing was missing from San Buenaventura, nor was there any knowledge of missing money. Without doubt, Altimira, like Ripoll, who paid for his passage from stipends which had accrued to him, used the same legitimate means. No information concerning Altimira's activity in Europe is available except for a report, recorded by Bancroft, that as late as 1860 the missionary was still living at Tenerife on the Canary Islands.

Altimira was a sort of "Young Turk" missionary, a type that would not be frustrated. If legal entanglements were in the way, he meant to take action nevertheless. He did found the last of the twenty-one missions, the only one established under Mexican auspices. The founding was not legitimate, but it was legitimatized.

[1] *Missions and Missionaries*, III, 181-182.

AMESTOY, MARCOS (1778-?)

Fray Marcos Amestoy was born at Treviño in the diocese of Calahorra, Spain, in 1778. He was recruited for the service of San Fernando College by the commissary, Baldomero López, leaving his native country in 1803 as a student preacher. He sailed on the *San Miguel* alias *Sagrada Familia* from Cádiz shortly after June 20 and arrived at Vera Cruz in August of the same year. At the time of his departure, Amestoy was described in the official government report as of regular height, of light complexion, with a pockmarked face, scant beard, black hair and eyes.

By December 22, 1803, at San Fernando College, he had already volunteered for the California missions and had received approval. With Friars Pedro de la Cueva, Pedro Múñoz, and José Sánchez, Amestoy set out from the college, continued on from Guadalajara, April 23, 1804, finally sailing from San Blas and arriving at San Francisco, August 14, that same year.

Amestoy's one place of service in California was at Mission Santa Barbara to which locale President Estevan Tapis had assigned him by October 1, 1804, and where he ministered until July 14, 1813.

At Santa Barbara, Amestoy was the associate, chiefly, of Fray Luís Gil y Taboada. There he witnessed the extensive building program that took place between 1804 and 1812, the year when the earthquake of December occurred. He officiated twice at Mission Santa Ines, in 1805 and 1810. It appears that Rancho San Marcos, belonging to Mission Santa Barbara but on the Santa Ines side of the mountains, was named after him.

Stricken with paralysis, which deprived him of the use of one arm and leg, he did not retire to the college until September 22, 1815. By the time he arrived at Tepic, however, his health had greatly improved. He soon asked to be disaffiliated from the college, which request was granted. The place and time of his death are unknown.

While Amestoy signed the annual reports of the mission and made many an entry in the Mission Santa Barbara registers, not a single letter written by him has been found either in the mission archives or in those of the archdiocese of San Francisco. Apparently, he was not involved in any particular issue, personal or public, was faithful to his duties, and served out his ten years.

AMORÓS, JUAN (1773-1832)

Fray Juan Amorós was born at Porrera, Catalonia, Spain, in the archdiocese of Tarragona, October 10, 1773, and was baptized on the following day.[1] He entered the Franciscan order at Gerona, April 28, 1791, and made his profession on April 30, in the following year. He was ordained a priest at Solsona in December 1797 and subsequently held the offices of preacher and confessor. Amorós, recruited for San Fernando College, Mexico City, by Baldomero López, left his province, March 4, 1803, for Cádiz, whence he sailed for America. On leaving Spain, he was described in official records as tall, thin, pockmarked, with black hair, and a scant beard.

After his arrival at Vera Cruz, he entered San Fernando College, July 26, 1803. By December 22 of that year he had received permission to serve in the California missions. He arrived in California, August 14, 1804, and was assigned to Mission San Carlos, Carmel, where he remained until 1819. From there he was transferred to Mission San Rafael, where he labored until his death in 1832.

At his first assignment, he saw the mission in the period of its fullest development and witnessed a rise in the number of baptisms from 2,487 to 3,154. Amorós labored faithfully so as to merit great praise from his superior, Vicente Francisco de Sarría, in 1817. He was known for his religious zeal, characteristic industry, and for his ability to conduct the temporal and mechanical activities of the mission. While at Carmel he also attended the presidio at Monterey and visited the neighboring ranches. "I consider him to have the qualification for office within a college or community," wrote Sarría. Three years later, Mariano Payeras stated that Amorós' "merit was outstanding, his aptitude for the apostolic ministry in both spiritual and temporal matters above the average and was, perhaps, fit for some official position in the Order."

Letters which he wrote and activities in which he engaged show Amorós to have been a man of vision — broadminded and candid. As a result of Otto von Kotzebue's visit in 1816, Amorós foresaw the growing fame of San Francisco as a port. When Governor Pablo Solá placed an excessive tax on foreign ships as well as on exported mission produce, Amorós showed that in mercantile matters he was ahead of the narrow Spanish policy with its trade monopoly. Foreigners, he said, were also children of God and, as such, brethren of the Spaniards. Hence it was neither honorable nor generous to charge them a maximum price and to resent their unwillingness to sell at a minimum price. Vessels should be thanked for coming, not taxed. Trade was good for the country, and a shortsighted policy might destroy it. He protested against the attempt to collect export duty on mission goods.

When he charged soldiers with wanton destruction of the cattle in a remonstrance to Solá, he added, "You well know that I am candid."

On August 10, 1809, with Friars Sarría and Estevan Tapis, he witnessed Governor José Joaquín Arrillaga's swearing of allegiance to Fernando VII in opposition to Joseph Bonaparte, who had invaded Spain. This oath had been required by the viceroy. In 1814, Amorós composed his treatise on the customs and habits of the San Carlos Indians in response to the request made by the Spanish government. From it one gleans the fact that he had a practical knowledge of at least two of the seven dialects of the region, Rumsen and Excelen.

In the summer of 1819 Amorós was transferred to Mission San Rafael to succeed Fray Luís Gil y Taboada. He administered his first baptism there on July 18, his last, June 24, 1832. He lived at that mission during José Altimira's illegal founding of Mission San Francisco Solano and was a target of Altimira's anger for opposing the latter's proposed suppression of Mission San Rafael, on which matter Amorós wrote a letter of protest to Governor Luís Antonio Argüello, May 17, 1823.

San Rafael flourished under Amorós' administration. Baptisms outnumbered deaths 2 to 1, and population nearly doubled despite the fact that 92 neophytes were transferred to San Francisco Solano. San Rafael reached its zenith in 1828 when it had 1,140 souls.

Amorós might be called a diplomat of the frontier. In 1822, when he learned that the Russians had discovered a silver mine during an expedition to Bodega, he notified Governor Argüello and urged the government to explore and develop the northern frontier. In 1823, the civil authorities were fearful of further Russian encroachments and as a result were taking precautionary measures. On this account, Amorós, on March 8, wrote to Fray Narciso Durán that he had entertained Russian officers at San Rafael but had prevented them from going to a place called Ros-Kosoff by enlarging upon the difficult terrain and other difficulties to be encountered in reaching it. In 1831, when Russians advanced to a place called Santiago, twelve leagues beyond Fort Ross, and were preparing to till the soil, Amorós' presence there during a visit he was making in pagan territory caused the Russians to make no further penetration into the region.

In the matter of political loyalty, subsequent to Mexican independence, Amorós declined to take the oath of loyalty to the Mexican constitution of 1824, stating that he would obey any government under which he lived. Nor did he ask for a passport. He was allowed to remain.

On June 16, 1832, San Fernando College, which was a declining institution by reason of the expulsion of its Spanish members — only six friars were left — elected Amorós as one of its counselors under the guardian Fray José Guzmán. This office, of course, he could not effectively exercise because of distance. Within a month, moreover, he would no longer be among the living.

Amorós died at Mission San Rafael at 3:30 on the morning of July 14, 1832. With him were Friars Buenaventura Fortuny and Tomás Esténaga. The latter sang the Requiem High Mass. Amorós was buried at five o'clock in the afternoon on the Epistle side of the antepresbytery. He was fifty-nine years old and had spent forty in the Franciscan order, thirty-five in the priesthood, and twenty-eight in the California missions.

Fortuny, who entered the death record in the local mission register on July 16, stated: "I knew this padre since the year 1792 and have always considered him a saint, having lived with him for a long time." He declared that Amorós had labored with "astonishing constancy."[2] In 1876 General Mariano Vallejo at the centennial celebration in San Francisco eulogized Amorós as follows: "Friar Juan Amorós was sanctity itself; . . . [a man of] brilliant qualities . . . a model of virtue, charity, humility, and of Christian meekness — a man without a blemish, of a candid heart, and of most exemplary life; he was the admiration of his contemporaries and the astonishment of the tribes of the aborigines."[3] Vallejo had known him at Monterey seventy years prior, and from him he had received his first sacraments. "I speak with so much feeling of kindness towards Father Amorós because I am cognizant of his great virtues, his pure heart and his sincere devotion."[4] The general stated that Amorós in appearance was very similar to Archbishop Joseph Alemany of San Francisco and that the two possessed similar virtuous qualities.

It appears that the only missions Amorós knew besides San Carlos and San Rafael were those of San Francisco and Santa Clara, though there are no records of his ministrations in their registers.

[1] Pedro Sanahuja, O.F.M., in *Historia de la Seráfica Provincia de Cataluña* (Barcelona, 1959), p. 465, gives Oct. 12, 1775, as the date of Amorós' birth. However, his Cádiz record of embarcation, early in 1803, gives his age as twenty-nine, while Sarría's biographical sketch of Nov. 5, 1817, gives his age as forty-four. Both data would indicate 1773 as the year of his birth.

[2] Burial Register, Mission San Rafael.

[3] [Patrick J. Thomas], *Our Centennial Memoir* (San Francisco, 1877), p. 115.

[4] Ibid., p. 116.

AMURRIÓ, GREGORIO (1744-?)

Fray Gregorio Amurrió was born at Bastida, in the diocese of Calahorra, Spain, in the year 1744 and entered the Franciscan order at Vitoria in the Franciscan province of Cantabria, March 18, 1760. As a member of the community of San Juan de Piedrola, he volunteered for the American missions and left for Cádiz, arriving there sometime before June 12, 1769. There, at the age of twenty-five, he was described

13

in passport records as tall, with a large face, and a pallid complexion. He held the office of preacher. Recruited by Fray Rafael Verger, Amurrió and thirty-nine other Franciscans set out for San Fernando College, Mexico City, which they reached on May 27, 1770.

Amurrió and nineteen others were accepted for the missions of Lower California. Under the leadership of Fray Juan Prestamero, they left the college in October 1770 and traveled as far as Tepic. The band of missionaries was delayed in the local friary until the beginning of February 1771, waiting for the arrival of the *San Carlos* at San Blas. Bound for Loreto, the ship had encountered a violent storm which drove it as far south as Acapulco and grounded it at Manzanillo. Seventeen of the friars, among whom was Amurrió, received orders from the viceroy, Carlos Francisco de Croix, to travel overland up the coast of Sinaloa opposite Loreto. They reached Tamasula, a distance of three hundred leagues. The governor of Lower California sent the ship, *Concepción,* to bring Amurrió and his companions to Loreto, where they arrived, November 24, 1771.

President Francisco Palóu assigned Amurrió as assistant to Fray Juan Sancho at Misión Santa Gertrudis, where he remained until the Lower California missions were handed over to the Dominicans in 1773. Palóu, Amurrió, and four other missionaries of the area set out from Velicatá with Sergeant José Francisco Ortega, July 21, 1773, and made the overland trip to San Diego, which they reached on August 30. Palóu, acting as ad interim president because of Junípero Serra's absence in Mexico, appointed Amurrió as supernumerary at San Diego, who performed his first baptism there on the day of his arrival. He remained at that mission until April 3, 1774.

When Serra arrived at San Diego by ship, together with Fray Pablo de Mugártegui, who had become ill, the president appointed Amurrió to replace Mugártegui as chaplain of the *Santiago,* bound for Monterey. He sailed from San Diego, April 6 and arrived at Monterey, May 9. From there Amurrió proceeded overland to Mission San Luis Obispo, stopping at Mission San Antonio, where he baptized on June 21. He ministered at San Luis Obispo from July 7, 1774, until October 1775.

When Serra was ready to found Mission San Juan Capistrano in August 1775, he appointed Fermín Francisco de Lasuén and Amurrió as its ministers. Lasuén joined Amurrió at San Luis Obispo, and the two proceeded as far as Mission San Gabriel. Amurrió remained there to gather cattle and church goods for the new mission while Lasuén continued to San Diego. Sergeant José Ortega, Lasuén, and soldiers set out from the southern port for the purpose of founding the mission, construction of which was begun on October 30, 1775. Amurrió departed from San Gabriel and arrived at San Juan Capistrano eight days after the founding. On that very day a messenger arrived from San Diego announcing the tragic news of the destruction of Mission San Diego and the death of Fray Luís Jayme at the hands of the Indians.

Ortega prepared to leave immediately and ordered the friars to follow him. Work on the mission was suspended. Friars Lasuén and Amurrió brought the church goods with them to San Diego and were subsequently forced to remain there for over a year until the dangerous situation had passed. The friars became restive and asked for retirement to San Fernando College.

While at San Diego, Amurrió witnessed and also participated in the events leading up to the declaration of excommunication of Fernando Rivera y Moncada because of his alleged violation of church asylum with regard to the Indian, Carlos, accused of murder.

After Serra had arrived in San Diego on July 11, 1776, from Monterey, he appointed Mugártegui and Amurrió to the previously abandoned Mission San Juan Capistrano. With Serra, Amurrió and soldiers set out from San Diego. On November 1, 1776, the seventh mission in the California system was refounded, and Amurrió baptized the first pagan Indian on December 19. Mugártegui arrived from San Luis Obispo late in November or very early in December. Amurrió's last baptismal entry at the mission is September 1, 1779. He was again at San Gabriel on November 4, 1778, assisting Serra in the administration of confirmation. The latter considered Amurrió to be a competent missionary.

Because of ill health, Amurrió requested permission to return to San Fernando College. Governor Felipe de Neve opposed his leaving without first obtaining gubernatorial permission. Serra maintained, however, that such permission was unnecessary according to the regulations laid down in *Recopilación de las leyes de los reinos de Indias.*

Amurrió sailed from San Diego in the autumn of 1779. On December 12, he had reached Guadalajara where he received from the college the requested papers of disaffiliation. He joined the Franciscan province of Jalisco, and he remained there for four years. On July 6, 1783, at his petition, the discretory gave him permission to re-enter the college. On March 16, 1784, he was elected vicar of the institution. No further account of his activities or of the place and year of his death have come to light.

ANZAR, JOSÉ ANTONIO (ca. 1792-1874)

Fray José Antonio Anzar was a native of Mexico. Neither the place nor the year of his birth is disclosed in Franciscan records, though judging from the year of his ordination to the priesthood, he was probably born around the year 1792. He became a Franciscan in the province of Jalisco, but, as a cleric studying for the priesthood, he became incorporated in the apostolic college of Our Lady of Guadalupe, Zacatecas. There he received all the grades of clerical orders from tonsure to priesthood between August 14 and August 24, 1815, from the hands of the Most Rev. Dr. Juan Cruz Ruiz de Cabañas, bishop of Guadalajara.

Anzar is first found as a missionary in Sonora in 1824. Since this field belonged to the college of Querétaro, Bancroft is inclined to think that Anzar had transferred to that college. When the California missions north of San Miguel were transferred from the Spanish Fernandinos to the Mexican Zacatecans, Anzar came to California with the advance guard of the latter in 1831. With Friars Mariano Sosa, Francisco Cuculla, and Jesús María Martínez, he traveled overland through Lower California and arrived at Mission San Gabriel where he presented himself to the Fernandino president, Fray José Bernardo Sánchez.

Anzar was temporarily assigned as assistant to Fray Antonio Peyrí at Mission San Luis Rey, where he baptized between July 1831 and April 1833. When Peyrí left the mission for his native Spain in January 1832, his place was taken by Fray Vicente Pascual Oliva of San Diego. Anzar continued service under him. By the end of 1831, 5,295 Indians had been baptized under the aegis of Mission San Luis Rey, while 2,819 were still living at the mission. Thus Anzar became familiar with California's largest and most prosperous mission before secularization and decay set in.

When the final band of Zacatecans arrived at Monterey, January 15, 1833, Anzar was called north to labor in their jurisdiction and was placed in charge of Mission San Juan Bautista, where he lived from May 30, 1833, until November 6, 1854. He received this mission from the well-known padre, Felipe Arroyo de la Cuesta. Indians to the number of 4,017 had been baptized since 1797 when the mission was founded. At the time of Anzar's arrival, about 916 were still living there.

Anzar was destined to see the mission decline through secularization and sale. He witnessed also the changes of the turbulent period resultant upon the American invasion and the gold rush. The mission was secularized in 1834, Anzar remaining in charge of spiritualities. A letter written by him to Governor José Figueroa, January 29, 1835, discloses the financial and social chaos brought about by secularization. The mission inventory was drawn up, May 9, 1835, and signed by the secular commissioners and Anzar. The sale of the mission was authorized by Pío Pico on October 28, 1845, and a second inventory was drawn up and signed by the commissioners and Anzar.

Meanwhile, Fray José María de Jesús González Rubio renounced the presidency of the Zacatecan missions, April 8, 1843, and Anzar was elected to replace him. His reelection occurred on December 11, 1845. Anzar was the last Franciscan to attend San Juan Bautista. He left for Mexico after November 6, 1854, the date of his last baptism, presumably going to Zacatecas. No data concerning him is available at the college except that he died at Colima in December 1874 at the probable age of eighty-two. Before his departure from California, a photograph had been taken of him in his gray habit and broad-brimmed hat. He is one of the few older friars whose picture we have today.

While stationed at San Luis Rey, Anzar baptized at Mission San Juan Capistrano on January 1, 1832, and en route to San Juan Bautista, he baptized at Los Angeles, April 6 and 11, 1833. During his period of service at San Juan Bautista, he visited Missions Santa Clara, San Carlos, and Santa Cruz at various times when he administered baptism. On November 18, 1853, he testified before the U. S. Land Commission concerning mission lands and properties which belonged to the Church.

Bancroft summarized Anzar's contribution to California's missionary effort with a short statement: "Though involved in occasional troubles, P. Ánzar seems to have been a priest of fair character and abilities."[1] On July 8, 1834, the California territorial assembly had on its agenda for a secret session charges against Anzar for maladministration of Mission San Juan Bautista. No details of the charges nor of the results of the deliberations are available.

On July 16, 1859, the diocesan priest of Mission San Antonio, the Rev. Doroteo Ambris, stated that Anzar had lived continuously at a ranch which, though under his brother's name, was publicly considered to belong to the former and that it was rare for Anzar to visit the mission under his charge. At the ranch the padre dedicated his time to agriculture, cattle raising, and running a store for a period of from four to six years, from which he realized all the profits. Ambris states that, according to trustworthy persons, the land he left to his brother's widow came to possess 12,000 head of cattle and large numbers of horses and sheep. "This padre," wrote Ambris, "is known for his avarice and for his tolerance among his [religious] subjects living in immorality, he being their prefect."[2]

Some light is thrown on Anzar's change of residence from Mission San Juan Bautista to Rancho Las Aromas in the "Libro Primero de Gobierno" of the diocese of Monterey.

On June 14, 1847, the Rev. Father administrator of the diocese, Fray José María de Jesús González Rubio, gave permission to the Rev. Father, Fray José María Anzar, President of the Missions of the North [the Zacatecan missions] empowering him to erect a rural chapel on the ranch where he actually lives, called Las Aromas, located in the jurisdiction of San Juan Bautista, so that the residents of the ranch as well as other ranches of the area could more frequently and with greater facility fulfill the precept of hearing Mass on days of obligation."[3]

In the confused and troubled times after secularization and American occupation, the alleged irregularities of Anzar would have to have more detailed and juridical proofs to admit their final acceptance in all their phases.

[1] *History of California*, II, 699.

[2] This letter has only recently come to light. The original is in the Archives of the Propagation of the Faith in Rome and was written during the controversy between Bishop Thaddeus Amat and the Franciscan college of Santa Barbara, 1857-1861. A photographic copy is in SBMA.

[3] Fol. 5, SBMA.

ARROÍTA, FRANCISCO JOSÉ (1762?-1821)

Fray Francisco José Arroíta, usually known as José, was a member of the Spanish Franciscan province of Cantabria and entered San Fernando College, Mexico City, in 1785. There he was described as a good man, fairly active but inexperienced. Together with five other friars he sailed for California where he arrived in September 1786, probably at Monterey. He baptized at Mission San Carlos, Carmel, for the first time on September 8.

For a period he was in the southern missions, baptizing at San Buenaventura, December 8, 1786, at San Juan Capistrano, December 26, 1786, and February 13, 1787, again at San Buenaventura, March 19, 1787, then at Santa Barbara, March 26. His first baptism at Mission San Luis Obispo, to which he had been assigned by President Fermín Francisco de Lasuén, occurred on April 7, 1787, and there he continued to minister until February 5, 1788.

Arroíta was assigned with Fray Vicente Fuster as one of the first missionaries for the new Mission Purísima, founded on December 8, 1787. Building operations, however, did not commence until the following April. Arroíta baptized there from April 9, 1788, until June 21, 1796. During that tenure, he also baptized at Mission Santa Barbara at various times between 1791 and 1794 and at Mission San Luis Obispo between 1788 and 1794.

On July 20, 1796, Lasuén notified Governor Diego de Borica that he had given permission to the missionary to retire to the college since he had served his ten years and was worn out by the hardships he had endured. Arroíta baptized at San Juan Capistrano between December 1796 and February 1797, probably on his way to San Diego to obtain ship passage. He died at San Fernando College at midnight, March 5, 1821. There is no record of his activity in Mexico. His California career was devoid of incident and consisted chiefly of his labors in building up the initial Mission Purisima at its first site. This mission was destroyed in the earthquake of 1812.

ARROYO DE LA CUESTA, FELIPE (1780-1840)

Fray Felipe Arroyo de la Cuesta, son of Matías Arroyo and Isabel de la Cuesta, was born at Cubo, district of Bureba, a section of Santa María de Rivarredonde, province of Burgos, Old Castile, Spain, April 29, 1780. He was baptized in the parish church of St. Millán, May 2. At the age of sixteen, on August 3, 1796, he became a Franciscan in the *convento grande* of Burgos and made his profession on August 6, the following year.

Having been ordained to the priesthood in 1804, he volunteered for the American missions. At Cádiz, twenty-five years of age and listed as a moralist, he was described in passport records as of regular stature, swarthy, broad-shouldered, with black hair and hazel-colored eyes, having thick nose and lips. Arroyo sailed on the *Gravina* on September 2, 1804, arrived at Vera Cruz the same year, and entered San Fernando College, Mexico City. In 1807 he volunteered for the California missions, setting out on December 14 with Friars Francisco Suñer and Francisco Xavier Uría and arriving at Monterey, August 13, 1808. Appointed to Mission San Juan Bautista by President Estevan Tapis and replacing Andrés Dulanto, Arroyo de la Cuesta served there from September 9, 1808, until April 2, 1833.

Arroyo de la Cuesta's missionary work at San Juan Bautista is almost coextensive with the history of the mission, which was founded in 1797. From the end of 1808 to the end of 1832, the number of baptisms increased from 1,856 to 4,017. The greatest number of Indians living at the mission in any one year was 1,248 in 1823. The banner year for cattle was 1820 with 11,000 head and for sheep in 1815 with 13,400 head. Building developments continued down to the twenties. The present mission church, whose cornerstone was laid on June 13, 1803, was gradually built up until its dedication on June 23, 1812. It was blessed by Fray Tapis in the presence of Governor José Joaquín Arrillaga. It is unusual among the mission buildings in having three naves.

Arroyo de la Cuesta brought with him a diversified talent and displayed a continuous zeal. He stands out for his contribution to linguistics and music. Concerning the former, Vicente Francisco de Sarría wrote of him, November 5, 1817:

From the beginning he was located as missionary at Mission San Juan Bautista where he has continued to this day. He applied himself most assiduously to learning the respective languages with such success that I doubt whether there is another who has attained the same proficiency in understanding and describing its intricate syntax. He even reduced to some sort of rules the confusing formation of its verbs, adverbs and the rest of the parts of speech which I understand may serve likewise for the other missions; for notwithstanding that their languages are very different, and that many of them have two or three idioms in the same district, they preserve their analogy with regard to expressing their ideas. I have animated him to compose a work on the subject. He has labored, as I understand, with good success, wherefore he may succeed in the work.[1]

The linguist-missionary composed a "Vocabulary and Phrase Book of the Mutsun Language of Mission San Juan Bautista" which consists of 2,884 phrases, accompanied with a Spanish translation. It was called an "Index" or "Collection." The padre wrote it for his own use and not for publication. The footnotes and explanations are in Latin, and the work was signed on April 2, 1815. This index was published for the first time by Dr. John Gilmary Shea under the auspices of the Smithsonian Institution in New York in 1852. In a composition book of over forty pages, Arroyo wrote a vocabulary or "Algunas espresiones de la lengua Nopthrathre o digamos Tulareños," dated July 15, 1823.

Less well known is his "Confesionario" in Mutsun, which the missionary wrote out on the unused pages of the first volume of a printed work, *Theología Christiana dogmático-moral*, by the Rev. Daniel Concina, O.P. (Madrid, 1770). Three pages of questions and answers on the commandments and Christian life, two exhortations, and the Acts of Faith, Hope, and Charity in Mutsun are accompanied by an explanatory note in Spanish dated October 24, 1818. The questions and answers go back as far as December 1811. Then follows a copy of the *interrogatorio* in Spanish by Sarría, of June 7, 1818. This same volume contains a list of all the mission books allowed for his own use, dated September 6, 1808, and is in the Santa Barbara Mission Archives.

Arroyo de la Cuesta also gave some attention to music. Father Owen Da Silva, O.F.M., in his *Mission Music of California* states that there are "jottings about the Indian music in his work on the Mutsun language, and attempts to set Indian words to some of the common mission melodies. At the Bancroft Library we also find a number of masses and hymns in his handwriting."[2] It also appears that Arroyo de la Cuesta had an excellent singing voice. On the occasion of a visit to the mission by Captain F. W. Beechey's men of the British Royal Navy in 1826, the padre sang a stirring rendition of the song, "España de la Guerra." His interest in music and song is further in evidence. In 1829, he reported the acquisition of an organ of three cylinders. Though this was only the barrel organ which Captain George Vancouver had given to Lasuén at Monterey, it was a noteworthy acquisition for the recreational facilities of that day. Each barrel contained ten tunes. Among the diversified pieces were "Spanish Waltz" and "Go to the Devil."

When Alfred Robinson visited the mission in 1831, he wrote that Arroyo de la Cuesta, "for amusement, when tired of study, . . . called in the children of the place and set them to dancing and playing their games. In his eccentric taste he had given them the names of all the renowned personages of antiquity, and Ciceros, Platos, and Alexanders were to be found in abundance."[3]

Arroyo de la Cuesta said the first Mass in the newly dedicated mission church of San Jose in 1809. In 1814 he composed the answers to the questionnaire of the Spanish government concerning the customs and habits of the San Juan Indians. When the question of allegiance to Mexico came up in 1826, Arroyo de la Cuesta reserved his for the king of Spain but took a modified oath to republicanism. Governor José María Echeandía recommended that he be given his passport and be sent back to Spain.

Already in 1813 the missionary had begun to be ill. Four years later Sarría, in his biographical sketches, wrote: "In the midst of all this he has been afflicted for four or five years with grave rheumatic pains which for a long time prevented him from celebrating holy Mass; but in the rest of his duties, he served in the regular management of mission needs, especially attending to instructions which his knowledge of language made it easier for him to do so far as his health allowed."[4]

In 1820, Mariano Payeras, in his biographical sketches, stated: "He is forty years of age and his merit is above average in his aptitude and disposition. Although very high in itself, it promises nothing owing to the grave infirmities which are already chronic and which for years have made him think at least of death."[5]

Concerning Arroyo de la Cuesta, Sarría wrote to Governor Echeandía in 1830: "At Mission San Juan Bautista the missionary Father is so incapacitated that, when there is necessity of hearing a confession or of administering Extreme Unction in the Indian village, he has to be bourne to the place on a stretcher. Even so he cannot visit the outside ranchos, so that I myself at times attend his sick."[6]

How Arroyo de la Cuesta himself felt about his situation is clear from his words to José M. Herrera, collector of customs at Monterey, August 10, 1826:

There are difficulties all around, and I am overburdened with cares which render life wearisome. There is hardly anything of the Religious in me, and I scarcely know what to do in these troublous times. I made the vows of a Friar Minor; instead, I must manage temporalities, sow grain, raise sheep, horses and cows. I must preach, baptize, bury the dead, visit the sick, direct the carts, haul stones, lime, etc. These are things incompatible, thorny, bitter, hard, unbearable. They rob me of time, tranquility, and health of both the body and the soul. I desire with lively anxiety to devote myself to my sacred ministry and to serve the Lord.[7]

When Arroyo de la Cuesta handed over his mission to his Zacatecan successor, José Antonio Anzar, in 1833, he was sent to Mission San Luis Obispo, where he was associated with Ramón Abella. While there, he served part of the time at San Miguel, 1833-1834. Though paralyzed and in a wheel chair, he loved to keep the attendant, Serrano, about him for the pleasure of conversation. From September 23, 1834, until March 1836, he was at Mission Purisima, but his health did not improve. Finally he was removed to Mission Santa Ines, where he baptized a few times between December 2, 1836, and July 25, 1837. There, after a long and painful illness, having received the sacraments "very much conformed to the will of God," Arroyo de la Cuesta died on September 20, 1840. Fray José Joaquín Jimeno interred his remains on the Gospel side of the sanctuary on September 22.

During his years at San Juan Bautista, the missionary baptized at times at Missions San Francisco, Santa Clara, and San Carlos. On September 13, 1820, he acted as secretary to Payeras on an official visitation to Mission Santa Cruz, where he signed the official books.

Engelhardt called Arroyo de la Cuesta "a most methodical man in everything. He was nothing if not methodical. Hence his time and means were so arranged that he effected wonders in his line while being a wonderful convert-maker."[8] Bancroft says he "was a scholar and always a student."[9] Besides his contribution to linguistics and to music, Arroyo de la Cuesta combined an interesting personality with religious zeal. Nothing short of the word heroic can be applied to him when one considers that he accomplished so much amid physical pain and mental distress. Many another missionary returned to Mexico or Spain for less reason than this able and self-sacrificing missionary had for relinquishing the field, even in his earliest years.

Angustias de la Guerra y Ord recalled that he had the reputation of a man of great learning. She related that he was "of average stature, but when I knew him in 1833 or 1834 his legs and hands were crippled. He could write but with effort. He had good countenance and color. Though he was then 50, he didn't appear old."[10]

According to Captain Beechey, the padre "appeared to be of an active mind, and had constructed a water clock which communicated with a bell by his bedside, and which by being arranged at night could be made to give an alarm at any stated hour."[11] There can be no doubt that the padre was interested in mechanical things. He possessed a set of the twelve volumes of William Guthrie, *Geografía Universal Descriptiva, Histórica, Industrial y Comercial, de las Cuatro Partes del Mundo* (Madrid, 1804-1808), which contained plates showing various mechanical devices with corresponding texts on their operations.

Beechey stated furthermore that Arroyo de la Cuesta divided his time "between the duties of his holy avocation and various ingenious inventions."[12]

Beechey's sailors found the missionary good-natured, cheerful, hospitable, amusing, generous, and a good conversationalist, with a fund of anecdotes and proverbs. He confided to the naval men that he had written a vocabulary and grammar in the local Indian language but was not disposed to show them to the visitors. When Beechey's men returned to San Juan Bautista unexpectedly at a later date, they found Arroyo de la Cuesta less cordial and less disposed to conversation.

A significant number of books which the missionary used in California are preserved today in the Santa Barbara Mission Archives. They reveal that he had a wide range of interests beyond theology. His many notations on flyleaves and on margins show that he had perused these volumes. His notes indicate that he had a precise mind and a regard for facts. At times he took to writing verse. Some of the verse and some of his notes are written in red ink. More than any other padre, Arroyo de la Cuesta did not hesitate to write on any usable page. While this might be bad for the book, it was good for history and biography.

Faxon Dean Atherton, who met Arroyo de la Cuesta at Mission Santa Ines on June 25, 1836, tells an amusing story which, if correct in all its details, reveals much about the padre. He had been called from Purisima that Sunday morning to attend Padre Marcos Antonio de Vitoria, very old and an invalid, who purportedly was at the point of death. Arroyo heeded the summons but on arrival found Vitoria in better health than usual. The whole thing was a bit of a joke to get the Purisima missionary to join the other friars in merriment. Atherton found him to be a "very talkative old man . . . possessed of good information. He kept me listening to his yarns for about two hours, and most of the time was endeavoring to make me understand *his* theory of the motion of the Planets, he believing or pretending to believe the Earth to be a plane and that the Sun revolves around it."[13]

If in 1830 Arroyo de la Cuesta at San Juan Bautista had to be carried on a stretcher to answer a sick call, and if later at San Luis Obispo he was forced to use a wheel chair, it is difficult to understand how he made the trip Atherton describes in 1836 unless a carriage was provided for him, an item that is not mentioned. And if what was jokingly reported as an urgent sick call turned out to be merely a ruse for a convivial meeting, Arroyo de la Cuesta must have possessed a sense of humor beyond the measure given to most mortals. Finally, could a paralytic condition of many years be so easily accommodated to the scene described?

[1] Engelhardt, *Mission Santa Ines*, p. 111.

[2] Los Angeles, 1941, p. 21.

[3] *Life in California*, p. 118.

[4] A translation similar to the author's may be found in Engelhardt, *Mission Santa Ines*, pp. 111-112.

[5] Ibid.

[6] Engelhardt, *Mission San Juan Bautista*, p. 43.

[7] Ibid., pp. 37-38.

[8] Ibid., p. 125.

[9] *History of California*, III, 662n.

[10] Price and Ellison, tr. *Occurrences in Hispanic California*, p. 34.

[11] *Narrative of a Voyage to the Pacific and Beering's Strait* (London, 1831), II, 53-54.

[12] Ibid., p. 50.

[13] Doyce B. Nunis, Jr., ed. *The California Diary ... 1836-1839* (San Francisco, 1964), p. 20.

BARCENILLA, ISIDRO (1766-?)

Fray Isidro Barcenilla was born in 1766 at San Manes in the diocese of Palencia, Spain. He received the Franciscan habit at Abrojo in 1785. Early in 1795 he was at Cádiz with twenty-two other Franciscans, awaiting embarcation for the Indies. His passport identification described him as of regular stature, of light skin, thick beard, with a mole on his right cheek and another above his left eye. He sailed on the *Santiago de España,* May 8, 1795, under the commissary, Manuel Arévalo, and disembarked at Vera Cruz, June 26.

Barcenilla entered San Fernando College, Mexico City, and in 1797 volunteered for the California missions. Sailing from San Blas on the *Concepción,* together with Fray Agustín Merino, he arrived at San Francisco, April 14, 1797, after a voyage of twenty-nine days. President Fermín Francisco de Lasuén appointed both newcomers to the newly founded Mission San Jose with Barcenilla as superior. They began their labors there on June 28.

Precisely at a time when the new mission required the presence of two healthy men with at least one experienced, both missionaries were plagued by illness within a short while. Merino became ill first. Even his mind became affected. As early as August 1799 Lasuén gave him permission to return to the college. Barcenilla, about the same time, wrote to Lasuén asking for a similar permission. He likewise revealed the condition of his health to Governor Diego de Borica. Overwork, worry, the illness of his companion, and his own discomfort, which developed from a hemorrhoidal condition, reacted on his nerves. Lasuén advised him to seek the aid of a physician at Monterey, which he did, for the records show him baptizing at Mission San Carlos, February 3, 1800. It appears that he obtained little or no relief.

Early in January 1800, Lasuén declared that Barcenilla confessed

24

to a bad disposition, a lack of sociability with other missionaries, and an impatience with the Indians. His new companion, José Antonio Uría, in no uncertain manner asked Lasuén to take Barcenilla out of Mission San Jose and replace him with another. Finally, on July 31 the president gave Barcenilla permission to return to Mexico, and in so doing, stated that the missionary was in a hysterical frame of mind, afraid of losing his reason, and, as a result, was deprived of rest, patience, and serenity. At the same time he praised Barcenilla for having been a good religious and for having labored eagerly and energetically despite his afflictions. On October 22, 1800, Barcenilla decided, nevertheless, to remain in California for another year. He continued to serve at San Jose until his successor, Luís Gil y Taboada, arrived at the end of March 1802.

Up to that time, 644 Indians had been baptized at the mission. During the same period, Barcenilla had visited Mission Santa Cruz in 1801 and 1802, Santa Clara in 1800, and San Juan Bautista the same year. He baptized at all three places. After leaving Mission San Jose, he went to Mission San Francisco at the invitation of the padres there. By the end of the year he felt well enough to receive an assignment to Mission San Gabriel where he remained a year and a half, ministering between December 9, 1802, and October 4, 1804, when he became ill again. He received a new permit to retire to Mexico from President Estevan Tapis and sailed in October. He continued to live at the college until May 9, 1807, when, at his petition, he was given leave to return to Spain.

Bancroft states that Barcenilla "was a very irascible man, always in trouble with the soldiers of the guard; but this characteristic was due mainly, it is believed, to a cerebral affliction and to piles, which so impaired his health that in July 1800, he obtained, after repeated applications, permission to retire."[1]

The Rev. Francis F. McCarthy, who devotes an entire chapter to Merino and Barcenilla, takes exception to Bancroft's blanket statement, calling it an "unjust generality." Both Lasuén and Barcenilla himself at least admitted this tendency to irascibility. This trend, however, did not necessarily enter into his relations on public affairs affecting the mission. The records of three public incidents refer to complaints centered around the trespassing on mission lands of cattle from the pueblo of San Jose, about which both Christian and pagan Indians became incensed, and to the misconduct of certain soldiers of the guard. The letters of protest were written "in firm but respectful terms."[2]

[1] *History of California*, II, 114, n. 44.
[2] McCarthy, *The History of Mission San Jose*, p. 81.

BARONA, JOSÉ (1764-1831)

Fray José Barona was born at Villanueva del Conde in the arch-diocese of Burgos, Spain. Bancroft places the date of his birth on March 24, 1764, while Engelhardt states that it occurred in July. It appears that neither is correct. Vicente Francisco de Sarría, in his biographical sketches, signed November 5, 1817, stated that Barona was fifty-three years and four months old. This would place his birth on about August 5, 1764. Barona received the Franciscan habit at Villa de Velardo in the province of Burgos, July 18, 1783. On September 2, 1794, he left the friary of Calahorra for the port of Cádiz to embark for the American missions under the commissary, Manuel Arévalo. At the time he was listed in passport records as preacher and confessor and was described as of regular build, with lemon-colored skin, hazel or dark brown eyes and hair, a thick beard, and with a scar on his forehead. With twenty-two other Franciscans, he sailed on the *Santiago de España* on May 8, 1795, disembarked at Vera Cruz, June 26 and entered San Fernando College, August 24.

Early in 1798 Barona was sent to the California missions together with seven other missionaries and arrived at Santa Barbara on the *Concepción*, May 8, 1798. Fermín Francisco de Lasuén assigned him to Mission San Diego, where Engelhardt places him between August 4, 1798, and January 24, 1811. Prior to that, he was at San Luis Rey, temporarily substituting for José Faura. With the exception of a brief stay at Mission San Gabriel from July 1829 until September 10, 1830, Barona filled out a long term of service at San Juan Capistrano from April 26, 1811, until August 6, 1831. Since 1827, he had also spent a considerable amount of time at San Luis Rey. At various times he baptized at San Gabriel and San Fernando.

In 1817, Sarría stated that Barona had laudably discharged his duties, "inasmuch as his weak constitution does not permit him to make greater exertions." For a year prior, Barona had sought permission to retire from the missions. The permit was withheld, owing to the fact that there was no one to replace him. In 1820, Mariano Payeras declared that Barona's merit as well as his aptitude were medium and that his service in the ministry was limited to work among the natives or to the regular life in a Franciscan community.

At San Juan Capistrano, Barona went through the terrifying earth-quake of December 8, 1812. Fifty Indians attending Mass were killed when the large church was destroyed — still in ruins today. It had taken nine years to build and was finally completed in 1806. On November 12, 1813, Barona was invited to dedicate the new and final mission church of San Diego. In December 1818 he witnessed the turmoil occasioned by the Bouchard invasion. Bancroft asserts that Barona and his associate,

Gerónimo Boscana, had not been energetic enough in removing valuables inland as had the padres of other missions. On the other hand, Engelhardt writes that José de la Guerra y Noriega, the Santa Barbara presidio commander, April 6, 1819, exculpated both the local soldiers and the padres from blame in the matter. This, however, is denied by Joseph A. Thompson in his *El Gran Capitán, José de la Guerra*.[1] Barona participated in the dispute between Mission San Juan Capistrano and the adjoining Rancho Santa Gertrudis on the question of trespassing cattle. Barona wrote up the case in defense of the mission and explained the history of the dispute.

The padre became involved in a sensational affair on January 23, 1823, at San Juan Capistrano, and which Boscana described as "the most scandalous case witnessed in California." Fray Antonio Peyrí had called Barona to Mission San Luis Rey. Since there was no military guard available to accompany him from San Juan Capistrano, he decided to travel alone. As he was about to mount his horse, three soldiers, armed with saber, lance, and with guns leveled at him, appeared before Barona, Boscana, and a group of mission Indians standing by. One of the three soldiers, José Cañedo, seized the bridle, trying unsuccessfully to prevent Barona from mounting. Once the padre was in the saddle, Cañedo gave the horse a kick which felled the animal to one side with Barona falling beneath it. Fortunately, he received no particular injury. The soldier contended that no missionary could leave a mission without a military escort. This was, indeed, the regulation from the earliest days.

The case was taken to Governor Luís Antonio Argüello, to the central government, and to the Franciscan superior. Apparently a military trial was held at San Diego, wherein Cañedo was exculpated and Barona censured. Sarría, the Franciscan commissary prefect, considered the trial a mistrial, since no one favorable to the missionary was present. He contended furthermore that Barona had the right to travel alone if in the exercise of his ministry. He censured Barona, however, for resisting the soldier's action and for not making a solemn protest to Cañedo over the ecclesiastical censure resulting from his action. The culprits were ordered to be absolved from their censure by the president of the missions, José Señán.

Concerning the incident Engelhardt remarks: "It seems that Fr. Barona never fully recovered from the indignity and shock suffered at the time . . . . The shock from the public insult and the fall from the horse must have aggravated his weak condition. In the Baptismal Registers one can notice plainly that Fr. Barona's signature long after the occurrence was made with an unsteady hand."[2]

When the question of loyalty to the Mexican regime came up, Barona, on June 12, 1826, declared that he was prepared to swear to uphold the federal constitution in everything that was compatible with his religious profession for as long as he remained in the territory. Governor José María Echeandía on June 7, 1829, declared that Barona, with several other missionaries, should be allowed to remain in California because of their age, infirmities, and virtues. He stated that Barona was sixty-six years old and broken in health.

Death came to Barona on the night of August 4, 1831, at Mission San Juan Capistrano after he had received all the final sacraments. Fray José María Zalvidea gave him ecclesiastical burial in the mission church on August 6. Barona had served in the missions for thirty-three years. About twelve hundred Indians had been baptized at San Juan during his presence there.

[1] [Los Angeles, cop. 1961], p. 52.
[2] Engelhardt, *San Juan Capistrano Mission*, p. 78.

BARRENECHE, JUAN ANTONIO (1749-1781)

Fray Juan Antonio Barreneche, son of Miguel and María Catalina Barreneche, was born at Lecaroz in the Valley of Bastón, diocese of Pamplona, kingdom of Navarre, Spain, in 1749. His parents were honorable people and modestly circumstanced. They allowed Barreneche at a very early age to go to Havana, Cuba, with a merchant, Don Martín de Alegría, in whose employ he worked. Desiring to enter the Franciscan order at the age of seventeen, he was first obliged to undertake a study of grammar for two years, after which he was accepted at Havana, headquarters of the province of Santa Elena. After his profession, he studied there the course of philosophy.

Following a meeting with Fray Enrique Echaso of the college of Santa Cruz de Querétaro, who had passed through Havana on his way to Spain, Barreneche expressed a desire to become a member of that college. Assured that he would be able to study theology there, he applied for permission, May 13, 1773. He was accepted on June 14 and left Havana on August 12. From the port of Tampico, where he disembarked, he walked the distance of 200 leagues to Querétaro, arriving on September 13. There he pursued the course in theology and was ordained probably in 1776, subsequently employed at the college chiefly as confessor.

In 1779, Barreneche was destined by his superiors to be the companion missionary to Fray Francisco Garcés in the new missions to be established among the Yuma Indians along the Colorado River in California. Three extant Barreneche letters of 1780 and 1781 from the Mission Purísima Concepción, located on the site of present-day

Fort Yuma, give a very clear picture of the nature of the missionary work and the local terrain. They also reveal his zeal and his desire to found an additional mission dedicated to San Lorenzo. At Fort Yuma, Garcés and Barreneche worked together in complete harmony. Of his assistant, Garcés wrote: "Fr. Juan is very much contented; he is of that caliber which conquers many; he is another St. Patrick."[1]

In the uprising of the Yumas against the Spaniards, Barreneche and the three other missionaries of the area met a violent death. He was killed at ten o'clock in the morning, July 19, 1781, on the same day as Garcés. He was thirty-one years old, thirteen a Franciscan and nine as an apostolic missionary of the college at Querétaro. When his remains were discovered with those of his companions, they were taken to the Franciscan mission of San Pedro y San Pablo, Tubutama, Sonora, for burial. Later all were removed to the college at Querétaro and given solemn interment, July 19, 1794.

Barreneche is described in the college chronicle as a man of deep religious spirit, entirely unworldly, given to rather severe bodily mortification, displaying zeal for souls, and in teaching and hearing confessions. Several documents were drawn up, giving details of his virtues and heroic practices.

[1] Engelhardt, *The Franciscans in Arizona*, p. 163.

BOSCANA, GERÓNIMO (1775-1831)

According to Bancroft, Fray Gerónimo Boscana was born at Lluchmayor, Majorca, Spain, May 23, 1776, while Vicente Francisco de Sarría in 1817 gave October as the month of his birth. Recent information obtained from entry Number 97 of the Baptismal Register of Lluchmayor gives the date and year of his birth as May 27, 1775, with his baptism occurring on the following day. He was the son of Miguel Boscana and Pereta Mulet. Baptized by the Rev. Jayme Sbert, he received the names Hierónimo Magín Ramón. His paternal grandparents were Miguel Boscana and Catalina Puigsever; his maternal grandparents, Gerónimo Mulet and Margarita Garau. When less than a year old, he was confirmed by the Most Rev. Juan Díaz de la Guerra, bishop of Majorca.[1]

Boscana became a Franciscan at the Convento de Jesús, Palma, Majorca, August 4, 1792, and was ordained to the priesthood, December 21, 1799. For a period of four years he was professor of arts in his province. Holding the offices of preacher and confessor, he volunteered for the American missions. At Cádiz, port of embarkation, the government report described him as small of body, dark in complexion, with hazel or dark brown eyes, bushy eyebrows, a heavy beard, and with a mole on his nose.

Boscana set sail from Cádiz in July or August 1803 on *Nuestra Señora del Pilar* or *La Fortuna,* arrived at Vera Cruz on October 24, and entered San Fernando College, Mexico City. On February 17, 1806, he set out for the missions of California, arriving at Monterey, June 6. Boscana was first appointed as supernumerary to Mission Soledad by President Estevan Tapis but was soon transferred to Mission Purisima, where he first signed the registers on December 10. He served there until April 5, 1811, meanwhile baptizing at Santa Barbara on March 27, 1808.

Boscana was next stationed at Mission San Luis Rey from 1811 until 1814. While there, he preached the sermon at the dedication of the final church of Mission San Diego, November 12, 1813, performed the funeral services for Fray Pedro Panto at San Diego, July 2, 1812, and baptized at Mission San Fernando, April 7 the same year. In 1814 he was transferred to Mission San Juan Capistrano, where he remained until early in 1826. He was chosen to sing the Mass of dedication of the final church of Mission Santa Barbara, September 10, 1820. Finally, he served at Mission San Gabriel between April 29, 1826, and July 6, 1831, assisting at times at the chapel of Our Lady of the Angels (the Plaza church), Los Angeles.

Boscana's chief title to fame emanates from his ethnological treatise, *Chinigchinich,* the only study of this nature produced by a California missionary. It is an account of the origin, customs, and traditions of the San Juan Capistrano Indians, called "the Acagchemen Nation." It is not known precisely when Boscana finished his work, but at the end he speaks of "the present time of Nov. 1825." He himself never published it, but it was found among his effects at his death. Alfred Robinson first published it in translation in New York in 1846. It has been republished twice in modern times. Dr. John P. Harrington, anthropologist, considered it "unique and excellent." Dr. A. L. Kroeber credits the author for writing in "a spirited style," with matter "based on unusually full knowledge" and "done with understanding."

The composition of this valuable treatise called for infinite patience on the part of the missionary and presupposed an unusual acceptance of him on the part of the Indians. Still, he might be called the pessimist among the California missionaries because of his statement that he did not think the Indians were capable of absorbing Christianity.

When Boscana was approached on the matter of civil allegiance to the Mexican constitution of 1824, he replied that he would swear to uphold it in so far as it was compatible with his religion and conscience. On March 29, 1829, when the Mexican government demanded that all Spaniards still in California leave within a month, Boscana asked for his passport, only to be refused by Governor José María Echeandía.

A report by the alcalde of Los Angeles to the governor in 1828 that Boscana and Fray José Bernardo Sánchez were secretly exporting money and other articles to the port of San Pedro was examined and found to be false.

Boscana's superiors in California, Sarría and Mariano Payeras, respectively in 1817 and 1820, appraised him somewhat differently. The former wrote: "His merit is that of an ordinary religious and his zeal is of the same character." Payeras stated: "I consider his merit above medium and his aptitude the same for ministry among the faithful and unbelievers as well as for some kind of office or commission."

There has existed a confused and unsubstantiated assessment of Boscana's moral character based on faulty and inconclusive interpretation of documents. Bancroft, citing both Sarría's biographical sketches and his report to Payeras, February 2, 1819, concluded that some doubt was felt about the qualifications of Boscana as "a spiritual guide," for which reason "it would not be well to leave him alone at a mission."[2]

In his biographical sketches Sarría actually says nothing at all about Boscana that is in any way disparaging. In the report of 1819, Sarría declared: "In regard to spiritual matters it appeared to me in my visitations that Father *Barona* [not Boscana] was capable of doing little, wherefore even in the case of the shortage of a minister at San Gabriel I never considered leaving him alone for a long period. Your Reverence already knows Father Boscana."[3]

Sarría was distinguishing the work at any mission divided between *"lo temporal"* and *"lo espiritual."* He was not talking about Boscana at all but José Barona, who because of his physical condition was limited to the amount of work he could do. *"Lo espiritual"* referred to saying Mass, administering the sacraments, giving instructions, and had nothing to do with the moral qualifications of a missionary.

More damaging was Bancroft's statement that Boscana's sudden removal from San Juan Capistrano to San Gabriel in 1826 lent credence to "the disparaging hints in reports of superiors [there were none such] as noted above give some weight to the charges of Vallejo and others that the padre was guilty of immoral relations with his *neófitas*" and that his conduct was not in all respects exemplary.

Boscana was not removed to San Gabriel to take him out of any immoral environment but to replace José María Zalvidea whose health was not good and who was sent to San Juan Capistrano, where his charge would be lighter. Bancroft cites no reference to Vallejo and the unknown "others," who remain anonymous. Unsubstantiated allegations are as worthless in history as they are in court.

Eulalia Pérez, who knew Boscana, states that he was an inveterate taker of snuff, was kind hearted, generous, and generally well liked. She considered him to be of less than medium stature, of a fair complexion. and considerably bent. She added that the drawing of Boscana's bust, reproduced in Robinson's *Life in California,* was a good resemblance of him. Angustias de la Guerra y Ord, however, considered Boscana to be a man of medium size, not yet gray but somewhat stooped with age.

Boscana died at Mission San Gabriel, July 5 or 6, 1831, after having received the final sacraments. He was assisted in his last hours by Fray Jesús María Martínez of the college of Zacatecas, who had recently arrived at the mission, and by Friars Francisco González de Ibarra and José Bernardo Sánchez. The latter buried Boscana on July 6 in the sanctuary of the mission, on "the side of St. Joseph," next to Fray Joaquín Pascual Nuez. He also entered the record of burial in the mission register. At the time of his death, Boscana was fifty-five years old, had been a Franciscan thirty-nine years, and a priest about thirty-two years.

[1] This new data on Boscana is found in Bartolomé Font Obrador, *El Padre Boscana Historiador de California* (Palma, 1966), pp. 22-24.

[2] *History of California,* III, 642n.

[3] MS in SBMA.

CABOT, JUAN VICENTE (1781- ca. 1856)

Fray Juan Vicente Cabot, son of Pedro Cabot, a sergeant, and María Ana Bestard, was born at Buñola, Majorca, Spain, March 9, 1781, and was baptized on the same day. On December 6, 1782, he was confirmed by Bishop Rubio Benedicto Herrero. Cabot joined the Franciscan order, August 3, 1796, at San Francisco, Palma, in the province of Majorca, and made his profession on August 5, the following year. He had finished his studies for the priesthood by 1803.

At the age of twenty-three he sailed for Cádiz to await passage for the Indies. Tall in stature, his face pockmarked, with wavy hair, Cabot was thick lipped and had a mole below his left eye. Embarking from Cádiz, September 2, 1804, he arrived at Vera Cruz, Mexico, on the *Gravina,* around October. He went to Mexico City and entered San Fernando College. Volunteering for the California missions, Cabot left the college, March 12, 1805, embarked at San Blas, June 2, and arrived at Monterey, August 31.

He probably traveled overland to his first assignment, Mission Purisima, for he baptized at San Luis Obispo on September 20, 1805. He ministered at Purisima from October 31, 1805, until September 1807;

at San Miguel from October 1, 1807, until March 12, 1819; then at San Francisco from April 17, 1819, until late in 1820; then at Soledad until October 3, 1824, and finally again at San Miguel from November 7, 1824, until November 25, 1834. During his first period at San Miguel, he was assistant to Fray Juan Martín; during the second period there, he himself was in charge.

While at San Miguel, he baptized at San Luis Obispo, April 9, 1811, and accompanied Vicente Francisco de Sarría as secretary for the official visitation of that mission, September 20, 1816. From San Francisco, on a similar visitation with Mariano Payeras, he visited Mission San Rafael, October 21, 1820. During his service at San Miguel (1824-1834), he baptized at various times at San Luis Obispo.

From San Miguel, on October 2, 1814, Cabot set out with a military expedition into the San Joaquin Valley to the region known today as Tulare. At Bubal, situated on a large lake, with a population of 700, he baptized twenty-four Indians, most of whom were very old and some of whom were in danger of death from illness. On October 5 the town of Sumatche, of equal size, was reached. The expedition proceeded across a river called San Gabriel, advancing into the vicinity of present-day Visalia. Cabot described the area as good for a mission site, and having passed through the towns of Guachame and Tache near the Kings River, he declared the surrounding area also a proper mission site. Cabot kept a diary of the expedition, which returned by a more northerly route, reaching San Miguel on December 3.

Cabot accompanied a second expedition under Juan de Ortega to Tulare Lake and the Kings River, November 4-15, 1815, and made a third exploration of the Tulare country in 1818. Though no mission was ever founded in the interior valley, a significant number of Tulareños were baptized at Mission San Miguel.

According to Alfred Robinson, Cabot erected a shelter house and place for bathing over a sulphur spring at Paso Robles, where many persons went who suffered from rheumatic afflictions.

In the matter of allegiance to Mexico, Cabot replied to the governor that he could not "accommodate his conscience to such a pledge." In the Solís revolt, the leader approached Cabot to request that Fray Luís Martínez of San Luis Obispo attempt to arouse the Indians to revolt. Instead, Cabot warned his confrere of the scheme, urging him not to become embroiled in the affair. Later, when Martínez was unjustly accused of disloyalty to Mexico, Cabot testified in his favor. Cabot himself was accused of planning to destroy mission cattle and of trying to incite an uprising in favor of Spain; the charges were ignored.

When Cabot was asked by Fray Narciso Durán in 1831 for an opinion as to the advisability of emancipating the Indians, he replied that, while he himself would be glad to be relieved from administering the temporalities, he considered emancipation inadvisable for fear of the mission estates going to ruin. If the land was parceled up among the Indians, they would soon be scattered over large areas, in which case a missionary could not be held responsible for their spiritual welfare.

Cabot had intended to retire from missionary service as early as 1819. In 1827 he was in poor health, and two years later Governor José María Echeandía recommended that he be given his passport. With permission of the governor and the father president, he sailed for Spain in 1835, succeeded at the mission by Fray Juan Moreno. Cabot baptized at San Diego, February 1 and 14, 1835, embarking probably from that port. According to an article in the *San Francisco Bulletin,* April 25, 1864, Bishop Thaddeus Amat of the diocese of Monterey and Los Angeles had heard of Cabot in Spain in 1856 and that he had died a short time afterward. Neither the place nor the date is recorded.

Concerning Cabot's character and ability, Sarría, in 1817, wrote that he had the merit of the regular discharge of his duties, "increased somewhat by the expeditions made into the interior of paganism especially in these last two years." In 1820, Payeras declared: "His merit rises above the mediocre and tends to the superior. His aptitude is such that he is fit for the entire range of activity within the apostolic ministry."

In 1829, when Cabot happened to be at San Luis Obispo, Robinson met him there and wrote of him: "Father Cabot was a native of Spain, and brother to Father Pedro Cabot of St. Antonio, but as unlike him in character and appearance as he could possibly have been. He was a tall, robust man of over fifty years, with the rough frankness of a hardy sailor, differing widely from the soft and pleasing manners of his brother, and celebrated for his good-humor and hospitality."[1] In California, states the author, Juan was referred to as "the sailor," while Pedro was called "the gentleman."

[1] *Life in California,* p. 94.

CABOT, PEDRO (1777-1836)

Fray Pedro Cabot, brother of Fray Juan Vicente Cabot, was born at Buñola, Majorca, Spain, October 3, 1777, at seven o'clock in the evening and was baptized on the following day, receiving the names Pedro Juan Francisco Buenaventura. He became a Franciscan at San Francisco, Palma, Majorca, December 22, 1796, and made his profession on December 23, the following year. In 1803, he sailed for Cádiz to join other friars bound for the Indies. At the time, he held the offices of preacher and confessor. He was tall, with dark hair and deep-set eyes and was, like his brother, thick lipped. He sailed June 30, 1803, on the *San Miguel* alias *Sagrada Familia* and arrived at Vera Cruz, Mexico, in August and finally at San Fernando College, September 9.

Having been approved for missionary work in California, he set out from the college in February 1804, together with a fellow Majorcan, Juan Sancho. They left Guadalajara, April 23 and arrived in California at Monterey, August 4. Cabot and Sancho were colaborers at Mission San Antonio from November 15, 1804, until Sancho's death in February 1830. From November 14, 1834, until September 2, 1835, Cabot was stationed at Mission San Miguel and from October 10, 1835, till October 11, 1836, at Mission San Fernando.

While at Mission San Antonio, Cabot baptized at San Miguel at various times between February 3, 1806, and April 10, 1833; at Soledad, between April 1818 and 1829, and at San Carlos between December 12, 1813, and April 1826. From Mission San Fernando, he also attended the town church in Los Angeles, baptizing there a number of times in 1836. He was employed as secretary for official visitations by Vicente Francisco de Sarría to Missions San Juan Bautista (November 15, 1816), Soledad (June 10, 1818), San Carlos (September 16, 1818), and by Mariano Payeras to Mission San Jose (October 14, 1820).

When Cabot arrived at Mission San Antonio, it had been in existence for thirty-three years, but this did not mean that he became a mere administrator of the existing establishment. Building operations went on apace down to the year 1829 and included the present restored church (dedicated in 1813) and significant portions of today's restored monastery and cloister as well as other buildings no longer extant; the development of the dam and irrigation system and several mission ranches. A description of the mission lands, signed both by Sancho and Cabot, was directed to Governor José María Echeandía on October 7, 1827. Earlier Cabot had written the ethnological report on the San Antonio Indians, February 26, 1814, which had been requested by the government. From the end of 1804 until the end of 1832, baptisms increased from 3,041 to 4,419. At the time of his arrival, the mission had 3,000 head of cattle and 8,200 sheep. These numbers rose respectively to 8,000 and 11,000 in 1828.

Cabot handed Mission San Antonio over to the Zacatecan friar, Jesús María Vásquez del Mercado, in 1834 and was sent to Mission San Fernando, where he replaced Fray Francisco González de Ibarra, who had fled from there in 1835 because of the troubles arising from lay administration. From a letter written by Cabot, August 24, 1836, it is clear that he intended to leave California and to return to Spain. He had his passport, and on October 2 in another letter he stated that he intended to sail from San Pedro. However, death intervened. He died on October 11 after having received the last sacraments. Fray

Ibarra, who had returned in the meantime to his post at the mission, gave him ecclesiastical burial in the cemetery of the mission and entered the record of his burial in the local register. Not knowing that Cabot had passed away, San Fernando College, December 3, 1836, elected him a counselor of the institution. At his death, Cabot was fifty-nine years old, had been a Franciscan for forty years, a priest at least thirty-three years, and had spent thirty years in the California missions.

A description of Cabot by Alfred Robinson sets Pedro in distinct contrast with his brother Juan: "I found [him] to be a fine, noble-looking man, whose manner and whole deportment would have led one to suppose that he had been bred in the courts of Europe, rather than in the cloister. Everything [at Mission San Antonio] was in the most perfect order; the Indians cleanly and well dressed, the apartments tidy, the workshops, granaries and store-houses comfortable and in good keeping."[1] He was known as "El Caballero" or the Gentleman by those who associated with him.

His superiors, Sarría and Payeras, respectively in 1817 and 1820, wrote that Cabot was "not inferior to Father Sancho in merit," whom Sarría described as one of the better missionaries. "His zeal induces him to go whithersoever he may be destined or necessity calls him to exercise the ministry. At the same time he is versed in the language of the Indians. He is equally well versed in other branches of learning especially moral theology. For these reasons I do not doubt but that he can discharge not only the ordinary offices at a college or in a community but even others with which one may desire to entrust him."

"His merit is like his application — grand and distinguished," wrote Payeras. "His aptitude is not limited to the ministry of the faithful and infidels but renders him fit also for the office of superior within the order as well as outside of it."

In view of these encomiums, Bancroft states that Cabot was "known as a dignified, scholarly, courteous man," a friar of "polished manners, retiring disposition and tendency towards asceticism," and known for his hospitality, knowledge of the native language, and his uncompromising loyalty to Spain.[2] He had refused to take the oath of allegiance to Mexico but promised to obey the authorities. Echeandía had recommended that he be given his passport, provided that a substitute could be found. As late as 1829 he was declared to be in good health and a man of strict religious conduct. Engelhardt characterized Cabot as "a man of profound learning and of untiring zeal for the conversion of the Indians. He must have also been of a winning disposition and attractive exterior."[3]

[1] *Life in California*, p. 91.
[2] *History of California*, III, 646, n. 11.
[3] Engelhardt, *San Fernando . . . Mission*, p. 112.

CALZADA, JOSÉ ANTONIO (1760-1814)

Fray José Antonio Calzada was born at Trinidad, Cuba, November 24, 1760, and was baptized in the parish church of that city. He was the son of José Calzada and Micaela de Cala. He received the Franciscan habit at the Convento de la Purísima Concepción, Havana, in the province of Santa Elena, February 3, 1780. Having taken his vows, and while pursuing his studies for the priesthood, he requested to be transferred to San Fernando College, Mexico City, where he was ordained, December 18, 1784. That same year he was appointed novice master. In 1787 he was assigned to the California missions and arrived at Monterey early in October with Friars José Señán and Diego García.

Calzada's first assignment under President Fermín Francisco de Lasuén was to Mission San Gabriel where he served from February 21, 1788, until October 19, 1792. During this period he baptized on occasion at San Juan Capistrano, was at Mission Santa Barbara from September 1788 to January 1789, probably for reasons of health, and for a period in 1790 at San Luis Obispo. Calzada himself asked for a transfer and was next assigned to Mission Purisima, where his baptismal entries record his presence from November 22, 1792, until the end of July 1796. During this period he also visited San Luis Obispo where he baptized at times.

As early as mid-1795 Calzada had insistently requested permission to return to Mexico because of the recurrence of his old ailments, hemorrhoids and headaches. On July 20, 1796, Lasuén petitioned the governor to allow his retirement, which was granted. When Calzada's health improved at San Fernando College, he offered to return to California. With seven other missionaries he arrived at Santa Barbara on the *Concepción,* May 8, 1798, remaining until September. Lasuén offered to send him to San Luis Rey, then to San Luis Obispo, both of which assignments he declined. Finally, he was sent to Purisima where he served from September 2, 1798, until August 25, 1804, when he was replaced by Mariano Payeras.

Together with President Estevan Tapis, Marcelino Ciprés, and Romualdo Gutiérrez, Calzada was present at the founding of Mission Santa Ines, September 17, 1804 — Calzada and Gutiérrez appointed as the missionaries. Calzada ministered there until his death, meanwhile visiting Santa Barbara from March through April 1806 and San Buenaventura. He was present at the dedication of the new church, September 9, 1809.

A stroke of paralysis forced Calzada into a supernumerary status. On October 1, 1813, Señán wrote to the college that Calzada was "so completely paralyzed that he ... [was] unable to move." A second report of April 17, 1814, revealed that he was no better. According to Tapis, Calzada had labored at Santa Ines with indefatigable zeal, both in spiritual and temporal matters, until overcome by his stroke. While at the mission, Calzada saw the initial church, dwellings, utility rooms, and the Christian Indian village come into being.

Having received the last sacraments, Calzada died on December 23, 1814, after four days of severe congestion of the chest. He was buried on the twenty-fourth in the temporary church in the presence of Friars Ramón Olbés, Antonio Ripoll, and Francisco Xavier Uría. Tapis conducted the funeral. On July 4, 1817, Calzada's remains were transferred to the new (present) church and were interred in the sanctuary near the communion railing on the Gospel side.

CAMBÓN, PEDRO BENITO (1738-?)

Fray Pedro Benito Cambón was born at Lugar de Leaya in the jurisdiction of the town of Malpica, archdiocese of Santiago, Galicia, Spain, in 1738. He became a Franciscan at the Convento de Santiago, Compostela, September 15, 1754. In 1769 he left the friary of Noya for Cádiz, to embark for the American missions. At the time he was described in official records as of medium height, with a long, thin face, scant beard, and somewhat bald. He held the office of preacher.

Cambón, one of a group of forty-nine friars recruited for San Fernando College by Rafael Verger, entered the college, May 27, 1770. He was chosen as one of thirty destined for missionary work in both Californias. With nine companions he left the college in October 1770 and sailed from San Blas, January 20, 1771. He arrived at San Diego on March 12 and at Monterey, May 21. There President Junípero Serra appointed him and Fray Ángel Somera as the founders of Mission San Gabriel. Reembarking on the *San Antonio* at Monterey, he set sail for San Diego, June 7 and arrived on the twenty-fourth.

Cambón, Somera, and escorting soldiers started out from San Diego, August 6 and traveled as far north as the Santa Ana River, where the party was halted by a group of armed Indians. The friars unfurled a banner of the Blessed Virgin whose image so captivated the Indians that they laid down their arms. The missionaries, not finding the area of The River of the Earthquakes a suitable locale for a mission, continued northwestward until they reached the southern limits of the present-day San Gabriel Valley. There they raised the cross and founded California's fourth mission with the name of San Gabriel, September 8, 1771.

Provisional buildings were erected, and the friendly Indians aided the friars. Soon, however, there was a native outbreak which, according to some reports, was owing to the prevalence of immoral relationships with Indian women on the part of the military. Cambón gave a detailed account of the incidents to the college, February 28, 1772. When Governor Pedro Fages with Friars Antonio Paterna and Antonio Cruzado arrived at San Gabriel on October 17 on their way to found Mission San Buenaventura and realized that a perilous situation existed at San Gabriel, the founding of the channel mission was postponed. Paterna and Cruzado were placed in charge of San Gabriel while Cambón and Somera, disgusted with local events, retired to San Diego.

Cambón in company with Francisco Dumetz was sent to Lower California to obtain supplies in an effort to stave off hunger at San Gabriel. Cambón remained at Misión San Fernando de Velicatá until September 1774, Francisco Palóu entrusting him with the guardianship of the goods of the Fernandino friars, who had relinquished the Lower California missions to the Dominicans. Cambón brought the goods to San Diego, September 26, 1774, then proceeded with them to Mission San Carlos, May 24, 1775. For a period of time thereafter, Cambón was at Mission San Antonio. In April 1776 Serra sent Cambón from Carmel with special letters to overtake Colonel Juan Bautista Anza whom he caught up with at San Luis Obispo on the nineteenth.

Serra had chosen Palóu and Cambón as the ministers of the future Mission San Francisco as early as July 2, 1775. With soldiers and settlers of the Anza expedition, the two missionaries reached the present site of the mission, June 27, 1776, and the first Mass was said on the twenty-ninth. Work on the presidio was formally commenced on September 17 and work started on the mission, August 1, which, however, was not formally founded until October 9. Palóu remained at San Francisco, while Cambón accompanied Lieutenant José Joaquín Moraga and Captain Fernando Quiros, of the *San Carlos,* on a survey by launch of San Francisco Bay and the lower reaches of the Sacramento River. They returned to San Francisco, October 8.

Cambón continued as assistant to Palóu for a little over three years. At the end of that period, because of his ill health, he was given permission to return to Mexico. He sailed from San Francisco on *La Princesa* which was then preparing for a hurried departure because of the outbreak of war between Spain and England. Cambón arrived at San Blas quite ill. Upon recovery, he decided to return to California and was appointed chaplain of the *Santiago.* Meanwhile, Viceroy Martín de Mayorga ordered *La Princesa* to the Philippines, and, since it had no chaplain, Cambón volunteered for the post. He was with the vessel until it reached California, anchoring at San Diego December 9, 1781. Again ill, Cambón remained there for a time and then journeyed to Mission San Gabriel.

There, on March 19, 1782, he met Serra, whom Governor Felipe de Neve had called south for the founding of the Santa Barbara presidio and channel missions. On March 26, Neve, José Ortega, Serra, Cambón, soldiers, and settlers left the mission for the channel. They camped at the site of Asumpta, the Ventura of today, so named by Juan Crespí in 1769. On Easter Sunday, March 31, California's ninth mission was founded by Serra, and Cambón was placed in charge temporarily. He was also expected to visit Presidio Santa Barbara from time to time to give spiritual ministrations. The presidio itself was founded April 21, 1782.

Cambón was next assigned to his original post, Mission San Francisco, where he ministered between August 22, 1782, and June 28, 1791. Suffering periodic ill health, Cambón retired at times to Mission Santa Clara, where he occasionally baptized, and to San Carlos. It was during this period that Cambón built the present mission church of Dolores, the foundations of which had been laid by Palóu.

In November 1791, his ill health continuing — a condition certified by three physicians — he received permission from President Fermín Francisco de Lasuén to return to San Fernando College. He sailed on the *San Carlos*. On July 2, 1792, he received permission to return to his native province of Galicia. He had served the college and missions for twenty-one years and was considered a zealous and useful missionary. The place and year of his death are unknown.

CARNICER, BALTASAR (1770-?)

Fray Baltasar Carnicer was born at Alcañiz in the archdiocese of Zaragosa, Spain, in 1770. He became a Franciscan in 1786 in the province of Aragon. As a deacon, while residing at the friary of Huesca, he volunteered for American service under San Fernando College. He sailed from Cádiz on the *San Nicolás*, June 11, 1793, having been recruited under Fray Manuel Arévalo. At the time of his departure, he was described as tall, light-complexioned, with dark eyes and hair, a light beard, and a pockmarked face.

Carnicer came to California on the *Concepción*, which arrived at San Francisco, April 14, 1797. Though originally destined for Mission San Juan Capistrano, President Fermín Francisco de Lasuén appointed him to Mission San Miguel, where he served from July 9, 1797, until August 26, 1798. During this period he also ministered a few times at Missions San Juan Bautista, Soledad, and San Antonio. Carnicer was next assigned to Mission San Carlos from October 18, 1798, until April 10, 1799. There he became discontented because of the services he had to render to the presidio at Monterey and because of the rudeness and sluggishness of the Carmel Indians.

Lasuén re-appointed him to San Miguel. While there, in December 1800, Carnicer was attacked, together with his companion, Juan Martín, and a visiting friar, Marcelino Ciprés, by violent stomach pains. All three recovered, but Francisco Pujol, who had come from San Antonio to relieve the sick friars, died. Until recent years the illness and death of these friars were attributed to poisoning by the Indians. The discovery of a letter by Lasuén, dated November 25, 1801,[1] discloses the fact that the Indians were guiltless and that the illness resulted from drinking mescal (a Mexican liquor) which had been kept in a copper container lined with tin and which in consequence had become spoiled.

Having witnessed the painful death of Pujol, Carnicer, out of fear, hesitated to remain at San Miguel. So, once more he was assigned to Mission San Carlos, where he arrived on March 29, 1801, and where he continued to serve until November 28, 1807. Bancroft states that Carnicer already wished to retire to Mexico in 1804 but did so actually in 1808. He remained at San Fernando College until his return to Spain in May 1820.

[1] Lasuén to Fray José Gasol in Kenneally, *Writings*, II, 253-254.

CARRANZA, DOMINGO (1770-?)

Fray Domingo Carranza was born in 1770 at Loza in the diocese of Calahorra, Spain, and became a Franciscan at Vitoria in the province of Cantabria in 1792. He enlisted for San Fernando College under the commissary, Fray Manuel Arévalo, in 1796 and took passage for Mexico from Cádiz. Passport records, before his departure, described him as of regular stature, with dark hair, blue eyes, with a dimple on his chin and a scar on his right side.

Carranza came to California in 1798 on the *Concepción,* arriving at Santa Barbara on May 8. Fermín Francisco de Lasuén appointed him as missionary to Santa Cruz, where his first entry in the registers appears on October 26. En route to his destination, he baptized at Mission San Antonio on August 6 and October 8. There he remained until August 1808, meanwhile baptizing occasionally at San Juan Bautista.

During his early years at Santa Cruz, conditions at the mission were far from good: 138 neophytes had deserted, leaving agriculture and stock raising in a state of decline; the mission church was damaged by a flood; and the proximity of Branciforte, the civilian pueblo, caused many difficulties. In August 1808, Carranza was transferred by President Estevan Tapis to Mission San Luis Rey to serve under Antonio Peyrí until late in 1810. Having obtained permission to return to Mexico, Carranza received his permit from Governor José Joaquín Arrillaga, October 29, 1810. He went to San Diego and, for the last time in California, baptized there on November 25.

41

Accompanied by Fray Norberto de Santiago, who was also retiring, he sailed on the *San Carlos* which then proceeded to San Blas. There the ship fell into the hands of Mexican insurgents, who had already gained possession of the port in their revolt against Spain. The two friars were condemned to death but were released from custody when royalists recaptured the vessel. Fray Agustín Garrijo, the guardian of the college, notified Tapis of the events, April 19, 1811, and stated that the friars were safe at Guadalajara. Here the historical trail of Carranza is lost.

CATALÁ, MAGÍN MATÍAS (1761-1830)

Fray Magín Matías Catalá, more popularly known as the Holy Man of Santa Clara, was the twin brother of Pedro Nolasco Antonio Juan Catalá, and was born January 29 or 30, 1761, at Montblanch, Catalonia, Spain. He was the son of Dr. Matías Catalá Roig, a public and royal notary, and Francisca Guasch Burgueras. His paternal grandparents were Ramón Catalá and Josefa Roig, his maternal grandparents, Joan Guasch, a merchant, and María Burgueras. There were four other children, three boys and a girl. The twin, Pedro Nolasco, became a Franciscan priest in the province of Catalonia. Magín and his brother were baptized on January 31 by the Rev. Joan Ferrer in the church of Santa María Mayor. He was confirmed on August 10, 1767, at Lilla near Montblanch by the Most Rev. Juan Lorio y Lancis, archbishop of Tarragona.

Catalá became a Franciscan at the Convento de San Francisco, Barcelona, April 4, 1777, and pronounced his vows in the following year. Having completed his study of theology in Barcelona, he was ordained to the priesthood at the Convento de San Francisco, Gerona, in February 1785 and that very year volunteered for the American missions, being recruited by Fray Juan Ocón, the commissary. With eight other Franciscans he sailed from Cádiz about September 1786. Catalá, on leaving Spain, was described in the government report as a man of good build, with dark hair, gray eyes, a thick nose, divided beard, and with a scar on the left side of his face next to his ear.

Catalá remained at San Fernando College, Mexico City, for six years. In 1793, the guardian informed Fermín Francisco de Lasuén that Catalá and José Espí de Valencia, both "peaceful men," were en route to California. They arrived at Monterey in July. At once, Catalá was assigned as chaplain of the *Aránzazu,* destined to explore northern Pacific waters as far as Nootka Sound. The *Aránzazu* returned to Monterey, July 2, 1794. Governor José Joaquín Arrillaga asked Catalá to accompany the vessel on a second voyage, but he courteously declined because of the hardships involved and because he was primarily destined to service as an Indian missionary.

In California, Catalá was first at Mission San Francisco, where he baptized and conducted funerals late in August 1794. His name appears for the first time in the registers of Mission Santa Clara on September 1. From that day until the day of his death in 1830, a period of thirty-six years, Catalá was stationed at Santa Clara. He left the mission rarely. He was present at the founding of Mission San Juan Bautista, June 24, 1797, and from there went to Mission San Carlos with Lasuén. There, he baptized on the twenty-seventh. He also baptized at the neighboring Mission San Jose between September 2, 1797, and August 22, 1800. Aside from some journeys in the direction of the San Joaquin Valley to win converts, there appear to be no records of any other journeys undertaken by him.

At the time Catalá arrived at Santa Clara, Fray Miguel Sánchez was in charge. When the latter was transferred to Mission San Gabriel in October 1797, Catalá became the superior. Fray José Viader became Catalá's associate in August 1796 and his assistant in the following year. These two friars were inseparable companions during the next thirty-three years. Though Catalá remained the superior, the greater part of the care of the temporalities fell to Viader, owing to the fact that Catalá was soon attacked with rheumatism which became more intense with the passing of the years.

The statistics of the mission registers reveal that from January 1, 1795, to the end of 1830, the total number of baptisms rose from 2,923 to 8,394. Engelhardt states that Catalá personally baptized 3,067 people between September 1, 1794, and October 27, 1827. The banner year for livestock was 1828 when the mission had 30,922 head. During their tenure of office, the padres built two successive churches at the mission, one in 1818-1819 and the final or fifth church which was dedicated, August 11, 1825. They also built a church in the pueblo of San Jose, the cornerstone laid, July 12, 1803. According to tradition, Catalá planted the poplar trees lining the alameda joining the pueblo of San Jose with Mission Santa Clara.

With regard to the controversy between the mission and pueblo of San Jose, which began in Serra's time and which flared up from time to time, Governor Diego de Borica, September 3, 1796, stated that it had been reported that Catalá had threatened the corporal of the guard at San Jose that he would destroy the houses in the town which admitted Christian Indians from the mission. The governor, however, did not believe this report, "as Father Magín is a friar, not a Robespierre." Bancroft states that Catalá's hostilities toward settlers were rebuked

43

but does not say by whom and that corporals Moraga and Vallejo were forced to apologize to Catalá for rudeness shown him.

When Lasuén, in 1796, received from the bishop of Sonora diocesan faculties with power to subdelegate them, he granted these same faculties to Catalá on March 26, 1797, to be exercised at Missions Santa Clara, Santa Cruz, and San Jose, as well as in the pueblo of San Jose. Lasuén also subdelegated his faculties as vicar forane, ecclesiastical judge, and military vicar at a later date. When Catalá was asked to take the oath of allegiance to the Mexican constitution of 1824, he replied on July 6, 1826, that, while he could not take it in conscience, he would swear to observe fidelity and obedience to the government and its appointed authorities. When Captain F. W. Beechey visited Mission Santa Clara in 1826, he found it one of the best regulated and cleanest of all the missions.

Catalá's early years at Santa Clara presaged anything but lengthy tenure at the mission by reason of his illness. As early as March 1797, he suffered from insomnia, and he pleaded with Lasuén to permit him to return to Mexico at the earliest opportunity. He reiterated his plea early in 1798, but Lasuén considered him "so good a worker" that he tried to retain him. Though he did receive permission to leave by the end of the year, Catalá agreed to remain a year longer, owing to the shortage of manpower caused by the departure of another missionary. Lasuén referred to him as "good Father Magín." Permission to leave was again granted by Lasuén, September 1, 1800, because of the missionary's continuing insomnia. He was praised for his good service, religious conduct, apostolic zeal, and notable success. To Governor Arrillaga, Lasuén wrote that he grieved to lose Catalá, since he was such a good worker and carried out his duties in the ministry "to perfection." Catalá decided to stay on, and by the end of 1801, the president could state that Catalá had regained his health.

Once again on July 1, 1804, President Estevan Tapis gave Catalá permission to retire for reasons of health and praised him for his zealous work. Still the missionary remained. In his later years because of rheumatism, he could only limp along painfully with the help of a servant. Nevertheless, he insisted at times on visiting the sick and consoling the afflicted. Thus he would visit neighboring Indian rancherias. In the last two years of his life he suffered intensely. When he could no longer ascend the pulpit nor even stand to preach, he addressed the people seated in a chair by the Communion railing. That Catalá was a good preacher is attested to by James Alonso Forbes, a Scotsman and British consul in California. He stated that he considered Catalá as zealous a man as St. John Chrysostom and as fully effective as a preacher.

Catalá died at seven in the morning on November 22, 1830. Friar

Viader, who made the death entry in the local register, stated that "his whole life was exemplary, industrious, and edifying, and much more so his death."[1] Burial took place on the twenty-third. Friar Narciso Durán of Mission San Jose preached the funeral sermon. Present were the Indians of Santa Clara and the townspeople of Pueblo San Jose. Catalá was buried near the presbytery on the Gospel side of the altar.

As early as 1779, Lasuén, in writing to Governor Borica, had referred to Catalá as "Blessed Father Magín." In 1817, Vicente Francisco de Sarría, in appraising his worth as a religious and missionary, stated that "his prudent conduct together with a tender and religious zeal . . . gain for him the merit of a commendable and evangelical missionary. . . . I do not doubt that this good father could fill other charges and offices . . . if the present state of his health did not embarrass him." Mariano Payeras in 1820 declared: "His merit is great, his services commendable and his aptitude for a perfect apostolic missionary both for the faithful and pagans and for offices in the Order is limited by the fact of his feeling the full weight of his years and suffering from rheumatic pains it being almost impossible for him to ride on horseback."

Engelhardt wrote of Catalá: "Despite his infirmities he observed the [Franciscan] rule strictly, used the discipline and penitential girdle, tasted nothing till noon, and then and in the evening would eat only a gruel of corn and milk. He never used meat, fish, eggs, or wine. The venerable missionary was famed . . . for his miracles and prophecies, as well as for his virtues."[2]

On April 2, 1860, his tomb was opened before a large gathering of Spanish, Mexican, and Indian people, Juan Crisóstomo Galindo, majordomo of the mission in Catalá's time, identifying the remains. Only the skeleton and parts of the Franciscan habit were in evidence. It was estimated that Catalá's height was about five feet, eight inches. The grave was again sealed.

As early as 1882, the Jesuits of Santa Clara communicated with Archbishop Joseph Alemany of San Francisco on the subject of Catalá's continued fame for sanctity. On November 22, they formally petitioned for the opening of the process towards eventual beatification. Permission was granted. Persons were interviewed who had known the missionary in life. These witnesses were called to Santa Clara in 1884 to offer their testimony officially. Alemany took these findings to Rome before retiring to Spain.

In 1904 Engelhardt published the first life of Catalá in *Dominicana* (San Francisco), which was based on an original manuscript written by the Rev. Andrew Garriga who was secretary at the official proceedings in 1884. In 1907, the Jesuits opened the tomb of Catalá, which was an unmarked grave in the church, and had the remains removed to the foot of the altar of the Crucifixion. The old coffin was found to be entirely decayed with only a few bones, some hair, and pieces of the habit. These remains were placed in a large tin box, the lid of which was fastened down hermetically, and lowered into the new sepulcher. Over this was placed a marble slab giving biographical data in gold lettering and bearing the Franciscan coat-of-arms and the biblical inscription: "His memory is in benediction."

In 1908 the Sacred Congregation of Rites, at the request of the Franciscan Postulator General, Francesco Maria Paolini, having examined the testimony of the process of 1884, decided to advance the cause of Catalá by the process of *De non cultu*. Archbishop Patrick Riordan of San Francisco issued a decree on November 6, calling for any writings of Catalá. On September 19, Engelhardt was appointed vice-postulator of the cause. Sessions began at Santa Clara, November 18, 1908, and ended February 20, 1909. The documents were sealed and sent to Rome. At present the cause is quiescent. In 1909, Engelhardt published *The Holy Man of Santa Clara,* which was translated into Spanish and published at Barcelona in 1924 by Fray Pedro Sanahuja, O.F.M., under the title, *Un Misionero Santo.*

[1] Engelhardt, *The Holy Man of Santa Clara,* p. 35.
[2] *The Catholic Encyclopedia,* IX (New York, 1910), 530.

CATALÁN, BENITO (1766-?)

Fray Benito Catalán was born at Alzola in the diocese of Tarragona, Catalonia, Spain, in 1766. He entered the Franciscan order at Zaragosa in the province of Aragón in 1786. In 1795 he enlisted for service at San Fernando College under the commissary, Fray Manuel Arévalo. That same year he sailed from Cádiz for Vera Cruz, Mexico. At his departure, he was described in passport records as of regular stature, pockmarked, having a large nose, reddish hair, blue eyes, a split beard, and with a mole on the right side of his chin.

Sailing from San Blas with ten other missionaries on the *Concepción,* Catalán arrived at San Francisco, April 14, 1797. President Fermín Francisco de Lasuén first appointed him to Mission San Antonio, where he served with Marcelino Ciprés during the absence of Buenaventura Sitjar who had gone to San Miguel for the founding of that mission and to manage its early development. Catalán remained at San Antonio until late in 1799. He also exercised the ministry at Purisima, April 30, 1798; Santa Barbara, May 6, 1798; and San Juan Capistrano, November 1 and December 6, 1799.

Catalán's California record revolves around his illnesses more than anything else. In May 1799, he developed a high fever, was unconscious for several days, and received the last sacraments. Lasuén informed the college that there was no hope for his life. Still he survived. Not long after his recovery, he experienced a nervous breakdown during which he was sent to San Miguel for a period, where he became extremely violent and had to be manacled to prevent him from harming himself and others. There was no alternative but to return him to Mexico, Lasuén signing his official permit, August 13, 1799. In January 1800 Catalán and another missionary in a similar condition, Agustín Merino, sailed from San Diego on the *Concepción* for Mexico. No further details on Catalán after his return to the college have come to light.

CAVALLER, JOSÉ (1740-1789)

Fray José Cavaller was born in 1740 at Falcet, archdiocese of Tarragona, Catalonia, Spain, and entered the Franciscan order, February 14, 1759, at Reus. He was a member of the community of Tarragona when he volunteered for the American missions. In passport records at Cádiz, where he embarked, he was described as of medium height, somewhat corpulent, and of a dark complexion. He arrived at San Fernando College, Mexico City, late in 1769 or early in 1770. As one of a group of ten friars, Cavaller set out for California under Fray Antonio Paterna in October 1770.

He sailed on the *San Antonio* from San Blas, reaching San Diego, March 12, 1771, and Monterey, May 21, where he was received by President Junípero Serra. Cavaller and companions lived at the combination Presidio-Mission San Carlos, Monterey. When Serra transferred the mission site to Carmel Valley (the mission began to function there, December 24, 1771), Cavaller and his fellow Catalonian, Domingo Juncosa, continued to live at the presidio as chaplains of the troops. As early as June 9, 1771, Serra officially named Cavaller and Juncosa as the founders of future Mission San Luis Obispo.

Governor Pedro Fages and Serra in August 1772 set out for San Diego, and, en route, Serra founded Mission San Luis Obispo, the fifth California mission, September 1. Cavaller accompanied them from Monterey, Juncosa being obliged to remain behind to supply for Serra in his absence. The site chosen was within shadow of the volcanic peak, Cerro del Obispo, near the Valley of the Bears. Five soldiers were left with Cavaller as a guard, and on the next day the governor and president continued on to San Diego. Several years later in 1784, Serra stated that in founding the mission in such impoverished circumstances he had trusted in the providence of God alone.

Thus at the age of thirty-two Cavaller was placed in sole charge of a new mission. His nearest neighbors, north and south, were the missionaries of San Antonio and San Gabriel, twenty and forty leagues distant respectively. A fortunate situation existed at San Luis Obispo owing to the friendliness of the Indians (of the Chumash tribe), who were grateful to the Spaniards for having ridded the area of ferocious bears the year before.

The first mission buildings at San Luis Obispo, as at other missions, were fashioned in the familiar palisade or log-cabin style, roofed with tule or earth. By the time of the arrival of the Anza expedition in 1776, the mission buildings had already been arranged in the usual quadrangular pattern. Only the church, built in 1775, was of adobe.

Mission San Luis Obispo was unfortunately exposed to damage by fires, three occurring during the administration of Cavaller. The first, on November 29, 1776, was started by a pagan Indian who tied a burning wick to an arrow which he shot into the dry thatched roof of the mission. Considerable damage was caused to buildings and furnishings. The second fire occurred on Christmas Day, 1781. Cavaller blamed the outbreak on the stupidity of a Lower California Indian in his careless use of firearms. Damage was considerably curtailed, owing to the fact that the congregation was at midnight Mass and a number of fire fighters could be quickly enlisted. The third occurred in November 1782.

No less an authority than Francisco Palóu states that the frequent fires at the mission led the missionaries to begin the use of tile for roofing, and he credits that mission with the first use of roof tiles. Other missions soon followed suit. However, Edith B. Webb in her monumental work, *Indian Life at the Old Missions* (Los Angeles, [1952]), showed convincingly that roof tiles were first used at Mission San Antonio, citing as evidence a letter by Serra of December 8, 1781.

The present mission church was started by Cavaller in 1788, though he did not live to see it finished. Between October 1, 1772, and the end of 1789, the year of his death, 877 baptisms were conferred at the mission, 203 Christian marriages blessed, and 270 burials performed. The number of converted Indians living at the mission at the end of 1789 was 578. Because of the fertile soil of its neighborhood, the mission through the efforts of Cavaller was able not only to maintain itself but by 1776 had surplus produce.

Apparently Cavaller did not leave San Luis Obispo often. He was at San Antonio on February 22, 1775, April 26, 1782, June 11, 1784, and September 15, 1788; at Mission San Carlos, February 23, 1777, and June 9, 1782; and at Mission Purisima on August 10, 1788.

Cavaller died on December 9, 1789, at about two o'clock in the afternoon when only forty-nine years of age. He baptized for the last time on November 20, Miguel Giribet making the entry and Cavaller signing his name with a trembling hand. Miguel Pieras made the entry in the Burial Register stating that Cavaller "died as a good religious having received the holy sacraments" and praised him for his "indefatigable zeal."[1] On December 10, Pieras buried his confrere on the Gospel side of the church near the sanctuary. Bancroft states that Cavaller had the reputation of a zealous and successful missionary.

[1] Burial Register, Mission San Luis Obispo.

CIPRÉS, MARCELINO (1769-1810)

Fray Marcelino Ciprés was born in 1769 at Huesca, Aragon, Spain. He became a Franciscan at the Convento de Nuestra Señora de Jesús, Zaragosa, in 1786, studied philosophy at Teruel and theology at Tarragona, whence he set out for San Fernando College, Mexico City. He sailed on the *San Nicolás* from Cádiz, June 11, 1793. At his departure he was described in passport records as tall, dark-complexioned, having blue eyes, dark hair, and a light beard. He arrived at Monterey, California, on the *Aránzazu,* August 24, 1795.

Ciprés was first assigned by President Fermín Francisco de Lasuén to Mission San Antonio where he made his first entry in the Baptismal Register, October 2, 1795, his last on July 8, 1804. On November 28, 1795, Lasuén wrote to the college that Ciprés was "not only a robust young man, the kind that is needed to help good Father Sitjar in his old age and infirmities, but he is also a person quite gifted in learning the dialect; and we should see to it that such a favorable opportunity is not missed at that mission."[1]

During Ciprés' stay at San Antonio, the number of baptisms rose from 2,143 to 3,041. He was at Soledad, baptizing on March 4, 1798. In December 1800, while on a visit to San Miguel, Ciprés, together with Friars Juan Martín and Baltasar Carnicer, was poisoned from drinking some mescal which had been kept in a tin-lined copper container.

Lasuén declared on June 26, 1802, that Ciprés was low in spirit and desired to retire in the following year. He had suffered a partial breakdown in health and at his own request was transferred to Mission San Luis Obispo. His first entry in the registers there occurs on August 22, 1804, his last on September 14, 1809. While at that mission, he baptized twice at San Antonio and San Miguel between 1804 and 1808 and was present at the founding of Mission Santa Ines, September 17, 1804. He died at Mission San Miguel, January 31, 1810, and was buried in the sanctuary of the church.

[1] Kenneally, *Writings,* I, 363.

CORTÉS, JUAN LOPE (1772-?)

Fray Juan Lope Cortés was born in 1772 at Torrejón de Ardoz in the archdiocese of Toledo, Spain, and entered the Franciscan order in 1788. At the time of his departure for America in 1795, while still a deacon, he was, according to his passport identification, tall, swarthy, with dark brown hair, hazel-colored eyes, and a scar on his forehead. He sailed from Cádiz on the *Santiago de España,* May 8, 1795, with twenty-two other friars under the commissary, Manuel Arévalo, and disembarked at Vera Cruz, July 26. After entering San Fernando College, he volunteered for the California missions some time before February 3, 1796. He was described by his superior, Antonio Nogueyra, as a person of proven conduct who had given complete satisfaction to the discretory.

Together with four other missionaries he arrived in California on June 18, the same year. He was assigned by President Fermín Francisco de Lasuén to Mission San Gabriel, leaving for his destination on June 30 (probably from Monterey), and making his first entry in the mission registers on August 19. He continued to minister there until April 22, 1798. Meanwhile he had been appointed cofounder of Mission San Fernando Rey with Fray Francisco Dumetz. This mission was established on September 8, 1797. Cortés baptized at San Fernando on September 26 and on later occasions. It appears that he went back and forth between San Fernando and San Gabriel to administer the sacraments and to perform other ecclesiastical functions.

Cortés was next assigned to Mission Santa Barbara where his first entry occurs on October 8, 1798, his last on September 18, 1805. While stationed there, he was the associate of Estevan Tapis in a period when the mission was making its greatest spiritual progress in the matter of conversions. The banner year was 1803, the number of converts being 831. During his ministry at Santa Barbara, Cortés paid visits to San Fernando, May 18, 1800; to Purisima, September 6, 1800, and September 4-8, 1803; and to Santa Ines, May 9, 1805. Having served a little short of ten years in California, Cortés asked permission to return to Mexico. On June 29, 1805, Tapis asked Governor José Joaquín Arrillaga to grant Cortés' request. It appears that he traveled overland to San Diego, for he baptized at San Juan Capistrano late in September 1805 and sailed from San Diego, November 5.

On July 11, 1812, Cortés was elected a counselor of the college and on July 11 was given the additional assignment of novice master from which office, however, he resigned on the following November 5. On August 8, 1818, he was again elected a counselor and named vicar of the college. On July 28, 1821, he was named procurator of the California missions, and continued in that same position again on May 22, 1824, which office he exercised until 1828. On December 20, 1827, the Mexican government issued a decree commanding all Spaniards to leave the country within six months unless they took the oath of allegiance. Though a dispensation had been obtained for Cortés to remain at San Fernando College, he declined to accept it and returned to Spain in January 1828 at the age of fifty-seven. No data is available concerning him in Spain.

CRESPÍ, JUAN (1721-1782)

Fray Juan Crespí was born at Palma, Majorca, Spain, March 1, 1721, the son of Joan Crespí and Joana Fiol, members of the parish of San Jaume. He was baptized at the cathedral by the Rev. Joseph Bauzá and received the names Joan Baptista Martí. He was confirmed at the same cathedral, March 15, 1724, by Bishop Juan Zabate of Palma. Crespí made his elementary studies in Palma together with Francisco Palóu. He entered the Franciscan order, January 4, 1738, receiving the habit from the provincial, the Very Rev. Pedro Barceló, at the Convento de San Francisco, Palma, and made his profession, January 9, 1739. With Palóu as a fellow student, Crespí studied philosophy under Fray Junípero Serra from 1740 to 1743, followed by three years of theology, both courses taken at San Francisco de Palma. After Crespí was ordained, probably in 1746, he was sent to the convent of Santa María de los Angeles de Jesús, the novitiate house outside the walls of Palma. It is not known in what capacity he served there.

Volunteering for the Indies, Crespí with two other Majorcans set sail from Palma, September 4, 1749, for Cádiz. Finally on December 29, 1749, he sailed from the latter port with twelve other friars for Mexico on the *Nuestra Señora de Begoña* under the commissary, Fray Pedro Pérez de Mezquía. This group reached San Fernando College early in April 1750. Crespí's physical appearance as a young man of twenty-eight was characterized by shortness of stature, light skin, pallid face, somewhat florid complexion, blue eyes, and black hair.

In 1752 Crespí was sent to the Sierra Gorda missions of Mexico. He served there until 1767, most probably continuously at the Misión San Francisco de Tilaco, the easternmost of the missions. His first signature in the registers is found on August 4, 1752; his last, July 14, 1767. In 1766 he was in charge of the mission. Whether he or his unnamed companion was the actual builder of the fine structure, begun sometime after 1752, is not definitely known.

Crespí was one of the missionaries chosen to replace the expelled Jesuits in the missions of Lower California in 1767. With five companions he went directly from the Sierra Gorda to Tepic through Querétaro and Guadalajara. He arrived at Tepic late in August and there joined Serra and his group who had come directly from San Fernando

College. Crespí was among the signers of the document protesting the Fernandinos' change of destination from Lower California to the Pimería Alta. The viceroy recognized the validity of the protest, and Crespí with the other members of the college, in accordance with the original plan, sailed from San Blas, March 14, 1768, on the *Concepción,* and arrived at Loreto, Lower California, April 1. On the sixth he was assigned by Serra to Misión Purísima Concepción de Cadegomó, thirty leagues northwest of Loreto, founded by the Jesuits in 1718.

When José de Gálvez, visitor-general of Carlos III, decided to occupy Upper California, Serra visited the missions of the peninsula as far north as Guadalupe, inviting missionaries to become volunteers for the new conquest, among whom was Crespí. Later Serra appointed him as chaplain and diarist of the first arm of the military expedition bound for San Diego under Fernando Rivera y Moncada. Crespí left his mission, February 26, 1769, and arrived without mishap though not without some suffering at San Diego, May 14, the same year. The two sea expeditions had already arrived on April 11 and May 1.

While awaiting the arrival of the second overland expedition, Crespí and Fray Juan González Vizcaíno with two Spanish officers explored the valley of the San Diego River and reported favorably on the locale as a proper site for a mission. This letter, dated June 22, 1769, was the first letter written by a Franciscan in Upper California. Meanwhile, sickness broke out in camp, and a number of sailors died. Crespí, Vizcaíno, and Fernando Parrón ministered to them spiritually.

Serra arrived with Gaspar de Portolá at San Diego, July 1. On the fourteenth, Portolá and his men started out on the first overland expedition of Upper California in search of the harbor of Monterey. Crespí was commissioned to accompany it as chaplain and diarist with Fray Francisco Gómez as companion. The expedition failed to recognize the harbor but accidentally discovered San Francisco Bay on October 31. The expedition returned to San Diego, January 24, 1770.

The diaries written by Crespí both in Lower and Upper California were meticulous and detailed. Crespí gave Christian names to the villages, rivers, and sites encountered along the way, yet of all the names he bestowed, only two remain, Los Angeles and Santa Cruz. The former was named on August 1 in memory of the Portiuncula Indulgence attached to the Franciscan chapel of Our Lady of the Angels at Assisi. Crespí and Gómez administered the first baptisms in California when they came across two dying Indian girls north of San Clemente on July 22. His diary records the first earthquakes experienced by Europeans in California and notes the La Brea tar pits in Los Angeles.

The Santa Barbara Channel area was minutely described, almost after the fashion of a census.

The situation at San Diego for lack of supplies became desperate after the return of the Portolá expedition, and the decision was made to return to Mexico if a relief ship did not appear by March 19. Crespí joined Serra in a determination to remain behind even in that event, taking refuge on the *San Carlos* in the harbor. However, on the very afternoon of March 19, about three o'clock, according to Crespí, the sails of the *San Antonio* appeared beyond the harbor and the expedition was able to remain.

A second overland march was undertaken to found an establishment at Monterey, again led by Portolá. Crespí joined it and kept another diary. The party set out from San Diego, April 17, 1770, and arrived at Monterey, after definitely identifying the harbor, May 24. Crespí participated in the founding of the second California mission, San Carlos, June 3.

Crespí lived at the presidio of Monterey until he was called to Carmel Valley, where Serra relocated the mission between August 24 and December 24, 1771, and on Christmas Eve Carmel became the residence of Crespí, who was to serve as assistant to Serra. Meanwhile, Crespí had administered his first baptisms in the area, January 1, 1771. At Monterey he also rewrote and polished his diaries. In the course of his missionary career, Crespí also baptized at San Antonio, May 6, 1773, San Francisco, November 1, and at Santa Clara, November 9, 1781.

When Governor Pedro Fages decided to make a reconnaissance of the San Francisco Bay area, Serra sent Crespí along as chaplain and diarist. This expedition left Monterey, March 20, 1772, and returned on April 5. On this occasion the East Bay area between present-day San Jose and Berkeley was reconnoitered and the Sacramento and San Joaquin rivers discovered.

Crespí became discontented on the Monterey peninsula because of the cold climate, foggy atmosphere, and the tiring trips he had to make between Carmel and Monterey for divine services. He asked Serra for a change of locale. An opportunity came when a packtrain of provisions had to be sent to San Diego. Crespí went along as chaplain, leaving Monterey, April 13, 1772. He was not long in San Diego, however, before he regretted the change and asked Serra to take him back to Carmel. Crespí returned on September 22, 1772, and was attached to Mission San Carlos until his death in 1782.

Together with Fray Tomás de la Peña, Crespí was sent by Serra to accompany the maritime expedition of Captain Juan Pérez to reconnoiter the northwest coast of North America. The friars sailed on the

Santiago, leaving Monterey, June 11, and returning August 24, 1774. The ship reached Queen Charlotte Islands off the coast of Canada. Again Crespí as well as De la Peña kept a log of this voyage.

Thereafter, Crespí left Carmel only once, at his own request, to visit San Francisco with Serra in 1781, and where, upon his arrival, Crespí was welcomed by his schoolmate of Palma days, Francisco Palóu. The two friars remained at San Francisco from October 28 to November 9, returning to San Carlos by way of Santa Clara in order to be present at the laying of the cornerstone on November 19 of the new church which Fray Jose Murguía had started to build.

Shortly after his return from San Francisco, Crespí fell ill and took to his bed. He developed chest trouble and suffered from inflammation of the legs. There was no doctor at Monterey at the time, so the friars consulted their *Florilegio Medicinal de Todas Las Enfermedades* and gave him the remedies they had at hand but to no avail. On the last day of the year, he received the last sacraments, and on the morning of January 1, 1782, about six o'clock, he died. Serra conducted the Requiem and buried him in the sanctuary on the Gospel side near the main altar of the then existing church of Carmel. Serra entered the facts into the Death Register. At some undisclosed time, Crespí's remains were transferred to the sanctuary of the present church, where they were first uncovered in 1856 and exhumed and identified in 1882 and 1943. The remains of Crespí are located today in the stone vault of the sanctuary closest to the wall on the Gospel side.

Palóu wrote of his lifelong friend and associate:

He was adorned with merits and exercised in the virtues which he had practiced from his youth . . . . I always knew him to be extremely exemplary. Among his companions he was known by the name of "Blessed" or "Mystic." He persevered in this manner for the rest of his life, with a dovelike simplicity. He was possessed of a most profound humility. He was so humble, in fact, that when he was a student cleric, if at any time he thought he had irked any of his fellow students, he would go to his cell, fall on his knees and ask his pardon. Since he had a poor memory and could not learn by heart or recite from memory the doctrinal sermons at Mass on Sundays . . ., he used to take along a book, and after the Gospel of the Mass for the people he would read one of the doctrinal sermons. By this means he instructed the people and edified all with his humility . . . . All of us who knew him and had dealings with him piously believe that he went directly to enjoy God . . . . The cries [of the neophytes at his funeral] . . . demonstrated the love they had for him as a father.

Palóu ended his encomium by stating that Crespí was a man of "blameless life and exemplary virtues."[1]

Professor Herbert E. Bolton, eminent authority on early California history, summed up his estimate of Crespí as follows:

Among all the great diarists who recorded explorations in the New World, Juan Crespí occupied a conspicuous place.... Gentle character, devout Christian, zealous missionary, faithful companion, his peculiar fame will be that of diarist. Of all the men of this half-decade, so prolific in frontier extension ... Crespí alone participated in all the major path-breaking expeditions: ... In distance he outtraveled Coronado.

In all these expeditions he went in the double capacity of chaplain and diarist.... Of all his expeditions he kept superb records.... These precious pages record nearly 2000 miles of land travel and a sea voyage of twice that distance. Missionary, globe trotter, and diarist he was; breviary, pack mule, caravel, and quill might decorate his coat of arms or his book plate.

Crespí's record was carved deep in the palimpsest of North America. His kindly deeds and his Christian teachings will never die.... The baptisms, marriages, and the burials of hundreds of neophytes are recorded in his distinguished hand. The archives of California, of Mexico, and of Spain are enriched by his correspondence with officials and friends. In his precious diaries the human toils, the adventures, the thrills, the hopes, the fears of three historic journeys on the Pacific Coast are embalmed.[2]

[1] Geiger, *Palóu's Life of ... Serra*, pp. 214-215.
[2] *Fray Juan Crespi*, pp. xiii-xvii.

CRUZADO, ANTONIO (1724-1804)

Fray Antonio Cruzado was born about May 1724 at Alcarazejo, diocese of Córdoba, Spain, and became a Franciscan in the province of Los Angeles in 1742. He left his convent of Palma de Ecija, September 29, 1749, for Cádiz where passport records describe him, before his embarking for the Indies, as tall, thin, light-complexioned, with scant beard, blue eyes, and somewhat reddish hair. Cruzado with twelve other Franciscans under the leadership of Pedro Pérez de Mesquía sailed on the *Nuestra Señora de Begoña*, December 31, 1749, and arrived at San Fernando College in April the following year.

Cruzado soon volunteered for the Sierra Gorda missions, where he served for twenty-two years, leaving in 1770. His name is found in the scant registers still existing such as at Tancoyol, November 27, 1756, and Tilaco, February 9, 1764. He was the companion missionary of Juan Crespí at Tilaco when the latter left for California in 1767. Cruzado had volunteered that same year for the California missions but could not be released at the time. Twice, June 22, 1769, and June 11, 1770, Crespí begged the guardian of San Fernando College to allow Cruzado to be sent to California. Only when the Franciscans handed over the five Sierra Gorda missions to the archbishop of Mexico City in 1770, was Cruzado finally able to set out for California. He reached San Blas by January 20, 1771, San Diego, March 12, and Monterey, May 21. He sailed on the *Concepción* with nine companions under the superior, Antonio Paterna.

At Monterey Cruzado met Junípero Serra and Crespí. Serra chose

55

Cruzado and Paterna as founders of the projected Mission San Buenaventura. They set sail with Governor Pedro Fages and missionaries destined for the southern missions on the *San Antonio,* July 7 and arrived at San Diego, July 14, 1771. Cruzado and Paterna with Fages, soldiers, and packtrain set out for San Buenaventura and arrived at Mission San Gabriel, October 17. Shortly before, hostilities had broken out between the Spanish soldiers and the Indians of the area, with the result that the founding of San Buenaventura was suspended. The two missionaries had no choice but to remain at San Gabriel, and when the two founders of the mission, Pedro Benito Cambón and Ángel Fernández Somera, retired to Mexico in 1772, Cruzado and Paterna were placed in charge, the former as superior after 1776. Cruzado remained at the mission until his death in 1804. Relations between the two were not harmonious, owing perhaps to differences of temperament. When Palóu was en route from Lower California to Monterey in 1773, he left Friars Fermín Francisco de Lasuén and Juan Figuer at San Gabriel, since he had learned in the meantime that Cruzado and Paterna had petitioned for permission to return to Mexico.

At San Gabriel in 1774, Cruzado met Captain Juan Bautista Anza together with Friars Francisco Garcés and Juan Díaz of the college of Querétaro and two years later when Anza again was leading the large body of soldiers and settlers for the founding of San Francisco.

The original Mission San Gabriel had been founded about a league southeast of the present site, along the slopes of the Montebello hills overlooking the present-day San Gabriel Valley. It was to this original site that Cruzado came in 1771 and there lived until November 1775 when the site was transferred to its present locale. In a detailed and revealing report in 1783, Cruzado described not only what had been accomplished at the old site but at the new.

At the new site, between 1775 and 1783, Cruzado built the structures, all of which were of adobe. The roofs, however, were of earth and grass. The compound formed a complete quadrangle, with a second one almost completed. By the end of 1789 all the buildings were roofed with tile. In 1804 the large mission building (the original quadrangle) acquired its corridor with pillars of brick and mortar. This may be clearly seen in the painting of Ferdinand Deppe done in 1832, before the mission was secularized.

A new stone and brick church, the existing one, was begun about 1795 and was largely completed by February 1803 but was not dedicated until two years afterward. As early as 1783 Cruzado reported the existence of a vineyard and orchard at the mission, and in 1799 Lasuén declared that grapes were eaten and some wine was produced at the mission.

56

Between 1771 and the end of 1804 a total of 3,891 Indians and 128 whites were baptized at the mission. At the end of the same period, 1,294 Christianized Indians were living at the mission. Livestock of all classes numbered 22,490 head, while 7,055 bushels of wheat, corn, and similar products were grown on the mission lands.

Cruzado was an eyewitness to the principal events of the area; and, besides those already mentioned, he observed the preparations for the founding of Los Angeles (September 4, 1781), San Buenaventura (March 31, 1782), and Santa Barbara (April 21, 1782). These foundations were directed by Governor Felipe de Neve out of San Gabriel. Cruzado was also among the first to receive the news of the massacre of padres and soldiers in the Yuma uprising of July 1781. The material prosperity of San Gabriel enabled that mission to provide for the soldiers and colonists of the Anza expedition and to aid less prosperous missions such as San Diego and San Juan Capistrano.

Cruzado outlived his companion missionary of twenty-eight years, Miguel Sánchez, whose funeral services he was probably too weak to conduct, for the burial entry was made by Fray Norberto de Santiago of San Juan Capistrano. Padre President Estevan Tapis notified Governor José Joaquín Arrillaga, October 1, 1804, that Cruzado was physically incapacitated — his last entry in the registers, November 17, 1800, was written in a feeble hand. He signed the last biennial mission report at the end of 1802.

Cruzado died at the mission which he had developed, probably on October 11, 1804, for he was buried on the following day. The entry in the register was made by Fray Francisco Dumetz. Cruzado was eighty years and five months old. He had served in the Sierra Gorda for twenty-two years and in Upper California for thirty-three years. Before death he received extreme unction. Dumetz does not state the precise place where Cruzado was buried in the mission church.

CUEVA, PEDRO DE LA (1776-?)

Fray Pedro de la Cueva was born in 1776 at Hornachos in the priorate of Llevena, province of Estremadura, Spain. Data concerning his entrance into the Franciscan order is missing. He was recruited for service at San Fernando College, Mexico City, by Baldomero López, commissary, in 1803, together with thirty-nine other friars. At Cádiz on May 3, the government report described him as of regular stature, with black hair, blue eyes, thick nose, and a mole below his left ear. He arrived at the college before December 22, by which time he had applied to serve in the California missions. He left Guadalajara, April 23, 1804, and arrived at San Francisco, August 14. En route to California, De la

57

Cueva caused trouble, and a report reached President Estevan Tapis that he was a friar whom it would be well to watch.

Tapis assigned De la Cueva to Mission San Jose, where he served until March 1, 1806. He baptized at San Juan Bautista, July 7, 1806. At Mission San Jose, De la Cueva came into the news of the day by reason of two sick calls answered in unusual circumstances. In January 1805, Indians from the San Joaquin Valley, about fifty miles from the mission, reported that some runaway neophytes who were in hiding among the Asisenes were seriously ill and had asked for a padre to prepare them for death. Following the regulations, De la Cueva asked for two soldiers to accompany him, a request which was granted. The majordomo and a few Christian Indians volunteered to accompany him also. Their destination was a place between the Calaveras and Stanislaus rivers.

One of the Indians of the party turned traitor and in a deep fog led the party among the pagan Leuchas who attacked it. The majordomo was killed, one of the soldiers wounded, and De la Cueva received an arrow wound in his cheek. The Spaniards retreated, and a messenger was sent to the mission for help. Meanwhile, De la Cueva and a soldier took refuge in a cave and continued to make their escape by night, eventually meeting the rescue party. While the sick Christians could not be aided in the circumstances, the expedition brought about the voluntary return of a number of fugitives and the arrival at the mission of a number of pagan chiefs who declared their innocence with regard to the hostilities.

About fourteen months later De la Cueva was asked to respond to another sick call, and, when soldiers refused to accompany him, he set out alone for a considerable distance. This action was reported to Governor José Joaquín Arrillaga, who in turn informed Tapis. The latter defended the missionary, stating that any missionary in his line of duty in similar circumstances would be willing to sacrifice his life, this being the highest form of charity toward the neighbor in spiritual need. De la Cueva's devotion to duty was all the more apparent when one realizes that he undertook the journey on horseback while suffering from a distressing fistula ailment.

During his service at Mission San Jose, De la Cueva had the opportunity of meeting the members of the Nikolai Rezánov party in 1806. The friar was on a visit to San Francisco at the time and was staying with the Argüello family. Dr. Georg von Langsdorff wrote of De la Cueva: "The sternness of Padre José Uría ... was in striking contrast with the vivacity of Padre Pedro de la Cueva. ... When the former spoke, all was silence and profound attention, but hardly had the latter opened his lips than laughter followed from the whole company. He seemed to abound in wit and humor, and entertained us in a most agreeable manner."[1] Langsdorff later visited De la Cueva at Mission San Jose, where the friar extended him both hospitality and aid. The Indians were given a day off from work, and they performed their native dances and exercises of skill for the prominent visitor. Langsdorff praised De la Cueva for his cordial reception: "I owe my public acknowledgments for his kindly reception and hospitality."[2]

De la Cueva, because of his ailments, sought medical advice from Dr. José Benítez at Monterey, who advised him to return to Mexico. Both Tapis and Arrillaga gave him permission, the release being dated July 11, 1806. De la Cueva was present at the dedication of the stone church at Mission San Juan Capistrano, September 7, and his name appears in the register of Mission San Diego for September 30, 1806. He sailed from the port in November.

There is another side to De la Cueva's activities, less edifying than his hospitality and devotion to duty, that is unusually well documented and this by his fellow Franciscans. De la Cueva was a confirmed alcoholic. During his brief stay at the college after his arrival from Spain there was no indication of this latent tendency, else he would never have been sent to the missions. But from 1804 until 1808, drink was his consuming vice. His behavior gave cause for scandal to his fellow friars, to the Indians, and to the laity of Mexico. Fray Romualdo Gutiérrez testified that on the way from Mexico City to San Blas, when en route to California, De la Cueva drank immoderately during the entire trip, despite warnings from his superior on the journey, Fray José Urrestí. He caused his fellow missionaries concern in Celaya, Salamanca, Guadalajara, Tepic, and San Blas. On several occasions he pulled out a dagger against individuals of the group. Almost on the eve of departure, when he could not be found at the port, a special courier was required to round him up in Tepic.

In California itself, Tapis wrote to San Fernando College requesting that De la Cueva be recalled. Fray José Gasol, guardian, relating the detailed escapades of the friar to Viceroy Pedro Garibay, November 7, 1808, stated that De la Cueva had embarrassed his missionary associates, scandalized the Indians, and tried the patience of his superiors because of his excessive drinking. During his return trip to Mexico in 1807, De la Cueva created a scandal in San Blas and Tepic in private homes where he had received hospitality.

Back at San Fernando College, De la Cueva frightened his fellow religious by his acts of violence. They had to lock themselves in their rooms for fear of their lives. Neither the advice of his superior nor the counseling of his brethren had any effect on him. On one occasion, Fray Joaquín García, of the community of San Francisco, Mexico

City, met De la Cueva near Puebla and accompanied him to the capital. García testified that his companion drank all along the way, and at San Martín de Texmelucan had addressed words of such an opprobrious nature to him that were De la Cueva not inebriated, García would have had him thrown into jail. At an inn De la Cueva sent his lay servant to buy some brandy, and on learning that the latter had no money, told the servant to steal the liquor.

Gasol next requested the provincial of the province of the Holy Gospel, who resided at the headquarters in Mexico City, to take De la Cueva "on deposit" and place him in one of the friaries in his province. This Gasol did out of commiseration for De la Cueva, stating that legally he could have had him returned to Spain. De la Cueva was accepted and given an obedience to reside at Quaquechula, where he arrived on July 23, 1807. He soon fell out with the superior, Fray Montés, for De la Cueva's drinking continued, and on the night of August 2 in an alcoholic rage he broke the furniture in his room, got hold of a knife, and sought to kill Montés. Fray Francisco Vila, who recounts the affair, with Montés was forced to flee at ten o'clock at night, seeking hospitality in the home of a government official.

Shortly thereafter De la Cueva appeared at San Fernando College asking to be sent to another friary. He was then sent to San Cosme near the city, a move which the provincial of the province made reluctantly only after repeated requests of Gasol. There De la Cueva continued his antics. On one occasion he submerged himself in an aqueduct with intent to drown himself. After that he was ordered confined. De la Cueva promised amendment and offered to make the spiritual exercises of a retreat, and was once more given a chance. He returned, however, to San Fernando College, where he was accepted more "by force than by favor." At the college, on the night of March 11, 1808, De la Cueva was in such a state of fury that he prepared to hang himself, which he was only saved from doing by the quick actions of his confreres. Since there was no lockup at San Fernando, the guardian had recourse to the great convent of San Francisco, where a jail cell existed for recalcitrants. De la Cueva was accepted there until the commissary general of the Indies could be contacted with regard to the friar's future disposition. At San Francisco, meanwhile, he loosened the brickwork and damaged the walls of his cell, for which behavior he was placed in stocks. After tolerating De la Cueva for five and a half months, the guardian of the friary asked that Gasol have him removed, for the guardian could no longer put up with a person who had no respect for superiors, who had a mordant tongue, and who damaged property.

With his charity and patience wearing thin, Gasol had now but one more source to which he could turn for help, and this was the viceroy. An *expediente* was submitted to him in which all of the friar's past was described in detail. Gasol requested that De la Cueva be returned to Spain and he offered to pay the expenses — always a touchy question with the viceroy when a friar had not completed his ten years of service.

Pedro Garibay gave the necessary permission on November 30, 1808. De la Cueva was disaffiliated from the college on February 7, 1809, and taken to Vera Cruz, orders being given to place him on the first ship going to Spain, detaining him in the meantime in the fortress of San Juan de Ulloa.

No further details are available on De la Cueva. Not only is this full story of the friar told in the *expediente* of 1808, in the Archivo General de la Nación, Volume LXI, in the section of the Californias, but the details of the attempted suicide at the college are recorded in the "Libro de Decretos" of the college itself, a volume now in the hands of the Mexican government. De la Cueva was a sick man, a genuine alcoholic, whom neither counsel nor confinement could cure.

[1] *Narrative*, p. 82.
[2] Ibid., pp. 108-109.

DANTÍ, ANTONIO (1760-?)

Fray Antonio Dantí was born at Sampedor, Catalonia, Spain, in 1760, and entered the Franciscan order at Barcelona in 1777. In 1786 he set out for America from the house of studies in Barcelona and was listed by the commissary, Juan de Ocón, as a moralist. In passport records at Cádiz, he was described as a man of regular stature, thin, with a large face, gray eyes, reddish beard, pockmarked, and lacking some upper teeth. He sailed from Cádiz for Mexico about September 1786 and subsequently entered San Fernando College, Mexico City, remaining there about three years as a preacher and confessor with faculties in the archdiocese of Mexico.

Together with Friars Estevan Tapis, Mariano Rubí, and José de Miguel, Dantí set out for California, arriving at Monterey on August 2, 1790. He baptized at Mission San Carlos on the twenty-seventh. President Fermín Francisco de Lasuén assigned him to San Francisco where Pedro Cambón, its cofounder, was directing its destinies. His name first appears in the mission registers, October 21, 1790, his last on February 22, 1796, though he remained there some time longer. When in November 1792 Captain George Vancouver anchored at San Francisco, he was welcomed by Dantí and his associate, Martín de Landaeta. The friars visited Vancouver aboard ship and later gave him a gracious reception at the mission.

On November 15, 1795, under orders of Governor Diego de Borica, a military expedition set out from Monterey to explore new mission sites. Led by Ensign Hermenegildo Sal and accompanied by Dantí, it explored the valley of the San Benito River and reached the East Bay area in the vicinity of present-day Oakland. A cross was raised at a place called San Francisco Solano. The expedition returned to Santa Clara on November 25. Dantí recommended the site of the future Mission San Juan Bautista, later founded on June 24, 1797, and made an actual survey of the future site of Mission San Jose, founded June 11, 1797.

It appears that Dantí came under the influence of two missionary malcontents, Bartolomé Gilí and Mariano Rubí, who were opposed to Franciscan administration of temporalities as out of harmony with the Franciscan rule, a view that was shared neither by the father president, Lasuén, nor the father guardian, Tomás de Pangua. The latter, writing to Lasuén, September 30, 1794, stated: "There has been discovered another *temporalista,* that is to say, a declaimer against temporalities. It is Father Antonio Dantí, whom without doubt the other two practitioners have imbued with their mode of thinking. Your Reverence will endeavor to convince them and make them see the fatal consequences of their opinion, and that far from being opposed to our religious state, the management of temporalities for the Indians is very acceptable to God."[1]

Bancroft wrote: "Of Antonio Dantí we only know that he was minister at San Francisco from October 1790 until July 1796; that he had a fiery temperament — *geniò de pólvora,* as Borica termed it — and was disposed to be unduly severe to his Indians; and that he was finally allowed to retire, suffering from some trouble with his legs and with inflamation of the eyes threatening blindness."[2] The first part of this characterization calls for correction.

Dantí had trouble with runaway Indians, and in an effort to secure their return, in March 1795 he directed fourteen Christian Indians to cross the bay. In their pursuit these Indians were attacked by pagans and seven of the Christians were killed. Dantí was deeply grieved and informed Lasuén, who comforted him and exculpated him from blame. Lasuén told him, however, that he should not use that method in the future unless there was a greater number of persons in the searching party and it was better protected.

On September 12, 1796, Fray José María Fernández, whose mind became deranged after he had been accidentally hit on the head, wrote to Governor Borica that Dantí and Landaeta did not appreciate his presence in San Francisco and that the desertion of Indians from that mission was a result of harsh treatment on the part of the missionaries. The governor, unaware of Fernández' condition, angrily wrote to Lasuén on the matter but, on receiving an explanation from him concerning Fernández, apologized and exonerated the missionaries.

While stationed at San Francisco, Dantí visited Mission Santa Clara a number of times and officiated there. He had already requested retirement by October 1794, and in the following year became quite querulous with Lasuén for not having received a reply from the college. In the friar's favor the president declared that Dantí was running the risk of going blind if he did not receive immediate treatment, and he was given the assurance that he would be permitted to retire in the following year. Lasuén issued the permit on July 29, 1796, explaining both to Governor Borica and to Viceroy Branciforte that he had granted the permit because the friar suffered from pains in the legs, a severe inflammation of the eyes, all the while fearing that he would sustain a complete loss of eyesight. His name appears in the Santa Barbara Mission Register, September 1 and at San Diego, October 20 and 29, 1796. He probably sailed for Mexico from the latter port shortly thereafter.

Evidently his maladies improved at San Fernando College, for in 1802 he was listed as novice master. In the chapter held in 1803 and again in July 1821, Dantí was elected a counselor of the college, and on March 27, 1822, he was appointed vicar, or second in command after the guardian. He was still in Mexico City in 1827 when the banishment of Spaniards was decreed by the government. Though Dantí, then sixty-three years of age, was allowed to stay, he chose to return to his native Spain.

[1] Engelhardt, *Missions and Missionaries of California*, 2nd ed. (Santa Barbara, 1930), II, 505.

[2] *History of California*, I, 713, n. 37.

DÍAZ, JUAN (1736-1781)

Fray Juan Díaz, son of Juan Marcelo and Feliciano Vásquez, was born in May 1736 at Alazar, archdiocese of Seville, Spain. The patronymic was given to him by his godfather, Alonso Díaz. When he received the Franciscan habit, he was known as Juan Marcelo Díaz, but after his profession he went by the name Juan Díaz only. At the age of eighteen he began his novitiate at the convent of Hornachos in the Franciscan province of San Miguel in Estremadura. He was ordained a priest at the age of twenty-seven. He volunteered for the American missions and entered the college of Santa Cruz de Querétaro in 1763. There he was known for the strict observance of the rule, for devotedness in prayer, zeal in hearing confessions, and in preaching.

When the Jesuits were expelled from their missions in the Pimería by Carlos III in 1767, Díaz was among the Queretaran friars chosen by his superiors to labor in that northern field. He proceeded to Tepic and, then, by way of San Blas and Guaymas, reached San Miguel de Horcasitas in May where he was assigned to the Misión Purísima Concepción at Caborca in Sonora. From there he attended the *visita* at Pitic, two leagues east, and the *visita* of Bisanig, six leagues west. The Pima Indians under his charge numbered 1,145. Employing firmness and sweetness, as occasion required, Díaz succeeded in developing the mission spiritually and materially, so that when the president visited it after six years, he was surprised at the progress made. In June 1775 Díaz was delegated by the president of the missions as official visitor for eight missions in Pimería Baja.

Together with Captain Juan Bautista Anza and Fray F. H. Garcés, Díaz went on the reconnaissance in 1774 to determine the feasibility of an overland route to the California missions. He was at Mission San Gabriel from March 22 to April 10, 1774, stopped at Mission San Antonio about the middle of April, and arrived at Monterey on April 21. Anza and Díaz visited Mission San Carlos at Carmel; San Antonio again on the return trip; San Luis Obispo and finally, from May 1 to 4, San Gabriel. Then Díaz returned to Sonora. He baptized at Mission San Gabriel on March 24 and visited Mission San Diego shortly before leaving San Gabriel. He kept a diary of his journey from Tubac to San Gabriel, January 8-April 5, 1774, and from San Gabriel to Tubac, May 1-26, 1774. Díaz subsequently became president of the Queretaran missions sometime before the year 1778.

With Garcés, Díaz set out on an embassy to the Yumas, August 1, 1779, and reached Sonoitac, where he remained with a group of soldiers while Garcés went on to the Yumas. Díaz joined him in October. When the commandant general, Teodoro de Croix, ordered the friars not to establish any missions among the Yumas because of impending trouble, Díaz returned to Arispe to confer with De Croix.

With the eventual founding of missions among that tribe, it was finally determined that a separation between the spiritual and temporal government would be desirable. Two Spanish pueblos were to be founded along the Colorado; the pagan Indians could join if they wished, while the missionaries, limited to spiritual matters, were to find and instruct the natives in Christianity as best they could. This pattern was a "new method of conquest," alien to the practices of the colleges.

The military, colonists, and missionaries came to the Colorado on the California side in 1780 and established the two pueblos, while the missions of Purísima Concepción at Fort Yuma and San Pedro y San Pablo at Bicuñer several leagues to the north were founded. Díaz was placed in charge of the latter mission.

The missionaries made the best of the situation, but their efforts met with ill success. When they saw that the Indians were about to revolt and that there was no chance to escape, they prepared the Spaniards to meet death. The attack on Bicuñer came on July 17, 1781. Díaz and his companion, Joseph Matías Moreno, were murdered with clubs. Díaz was forty-five years old and had been a Franciscan for twenty-seven years, a priest for seventeen, and had been an Indian missionary for thirteen years.

The remains of Díaz and Moreno had lain unburied for five months when they were discovered. Díaz' head was missing, but the remains were identified by the survivors by means of the patched habit, the cord, and the crucifix which Díaz always wore on his breast. The bodies were taken to the mission of Tubutama in Sonora. In 1794 they were transferred to the college of Santa Cruz de Querétaro, where solemn and final interment took place.

DULANTO, ANDRÉS (1774-1808)

Fray Andrés Dulanto was born in 1774 at Suzarra, archdiocese of Burgos, Spain, according to his record of emigration, while his death record gives the place of his birth as Miranda de Ebro. He became a Franciscan in the province of Cantabria and on volunteering for the Indies, he held the offices of preacher and confessor. Dulanto was a man of regular stature, of florid complexion, with hazel-colored hair, gray eyes, thick nose, and scant beard. He sailed from Cádiz shortly after June 20, 1803, on the *San Miguel* alias *Sagrada Familia* and arrived at Vera Cruz, Mexico, in August. By December 22, at San Fernando College, he had volunteered for the California missions.

With nine other Franciscans Dulanto left Mexico City at the end of March or beginning of April 1804. The group left Guadalajara, April 23 and arrived at Monterey, August 15, 1804. Fray José Antonio Urrestí was the superior. Dulanto was assigned to Mission San Juan Bautista and officiated at a baptism there for the first time on September 4. He served under Fray Domingo Iturrate who had been at the mission since 1801. Dulanto saw a significant section of the present church rise. The mission had 1,000 convert Indians. He visited Mission Santa Cruz at least on two occasions, January 12, 1806, and February 23, 1807, when he baptized.

Dulanto's last entry at San Juan Bautista was on May 19, 1808, after which illness forced him to retire to Mission Santa Barbara at a doctor's behest. He died there, September 11, after receiving the sacraments, and was buried by Marcos Antonio de Vitoria on the following day in the third church built at the mission. Dulanto was only thirty-four years of age.

At San Juan Bautista, Friars Felipe Arroyo de la Cuesta and Domingo de Iturrate also made an entry in their Burial Register. They stated that Dulanto labored "with the greatest efficacy and solicitude for souls as was observed in his preaching, in the confessional and in his grand example among the neophytes."[1]

When the fourth and final church of stone at Santa Barbara was dedicated, September 10, 1820, the remains of Dulanto were removed from their original burial site to the new vault beneath the sanctuary, President José Señán officiating at the ceremony.

[1] Burial Register, Mission San Juan Bautista.

DUMETZ, FRANCISCO (1734-1811)

Fray Francisco Dumetz, also spelled at times Dumete, was born at Palma, Majorca, Spain, in 1734 and entered the Franciscan order in his native city at the Convento de Jesús, October 15, 1751. From that same friary he left for the Indies in 1770. At Cádiz he was described in passport records as aged thirty-six, of medium build, of florid complexion, and bald. He and twenty-nine other friars sailed for America under the leadership of Fray Rafael Verger. Arriving at San Fernando College that same year, he was already destined in October as one of ten to serve in the Upper California missions.

With Antonio Paterna as leader of the group, Dumetz traveled to Tepic, where he remained, residing at the hospice of Santa Cruz de Zacate, until passage could be obtained out of San Blas for California, January 20, 1771. He arrived at San Diego on the *San Antonio,* March 12, where he replaced Fray Francisco Gómez who was suffering from scurvy and who wished to return to Mexico. Dumetz stayed at San Diego until September 1772 and while there was employed by Governor Pedro Fages in obtaining the return of some military deserters to their post. Also, when supplies were running low there and at San Gabriel, Dumetz and Pedro Cambón went to Lower California to replenish them. Dumetz in company with Tomás de la Peña returned with the first sheep introduced into Upper California.

Dumetz next made the overland journey to Mission San Carlos with Juan Crespí, who at the time was temporarily at San Diego. En route, Dumetz baptized at San Gabriel on November 1 and 2, 1772. He remained at San Carlos for the greater part of the next ten years, his last entry occurring on May 18, 1782. Serra later stated that he had "good grounds" for transferring Dumetz from San Diego, replacing him with Tomás de la Peña.

It was during Serra's absence in Mexico City that Dumetz with Crespí received the interim president of the missions, Francisco Palóu, November 13, 1773. When Captain Juan Pérez and Friars Crespí and De la Peña were absent from Monterey for their northwest exploration by sea, June 10, 1774, he officiated at the solemn Mass. Later he officiated at Mission San Antonio, July 25, 1774, and temporarily served there with Buenaventura Sitjar from about December 18, 1775, to the middle of April 1776 and again from November 7 to 23, 1777.

During the first half of 1775 Dumetz was again in Lower California, leaving Monterey, January 13. On this occasion he accompanied the transfer of the personal goods of the Fernandino friars north to Monterey from Misión San Fernando de Velicatá where they had been deposited after the Lower California missions had been given up to the Dominicans, returning with his companion Cambón, May 24, 1775.

Dumetz was at Mission San Carlos when Serra administered the sacrament of confirmation for the first time in California, June 29, 1778, and assisted Serra in its administration. When Felipe de Neve arrived at Monterey, February 3, 1777, as the first resident governor of the new capital of both Californias, Dumetz and Serra were on hand to greet him. Dumetz was at Mission Santa Clara, August 12, 1781, for the celebration of the mission patron, on which occasion he baptized.

After a delay of thirteen years on the part of the government, Mission San Buenaventura was finally established, March 31, 1782, by Serra, who placed Cambón temporarily in charge. Upon Serra's return to San Carlos, Dumetz and Vicente de Santa María assumed charge. They arrived about May or June 1782 and served there together for fifteen years, Dumetz' last entry in the registers occurring June 29, 1797. While there, Dumetz met Captain George Vancouver, who visited the mission in 1793. The navigator named Point Dume, between Point Mugu and Malibu, in memory of the friar. Dumetz visited Mission Santa Barbara on July 21, 1787, in February, June, and December 1788, and on March 3, 1792. He was there again in February 1793, where he administered the last rites to Paterna, the mission's first superior, gave him ecclesiastical burial, and made the entry in the local register.

President Fermín Francisco de Lasuén called upon Dumetz to join him in founding Mission San Fernando Rey, September 8, 1797. Dumetz performed his first baptism there on the thirteenth and remained there until December 13, 1805. He erected the initial buildings, completed the second church and quadrangle, and Christian Indian village, and began the third and final church in 1804, which was dedicated on December 6, 1806, after Dumetz' departure. Indians to the number of 1,534 had been baptized by the end of 1805. While at San Fernando, Dumetz officiated at San Gabriel, June 3, 1801, and August 31, 1803. Out of San Buenaventura he had also officiated there, October 3, 1782, and April 19, 1787.

When Dumetz was assigned to Mission San Gabriel in 1805, that mission had been in existence for thirty-five years. The building program had been completed, and at the end of that year, 4,045 Indians had been baptized, and 1,314 Christians were living at the mission. The mission livestock numbered 18,206. Dumetz officiated at his last baptism, October 22, 1810, three months before his death on January 14, 1811. He received the sacraments and was buried on the following day by Fray José María Zalvidea in the mission church. Dumetz was seventy-seven years old, had been a Franciscan for sixty years, and a California missionary for forty. At the time of his death he was the oldest missionary in the territory and the only surviving companion of Serra in the province.

Bancroft states concerning him: "Though he appears to have been an efficient and zealous worker, he is perhaps the least prominent of all the old padres in the missionary records. Not a single document bears his name in my list of authorities."[1] According to José María Romero, a contemporary soldier, Dumetz was tall, stout, addicted to the use of snuff, "traces of which were also unpleasantly visible."[2]

[1] *History of California*, II, 355, n. 40.
[2] Bancroft Library MS.

DURÁN, NARCISO (1776-1846)

Fray Narciso Durán was born December 16, 1776, at Castellón de Ampurias, diocese of Gerona, Catalonia, Spain. He became a Franciscan at Gerona, May 3, 1792, and was ordained a priest, December 20, 1800, by Bishop Pedro Díaz y Váldez in the episcopal chapel at Barcelona. Three years later he and Fray Buenaventura Fortuny left Catalonia for Cádiz where they sailed for Vera Cruz, Mexico, on May 3, 1803, arriving there about July. Durán was a preacher and confessor. He was tall, had dark hair, blue eyes, a heavy beard, and a large scar below the left eye. In later years he was described as medium in height, somewhat stout, of fair complexion, with blue eyes. The engraving of him in Eugène Duflot de Mofras' *Exploration* (1844) was considered by José María de Jesús González Rubio to be a tolerable likeness.

On February 17, 1806, Durán and three confreres left San Fernando College for California, arriving at Monterey, June 6, probably on *La Princesa*. Soon Durán was assigned by President Estevan Tapis to Mission San Jose, which had been in existence for nine years. Georg von Langsdorff, the Russian naturalist, who had been entertained there in April 1806, just a few weeks before Durán's arrival, described the mission as having buildings and grounds of considerable extent, the soil everywhere fertile and rich with the vineyards producing excellent wine. The Christian Indians still lived in their conical-shaped huts. Trees in the area were scarce, but the soil was excellent for manufacturing adobe bricks.

Fortuny, who had come to California with Durán, was also sent to San Jose with him. Their association at that mission lasted from June 1806 until 1826 when Fortuny was transferred to Mission San Francisco Solano. At San Jose, Fortuny was the superior until 1826 when Durán succeeded him. Durán continued to supervise the mission and its activity until 1833. The new church, which had been begun by José Antonio Uría in 1805, was finally blessed by President Tapis, April 22, 1809. Between 1809 and 1827 building continued, including a Christian Indian village, a dam across Mission Creek, a flour mill, a soap factory and tannery, a new cemetery, two large gardens, and massive two-story living quarters for the padres. That Mission San Jose together with its neighbor Santa Clara exceeded the other missions in the traffic in hides is attested to by Richard Henry Dana in *Two Years before the Mast*.

Between the end of 1806 and the end of 1831 the Indian community grew from 662 to 1,886 members. The number of baptisms between those years grew from 1,556 to 6,637. Cattle increased from 4,500 to 12,000 head, sheep from 8,000 to 13,000, and horses from 4,800 to 13,000.

Though no professional musician, Durán developed at Mission San Jose and later at Mission Santa Barbara the innate musical ability he had. It was Durán and José Viader of Santa Clara who directed the combined choirs of Missions Santa Clara, San Francisco, and San Jose when the church of the last-named mission was dedicated in 1809. When Alfred Robinson visited Mission San Jose in 1831, he wrote that "the music was well executed, for it had been practiced daily for more than two months under the particular supervision of Father Narciso Duran. The number of musicians was about thirty; the instruments performed upon were violins, flutes, trumpets and drums. . . ."[1]

When Durán arrived at the mission, he found the choir in poor shape and on recognizing the Indians' native ability to sing and to play, he adapted European music to his local purposes. He wrote his "Prológo" in 1813 to explain his method, declaring that if his system of adaptation were followed it would make no difference who was in charge of the choir. He maintained that instrumental music should always accompany singing and that the number of singers should be large. The notes he used were square shaped and written large so that they could be seen from a distance, and they were in three colors corresponding to three voices. Durán composed a choir book, with propers for Masses and other liturgical music. The Masses, *Misa de Cataluña* and *Misa Vizcaína*, are attributed to him. Without doubt Padre Durán was the padre musician par excellence of the mission period.

At Mission San Jose Durán met a number of foreign visitors who recorded their impressions of him and his work: Otto von Kotzebue in 1816; Camille de Roquefeuil in 1817; and Captain Frederick Beechey in 1826, who found the mission "was all neatness, cleanliness and comfort," and who praised the choir, hospitality, and character of the resident missionaries. In 1827 Auguste Duhaut-Cilly spent a day there and said of Durán that he was a well-educated man and read much but characterized him at the same time as a cheerless personality.

Jedediah Smith, the trapper, came to the mission in 1827. Durán, who had orders from the governor to arrest him, placed him in charge of the corporal of the guard until his purpose in California became clear. On a subsequent visit, Smith was given full hospitality. Kit Carson and his men arrived at Mission San Jose in 1830 and were hospitably entertained. Robinson wrote in 1829 that Durán was "generous, kind and benevolent" and that "the natives not only revered him, as their spiritual father and friend, but seemed almost to adore him. He was universally beloved, and the neighboring [Indian] village bore testimony to his charitable heart, while many a transient traveler blessed him, and thanked God, that such a man existed among them."[2]

However revered Durán was, he had his Indian troubles. The revolt of Estanislao, the alcalde of the mission, 1828-1829, was a serious one. As a result, some five hundred Indians from Missions San Jose, Santa Cruz, and San Juan Bautista, joined by some pagan Indians, left the area of the missions and went into the San Joaquin Valley. Only after three military expeditions were sent against them, were they overcome. Estanislao appears to have been a veritable firebrand; but in the end he asked for sanctuary, and Durán begged Governor José María Echeandía to pardon him. The pardon was granted, and the chief and his people returned to the mission.

While at Mission San Jose, Durán officiated a number of times at Mission Santa Clara and was at Mission Santa Cruz when Andrés Quintana was murdered. He conducted his funeral services on October 13, 1812. In May the following year he visited Mission San Francisco, baptizing there on the seventeenth. At the same mission he acted as secretary to Vicente Francisco de Sarría, commissary prefect, December 2, 1816. In May 1817 together with Ramón Abella, Durán accompanied Lieutenant Luís Argüello on an expedition along the Sacramento and San Joaquin rivers, primarily to seek new mission sites. The company left San Francisco May 13 and returned on the twenty-sixth. Durán kept a diary of this reconnaissance. He was also present at the establishment of Mission San Rafael, December 14, 1817.

In 1809, Durán was involved in a dispute with the citizens of Pueblo

San Jose concerning the encroachment of the pueblo cattle on mission lands, but he lost his case. In 1817 he sent a vigorous protest to Governor Pablo Solá, who sought to impose an export tax on mission products. In 1822, he protested to Governor Luís Argüello against the forced contributions by the missions to maintain the military establishments. In 1823, Durán was active in preventing the dissolution of Missions San Francisco and San Rafael in favor of San Francisco Solano, fostered by José Altimira, and wrote a letter to the governor on the danger of Russian encroachment in California. In 1826, he protested against the government request that 10 percent of all new-branded cattle belonging to the missions be given over to the military. About the same time he was the first to suggest the appointment of a bishop for California, since the sacrament of confirmation had not been administered in the territory for fourteen years.

With regard to the question of his political loyalty, Durán declined to take the oath in favor of the Mexican constitution of 1824. He contended that oaths had become mere playthings. When Echeandía peremptorily ordered him to appear at San Diego, he refused on the ground that he was alone at the mission and could not leave it unattended. Durán offered to swear fealty to the existing government and to promise not to act against it. Otherwise, he was resigned to go into exile. He was let alone.

Durán's superiors, Sarría and Mariano Payeras respectively, in 1817 and 1820, considered him an excellent missionary and a capable man. Of him Sarría declared that "his aptitude for other offices cannot be doubted." Payeras declared that "his merit is distinguished and his aptitude is for a complete apostolic man in both fields [spiritual and temporal matters] and for such offices and prelacies which may be deemed best to bestow upon him." Payeras furthermore wrote on April 20, 1820, that Durán was a missionary of talent and of religious spirit. Hence it is no surprise to learn that Durán became president of the California missions though in a novel way. When Sarría was elected commissary prefect to succeed Payeras in the chapter of May 24, 1824, the superiors of the college gave Sarría the privilege of choosing the new president. Sarría chose Durán, and the latter notified Governor Argüello of his appointment, April 2, 1825.

When Durán opposed Echeandía's plan for emancipation of the Indians, he became *persona non grata* to the Mexican officials. As a result, in the election at San Fernando College of 1827, the college was notified that Durán would not be acceptable as president. Fray José Bernardo Sánchez of San Gabriel was chosen to succeed him, June 9, 1827, and Durán continued to labor at San Jose as a simple missionary.

When the decree expelling all Spaniards from Mexico became the law in 1827, Durán was listed among those destined for exile, but he was allowed to remain since no replacement could be obtained.

On May 26, 1830, Durán was again elected president of the missions, though notice did not reach him until June 1831. When Sarría's term as commissary prefect was terminated in June 1830, Father Ildefonso Arreguín of San Fernando College was elected to that office, but he appointed Durán as vice-commissary prefect. A considerable interval elapsed until he was notified. He first signed himself in that capacity on September 18, 1832. At the same time he was named vicar forane and ecclesiastical judge for California by the bishop of Sonora. Thus he became the chief ecclesiastic in California.

When Anastasio Bustamante became president of Mexico, he wrote to Durán, asking him for a statement of conditions in the territory. Durán answered in lengthy letters on May 10 and September 10, 1830, describing the situation and making recommendations. When Echeandía issued his plan for the secularization of the missions, Durán refuted the governor's articles in a long exposé.

After twenty-seven years at Mission San Jose, Durán was forced to leave, since all the missions north of San Miguel were to be handed over to Franciscans from the college of Zacatecas. These friars, all Mexicans, arrived at Monterey with the new governor, José Figueroa, January 15, 1833. Fray José María de Jesús González Rubio replaced Durán, although the latter remained with the new missionary for several months and administered his last baptism at the mission on April 8. He was still president of the missions from San Miguel to San Diego. Durán betook himself to Mission Santa Barbara, where he maintained his headquarters until his death in 1846. He retained his office as president of the Fernandino missions until 1838 when he became commissary prefect, an office he retained until 1846.

Durán's years at Santa Barbara placed him in the role of watching the slow death of the mission system. He fought its dissolution every step of the way, defending the rights of the Indians and condemning the despoilers. In the very nature of the case he had a vast correspondence with the civil officials, a correspondence that is alive with the legal aspects of the secularization issue. He advised Governor Figueroa, and through him the central government, against general emancipation of the Indian. Secularization was nevertheless decreed by Mexico on August 17, 1833. The California missionaries were restricted to spiritual functions.

When Governor Mariano Chico required the people to swear to the new centralist constitution of October 23, 1835, Durán declined to accompany the civil ceremonies with religious services. When the same governor asked Durán whether the missions were obliged to aid the state out of justice or merely out of charity, the commissary prefect stated that the missions were not part of the public domain and would help the state only out of charity and according to ability. Chico asked the territorial assembly to have Durán banished. The people of Santa Barbara rose en masse and prevented his departure.

In 1836 California declared itself free and independent from Mexico, Juan B. Alvarado becoming the leader of the *Californios*. He came to Santa Barbara and asked Durán to bless the new flag. This the padre refused to do, fearing that in so doing he would jeopardize the entire Franciscan order in Mexico. When Mexico finally acknowledged Alvarado as California's governor, the territory remained united with Mexico. When Spain acknowledged Mexico's independence, Durán took the oath of loyalty to Mexico, July 9, 1839. William Hartnell, appointed as inspector of the missions by Alvarado, placed Durán in charge again of Santa Barbara's temporalities, a duty the padre assumed as a work of charity. Then, on March 27, 1842, Governor Manuel Micheltorena restored the temporal control of the missions to the Franciscans. Under Governor Pío Pico the missions were rented to civilians and finally sold. Thus Durán lived to see the complete destruction of the system and died shortly before the American flag was raised at Monterey in 1846.

Even though California became a diocese in 1840, and its first bishop resided at Mission Santa Barbara between 1842 and 1846, Durán retained his office as commissary prefect. Before his death, Bishop Francisco García Diego y Moreno appointed Durán and González Rubio joint vicars-general and administrators of the diocese. The Santa Barbara registers attest to the fact that Durán frequently officiated at the presidio chapel as well as at the mission and that he was empowered to administer the sacrament of confirmation. Durán outlived the bishop only a little over a month, his death occurring on June 1, 1846. He was buried two days later in the friars' vaults beneath the sanctuary of the mission church by González Rubio. He had received the last rites. He was seventy years old and had been a missionary nearly forty years. Twenty-seven had been spent at Mission San Jose and thirteen at Santa Barbara. He had been president of the missions for eleven years and commissary prefect for eight, vicar-general and administrator of the diocese for a month, and vicar forane for the bishop of Sonora for eleven years. He was the first president to administer the full twenty-one missions. He was in touch with all the important men of his time and area.

Shortly after Durán's death at five o'clock in the afternoon, González Rubio, the surviving vicar-general, wrote the following lines to Pío Pico, the governor:

He was such a beloved friend and above all a zealous priest and a missionary so beloved by these towns that he cannot but move also the soul of Your Excellency for you know very well how much gratitude California owes to this venerable man. Despite the virtues and learning he possessed which in his own country or in any other would, no doubt, have served him in carrying out a brilliant career, he abandoned all, country, parents, friends, hopes and comforts to come here to consecrate to God his services as has been laudably demonstrated in the lengthy period of forty years he spent here.[3]

Bishop García Diego y Moreno had referred to Durán as a man of learning and virtue. Angustias de la Guerra y Ord, personally acquainted with him wrote:

[He was] a great friend of my parents and of everyone here in Santa Barbara. He settled here in 1833 and he soon made everyone love him to the point that all were willing to sacrifice for him. He accomplished many things during his long life, particularly after the political upheaval, especially the winning of minds and prevention of the flowing of blood. He could not always quiet the tempest, but I can only believe that his good advice and influence contributed to making these disturbances less deplorable. . . . In 1833 Padre Durán appeared to be a man of about 58 or 60 years. He was a Catalan of regular stature. Somewhat gray, white in color. He was blue-eyed. He did not wear sandals like the other friars because he suffered from rheumatism in his feet. This affliction ended his existence in 1846 at the Mission of Santa Barbara. . . .The death of Padre Durán was deeply felt by everyone, natives and aliens, because he had a kind deed or word for everyone.[4]

Michael C. White, who had been in California since 1828, reported the following recollection of Durán in 1877: [He] "stood 5 feet 8 or maybe a little more, quite stout when I made his acquaintance (in 1829). He was extremely fond of a joke, and was constantly letting off jokes. He was a man of fine education and intelligence, amiable to everybody, and constantly attending to his ministerial duties."[5]

Bancroft summarized Durán's personality and accomplishments in these words:

He was a most earnest and successful missionary, the only fault ever found with him in this respect being an excess of zeal in the forcible conversion of gentiles for his mission of San José; while as prelate he was a worthy successor of Sarría, Señan, and Payeras. Throughout the troublous times of secularization he managed the mission affairs with marked ability . . . . He was a politic and practical man, contenting himself with a part when all could not be won. Though an able and bitter foe to secularization, yet as a choice of evils when he realized that secularization could not be prevented he gave honest and valuable advice respecting the practical working of the successive schemes. Though he often became impatient and despondent, these moods never lasted long; and though he engaged in many controversies and wrote many bitter and sarcastic things, he yet retained the esteem of most adversaries, and was always beloved by people of all classes, being especially popular and influential in Sta. Bárbara in the later years.[6]

74

Finally, Engelhardt declared: "During the troublous times of the secularization and sale of the missions it was Father Durán who fought the pillagers step by step, though in vain, and fearlessly unmasked the real aims of the despoilers. His numerous letters to the Government on the subject are masterpieces of close reasoning, pungent sarcasm, and unanswerable argument . . . . For virtue, learning, and missionary zeal [he] ranks with the most brilliant of his predecessors."[7]

[1] *Life in California*, p. 124.

[2] Ibid., pp. 85-86.

[3] Doc. No. 2336, Taylor Collection, Archives of the Archdiocese of San Francisco. Phs. in SBMA.

[4] Price and Ellison, eds. *Occurrences in Hispanic California*, p. 36.

[5] *California All the Way Back to 1828*, p. 93.

[6] *History of California*, V, 633-634n. With regard to the alleged forcible conversions, Beechey, *Narrative*, II, 17, questions the validity of this view.

[7] *The Catholic Encyclopedia*, V (1909), 206.

ESCUDÉ, JAYME (1779-?)

Fray Jayme Escudé was born at Gandesa, Catalonia, Spain, in July 1779 and became a Franciscan at the Recollect friary in Tortosa, November 18, 1799. On March 29, 1810, he embarked at Cádiz and arrived at San Fernando College, July 13, the same year. On June 11, 1811, with five companions, he left Mexico City for San Blas. Owing to the dangerous conditions arising from the Mexican insurrection against Spain, he and his fellow missionaries went to Acapulco, where he met further delay because of the outbreak of pestilence. Escudé and four others embarked on the *San Carlos* and reached El Cabo only after four months. They were the guests of the Dominican missionaries at Loreto until April 23, 1812. In May Escudé with a single companion made the long overland journey to San Diego where he arrived July 15.

From the southern port Escudé went on to Mission San Luis Rey, remaining for several months as a supernumerary under Fray Antonio Peyrí. Then he was directed to go to Mission Santa Cruz to replace the murdered Fray Andrés Quintana. En route he baptized at Mission San Carlos in January 1813. His first entry in the registers of Santa Cruz was on March 5, 1813. There he continued to officiate until February 8, 1818.

Between November 3 and December 3, 1815, Escudé accompanied a military expedition under José Dolores Pico from San Juan Bautista to the San Joaquin Valley. Early in 1818 Escudé accompanied Vicente Francisco de Sarría, the commissary prefect, on an official tour of the southern missions in the capacity of secretary. He was at San Diego by July 23. Then he was assigned to Mission San Luis Rey, where he remained until 1822. He was the only friar in California who at first was reluctant to take the oath of allegiance to the Iturbide regency in 1821, though he finally decided to conform.

Having served ten years in California, Escudé applied to Governor Pablo Solá for permission to return to Mexico. He sailed either in December 1822 or in January 1823, probably from San Diego. On arriving at Tepic he notified the guardian of the college of his presence there and stated that he would remain there for a period because of the shortage of priests. At the same time he asked for and was subsequently granted letters of disaffiliation from the college. He returned to Spain via the Philippines, for on August 10, 1823, he notified Luís Argüello that he had arrived at Manila on the previous July 3.

In 1817 Sarría had described Escudé as a zealous missionary of edifying conduct. In 1820 Mariano Payeras declared that he was capable and worthy of being placed in charge of a religious community.

ESPÍ DE VALENCIA, JOSÉ DE LA CRUZ (1763-1838)

Fray José de la Cruz Espí de Valencia was born at Turis, Valencia, Spain, January 3, 1763. He was the son of Pablo de la Cruz, an official of the revenue department, and Eulalia de Valencia. The parents were well to do. As friar he always wrote his name Espí, while others employed the form Espit. Later on De Valencia was added. In his youth he attended the Colegio Calasancio in Valencia and received the Franciscan habit, August 13, 1777, at Santa María de los Angeles outside the walls of Valencia. On leaving Cádiz for the Indies, he was described in passport records as having a well-formed body, a lemon-colored complexion, large gray eyes, a large thick nose, a parted beard, and thin hair. The government report gave his name as Espí Beferrul. He sailed for Vera Cruz about September 1786 and entered San Fernando College, Mexico City. There he was ordained a priest in 1787.

In the years 1788-1789 as chaplain he accompanied the maritime expedition of Estevan Martínez to Nootka on *La Princesa*. Not until 1793 was Espí assigned to the California missions. He arrived at Monterey together with Magín Catalá on the *Aránzazu*. Espí served at Mission San Antonio between September 13, 1793, and June 6, 1795, meanwhile also officiating at San Luis Obispo during April and May of 1794, at Santa Clara in December 1794 and January 1795, and at Soledad from September 29 to December 23, 1795. He was at Mission Santa Cruz from November 29, 1796, to May 10, 1797, and at Mission San Francisco from June 21, 1797, to June 6, 1799. He also officiated at Mission Santa Clara on May 2, 1797, at Mission San Jose, April 22, 1799, and at Mission San Carlos in March and May of 1796 and again in 1799.

While at San Francisco he was subdelegated by Fermín Francisco de Lasuén military vicar for the bishop of Sonora with faculties for the soldiers.

Espí was permitted to retire to San Fernando College in 1799, and sailed from San Diego, January 16, 1800. In 1802, he acted as secretary to the guardian, Fray Miguel Lull, at Havana, Cuba, probably on an official visitation. While there, on July 27, Espí asked for disaffiliation from the college in order to return to Valencia. Actually, disaffiliation was not granted until December 18, 1809, the official declaration stating that Espí had been absent from the college for seven years, and though called back several times had been unable to comply for reasons beyond his control.

Instead of returning to Spain, he remained in Cuba, where he became attached to the Franciscan province of Santa Elena. While living at the Convento de San Francisco in Havana, he evinced a special commiseration for the poor. In 1809 he was transferred to Trinidad, Cuba, to rebuild the Franciscan friary, which was in ruins.

Espí was a fervent and assiduous preacher but was suspended for a period probably because of some false accusations. Known for his great charity, mortification, and spirit of poverty, he was sent out on various missions.

While Espí was on a mission at Puerto Príncipe in 1813, the town council petitioned for him to remain there, a permission which was granted in midyear 1814. There, his charitable work continued. He built San Lázaro, a hospital for lepers, of which he became the chaplain, May 6, 1816, and its church, which was completed in 1817. Later the place was known as Asilo de Padre Valencia and as such was known well down to modern times. El Carmen, a hospital for women with an adjoining church, was commenced in 1815. He then founded the hospice of San Roque with its chapel for pilgrims in 1826 and inaugurated a convent of Ursuline nuns, completed in 1825. He also built a school dedicated to Our Lady of Loreto and commenced a *colegio* which he did not live to see completed.

Espí was considered a saintly ascetic, friend of the poor, and Christian social worker and was called the Holy Man by the people among whom he labored. He died at Puerto Príncipe, May 2, 1838, about midmorning and was buried in the sanctuary of the church of San Lázaro, on the Gospel side. The funeral was attended by a large concourse of people. In 1851, his grave was opened, and his remains were found to be incorrupt. They were exhumed again in 1876 when they were placed in a new sepulcher. When the sepulcher was opened in 1902, the bones were found to be in good condition, together with pieces of his habit. A bust of Espí exists at Camagüey.

It appears from the evidence produced by his superior, President Lasuén, that Espí was far from being completely happy in California and gave cause for concern to his leader. Lasuén states that Espí accepted his assignment to Santa Cruz with great joy but within a few days of arriving there, he objected to the place vehemently and asked for a prompt change. Lasuén was obliged to complain to the college that Espí was a problem, adapted himself poorly anywhere, and had no taste for the work that was necessary for missionaries to perform.

When Espí asked for a change from San Antonio, where he had been stationed, he was sent to Mission Soledad at the request of Diego García. Even so, Lasuén had no assurance that Espí was satisfied. In 1797 the president wrote that Espí "gets sick very readily," and in June 1797 he tried to pacify the friar by assigning him to San Francisco, where he had expressed a desire to go, and in response to Martín de Landaeta's request for his presence there. Espí had already requested retirement in May of that year, and he reiterated the request in 1798. Finally, on August 6, 1799, Lasuén gave him his formal permit to retire, emphasizing the fact that Espí had served his ten years in a praiseworthy and apostolic manner and overlooking his peculiar tendency to be dissatisfied. Lasuén declared that Espí had made "repeated, formal and forceful representations" to retire and in one such communication, which "no superior could tolerate from a subject," had shown "a strong, obstinate and inflexible urge to retire."

The Espí of California days and the man of Cuba do not appear to be the same individual — the problem child of the province, the saint of the island. The most plausible explanation is that in the first instance he was misfitted for the type of work and that in the second case, the field of operations conformed perfectly with his temperament and character. In Cuba he found himself.

ESTÉNAGA, TOMÁS ELEUTERIO (1790-1847)

Fray Tomás Eleuterio Esténaga was born at Anzuola, Vizcaya, Spain, in 1790, and entered the Franciscan order in the province of Cantabria. He came to San Fernando College, Mexico City, at private expense in 1810, and there finished his studies and was ordained a priest. In 1815 while still a student, he requested disaffiliation from the college for reasons of health. When this was granted, he joined the province of the Holy Gospel, whose headquarters were in Mexico City. However, on September 15, the same year, he asked and was subsequently granted permission to be readmitted to the college.

Esténaga was assigned to the California missions in 1820 and arrived at Monterey on August 8 or 9, on *El Señoriano y San Francisco*. Mariano

Payeras described him as a person manifesting a spirit of religion and prudence, sufficiently apt for the ministry but in poor health. The record shows that he baptized at Mission San Carlos on September 13 and November 23, 1820. After serving there as supernumerary for a few months, he was sent to Mission San Miguel, where his first entry in the register was made on February 5 and his last on June 23, 1821. He is next found at Mission San Francisco, first signing the register on November 25, 1821, and last on February 29, 1833. He also attended Mission San Rafael during this period, where the records show that he officiated from July 21, 1832, until March 14, 1833.

When Captain Frederick W. Beechey of the British navy visited San Francisco in 1826, he stated that he had been hospitably received by the military commander and by Esténaga, the latter supplying him with horses for his men, free of charge, to make a trip to Monterey. He found that Esténaga had genuine humor, was an affable friend, and that his conversation was as palatable as his cheer.

At the same port Auguste Duhaut-Cilly met the friar in 1827, where "he came to receive us with great demonstrations of friendship; a welcome which the behavior of this religious never, furthermore, belied in the numerous relations I had later with him." Esténaga was glad to hear news from Spain to which California no longer owed allegiance, glad "to find at last a Christian stranger with whom to converse; for all those heretics (meaning the English and Americans) open their mouths only to lie and to vomit blasphemies."

Duhaut-Cilly stated that at the time of his visit, the mission was in a state of deterioration, "one of the poorest on the whole coast." Esténaga was "an excellent man, whose poor health made him indifferent to the handling of his business, and he willingly gave up the care of it to administrators, that he might enjoy the quietness he needed."[1] Esténaga gave Duhaut-Cilly all the information he sought concerning trade in the territory.

General Mariano Vallejo in 1876 recalled that Esténaga was in charge of the choir at Mission San Francisco for the patronal celebration held there in 1830 — "a young man of medium height, the personification of activity, of jovial disposition, select and varied in his conversation, an excellent and very sincere priest. He had seen a great deal of the war of the Revolution in Spain, and was there during the French invasion, when Napoleon I. and his brother Joseph tried to appropriate to themselves that privileged land."[2]

The friar refused to take the oath of allegiance to Mexico on the basis of the constitution of 1824 and was among those recommended for exile by Governor José María Echeandía if a replacement could be found. He took the oath finally in 1843. After Esténaga had handed

79

over Mission San Francisco and Mission San Rafael respectively to the Zacatecan friars, Lorenzo Quijas and Jesús María Vázquez del Mercado, in March 1833, he was assigned to Mission San Gabriel, in which jurisdiction he first baptized on April 2. Thereafter, Esténaga was mostly alone at the mission until December 28, 1846, when he made his last entry in the registers.

In a letter written to Governor José Figueroa, May 26, 1834, Esténaga was accused together with Fray Narciso Durán and Captain José de la Guerra y Noriega of conspiring against the government. Inquiry proved that a conference held by the three had dealt with the sale of a piece of property, nothing more. On learning the truth, the governor dropped the false charge.

At San Gabriel Esténaga experienced the troubles attendant upon secularization. The Indians at Rancho San Bernardino went so far as to steal the sacred vessels kept there, and when Esténaga went there to investigate the matter, they held him prisoner for a period. In June 1835, Esténaga and Francisco González de Ibarra of Mission San Fernando, utterly discouraged with prevailing conditions, left their missions without the leave of their religious superior and went to Sonora. The action of abandoning their missions without permission was akin to apostasy from the order, but Father Durán, the commissary prefect, thoroughly understanding their discouragement, sent them their licenses to retire, legalizing their illegal departure. They returned to their posts a year later, however, Esténaga arriving in August 1836.

When he had first come to San Gabriel in 1833, he found that all the cattle had been killed in resentment against secularization. He himself went to the extreme of allowing neighbors to enter the mission property, unroof the buildings, convert lumber into firewood, dispose of tools and utensils. He even ordered the vineyards to be razed to the ground, but this the Indians refused to do. By 1844 the mission had nothing left but some badly deteriorated vineyards, cared for by about thirty neophytes.

From time to time he officiated also at Mission San Fernando, the first occasion on October 27, 1836, after the death of Pedro Cabot, until the arrival of Blas Ordaz in May 1837, baptizing there for the last time on June 11, 1837. He was at San Juan Capistrano, baptizing on May 10, 1843. On November 4, 1841, he blessed a cemetery in Los Angeles which had been acquired through the subscriptions of its residents.

There is no existant death record of Esténaga, for the Burial Register of Mission San Gabriel is missing. Nor is there any account in that of Mission San Fernando. Mrs. Catalina López, old-time resident of San Fernando, however, told the Franciscan historian Engelhardt in 1904 that she was present at Esténaga's funeral and that he was buried in the church near the pulpit, pointing out the spot. She added that Esténaga died early in 1847 in one of the rear rooms of the long building near the chapel. This same woman, as well as Doña María de las Angustias, told Father Eugene Sugranes, C.M.F., that Esténaga had become quite ill at San Gabriel and had been removed to San Fernando by Don Juan Manso and Don José Arnaz and that he died a few months later and was buried in the mission. Before receiving the Viaticum, he asked forgiveness from anyone he might have offended or scandalized.

According to Eulalia Pérez, old-time resident at San Gabriel, Esténaga was somewhat tall, thin, quite light in complexion, and "very intelligent in the management of the little that remained at the mission. . . . He treated all with much amiability."[3]

[1] Carter, "Duhaut-Cilly's Account of California in the Years 1827-28," pp. 142-143.

[2] [Patrick J. Thomas], Our Centennial Memoir, p. 115.

[3] "Una Vieja y sus Recuerdos," Bancroft Library MS.

ESTEVAN, PEDRO DE SAN JOSÉ (1751-?)

Fray Pedro de San José Estevan was born in the region of Castile, Spain, in 1751, and joined the Franciscan order at Havana, Cuba, in 1783, thus becoming a member of the province of Santa Elena. From there he was admitted to San Fernando College, Mexico City, 1793. According to the guardian, Tomás de Pangua, Estevan was considered "a commendable subject." With five fellow friars, he was sent to California about January 1795 and arrived at Monterey on the Concepción the same year.

President Fermín Francisco de Lasuén first assigned Estevan to Mission San Antonio, where his name is found in the Baptismal Register between April 21 and September 15, 1795. It was not long, however, before Estevan became a malcontent. Already on July 30, 1795, Lasuén declared: "To the regret of all who have come to know him, Father Fray Pedro Esteban has declared that he is no longer fitted for the work here."[1] When the president offered him the post of Santa Clara, he declined peremptorily. Lasuén then sent him to Mission San Diego. En route he baptized at San Juan Capistrano, November 2 and ministered at San Diego from November 14, 1795, till July 1, 1797.

Next Lasuén moved him to San Buenaventura but in October 1797 assigned him to Mission San Gabriel where he was to assist the two resident missionaries, especially in the pueblo of Los Angeles and in the surrounding ranchos. At the mission his name appears repeatedly in the registers from August 2, 1797, till July 27, 1802. During his stay there he visited Mission Purisima on October 17, 1797, where he baptized, and was frequently at San Juan Capistrano between July 19,

1797, and October 24, 1800, also assisting in baptisms. While there in 1800, he conducted the funeral services of Fray Vicente Fuster on October 22 and made the entry in the Burial Register.

It was during Estevan's last years in California that Lasuén revealed his full dissatisfaction with his subject. On September 7, 1801, he wrote: "We can no longer tolerate his extreme eccentricities. Always extremely self-satisfied, he is at peace with no one, and it is hardly possible for anyone to keep peace with him. If one tries to correct him, it makes him worse, and he rails bitterly and harshly against me and all the missionaries he has known. He keeps the Fathers at San Gabriel so perturbed and disturbed that he wears them out. He is a nuisance to the neighboring missions, and he is very annoying to the Indians."[2] On the basis of these difficulties, Lasuén asked the college to call him home. In the following year he reiterated his plea.

Estevan's license to return was signed by the viceroy, February 8, 1802, and by the governor, August 21. He baptized at San Diego from September 5 to October 3 and sailed for Mexico from that port, November 4, 1802, returning to San Fernando College. On the day before sailing, he wrote a letter to Lasuén, admitting his faults of "great blindness and pride" and asked forgiveness. He considered himself the victim of a disordered imagination. Lasuén was highly edified by this confession and wrote to Estevan, pardoning him and praising his confession of fault. It was in his departure that Estevan found his finest hour.

[1] Kenneally, *Writings*, I, 343-344.
[2] Ibid., II, 243.

FAURA, JOSÉ (ca. 1773-?)

Fray José Faura was born at Barcelona, Catalonia, Spain, about 1773, joined the Franciscan order in that province, and left Spain for admission into San Fernando College, Mexico City, in 1798. Soon after his arrival there, he was assigned to the California missions. He sailed on the *Concepción,* arriving at Santa Barbara, May 8, 1798, and from there went to Mission San Luis Rey. He arrived on June 18 and served until May 1800. While there he also baptized on occasion at Missions San Fernando, San Juan Capistrano, and San Diego, and at San Diego, he conducted the funeral services of Fray Juan Mariner, January 30, 1800.

Faura had been ailing and asked for a change of climate. President Fermín Francisco de Lasuén then sent him to San Juan Capistrano, where he remained till September 19, 1809. There he assisted Fray Norberto de Santiago in building the stone church, work on which began in February 1797 and which was dedicated on September 7, 1806. When the remains of Fray Vicente Fuster were transferred from the old church to the new, September 9, Faura delivered the sermon.

Faura was at San Juan Capistrano during its prosperous period. He and Santiago baptized 940 converts during the decade. The Indian community grew from 741 to 1,046. In the raising of sheep, the mission was far ahead of all others with 17,000 head.

At the close of 1809, Faura petitioned President Estevan Tapis for permission to return to San Fernando College, which he granted. After remaining at the college for nearly two years, on March 16, 1811, Faura requested and was given permission to be transferred to the province of the Holy Gospel, the headquarters of which were also in Mexico City.

Faura eventually returned to his native province in Catalonia, June 30, 1816, residing in the Convento de San Francisco in Barcelona. In 1818, he was appointed collector of religious for the province of Santiago, Jalisco, Mexico, by Fernando VII, an office he fulfilled for three years. A great plague broke out in Barcelona in 1821 during which a conservatively estimated twenty thousand people died, among them thirty Franciscans who perished as victims of charity and service. Faura also attended the sick and the dying, but, fortunately, he survived. Faura later entered a Trappist monastery where he was reported to be leading an edifying life in 1828.

FERNÁNDEZ, GREGORIO (1754-?)

Fray Gregorio Fernández was born at Burgos, Spain, in 1754 and entered the Franciscan order in the same province in 1772. Upon ordination, he was commissioned as a confessor and preacher. He arrived at San Fernando College, Mexico City, in 1785, and was appointed novice master of that institution, July 1, 1786. Fray Tomás de Pangua, the guardian, in writing to President Fermín Francisco de Lasuén concerning Fernández' coming to California, stated that he was a person of good conduct and enjoyed robust health. Fernández set out from the college about January 1794 and sailed from San Blas on the *Concepción*.

Apparently he arrived at San Francisco, for records show that he was baptizing there on June 23, 1794. For a short period he was at Santa Clara, but in late June Lasuén sent him to Mission San Luis Obispo where he remained until July 2, 1796. It appears that he was somewhat overzealous and severe with the Indians; he was reprimanded when certain natives of San Luis Obispo and Purisima threatened to revolt.

About midyear 1796, Fernández succeeded to the management of Purisima after Friars Francisco José Arroíta and José Antonio Calzada left there for other missions. He remained at Purisima until September 21, 1805. While stationed there, he visited Mission Santa Barbara from May 24 to 28, 1800, and Mission San Luis Obispo on August 19, 1804, when he administered a baptism. Fernández sailed for Mexico on November 6, 1805.

Bancroft writes that Fray Fernandez was styled *"un ángel"* [by Pablo de Mugártegui] when he came to California; "and there is nothing to show that his angelic qualities deteriorated in California."[1]

[1] *History of California*, II, 123, n. 78.

FERNÁNDEZ, JOSÉ MARÍA (1770-?)

Fray José María Fernández was born in 1770 at Madrid, then in the archdiocese of Toledo, and became a Franciscan at Guadalajara, Spain, as a member of the province of Castile, in 1786. The year 1791 found him a student of theology at San Diego de Alcalá. In 1795 he sailed from Cádiz for Vera Cruz. On leaving Spain, he was described in passport records as of medium stature, of light complexion, with hazel-colored eyes, and dark hair. Upon his arrival in Mexico City, he entered San Fernando College.

In February 1796, he sailed for California on the *Aránzazu*, arriving at San Francisco on June 18, 1796, and ministered at the mission until September 1797. On February 23, 1796, Fray Antonio Nogueyra of San Fernando College had recommended Fernández to the viceroy as a religious of "proven conduct and entirely satisfactory to this venerable discretory." However, in California, an accidental blow on the head so injured him that his mind became affected. He suffered from hallucinations that led him to believe that he was not appreciated by his fellow missionaries and was not made a party to their counsels and plans.

As his condition grew worse, he wrote to Governor Diego de Borica, complaining that his associates were cruel to the Indians and that this circumstance was causing the natives to desert the mission. Unaware of Fernández' mental state, Borica responded with a sharp letter to President Fermín Francisco de Lasuén, September 22, 1796. Subsequently apprised, however, of the true nature of the affair, the governor disregarded letters from Fernández written in 1797 and later referred to him as "a good religious whose mind was somewhat deranged." According to Lasuén, November 2, 1796, Fernández and Fray Diego García had tried "with fanatical zeal" to oust Martín de Landaeta from the mission.

In May 1797, Fernández insisted upon permission to return to Mexico because of his infirmities. The missionary's physical and mental condition and his unserviceability were certified by a physician of the *Real Armada*, Dr. Luís Paba, on May 13. Despite the fact that he had served only a little over a year in California, Lasuén gladly gave the permission. On July 8, 1797, he petitioned Borica for Fernández' license to retire, which the latter granted the same day.

Fernández sailed on the *Concepción* in September with Antonio de la Concepción Horra of San Miguel, who had become demented after only a few weeks in California. In Mexico he presumably joined the province of the Holy Gospel — official records of his arrival July 6, 1818, at Cádiz reported him as having proceeded from there. In August 1819, in good health, he was living at the Convento de San Francisco, Madrid.

FERNÁNDEZ, MANUEL (1767-?)

Fray Manuel Fernández was born at Villar, diocese of Tuy, Galicia, Spain, in 1767, and became a Franciscan at Compostela in 1784. In 1793 he left the friary of Cabeza de Alba with the office of preacher and sailed from Cádiz on the *San Nicolás,* June 11, arriving that same year at San Fernando College, Mexico City. He was tall, light-complexioned, had blue eyes, and graying hair.

He was sent with good recommendations to California in January 1794 in company with four other friars, arriving there on the *Concepción.* At Mission Santa Clara, his first assignment, he was, according to Bancroft, impetuous, violent, cruel, and a bad manager of the neophytes, or at least overzealous in converting pagans, and because of this latter tendency was admonished by President Fermín Francisco de Lasuén.

Fernández was at Mission San Francisco for much of early 1795. He was then stationed at Santa Cruz until 1798, where in rather gloomy terms he described difficulties owing to runaway Indians, the death of livestock, inundations, and the encroachment of wild animals.

With regard to his character and attitudes, Lasuén wrote on August 19, 1794: "I am told that nothing suits him; and I notice that none of the missionaries who have known him like him."[1] On May 23, 1796, he wrote concerning charges made against Fernández during an expedition: "Some similar examples of inconsiderate haste have been observed in that religious, and I do not know where we will end."[2] On October 20, 1798, Lasuén informed the viceroy that he had given permission to Fernández to retire because of various disabilities from which he suffered and because of "an insuperable disgust and repugnance for the country, and towards working in it."[3] He sailed that year for Mexico on the *Concepción.* Further details on him are not available.

[1] Kenneally, *Writings,* I, 316-317.
[2] Ibid., I, 381.
[3] Ibid., II, 97.

FERNÁNDEZ DE ULIBARRI, ROMÁN FRANCISCO (1773-1821)

Fray Román Francisco Fernández de Ulibarri was born on February 28, 1773, at Alí, near Vitoria, diocese of Calahorra, Spain, and became a Franciscan in the province of Cantabria at Vitoria in April 1794. On leaving Spain in 1803, he held the offices of preacher and confessor and was described in passport records as tall, light-complexioned, ruddy, with blue eyes, and a scar on the chin on the left side. He sailed from Cádiz, June 20, on the *San Miguel* or *Sagrada Familia* and arrived at Vera Cruz, Mexico, in August. At San Fernando College, Mexico City, he remained for five years, most of the time in poor health and generally not able to follow the routine of the institution. Nevertheless, he volunteered for the California missions, and there he found surprisingly good health and a robust vigor.

He arrived at Monterey, June 22, 1809, and was assigned to Mission San Juan Bautista where he served from September 4, 1809, to September 26, 1814, and to Mission Santa Ines from February 23, 1815, to November 20, 1819, except while temporarily at Mission Purisima, October 15, 1818, to July 3, 1819, and finally to Mission San Fernando, May 31, 1819, to December 22, 1820. He baptized at Mission Santa Barbara in May 1816 and at Mission San Miguel, January 30, 1815.

In 1817 Vicente Francisco de Sarría wrote that in the missions Ulibarri showed a "Christian zeal accompanied by a religious firmness." Mariano Payeras in 1820 declared that "considering all the circumstances, his merit is but regular as also his aptitude for the ministry among the faithful and pagans and perhaps for one or other assignment [in the order]." A further index to his character may be obtained from a letter of Payeras to the guardian of the college, May 20, 1820, in which he reported that he had sent Ulibarri to Mission San Fernando to replace Vitoria, and he expressed the opinion that Ulibarri was a fine religious, but was apt to be a little too zealous with the Indians, though if watched by the president would "tend towards moderation."[1]

In 1821 at Mission San Fernando he became ill. Francisco González de Ibarra, his companion, wrote to Captain José de la Guerra y Noriega on February 23: "My companion is very feeble and has a high fever, while his breast is much oppressed. On Sunday, during the night, he vomited very much blood."[2] Ulibarri was urged to go to Mission San Gabriel where he could receive better care. He followed the advice, but death nevertheless overtook him there on June 16, 1821. He received the sacraments, and José María Zalvidea buried him in the mission church on the same day. He had been bedridden for four months in patient suffering.

[1] Doc. No. 1943, California Mission Section, SBMA.
[2] Engelhardt, *San Gabriel Mission*, p. 290.

86

FERNÁNDEZ SOMERA Y BALBUENA, ÁNGEL (1741-?)

Fray Ángel Somera, whose full name was Ángel de Jesús María Fernández Somera y Balbuena, was born at Maravatio, Michoacán, Mexico, in 1741. He was the son of Pablo Fernández de la Somera, native of Halpujagua, and Ana María Balbuena, native of Maravatio. Somera spent his early years at Halpujagua. On February 5, 1758, he became a Franciscan at San Fernando College, Mexico City, and made his profession, February 6, the following year, when he took the names Jesús María. His novitiate was made during the guardianate of Juan Antonio Pico and under the novice master, Matías de la Parte.

With nine others he left the college in October 1770 and sailed from San Blas on the *San Antonio,* January 20, 1771. He arrived at San Diego, March 12 and at Monterey, May 21. Appointed by President Junípero Serra to be cofounder of Mission San Gabriel with Fray Pedro Benito Cambón, he went by ship back to San Diego and from there set out for the mission site with Cambón and a military escort on August 6. Within the present-day limits of Orange County the party was attacked by a mob of painted and shouting Indians prepared for war. One of the missionaries unfurled a banner of the Blessed Virgin. This quick thinking saved the day, for the warriors, who were immediately captivated by the beautiful painting, laid down their bows and arrows before it and left the Spaniards unmolested.

The mission was founded on September 8, 1771, several miles southeast of the present site at the southern extreme of San Gabriel Valley near the Montebello hills. Somera was stationed at San Gabriel until September 1772 and experienced the difficult period of conflict between the Spanish soldiers and the natives because of the misbehavior of the former. Somera became ill within a short time and was permitted to retire to Mexico. He baptized at Misión San Fernando de Velicatá in Lower California, September 27, 1772, and embarked at Loreto, October 19, for San Blas, where he arrived on the thirtieth, and from there returned to the college. Because of his continued ill health, he transferred from the college to the province of Michoacán, October 17, 1780.

FIGUER, JUAN (ca. 1742-1784)

Fray Juan Figuer, a native of Anento, Aragón, Spain, was born about the year 1742. He joined the Franciscan order at Zaragosa, June 12, 1761. Prior to sailing for the Indies, he was described as a person of good body, somewhat swarthy, though his face was light-complexioned. Figuer entered San Fernando College in October 1770. Shortly thereafter, with twenty-nine other friars, he arrived at Tepic where he was compelled to wait for four months before shipping was available. With nineteen of the group, he sailed on the *San Carlos* for Loreto, Lower

California, but the vessel was driven south to Acapulco, and when it returned north was grounded at Manzanillo. Figuer and Fray Marcelino Senra were able to board the *San Carlos* again after repairs were made and finally reached Loreto in August 1771.

President Francisco Palóu assigned Figuer and Senra to Misión San Francisco de Borja, for which the missionaries set out on September 9, 1771. Figuer next went to Misión Todos Santos and finally was named among those who were to be sent to Upper California. In August 1772, Palóu instructed him to go to Misión San Fernando de Velicatá and from there to proceed to San Diego. This he did in company with Fray Juan Usón, arriving at San Diego early in November. Figuer was intended to be one of the founders of Mission San Buenaventura, but when its founding was delayed, he was sent to Mission San Gabriel, where he baptized between May 10, 1773, and August 3, 1774.

Figuer was then transferred to Mission San Luis Obispo where he made his first entry in the registers, August 28, 1774. With Friars José Cavaller and Pablo de Mugártegui, he welcomed there the members of the Anza expedition on February 21, 1776. In 1777, Figuer was assigned by President Junípero Serra to Mission San Diego. He administered his last baptism at San Luis Obispo on June 13 and his first at San Diego on August 31. At San Diego he served under Fermín Francisco de Lasuén.

Beyond any doubt, San Diego was the least promising of the missions. Continuous unrest prevailed among the natives of the area and sometimes erupted into outright rebellion. At this period, because of the character of the Indians, both Lasuén and Figuer became discouraged and asked to return to Mexico. But Serra pleaded with Figuer to remain, and he did so until his death. With Lasuén he succeeded in building a new church and enlarging the mission compound — the mission had been destroyed in the Indian uprising of November 1775 — and before his death saw the thousandth Indian baptized there. While Figuer was at the mission, the alcalde system was introduced by Governor Felipe de Neve in 1779, a system of which the missionaries disapproved. Other missions at which Figuer had baptized were San Antonio, November 13, 1776, and San Juan Capistrano, June 22, 1780.

Figuer died at Mission San Diego, December 18, 1784, and was buried in the mission church by Lasuén, December 19. He had received the last sacraments. On April 26, 1804, the remains of Figuer, together with those of Luís Jayme and Juan Mariner, were exhumed by Mariano Payeras and were reburied in the new church, the remains of each in separate coffins, but all were placed in a common vault. Only the bones of Figuer had been preserved. The stone covering the vault was the third one removed from the altar of Nuestra Señora del Pilar and faced south.

FORTUNY, BUENAVENTURA (1774-1840)

Fray Buenaventura Fortuny was born in 1774 at Moster, archdiocese of Tarragona, Catalonia, Spain, and joined the Franciscan order at the Convento de San Francisco, at Reus, October 30, 1792. Prior to embarking at Cádiz, as a student preacher, with Fray Narciso Durán, May 3, 1803, Fortuny was described in official records as tall, with thick, dark hair, hazel or dark brown eyes, scant beard, and pockmarked face.

Fortuny arrived at Vera Cruz about July and shortly thereafter entered San Fernando College, Mexico City. He remained there for three years, serving both the community and giving missions to the faithful. In February 1806, he and Durán were sent to California and upon their arrival at Monterey, June 6, President Estevan Tapis assigned both Fortuny and Durán to Mission San Jose where they remained together for twenty years, Fortuny being the superior. His first baptism was recorded in September 1806, his last on September 5, 1826.

Fortuny's predecessor, José Antonio Uría, had begun the final church building, but the greater part of it had yet to be completed by the new missionaries. It was blessed by President Tapis on April 23, 1809. Fortuny continued to expand and develop the mission throughout his tenure of office: building a Christian Indian village, a dam, a flour mill, a soap factory and tannery; laying out a cemetery, two large gardens; and constructing a large two-story friary as living quarters.

At the end of 1806, 662 Indians were living at the mission. At the end of 1826 their number had increased to 1,783. By the end of 1806, 1,556 Indians had been baptized. The number of baptisms had risen to 5,597 by the end of 1826. In the same period cattle increased from 4,500 to 15,000, sheep from 8,000 to 20,000. Fortuny made out all the annual and biennial reports during his term of office, and these were countersigned by Durán. He also composed the answers to the government questionnaire on the customs and habits of the local Indians which he signed on November 7, 1814. Mission San Jose had become the second largest mission after that of San Luis Rey and together with that of Santa Clara was the largest exporter of hides.

On October 15, 1811, Fortuny, in company with Ramón Abella of Mission San Francisco, set out from that port in launches on an expedition under Sergeant José Antonio Sánchez. After stopping at Angel Island, they continued on until they reached the confluence of the San Joaquin and Sacramento rivers. The party traveled for some distance up the Sacramento and returned to San Francisco, October 30. At

Mission San Jose, Fortuny met the foreign visitors Otto von Kotzebue and Camille de Roquefeuil successively in 1816 and 1817. It appears that Fortuny served temporarily at Mission Soledad from July 31 to October 20, 1820, and at Mission San Juan Bautista from December 29, 1825, till June 12, 1826. Earlier he had baptized at San Francisco on October 22, 1810, and in March 1819. He was secretary to Vicente Francisco de Sarría ·on formal visitations at Mission Santa Clara in 1816 and 1818 and at San Francisco and San Rafael in 1825.

Sarría and Mariano Payeras respectively in 1817 and 1820 considered Fortuny an able and useful missionary. The former stated that he had greatly advanced Mission San Jose and that he was "an adjusted religious without being a burden to others, and a missionary given over to the performance of his duties without meddling in affairs not coming under his competence." Payeras declared that "his merit is as laudable as his simplicity and zeal. His aptitude for being a good missionary renders him suitable for labor among both the faithful and infidels."

In 1826 Fortuny refused to take the oath of allegiance to Mexico but promised to be respectful and obedient to the government authorities. He was one of the thirteen missionaries whom Governor José María Echeandía exempted from the order of expulsion, and the governor recommended to the central government that Fortuny be retained in California. In that same year Fortuny succeeded José Altimira at the recently established Mission San Francisco Solano at Sonoma. It had been abandoned for a while because of the raids of hostile Indians, but it was rehabilitated by "the virtuous Fr. Fortuni." His first baptism took place there, September 30, 1826. He served alone until he handed the mission over to his Zacatecan successor, Fray José María de Jesús Gutiérrez, administering his last baptism there, March 15, 1833. At this period Fortuny was described as a holy man, praying incessantly inside or outside the church, and he had the reputation of being learned, affable, humble, and apostolic.

San Diego was the next mission to which Fortuny was sent. He baptized there from September 22, 1833, to July 27, 1834. En route, he administered the sacrament at San Buenaventura, April 18. Durán begged Fortuny "for God's sake and out of necessity" to take over Mission San Luis Rey because of the disorders there. Many Indians refused to work, others left, and they took with them horses and cattle. In course of time many returned. Fortuny remained at San Luis Rey from April 1833 until June 1837, evidently commuting between San Luis Rey and San Diego for a period. When San Luis Rey was secularized in 1834, Fortuny handed the mission over to Captain Pablo de la Portilla.

Following this assignment, Fortuny was sent to Mission San Buenaventura where he administered his first baptism on July 16, 1837. He remained there until 1840, during its period of decline. His last entry occurred on November 22. His health having been undermined, he went to Santa Barbara where, at the home of José Antonio Aguirre, he received medical aid and care, and there he died on December 16, having received the last sacraments. Fray José Joaquín Jimeno of Mission Santa Barbara buried him in the crypt under the sanctuary of the church, December 18.

Angustias de la Guerra y Ord stated that Fortuny had been generous to the poor.

FUSTER, VICENTE (1742-1800)

Fray Vicente Fuster was born in 1742 at Alcañiz, archdiocese of Zaragosa, Aragón, Spain, and became a Franciscan at the Convento de San Francisco, Zaragosa, February 19, 1759. He left the friary of Balbastro in 1769 for Cádiz, where he joined thirty-nine other Franciscans whose destination was Mexico City. At the time of his departure, Fuster was described in government records as possessing a good body, a light complexion, thin face, dark hair, and medium beard. He held the office of preacher.

Arriving in Mexico in 1770, Fuster entered San Fernando College. In February 1771 with fourteen companions, he sailed on the *San Carlos* from San Blas for Loreto in Lower California — a trip that was fraught with hardship and mishaps. President Francisco Palóu assigned Fuster to administer missions Santa María de los Angeles and San Fernando de Velicatá. When the Fernandinos gave the Lower California missions over to the Dominicans, Fuster was appointed to Mission San Diego. Leaving Velicatá on August 3, 1773, he arrived at San Diego on the thirtieth. There he became the companion of Fray Luís Jayme. He served at San Diego until the summer of 1777, his last entry in the registers occurring on July 22.

At San Diego Fuster witnessed the events of the tragic night of November 5, 1775, when perhaps as many as eight hundred Indians burned the mission and murdered Fray Luís Jayme. Fuster himself barely escaped death and helped to repel the invaders. He wrote a graphic and detailed account of the event, November 28, which he forwarded to President Serra in Carmel. Because of the disaster, Fuster conceived a deep repugnance for the San Diego Indians, so that Serra was eventually obliged to transfer him.

While at San Diego, Fuster had an encounter with Captain Fernando Rivera y Moncada whom the padre declared excommunicated for forcibly extracting from the church, the Indian, Carlos, who had taken refuge therein with Fuster's permission and who had been implicated in the revolt. After Serra's arrival, Fuster aided him in reconstructing the registers which had been burned in the fire. Fuster, Fermín Francisco de Lasuén, and Gregorio Amurrió, all of whom were in San Diego, petitioned to return to Mexico, but their requests went unheeded.

Fuster next served at Mission San Gabriel until July 8, 1779, when he was appointed to succeed Amurrió at San Juan Capistrano, where he baptized for the first time November 4, 1779. When Lasuén founded California's eleventh mission, Purisima, he selected Fuster and Francisco José Arroíta as the first missionaries, though they were not present at the founding, December 8, 1787. Building commenced only in April the following year when a military escort from Santa Barbara arrived at the site. Records show that Fuster baptized at San Juan Capistrano on January 16, 1788, and that he and Arroíta arrived at Purisima in the company of Lasuén in April. He remained there until the summer of 1789, baptizing the last time on August 15. Thereupon he was again sent to San Juan Capistrano, where he remained for the next eleven years. His first entry in the registers was on November 4, 1789, his last on August 30, 1800. Work on the stone church began three years before Fuster's death. By the end of 1800 nearly two thousand Indians had been baptized at the mission.

When Lasuén was asked by San Fernando College to suggest three missionaries who would be likely candidates for the presidency of the California missions, he named, on September 3, 1796, Fuster, Hilario Torrent, and Estevan Tapis. Fuster had baptized at least twice at San Diego — after he had been reassigned — August 5, 1780, and February 23, 1783, and twice at Mission San Luis Obispo in April and September 1788.

For years Fuster had suffered from a chest ailment. He died as a result of it on October 21, 1800, and was buried on the following day by Pedro de San José Estevan on the Epistle side of the altar. He had received all the last sacraments. Assisting at the funeral were Friars Norberto de Santiago and José Faura. On September 9, 1806, after the dedication of the new stone church, President Tapis removed the remains of Fuster to the Epistle side of the new sanctuary. Pedro de la Cueva celebrated the Requiem Mass and José Faura preached the sermon.

GARCÉS, FRANCISCO HERMENEGILDO (1738-1781)

Fray Francisco Hermenegildo Garcés was born at Morata del Conde, Aragón, Spain, April 12, 1738, the son of Juan Garcés and Antonia Maestro, and was baptized on the following day. His early education was left to an uncle, the Rev. Moses Garcés, curate of the same town. Garcés entered the Franciscan order in the province of Aragón at the age of fifteen, studied his theology in the friary of Calatayud, and was ordained at the age of twenty-five. At Madrid he offered his services as an Indian missionary to Fray Juan Crisóstomo Gil, commissary from the college of Santa Cruz de Querétaro, Mexico, who accepted him. He entered the college in 1766, and was employed there as a confessor.

In 1767, by reason of the expulsion of the Jesuits, the missions of Sonora left vacant were entrusted to the college of Querétaro. Garcés was among those chosen to go among the Indians. After a delay of three months at Tepic, he and his companions took ship at San Blas, January 20, 1768, reaching the port of Guaymas about three and a half months later. At Horcasitas, Garcés was assigned to Mission San Xavier del Bac, near Tucson, Arizona, then the northernmost mission of the Pimería and open to Apache raids, and arrived there on June 30.

From the beginning Garcés showed himself a true missionary, adapting himself to the life of the Indians, showing himself kind and gentle, and offering them his counsel. The natives came to call him the Old Man, despite the fact that he was but thirty years old. The epithet was one of affection and respect. His missionary life was a combination of spiritual ministrations and tours of exploration to points no white man had reached. He became a missionary scout, preparing the Indians for the reception of the gospel.

In August 1768, absolutely alone, he made his first tour among the Indians living along the Gila River. In 1769 he entered the country of the Apaches. A year later, when a severe epidemic broke out in the Gila region, he hastened thither and baptized as many dying children as he could. On a very extensive journey in 1771, he reached the Colorado River near its mouth and returned to San Xavier after an absence of almost three months. He had reached Caborca in Sonora during that journey, and though his legs were swollen when he set out, he was in an improved physical condition when he returned. Garcés made known to Viceroy Antonio María Bucareli y Ursúa the results of his explorations. His findings were later reported to the king of Spain.

When Junípero Serra was in Mexico in 1773 consulting Viceroy Bucareli on California mission affairs, the latter brought up the question of the feasibility of a land route from Sonora to the Pacific Coast. Serra favored the idea, while Bucareli proposed its opening to his council. It was determined that Juan Bautista Anza, stationed at Tubac in present-day Arizona, should undertake to open the road, with the understanding that Garcés and a companion friar should go along with them. Garcés in company with Fray Juan Díaz left Tubac on January 2, 1774, with the Anza party and arrived at Mission San Gabriel, California, March 22. From San Gabriel, Garcés returned to the Colorado and to San Xavier, reaching his mission in the latter part of May. While in California he traveled from San Gabriel to San Diego, returning from that port with Serra who had recently arrived from Mexico.

In 1775, Garcés joined the second Anza expedition at Santa Eulalia and then retraced his steps to the rancheria of Chief Palma near present Fort Yuma, arriving January 3, 1776. On February 14 he set out with two Indian companions on what was to be his longest exploration. He traveled along the Colorado to a point near the present location of Needles. Turning westward into the Mojave, he subsequently discovered the Mojave River. He continued on across the Mojave desert, followed Cajon Pass into southern California, and reached San Gabriel a second time.

From there he traveled through San Fernando Valley, the Antelope Valley, as they are known today, and the Tehachapi range into the San Joaquin Valley to the area of Bakersfield and to the Kern and White rivers. Retracing his steps, from Mojave he turned east to the territory of the Moqui Indians of northern Arizona. On July 4 he left for the Colorado, traveled along it until he reached Fort Yuma, August 27, and finally returned to San Xavier del Bac, September 17, 1776. He had been away eleven months, had traveled about seven hundred leagues, and had contacted 24,500 Indians.

Chief Palma showed himself favorable to Christianity and asked for missionaries. The commandant general, Carlos de Croix, received orders from the king to establish missions and presidios along the Colorado. Under De Croix's orders, Garcés again visited the Yumas, but he found their attitude considerably changed. Nevertheless, soldiers, settlers, and missionaries set out for the river area. And though Garcés had warned against it, the viceroy ordered the missions established, bereft of their usual economic aspects. The cavalcade reached the river in the fall of 1780 where two missions were established, Purísima Concepción at Fort Yuma and San Pedro y San Pablo at Bicuñer, some miles upstream. Two missionaries were placed at each mission, Garcés and Juan Antonio Barreneche being at Fort Yuma.

The natives resented the use of their agricultural lands by the whites, and the succeeding ten months convinced the missionaries that the colonies and missions were doomed. When disaster was imminent, the missionaries did all they could to prepare the Spaniards spiritually for the inevitable. The native outbreak occurred on July 17, 1781, while Garcés was saying Mass. The friar and his companion survived the fury of the first day, hearing the confessions of the dying Spaniards, and finally found refuge among some Indians who had remained faithful. Despite the fact that Chief Palma had given orders to spare Garcés, on the nineteenth an underling discovered him and Barreneche and both were killed with clubs. The remains of the four slain missionaries were recovered in December 1781 and were first removed to the mission of

San Pedro y San Pablo, Tubutama, Sonora, and then were solemnly buried in the college of Querétaro, July 19, 1794.

Elliott Coues, commenting on Garcés' diaries, states: "Of the high historical value of the Diary of Garcés there can be no adverse opinions among those qualified to judge.... There could hardly be a better introduction to a considerable amount of United States history than such a knowledge of its southwestern corner as the Diary of Garcés affords."[1]

He declared furthermore: "Garcés is the first white man known to have reached the Grand cañon from the west; perhaps he is also the first to view it at this particular point and give it a specific name, as distinguished from that of the river flowing through the chasm."[2]

Professor Herbert E. Bolton in his several writings on southwestern history and particularly in his edition of Escalante's diary applied to Garcés such epithets as "intrepid" and "hardy," "heroic" and "fearless," and a "dynamic factor in frontier exploration." He described him as "a far western Daniel Boone in Franciscan garb,"[3] and said that "adventure rode with the restless Garcés. Like many another Franciscan all the world over, he manifested his zeal for saving souls both by physical endurance and by religious ministrations.... This human approach was an important factor in his notable success."[4]

John Galvin, in the latest edition of Garcés' diaries, states:

> As an observer of Indians he had a sharp and knowing eye. He recorded a large number of details, enlarging the Spaniards' knowledge of Indian life; and the modern ethnologist, too, has learned from him.
>
> It is from his own recital of his relations with the Indians that one best sees Garcés himself, a hardy, generous, essentially warmhearted man. His approach to the heathen was direct and friendly....
>
> Father Garcés was a devoted priest; at the end of his life, a martyr. He was a pathfinder worthy of remembrance, an indefatigable traveller, uncomplaining under stress of hardship, bold under challenge. In sum, he is one of the most attractive and respectable figures in all the early history of the Southwest.[5]

Monuments have been erected to Garcés at Bakersfield, Arvin, and Fort Yuma, California, and along El Camino de los Padres in Arizona. A high school in Bakersfield and the Santa Fe Railroad building at Needles, California, are named after him.

---

[1] *On the Trail of a Spanish Pioneer*, I, xxiii-xxv.

[2] Ibid., II, 349.

[3] Silvestre, Vélez de Escalante, *Pageant in the Wilderness* (Salt Lake City, 1950), p. 3.

[4] Ibid., pp. 3 and 4.

[5] *A Record of Travels in Arizona and California 1775-1776* (San Francisco, 1965), pp. viii-ix.

GARCÍA, DIEGO (1744-?)

Fray Diego García was born at Araal, near Seville, Andalusia, Spain, in 1744, and became a Franciscan at Santa María de los Angeles in the province of Los Angeles in 1759. He had been a member of the missionary college of Tarifa for ten years when he volunteered for the American missions. He left the friary of Peñaflor in 1786 and sailed from Cádiz for Vera Cruz under the commissary, Juan de Ocón, shortly after September 2 that same year. He held the offices of preacher and confessor. At the time of his departure, he was described as a person of regular stature, of robust build, with grayish eyes.

Having set out from San Fernando College in 1787 for California, he arrived early in October and was first assigned to Mission San Francisco where he served until September 23, 1790. On October 9, 1791, he was named by President Fermín Francisco de Lasuén to found Mission Soledad together with Fray Mariano Rubí. There he remained until January 28, 1792. In the meantime he officiated a number of times at Santa Clara. García is next found at Mission San Antonio where he baptized from March 1 to November 25, 1792. He was then returned to Soledad and labored there from February 9, 1793, until April 2, 1795. He was at Mission Santa Cruz in December of the latter year and at San Francisco again from April 18, 1796, until May 18, 1797.

Bancroft states that García's frequent changes from one mission to another stemmed from the fact that he was regarded as a supernumerary and that his services were not in great demand. He adds that in one year García failed to sow grain, causing a serious food shortage and that he made himself obnoxious to his associates. He was of the opinion furthermore that García, if not practically insane, was very unpopular and had gone so far as to be disobedient when he refused to accept charge of Mission San Jose. Although Engelhardt denies all the above-mentioned allegations, the facts, however, are not so easily dismissed. Lasuén had a number of uncomplimentary things to say about García. Writing to Pablo de Mugártegui, February 24, 1792, the president declared that García and his companion Rubí berated each other in the presence of the governor, and that the dissensions and disagreements between the two friars were of a most clamorous nature and that García could not easily adapt himself to new situations. In the following year he spoke of "the odd escapades of this Andalusian which have become public only too frequently" and "put everyone on his guard."

Lasuén, who did not regard García as a fit administrator, on September 1, 1795, spoke again of García's "peculiar disposition," of his physical ailments, of his little use as a missionary, and of the fact that none of the other missionaries were willing to have him as an associate.

Late in 1795, Lasuén offered García a post at Santa Clara, which he declined. When assigned to San Francisco, he and Fray José María Fernández, who was mentally afflicted, tried "with fanatical zeal" to oust from his position Fray Martín de Landaeta, the mission's minister — action characterized by Lasuén as "irresponsible" and "utterly imprudent." García and Fernández ascribed to Landaeta, "inhuman atrocities" which Lasuén declared were nothing more than "unfortunate incidents," and he attributed García's behavior to the disorders of a "diseased mind." García was piqued because of his removal from Soledad and because, at San Francisco, he considered himself without influence in mission matters. Through his actions, declared Lasuén, García lost in great measure the esteem of his associates, largely because of his "tall tales."[1]

García had accompanied Lasuén in his examination of the future site of Mission San Jose and was present at its founding, June 11, 1797. When Lasuén offered the mission to him to develop, he declined, the circumstance to which Bancroft referred. The president then sent him to Santa Cruz with the understanding that in the following year he could return to Mexico. Because of García's physical ailments, Lasuén signed his permit for retirement on July 8, 1797. He sailed on the *Concepción* from Monterey in the fall of 1797. On November 25 of that year he asked for disaffiliation from the college with the expressed intention of joining the province of the Holy Gospel, Mexico City. However, on January 13, 1800, he was in the province of San Pedro y San Pablo in Michoacán, when he petitioned to return to San Fernando College and was favorably answered.

[1] See Kenneally, *Writings,* I, 248 and passim.

GARCÍA, JOSÉ (?-?)

There is no data on the early years of Fray José García other than that he was a native of the province of Cantabria, Spain; that he was ordained a priest at San Fernando College, Mexico City, December 23, 1797; and that he came to California, leaving the college on February 3, 1800, and arriving at Monterey in August the same year. He was assigned to Mission San Luis Rey where he served under Fray Antonio Peyrí until 1808. His name appears on the registers of Mission San Carlos in September 1800, on October 19 at San Miguel, on November 9, at San Fernando, a few times at Mission San Juan Capistrano in 1801, 1802, and 1803, and at San Diego in 1807 and 1808. Fermín Francisco de Lasuén, on October 22, 1808, stated that García was in poor health and had a very poor disposition. Owing to these facts, he received his permit to retire both from Governor José Joaquín Arrillaga and President Lasuén. He sailed from San Diego in November

1808. In 1810 he requested permission to join the province of the Holy Gospel, which was granted. On March 27, 1811, he asked to be readmitted to San Fernando College.

GARCÍA DIEGO Y MORENO, FRANCISCO (1785-1846)

Fray Francisco García Diego y Moreno was born at Lagos, Jalisco, Mexico, September 17, 1785, of well-to-do parents, Francisco Diego of León and Mariana Moreno of Lagos. He was baptized when six days old in the parish church at Lagos by the Rev. Ignacio Ramos. In 1797 he became a student in the conciliar seminary at Guadalajara where he spent three years, becoming known for his talent and application. He joined the Franciscan order at the apostolic college of Our Lady of Guadalupe near Zacatecas and made his vows, December 21, 1803. He was ordained a priest, November 13, 1808, at Saltillo, by the Most Rev. Primo Feliciano Marín de Porras, bishop of Monterrey.

At the apostolic college García Diego was employed in offices at home and as a missionary among the faithful, preaching in the towns of Zacatecas and Jalisco. In 1815 he represented his community in the inauguration of the new college of Zapopan near Guadalajara. On June 6, 1816, he was elected master of novices, an office he held until 1820, when he was appointed lector of philosophy. On July 22, 1822, and again on July 21, 1828, he was elected a counselor of the college and in the latter year also commissary prefect of the missions. He became vicar of the college in 1832.

When the northern California missions of the Fernandinos were handed over to the Zacatecans, García Diego sent several of the friars ahead to California to prepare for the transfer. These friars, under Mariano Sosa, came to San Gabriel in 1831 and dealt with Fray José Bernardo Sánchez, president of the Fernandino missions. Upon Sosa's return to Mexico, García Diego and nine missionary companions set out from the college of Guadalupe traveling to Tepic where they gave missions while awaiting for embarcation. Finally, they sailed from San Blas in the *Catalina*, August 13, 1832. When the ship called at San Lucas, however, to take on the new governor of California, José Figueroa, the sailors seized the opportunity to mutiny. García Diego and his companions decided to travel overland to Upper California and had progressed as far as San José del Cabo, when it was learned that the mutiny had ended. They retraced their steps to La Paz and sailed from there late in November, arriving at Monterey, January 15, 1833.

García Diego traveled to Mission San Jose to arrange there with the commissary prefect of the Fernandinos, Narciso Durán, for the transfer of the northern missions, those from Soledad to San Francisco Solano. García Diego chose Mission Santa Clara as his headquarters, and there he lived until 1836. He accepted that mission from the aging José Viader, who had spent forty years in California.

The Zacatecans came to California after the days of the missions' zenith and were to experience their gradual passing and final decay. When Figueroa asked García Diego, August 2, 1833, which of his missions were fit to be secularized, he replied that, owing to the condition of the Indians, none were found to be in that category. Figueroa was in favor of gradual emancipation and made a recommendation to that effect to Mexico, but before his statement arrived, the National Congress passed the Secularization Act on August 17, 1833. García Diego counseled his friars to submit to the new situation. As commissary prefect, he also visited various missions under his jurisdiction, baptizing at times and administering confirmation.

García Diego went to Santa Barbara in May of 1835 to confer with Durán who resided there as president of the Fernandinos. Together they drafted a letter to Governor Figueroa on the existing mission system. Both prelates agreed that García Diego should go to Mexico and lay before the government a plan for a bishopric in California. García Diego returned to Monterey where he attended the dying Figueroa and celebrated his obsequies. Having appointed Fray Rafael Moreno as vice-commissary, García Diego and his secretary, Fray Bernardino Pérez, embarked at Monterey, November 17 for San Blas, staying at San Diego for about a month en route. They arrived at the Mexican capital in June 1836.

The commissary prefect submitted to the Mexican government two memorials on the mission system and secularization. On September 19, 1836, Congress adopted a resolution favoring the establishment of a bishopric in California. The matter was submitted to the metropolitan chapter of Mexico City which on October 12 requested the friar to submit a report on the subject. This accomplished, he returned to the college at Zacatecas and awaited developments. Not until June 22, 1839, however, did the chapter act on his request and that of the government by submitting three names for the proposed see, García Diego's heading the list. This action was approved by President Anastasio Bustamante, who had been a classmate of the future bishop. Instructions were sent to the Mexican ambassador at Rome who presented his petition on April 6, 1840. On April 27, Pope Gregory XVI erected the diocese of Both Californias and appointed García Diego its first bishop.

Meanwhile García Diego conducted the canonical visitation of his own college and presided at its triennial chapter wherein Fray José María Guzmán (also on the list of candidates for the California bishopric) was elected guardian, and Fray Rafael de Jesús Soria, then in California, was elected commissary prefect to succeed García Diego. José María de Jesús González Rubio of Mission San Jose was confirmed as president of the Zacatecan missions.

When he was notified of his election to the episcopate, García Diego went to Mexico City, staying at San Fernando College. In the capital he took the constitutional oath before the president, September 19, 1840, and was consecrated bishop in the basilica of Our Lady of Guadalupe, October 4 by its abbot bishop, the Most Rev. Antonio María de Jesús Campos. The new bishop next dealt with the government concerning the payment of revenues promised him and appointed Pedro Ramírez his lawyer and agent for the new diocese. The properties of the Pious Fund Estates were handed over to him to administer on November 2. The bishop was notified that on November 17 the president had requested the governor of California to restore the missions and the management of their properties to the friars in compliance with the law of November 7, 1835, suspending the earlier secularization.

García Diego issued his first pastoral letter on October 28, 1840, and notified the governor of California and Durán of his appointment as bishop. In Mexico he enlisted priests and seminarians to accompany him to his new see. At Zacatecas, at the request of his brethren, he composed his "Metodo de Misionar" or "Method of Giving Missions" as was traditional at the college. On February 22, 1841, he consecrated the church of San Diego at Zacatecas, which later became the cathedral.

With his niece and an elderly woman, two Franciscan priests, and several seminarians and laymen, the bishop left Zacatecas for San Blas near the end of October. On November 5, he arranged with Henry J. Crouch to transport him and his party to San Diego on the *Rosalind*. They arrived at the port, which had been designated the seat of the diocese, December 10 and on the following day took up residence in the home of Juan Bandini. At the presidio chapel he administered confirmation to 125 persons and conferred the tonsure and minor orders to several of the seminarians, these the first ordinations in California.

The bishop found San Diego unfit and inadequate for his residence. (The place had only 150 inhabitants and accommodations were poor.) He decided to go to Santa Barbara, sailing with his party on the *Guipuzcoana*, belonging to José Antonio Aguirre. Landing at Santa Barbara on January 11, 1842, the bishop was given a cheerful and ceremonial reception by the townspeople. He was taken to the mission, which he made his procathedral while he lived as a guest in the friary. A large number of people requested that the bishop make Santa Barbara his permanent home, and he notified the governor and the pope to that effect.

In his extensive diocese García Diego had only twenty-one priests, five in Lower, sixteen in Upper California. In Lower California were the Dominicans, in southern California were the Fernandinos, and in northern California, the Zacatecans. At Mission Santa Barbara on Holy Thursday, 1842, the bishop consecrated the holy oils for the first time and on June 24, the same year, ordained the first priest in the territory, the Rev. Miguel Gómez. González Rubio, at the bishop's request, had left his mission at San Jose to come to Santa Barbara as the bishop's secretary and confessor in mid-March 1842.

On February 4, 1842, the bishop issued a pastoral letter outlining his projects of establishing a diocesan seminary, a cathedral and episcopal residence, a girls' academy, and primary schools. He decided on the tithing system to support the church, the income to be obtained from the produce of field and cattle. In the same year the first two parishes in the state, Missions San Luis Obispo and San Miguel, were created when Durán handed them over to the bishop. San Buenaventura followed in 1843.

When President López María de Santa Ana came to power in Mexico, he confiscated the Pious Fund Estates, February 8, 1842, with the result that many of the bishop's plans for the development of religion came to naught. Despite his repeated protests, even his salary was not paid. A building fund which he started produced very little, nor did the tithing system meet his needs both because of the poverty of most of the people and the unwillingness of others to contribute, despite the issuing of another pastoral letter pointing out their obligation to do so.

A pastoral letter of January 4, 1843, dedicated the diocese to Our Lady of Refuge. Gabriel Ramírez, O.P., was appointed vicar forane in Lower California since the bishop himself found it impossible to visit the extensive southern territory. The bishop visited Missions Santa Ines and San Gabriel on a canonical tour, and on May 4, 1844, having obtained from Governor Manuel Micheltorena six leagues of land, García Diego opened his diocesan seminary at Mission Santa Ines. On the following day he set out for the north, visiting the missions and churches as far as San Francisco. At Monterey he was given a civic reception.

The final dissolution of the missions occurred under Governor Pío Pico when the territorial assembly voted to rent and lease the missions and finally arranged for their sale. Exempted were the mission buildings of Santa Barbara and Santa Ines. On April 19, 1846, García Diego appointed González Rubio and Narciso Durán as joint vicars-general and administrators of the diocese in the event of his death. He died at midnight, April 30, 1846, after a long and painful illness.

The subprefect of Santa Barbara, Anastasio Carrillo, notified Governor Pico and suggested that the deceased be given the burial honors of a grand marshal. At Santa Barbara a cannon boomed every fifteen minutes in his memory. "Divine Providence," wrote Carrillo, "has taken from us a grand man, a just soul."

The funeral took place on May 3, 1846, with only Friars Durán, González Rubio, and Antonio Jimeno present. At his own request, the bishop was not buried in the vault beneath the sanctuary containing deceased friars and notable secular persons. His remains were placed in a corner of the sanctuary on the Epistle side and marked with an entablature along the wall. The very small sum of money which he had at his death was left to the diocese.

Despite the fact that the bishop had been enthusiastically received by the people of Santa Barbara in 1842, it appears for reasons that are not very clear that in course of time he became none too popular. Captain George Simpson, who visited him early in the same year of his arrival, stated that all but the better classes were unfriendly to him, for "the provincial authorities regarded him with an eye of jealousy as a creature and partisan of the central government, and the mass of the people dreaded any symptom of a revival of a system which had, in their opinion, sacrificed the temporal interests of the colonists to the spiritual welfare of the aborigines."[1]

On two occasions during his residence at Santa Barbara, not only was dislike expressed against him, but actions were shown that were nothing short of contempt. One occurred on an evening while the bishop and his secretary were taking a ride in his carriage from the mission to the outskirts of the pueblo. A bull, enraged by the crowd of people on foot and on horseback, attacked the carriage, upsetting it and killing the mule. The bishop was forced to return to the mission on foot, no one giving him any assistance. The commissary prefect Durán was so offended by the incident that he censured the people from the pulpit. On another occasion when the bishop invited the people to spiritual exercises at which he was to preach, few attended while a number even engaged in horse racing and other noisy diversions near the mission at the time of services. Nor did the bishop always enjoy his stay as a guest at the mission itself. The incidents, as recorded in documents, were reported during the heated controversy which ensued between his successor and the friars, and may have been somewhat colored by the partisans to it. Nevertheless, there appear to be grounds for accepting their substantial truth, while they will always be difficult to evaluate, because of the circumstances in which they were later disclosed.

García Diego's episcopal life was largely one of disappointment and frustration. In view of the difficulties which arose from the attitudes of the federal and territorial governments and from the apathy and poverty of the people, he could accomplish but little. The era was one of decay, dissolution, and disintegration in morals and politics. It was the end rather than the beginning of an era.

The centenary of the consecration of California's first bishop was celebrated throughout the state in 1940 in each of the then existing five dioceses and at Santa Barbara. At Los Angeles the celebration in the magnitude of its religious ceremonies was unprecedented in the history of the Pacific coast. A number of the bishop's artifacts and documents are preserved at Mission Santa Barbara, and in the city itself García Diego Catholic High School, García Road, and Moreno Road recall his memory.

[1] *Narrative of a Journey Round the World, during the Years 1841-1842*, 2 vols. (London, 1847), I, 388.

GARCÍA RIOBÓ, JUAN ANTONIO (1740-?)

Fray Juan Antonio García Riobó was born in 1740 at Malpica, archdiocese of Santiago, Galicia, Spain, and became a Franciscan in Salamanca, March 4, 1762. He left his convent in Salamanca for America in 1769. Riobó held the office of preacher and was described in official records as of medium height, stout, with a thin face, and chestnut-colored hair. He arrived at San Fernando College, Mexico City, in 1770, and with twenty-nine other Franciscans he set out for the missions of Upper and Lower California later that same year. Riobó sailed with Governor Felipe Barri on the *Concepción*, which arrived at Cerralvo, Lower California. President Francisco Palóu assigned him temporarily to the Indian towns of San José del Cabo and Santiago. In May 1773, when the missions of the peninsula were handed over to the Dominicans, Riobó and five others returned to San Fernando College, sailing from Loreto on the *Concepción*.

On February 12, 1779, Riobó and Fray Matías Noriega, as chaplains of *La Princesa* alias *Nuestra Señora del Rosario*, sailed on a voyage of discovery to northwest Pacific waters. In the northwest the ship anchored at a bay called Nuestra Señora de la Regla, later known as Prince William Sound. Mount St. Elias in Alaska was sighted on August 2, and the harbor in its proximity was named Santiago. The cross was planted, a High Mass was sung, and a sermon preached. The vessel eventually anchored in San Francisco Bay on September 14, and subsequently left for San Blas. Riobó then returned to San Fernando College.

On June 2, 1783, Riobó with Fray Diego Noboa arrived at San Francisco, this time as an Indian missionary. President Junípero Serra assigned him to Mission San Carlos, then to Mission San Diego, where he baptized between September 28, 1785, and November 7, 1786.

Besides baptizing once at Santa Clara, he officiated at Mission San Gabriel between June 27, 1784, and September 1785, and at San Juan Capistrano on February 15, 1784. His name does not appear in the California mission registers after November 7, 1786. He returned to Mexico probably from the port of San Diego.

GIL Y TABOADA, LUÍS (1773-1833)

Fray Luís Gil y Taboada was born at Santa Fe, Guanajuato, Mexico, May 1, 1773, of Spanish parents. He became a Franciscan at the Convento de Nuestra Señora del Pueblito near Querétaro in the province of Michoacán, July 24, 1792. Early in September 1800, he entered San Fernando College, Mexico City. In the following year, he sailed on the *Concepción* and arrived at Monterey, August 9, 1801.

President Fermín Francisco de Lasuén first assigned Gil y Taboada to Mission San Francisco where he labored until April 1802, succeeded by a period of service at Mission San Jose until 1804. At that time he was sent back to San Francisco where his name appears in the registers from June 21, 1804, until February 28, 1806, while he baptized also at Mission San Carlos and again at San Jose. Governor José Joaquín Arrillaga and other officials conferred with him during this period concerning the land dispute between Mission San Jose and the civilian pueblo of the same name.

Gil y Taboada was next appointed to Mission Santa Ines where he served from August 1, 1806, until February 13, 1810, and while there, he visited Mission Santa Barbara, baptizing on two occasions, and was present at the blessing of the new mission church at San Buenaventura, September 9, 1809. He was transferred to Mission Santa Barbara and served there until April 26, 1815, experiencing the severe earthquake of December 1812 and its aftermath, which he described in his annual report. In August 1814, he laid the cornerstone of the Plaza church in Los Angeles.

Gil y Taboada was next assigned to Mission Purisima where his first entry was made June 1, 1815, his last, October 29, 1817. During these years he also baptized at San Gabriel in 1813 and 1814 and at Mission San Fernando in 1810, at San Miguel in 1815, at San Luis Obispo in 1815, and at Santa Ines in 1816 and 1817.

The padre offered to live among the Indians who were being moved from San Francisco to San Rafael, stating that he was ready to sacrifice himself in the service of those poor Indians "even to the shedding of my blood, if necessary." The *asistencia* of San Rafael was founded as a hospital or sanatorium of a sort for the ill at San Francisco. A cross was raised there, and a *Te Deum* sung December 13, 1817, and the following day Mass was said. With Gil y Taboada at these ceremonies were Friars

V. F. de Sarría, Narciso Durán, and Ramón Abella. At the time about two hundred and thirty Indians resided there. Thus he became the first resident missionary north of San Francisco Bay.

On September 26, 1818, he was at Mission Santa Cruz as secretary to Sarría, who was making an official visitation, and Gil y Taboada was assigned there from 1820 to 1827, after service at San Francisco between July 11, 1819, and August 3, 1820. When Auguste Duhaut-Cilly visited Mission Santa Cruz in 1827, the missionary gave him a cordial reception. The municipal authorities of Los Angeles petitioned President Mariano Payeras, during this interval, to appoint Gil y Taboada as the pastor of the pueblo, but this request was refused because of the padre's poor health. As early as 1816 he had asked to be relieved of his missionary duties for this reason, a request he repeated on November 24, 1821. His petition could not be granted, owing to a lack of a replacement. He had baptized at Mission Soledad in 1820 and at San Juan Bautista much later in 1830.

After Luís Antonio Martínez had been banished from Mission San Luis Obispo and Fray J. J. Jimeno had taken it over temporarily, Gil y Taboada was sent there in December 1830, and made his first entry in the registers on the twentieth, his last on November 21, 1833. He found conditions there deplorable.

In December 1833, Gil y Taboada went to Rancho Santa Margarita to say Mass for the Indians engaged in planting. He was attacked there by a violent spell of dysentery and vomited blood. A neighboring padre was called to administer the last sacraments, with the exception of the Holy Eucharist, and Gil y Taboada died on December 15. His remains were taken to San Luis Obispo where Fray Juan Cabot buried him in a vault on the Epistle side of the altar, nearest to the center of the sanctuary.

In 1817 Sarría stated that Gil y Taboada had learned the Chumash language well. He was praised also for his dexterity in performing Caesarian operations, "a very worthy skill for a missionary in these parts," by means of which he was able to baptize the unborn. Payeras declared in 1820 that his merit was distinguished and his aptitude very satisfactory but that his health was not good.

Pedro Amador, in his "Memorias," states that at Mission Santa Cruz, Gil y Taboada occasionally went in disguise into gambling establishments and took a hand in card games for the purpose of detecting the gamblers and of confiscating the cards. In 1826 he was accused of smuggling and of occasional immorality. Concerning the charge of gambling, he wrote to José M. Herrera, a customs officer, April 26, 1826: "I have never attempted to defraud anyone, much less the Nation in any way."[1] Of the insinuation of immorality, according to Bancroft, the padre's superiors were inclined to consider him innocent though imprudent. Engelhardt dismissed the insinuations as worthless.

[1] Engelhardt, *Mission San Luis Obispo*, p. 199.

GILÍ, BARTOLOMÉ (1759-?)

Fray Bartolomé Gilí was born at Artá, Majorca, Spain, February 16, 1759, the son of Bartolomé Gilí and Catarina Espluego. He took his vows as a Franciscan at the Convento de Jesús outside the walls of Palma, June 4, 1776. At the large Convento de San Francisco, Palma, he was employed as an organist. In official records, before leaving for America, he was described as of regular stature, with a swarthy complexion, round of face, with honey-colored eyes, a red beard, dark hair, and with a mole on the left side of his tonsure. He sailed under the commissary, Juan de Ocón, and arrived at San Fernando College, Mexico City, early in 1788.

Neither at the college nor later in the California missions did Gilí prove to be a satisfactory religious or missionary. At the college both Gilí and Mariano Rubí, a fellow Majorcan, conducted themselves in such a manner that they were reprimanded twice by the viceroy, on April 28, 1788, and April 6, 1789. Pretending to be ill, both retired to the infirmary to avoid the daily routine of religious exercises and slept (except at mealtime). They then made the nights wretched for the other observant and hard-working friars when they loosened bolts on storeroom doors to rob their contents, beat kettles in the manner of drums, and rolled balls, which the more normal friars used for recreation during the day, down the corridors. If San Fernando College had known the modern phrase, the two mischievous men would have been described as psychopaths.

On April 28, 1788, Gilí asked the viceroy to be transferred to one of the Franciscan provinces of Mexico. His request was refused.

Passing over the heads of their superiors, both Gilí and Rubí appealed directly to the viceroy to send them to the California missions. He consented, though their own religious superiors balked at the idea, fearing that they would do much harm to the new Christians. As vice-patron of the king in external affairs of the Church the viceroy could hardly be gainsaid. He had refused to send them back to Spain, for they had come to America at the king's expense and had not yet served their ten years. The college authorities were finally persuaded that a change of climate and activity might effect a change of mind and heart in the miscreants. A viceregal order in 1790 settled the matter, and the warning was added that if they did not amend they would be sent back to Spain nevertheless.

Gilí was first stationed at Mission San Antonio, July 1791, and served there for about a year. In March 1792, President Fermín Francisco de Lasuén sent him to Mission Soledad as assistant to Rubí after Fray Diego García who had had some disagreements with Rubí had withdrawn to San Antonio. Gilí's first entry in the registers was on March 5, 1792. There appears to have been no trouble at that mission where the two former associates worked together, bringing in a considerable number of converts. García was recalled from San Antonio to Soledad at the beginning of February 1793, where, according to Lasuén, for the brief time that García and Gilí were together, they had four public quarrels. Gilí's last baptism at the mission was on January 20, 1793.

At the end of 1792, Gilí went to the presidio surgeon at Monterey to seek relief from his physical ailments. Lasuén considered him to be seriously ill, but at the same time it was his opinion that no matter to which mission Gilí would be assigned, he would need to see a physician. The president revealed his thoughts on Gilí to the guardian, Tomás de Pangua, February 22, 1793, stating that the missionary was not fitted for appointment to any mission for the simple reason that he had no spirit for the kind of work necessary in California. Shortly after this in another missive Lasuén wrote that Gilí's trouble was simply an aversion to California and that there was no alternative but to recall him.

Lasuén finally sent Gilí to Mission San Luis Obispo where Fray Miguel Giribet, who was known for his gentility, was in charge. Gilí's first entry in the registers was made there on April 9, 1793, and he continued to serve for about a year. He was present at the dedication of the new church at Mission Santa Cruz, May 10, 1794. He served at Mission San Diego for a short period in 1794, baptizing meanwhile at Mission Santa Barbara on December 5 and at San Juan Capistrano, November 9, 1793. Dr. Pablo Soler of Monterey declared him absolutely unfitted for service in the territory because adverse to the type of work required as well as to the country itself. Already in July 1794 he had received his permit from the viceroy to return to Mexico. He sailed from Monterey on the *Concepción,* August 12, 1794, in the company of Friars Tomás de la Peña and Diego Noboa.

Prior to this time, on August 28, 1793, Pangua had written to the viceroy that Gilí had made several requests for transfer from the college to a province, a request which the college declined to grant. Pangua further declared that Gilí had shown disgust with religious observance, had disregarded advice, had associated with other troublemakers, had found missionary work in California distasteful, and found no companion who was congenial. While he alleged illness, his one reason for wanting to get out of California was his dislike of it. Gilí had publicly stated that the infirmary at San Fernando was a dismal enough place, yet he preferred it to California.

Gilí arrived at Acapulco. There he informed Pangua that the captain of the *Concepción* had compelled him to go on with him to Manila. From there he wrote to the college asking disaffiliation from San Fernando College and for permission to return to Majorca. This was granted December 29, 1797, no doubt with "deliberate speed." Gilí had been a mentally sick man throughout his public life. In 1797, he was incorporated into the province of San Gregorio de Filipenas. He returned to Cádiz, June 7, 1803.

There were charges of immorality, and with regard to them nothing appears to be provable. On this matter Lasuén communicated with the viceroy in general terms saying that he found nothing against either Gilí or Rubí concerning their faults or excesses that called for them being brought before the royal judges.

GIRIBET, MIGUEL (1756-1804)

Fray Miguel Giribet was born at Agramont in Catalonia, Spain, June 1, 1756, and was professed as a Franciscan at Barcelona, September 27, 1774. He arrived at San Fernando College, Mexico City, shortly after February 6, 1785, and was assigned to the California missions the same year. Giribet served first at Mission San Francisco from September 10, 1785, until October 12, 1787, baptizing a few times at Mission Santa Clara. Next he ministered at Mission San Luis Obispo where his name is found in the registers between December 23, 1787, and October 2, 1799. He baptized at Mission San Antonio, November 25, 1787, at Mission Purisima various times between May 14, 1789, and April 3, 1796, and at Santa Barbara, May 8, 1782.

In 1798, President Fermín Francisco de Lasuén, as vicar forane of the bishop of Sonora, subdelegated to Giribet his faculties over Spaniards at the missions of Purisima, San Luis Obispo, and San Buenaventura. He is described as a zealous and successful missionary, but he nonetheless suffered from ill-health and was unequal to the tasks imposed upon him. His character was that of a man of gentility.

After Giribet had made "repeated, strong and formal" representations to retire, Lasuén granted his request on August 12, 1799, and this to "my great sorrow," he added. The president stated that Giribet had served with "religious propriety, apostolic zeal and ceaseless activity." Giribet embarked at Santa Barbara for San Diego, and having baptized there for the last time on January 12, 1800, he sailed for Mexico on the sixteenth.

At the college on May 24, 1800, Giribet was elected novice master and counselor at the triennial chapter. While still holding these positions, he received permission to return to his native province for reasons of ill health. Bancroft states that he died at San Fernando College in 1804. However, Pedro Sanahuja, historian of the Franciscan province of Catalonia, writes that Giribet returned to Spain in January 1800 and died at Agramont on August 13, 1804.

GÓMEZ, FRANCISCO (1729-1784)

Fray Francisco Gómez was born at Lugar del Castillo de Laya, archdiocese of Burgos, in 1729 and became a Franciscan in the province of Concepción in 1748. He was recruited for San Fernando College, Mexico City, by Pedro Pérez de Mezquía. He left his friary of Nuestra Señora de la Esperanza, Rioseco, and sailed for Mexico from Cádiz on *El Jasón*, September 5, 1759. At the time of his departure, he was described in official records as a person of medium stature, swarthy complexion, with dark eyes and hair and a light beard.

In 1767 he was one of the sixteen missionaries who set out from the college to take over the ex-Jesuit missions of Lower California. Gómez left Mexico City, July 16, 1767, and reached Tepic, August 21. While awaiting transportation, he and his companions gave missions in and about Tepic.

On March 14, 1768, he set sail from San Blas on the *Concepción* and arrived at Loreto, April 1. On the third, President Junípero Serra assigned Gómez to Misión Pasión or Dolores, for which he set out on the sixth. In September of that year, however, when José de Gálvez, royal visitor-general, suppressed that mission, Gómez was transferred to Santa Rosalía de Mulegé, where he served until January 1769. Assigned to service in Upper California, Gómez in company with Fray Juan González Vizcaíno sailed on the *Concepción* from Port San Lucas and arrived at San Diego, April 11.

Gómez was chosen by Serra to be the companion of Fray Juan Crespí to accompany the first Portolá expedition to go in search of the harbor of Monterey. The expedition set out from San Diego, July 14, 1769, and returned January 24, 1770. En route northward near present-day San Clemente Crespí and Gómez baptized two dying Indian girls, these becoming the first baptisms in the present state of California. The expedition failed to recognize the harbor of Monterey but discovered the bay of San Francisco.

At San Diego Serra appointed Gómez and Fray Fernando Parrón as the first missionaries in charge of Mission San Diego de Alcalá, which he had established July 16, 1769. When a new band of missionaries arrived at San Diego in 1771, Gómez sailed with them on the *San Antonio* leaving San Diego, April 14, and arriving at Monterey, May 21. Because he was in a poor state of health, Gómez obtained permission from Serra to return to Mexico. He set sail from Monterey on July 21. At San Fernando College Gómez was employed as a home missionary. In 1777 together with Fray Juan Vizcaíno he gave a mission at Valladolid (today Morelia). In the chapter of June 17, 1780, Gómez was appointed novice master. Later he was appointed vicar of the college. He died there sometime before March 16, 1784.

GONZÁLEZ, FRANCISCO (ca. 1774-?)

Concerning this friar very little is known except that he was a Spaniard and that as a member of San Fernando College he became a California missionary. González sailed from San Blas on the *Concepción* and arrived at San Francisco, April 14, 1797. In May of the same year President Fermín Francisco de Lasuén sent him to Mission Santa Cruz where he served for eight years. In 1802 he was already reportedly in poor health. Early in 1803 he notified Lasuén that one of his eyes was completely useless for reading or writing and that the other was not very good and asked for permission to retire. In 1805 his condition was such that he again made the request and was permitted to sail on *La Princesa*, November 6, 1805, from San Diego. In the chapter held at San Fernando College, July 22, 1815, González was elected a counselor. While in California he had also baptized at Mission San Carlos, May 28, 1798, at Santa Clara, several times in 1799 and 1801, and at San Juan Bautista, December 19, 1802, and in February 1805.

GONZÁLEZ DE IBARRA, FRANCISCO (1782-1842)

Fray Francisco González de Ibarra was born at Viana, Navarre, Spain, in 1782, and entered the Franciscan order in the province of Burgos. He sailed from Cádiz shortly after April 9, 1819, on *El Cometa* and entered San Fernando College, Mexico City, that same year. He sailed for California, disembarking at Monterey early in August the following year. Ibarra, as he is generally referred to, was sent to Mission San Fernando where he served from November 4, 1820, till June 19, 1835. In his biographical sketches, Mariano Payeras stated in 1820 that Ibarra promised to be active and efficient and that he had ordinary talent. Román Fernández de Ulibarri was in charge of San Fernando when Ibarra arrived, but he died on June 16, 1821, at Mission San Gabriel. For the rest of the period Ibarra was alone at San Fernando.

At the end of 1820, 2,442 baptisms had been administered at the mission since its founding in 1797, while 1,028 Christian neophytes were living there. At the end of 1835 the number of baptisms rose only to 2,854. During the same years the mission cattle dwindled from 12,000 to 7,000 head while the sheep diminished from 7,600 to 4,000. Ibarra came to the mission after its halcyon days had passed. In his early years there he had to contribute heavily toward maintaining the presidio of Santa Barbara, and this caused some sharp correspondence between him and the commander, Captain José de la Guerra y Noriega. Engelhardt considered Ibarra an example of "missionary intrepidity" in defense of the Indians and the missions.

With regard to his political views, Ibarra answered Governor José María Echeandía in 1826 by declaring that he obliged himself to guard and observe the federal constitution whenever "it is not contrary to my conscience and religious character." Mission San Fernando was secularized in 1834, the temporal management passing from the hands of Ibarra to Lieutenant Antonio del Valle, May 29, 1835. Ibarra's last entry in the Baptismal Register occurred on June 19, 1835. He had also administered baptism during this period at Santa Ines, October 17, 1820, and June 20, 1822.

Seeing the destruction of everything he had tried to build up and protect, the padre became discouraged, and together with Fray Tomás Esténaga of Mission San Gabriel, left the mission without license and went to Sonora. His action was irregular and was tantamount to apostacy from the order. Narciso Durán, commissary prefect of the Fernandinos at Santa Barbara, sent both missionaries their permits to retire, sympathizing with their plight. He reported to San Fernando College on September 25, 1837, that the padres had been absent for over a year from their posts and that he had sent them their permits lest they be regarded as apostates. When the Mexican government reversed the secularization law, the two padres returned.

Meanwhile San Fernando had been entrusted to Fray Pedro Cabot. He died, however, October 11, 1836, and Ibarra returned in time to bury him. Ibarra was next sent to Mission San Luis Rey where he also served in trying circumstances with Pío Pico as civilian administrator of the mission. Durán, writing to William Hartnell on March 5, 1840, declared: "The friar upon whom I look with most compassion is Fr. Ibarra, who is with Pío Pico. He has complained so much to me during the past summer when he was here, about the despotism and arrogance of Pico."[1] Eugène Duflot de Mofras visited the mission in 1842, describing it as the most beautiful, the most regular, and the most solid in the whole of California. Still, while 3,000 Indians had lived there ten years before, at the time of his visit there were only 400 attached to the mission, and these were distributed in various ranches. Of Ibarra he wrote:

The religious at San Luis Rey is Fr. Francisco González de Ibarra, a Spaniard already advanced in years, who had been able to save some of the fragments of the Mission and to reunite four hundred Indians on the Rancho de las Flores, where they are dwelling together with one white family. The friars of San Luis Rey were reduced to the most deplorable condition. We have seen Fr. González (Ibarra) compelled to sit at the table of the administrator and to endure the rudeness of cowboys and mayordomos, who a few years before esteemed themselves happy if they could enter the service of the friars as common servants."[2]

The register of Mission San Diego shows that Ibarra went there at times, for he baptized at the mission on December 11, 1837, September 7, 1838, and again in January 1839. The registers of San Luis Rey are lost so that it is impossible to study his record of daily activity there. He was alone at that mission, and there he died, leaving no record of his last illness, death, and burial in 1842. Silvestre Marrón, an old settler who had been in the area since 1841, stated that José María Zalvidea of Mission San Gabriel gave Ibarra burial in the sanctuary of the church on the Epistle side. He added that the padre was short of stature, very old, and had white hair.

Bancroft writes that Ibarra was liked by the Indians for his sunny disposition and his plain, unassuming manners, and because of this latter trait they called him *Tequedeuma*. Angustias de la Guerra y Ord wrote of him: "Padre Francisco Gonzáles Ibarra of the Mission of San Fernando — I knew him when he came to Santa Barbara. He was known and called by the public and my father Padre Napoleon — I don't know why he was called that. My father joked a great deal with him because the Padre was witty and merry."[3] Bancroft adds that Ibarra was nicknamed Napoleon because of his disposition to boast of everything at his own mission and for the independent style in which he criticized the authorities in secularizing the missions.

When Alfred Robinson visited Mission San Fernando in 1827, he penned a less pleasing portrait of the friar.

St. Fernando . . . 1797 . . . was governed by the reverend father Francisco Ybarra; a short, thick, ugly-looking man, whose looks did not belie his character. In his own opinion no one knew so much as himself; nothing was so good as that which he possessed; and, being at the head of his establishment, no one ever presumed to call his sentiments into question. The niggardly administration of this place, compared with the liberality and profusion of the other missions we had visited, presented a complete contrast; and the meanness and unpopularity of our host had gained for him the nickname of *"cochino"* or "hog." At supper I was amused at the economy displayed in the arrangement of his table, which seemed perfectly in accordance with the narrowness of his mind. . . .

Distrustful of every one who wished to purchase his tallow or hides, he had accumulated an immense amount in his storehouse, where many of the latter had been destroyed by the length of time they had remained deposited. The tallow he had laid down in large, arched, stone vats, of sufficient capacity to contain several cargoes.[4]

[1] Engelhardt, *San Luis Rey Mission*, p. 114.

[2] Ibid., p. 127.

[3] Price and Ellison, tr. *Occurrences in Hispanic California*, p. 34.

[4] *Life in California*, pp. 47-48.

GONZÁLEZ RUBIO, JOSÉ MARÍA DE JESÚS (1804-1875)

Fray José María de Jesús González Rubio, the son of José María González Rubio and Manuela Gutiérrez, both Spaniards, was born at Guadalajara, Mexico, June 6, 1804, and was baptized on the tenth at the cathedral, when he received the names José Norberto Francisco. His paternal grandparents were Antonio González Rubio and Francisca Gómez, his maternal grandparents, Manuel Gómez and Petra Valdivia. As a youth he attended the conciliar seminary of Guadalajara where he received the baccalaureate in philosophy, January 20, 1820. He entered the Franciscan order at the apostolic college of Zapopan near Guadalajara and made his vows January 10, 1825. He received the tonsure, minor, and major orders that same year and was ordained a priest, December 22, 1827, in the episcopal chapel in Puebla, by the Most Rev. Antonio Joaquín Pérez. On December 10, 1829, he received faculties to preach and hear confessions.

His college having no Indian mission field, González Rubio applied to the college of Zacatecas for incorporation in order to become a California missionary. He was incorporated on May 19, 1832. Letters patent were issued by Francisco García Diego y Moreno, commisary prefect of the missions, May 30, 1832, naming him a missionary to California. González Rubio joined the other Zacatecans bound for California. He sailed from San Blas on the *Catalina*. On reaching Cape San Lucas in Lower California, the sailors mutinied and the friars were temporarily stranded. At La Paz they boarded the ship again, which was bringing the new governor, José Figueroa, to California. The party arrived at Monterey, January 15, 1833.

González Rubio was assigned to Mission San Jose as successor of the Fernandino missionary, Narciso Durán. He remained there until March 1842. Thus he came to know that mission just before its secularization. Concerning this period the missionary later wrote to the Rev. Joaquín Adam in 1864: "In the inventory made in January, 1837, the result showed that said Mission numbered 1,300 neophytes, a great piece of land, well tilled; the store-houses filled with seeds; two orchards, one with 1,600 fruit trees; two vineyards — one with 6,039 vines, the other with 5,000; tools for husbandry in abundance; shops for carpenters, blacksmiths, shoemakers, and even tanneries, and all the implements for their work."[1]

There were 20,000 head of cattle, 15,000 sheep, 459 horses, 600 two-year-old colts for the saddle, and 1,630 mares. Twice a year clothing, which amounted to $6,000.00, was given out to the neophytes, and when the mission was handed over to the majordomo at secularization, there was $20,000.00 in cloth and other articles in the store-house. Thirty musicians served in the choir and wore what was described as a very neat dress for feast days. González Rubio stated that the secularization took place in 1836, attributing the cause of the downfall of the mission, not so much to the fact that the temporalities were taken out of the hands of the missionary, but to the salaries paid to the majordomo and his civilian associates.

In his annual report for December 31, 1840, the missionary could state that since the mission's founding in 1797, 8,012 persons, mostly Indians, had been baptized and that the number of Indians still enrolled as belonging to the mission was 1,322, although the majority were either among the pagan Indians or in ranches or at other missions.

González Rubio composed three inventories while at San Jose between 1833 and 1842: one a complete inventory of movable and immovable goods of the mission in 1837; another of March 1, 1842; and another undated one. This last contained the list of books of Mission San Jose, of which 176 volumes were left there by Durán and 107 which González Rubio had brought from Mexico for his own use.

While at San Jose, González held several offices. On June 24, 1835, he was named president of the Zacatecan missions (Soledad to Sonoma) when García Diego y Moreno went to Mexico. However, he resigned the position, which resignation the college accepted on September 18. Still, on June 19, 1837, he was again elected president and was told that he could not refuse to accept. He retained that position until he resigned again, this time because he was made secretary to the bishop at Santa Barbara. His resignation was accepted on April 8, 1843. José Antonio Anzar succeeded him. In 1837 he was made vice-prefect of the missions. In addition to these responsibilities, he also baptized at various times at Mission Santa Clara and exercised the faculty of administering confirmation at the missions under his charge.

Three excellent character testimonials concerning González Rubio have been preserved for the period of his service at Mission San Jose. When Faxon Dean Atherton visited Mission San Jose in May 1836, he "found the Padre, José Jesús González, to be in appearance and manners very much of a gentleman and should infer from his way of conducting the affairs of the Mision that he was a very capable man.'"[2]

William Heath Davis, a prominent merchant, wrote of him:

The last of the Mexican priests was Father González, who presided in '38 at the Mission of San José. . . . He was a noble man, a true Christian, very much respected and beloved by his people, and by all who knew him. Whenever I went there he always welcomed me in the most cordial manner, and the moment I saw him I felt drawn toward him as by a lodestone. He would take me in and say, *"Sienta Usted, hijito,"* (sit down, my little son), and seating himself close by my side, he entertained me in such delightful manner by his conversation, that one hardly realized that he was only an humble priest. His people greatly honored and loved him and he was known among them as "The Saint on Earth."[3]

When Sir George Simpson met him at Santa Clara in the early forties, he stated that González Rubio was "a truly worthy representative of the early missionaries" and that his mission was "in a more perfect state of preservation than almost any similar establishment in the country."[4]

When García Diego y Moreno became bishop of Both Californias, he petitioned the college of Zacatecas to release González Rubio from the duties of the presidency of the missions so that he could become the bishop's secretary. The guardian, Rafael de Jesús Soría, informed González Rubio to this effect, February 9, 1841. On December 12, García Diego from San Diego asked González Rubio to direct his steps to Santa Barbara, where he would be locating the diocesan see. The missionary made his last entry in the registers of Mission San Jose on March 1, 1842, and arrived at Santa Barbara about the middle of the month. Santa Barbara was to be his home for the rest of his life.

As secretary González Rubio kept the "Libro Borrador" and the "Libro Primero de Gobierno" of the bishop, containing the official decrees and acta of the diocese; he accompanied the bishop on his visitations to the missions and churches and was present when the bishop opened his seminary at Santa Ines May 4, 1844. Shortly before the bishop died, he appointed González Rubio and Narciso Durán conjointly, April 19, 1846, as vicars-general and administrators. After the death of the bishop on April 30 and of Durán on June 1, González Rubio ruled the church in the Californias from 1846 until 1850.

He administered the diocese in a most difficult and trying period. Priests were few. The missions had been secularized, then rented and sold. The American occupation, the gold rush, and California's admission to the Union followed in rapid succession. On May 30, 1848, González Rubio issued a pastoral letter on the sad condition of the Church, and another on July 14 complained about the neglect in paying tithes to support the Church. On December 28, 1849, he issued a circular letter on mixed marriages. In conformity with a proclamation of Governor Bennett Riley, October 28, 1849, González Rubio ordered the first Thanksgiving Day in California to be celebrated religiously in all the churches and this the administrator called a "so rational and pious a custom."

González Rubio obtained clergy by appealing to the Sandwich Islands, the archbishop of Oregon, and to the Jesuits. He brought the Picpus Fathers to the state and placed them in charge of the Santa Ines Seminary while the Jesuits founded Santa Clara College, later to become a university.

When Joseph Sadoc Alemany became bishop of Monterey in 1850, he traveled to Santa Barbara to present his official papers of appointment to González Rubio who in turn handed over the official books and pontificalia to the new bishop, January 2, 1851. He also briefed the new incumbent on the historical background of the missions, needed for the proper government of the diocese. On January 24, 1851, Alemany made González Rubio his vicar-general for all that portion of his diocese south of San Miguel and which reached to the tip of Lower California. He took the oath of office on January 28. For all intents and purposes he was the "bishop" of the great stretch of land about one thousand miles long. At the first synod in the state, held in San Francisco in March 1852, González Rubio was vice-president. Later, when Alemany attended the First Plenary Council of Baltimore, González Rubio was appointed vicar-general for the whole diocese of Both Californias.

At a meeting at Mission Santa Barbara early in January 1853, Alemany handed over to the few remaining Franciscans a document from Rome authorizing them to establish an apostolic college. J. J. Jimeno was made superior of the mission, which for the time being was maintained as a hospice. González Rubio was pastor of the town.

In 1853, the archbishop of Mexico City advised González Rubio that he had been chosen vicar apostolic of Lower California. Twice he declined the promotion. In that same year Pope Pius IX erected the metropolitan see of San Francisco, advancing Alemany from that of Monterey. The Rev. Thaddeus Amat, C.M., became bishop of Monterey, while Alemany was made administrator of Monterey until Amat could arrive. He appointed González Rubio his vicar-general for the governance of the Monterey diocese, November 19, 1853.

Meanwhile, González Rubio's own college, Zacatecas, was calling him home, and on May 15, 1855, elected him guardian of the institution. He sent in his renouncement of the office while Archbishop Alemany urged him to remain in California to help him govern the diocese. Zacatecas declined to accept his resignation, and on the second order to return, González Rubio resigned his vicar-generalship, bade good-bye to his parishioners and prepared to sail for Mexico. When he proceeded to the wharf at Santa Barbara on January 22, 1856, he found himself surrounded by the entire population of the town — Catholics and Protestants, Anglo-Saxons and Hispanic people — forming a physical barrier against his departure. Despite his protests, the people would not give way. He was taken back to the Apostolic College of Our Lady of Sorrows (only recently established on July 23, 1854). Archbishop Alemany was urged to intervene, and the college of Zacatecas, when advised of the situation, finally relented and allowed the friar to remain, April 19, 1856.

The new bishop of Monterey, Thaddeus Amat, chose to make his headquarters at Santa Barbara, where he arrived December 2, 1855. He lived at the mission, and he reappointed González Rubio as his vicar-general, February 23, 1856. He asked the friars to exchange with him their college property in town for the mission and for them to return to it. This was effected through the Holy See. González administered his last baptism in the town parish on March 26. At the college both in town and at the mission González Rubio taught the clerics philosophy and theology.

When the first canonical visitation was held at the mission college in the summer of 1858, the visitor-general, Francisco Caro, appointed González Rubio guardian, which was equivalent to being provincial of a province. He held this office until 1872. When Amat heard of this, he asked González Rubio to resign his vicar-generalship, for he considered the two offices incompatible. González Rubio complied. The bishop was on the point of leaving for Rome to adjudicate the matter of a growing schism among the townspeople: those in favor of the bishop, and those who were partisans of the friars. Amat then notified González Rubio and the two other friars with him at the college that they were deprived of diocesan faculties. These were restored only in 1861 when the bishop returned and this at the insistence of Rome.

Amat tried to have the remaining Franciscans move out of the diocese. Failing in this, he sought to have them transferred to San Luis Rey. This move also failed, and it was finally agreed in Rome that a number of European friars were to be sent to Santa Barbara and that after a time the few remaining Mexican friars, including González Rubio, return to Mexico. However, when Amat could not pay the traveling expenses for the European friars because of heavy diocesan debts, the Mexican friars remained in California until their deaths.

Amat came as a reforming bishop where reform was greatly desirable but where the people were not inclined to submit to a new regime. The loss of Amat's patronage and the strictures against the friars caused great sorrow to González Rubio, which he bore with much patience and fortitude as his many documents on the case reveal. The guardian became involved with Amat in a second controversy which had to be taken to Rome when Amat refused to accept dimissorials from González Rubio for the ordination of his clerics on the ground that the guardian of the college was not empowered to issue them. As a result Archbishop Alemany was appointed apostolic visitor to handle the matter, which he did in favor of the friars. A third controversy arose between bishop and guardian when Amat declined to give to the mission the deed signed by Abraham Lincoln acknowledging the mission and adjoining lands as church property. The friars had given the deed to their property in town to the bishop when the property was exchanged, but the bishop maintained that the mission merely had the perpetual use of the buildings and of some of the land. The matter was not settled in the lifetime of either prelate.

In 1864 Amat asked González Rubio to start an educational venture at the mission, a secondary school for boys, which was gladly undertaken after financial means were obtained and necessary building repairs made. The Colegio Franciscano opened its doors on March 2, 1868, and continued in existence until June 1877 when it was forced to close its doors because of mounting debts.

Feeling the weight of his years, González Rubio petitioned Rome to appoint a successor as head of the apostolic college. The choice was José María de Jesús Romo, a Mexican friar of Zacatecas, serving in the Custody of the Holy Land. He arrived at Santa Barbara in January 1872, but the official papers did not come until June 2.

On November 30, 1872, González Rubio suffered a very serious stroke, and the last sacraments were administered to him. Though he recovered somewhat, he was never the same again. His eyesight began to fail; in the end he was almost blind. He bore his physical ailments with great patience and devoted himself to prayer. He died at 4:45 in the afternoon, November 2, 1875, lying on a mattress on the earthern floor in one of the mission rooms "as calmly as a baby going to sleep, lying on his right side with the crucifix in his hands."[5]

The people of Santa Barbara subscribed for the purchase of a special coffin for his remains. The funeral was held in the parish church in town by order of Amat, who was present but who at the same time forbade a sermon. The Requiem was said by the pastor, Jaime Vila. The remains were placed in the friars' crypt beneath the sanctuary of the mission church but not in any particular niche. On November 8, 1899, the coffins of González Rubio and Francisco Sánchez were removed from the crypt and transferred to the newly constructed friars' vaults in the mission cemetery. Through the glass covering at the head of the coffin witnesses saw that "the remains were well preserved, the features of the face even recognizable."[6]

A portrait of González Rubio was painted at Santa Barbara in 1850 by the Italian artist, Lorenzo Barbieri, and was paid for by the people of Santa Barbara, of both Hispanic and Anglo-American extraction. It shows him at the age of forty-six, thin of body and with somewhat swarthy skin and brown eyes. The features are marked with serenity and dignity. In a corner of the painting are the words: "The Most Illustrious Father José María de Jesús González Rubio of the Franciscan Order, Governor of the Sacred Miter of Both Californias, which the people of Santa Barbara had painted in testimony of their keen affection and public acknowledgement, to be preserved as a precious memorial of his eminent virtues and as a grateful memento of his unquenchable charity towards the poor and his love for all."[7]

Father Romo, his superior at death, said of him in the necrology of the college: "With the fame of uncommon virtues, especially with that of prudence and exquisite tact in governing, deeply mourned by the whole population of Santa Barbara, and much more by his brethren in the Order, and after a long and painful illness the result of paralysis, and fortified with the spiritual aids, he peacefully surrendered his soul to his Creator at this College."[8]

Bancroft characterized González Rubio as "the last survivor of the Cal. missionaries, a man respected and beloved by all from the beginning to the end of his career; one of the few Zacatecanos who in ability, missionary zeal, and purity of life were equals to the Span. Fernandinos."[9] The visitor-general to the college in 1858, Francisco Caro, described González Rubio as angelic in character.

Archbishop Alemany, writing to Rome in the late fifties, declared concerning González Rubio: "I have not seen a man so observant and so venerated in all California for his knowledge, prudence and virtue as the Rev. Fr. José González." Again he stated that he was "very virtuous, prudent, full of knowledge and ability, and esteemed not only for his works but for his merits." Finally, he was "universally venerated by all as truly prudent, learned and of good conduct."[10] Earlier, Colonel Jonathan Stevenson, May 1, 1848, wrote to a member of the American episcopate in the East that Padre José María González "is a man distinguished for his piety and learning and commands the respect of all who know him."[11]

José Arnaz, a Spaniard, in his "Recuerdos" recalls: "In the north the missions were administered by the Mexican fathers of the College of Guadalupe, Zacatecas, whose morals were not highly commendable and whose example had a bad influence. An exception was the Rev. Father José María de Jesús González who on the contrary was a model of virtue and of all the good qualities that adorn a genuine religious and to these he united sprightly talents and a wide learning together with a manner affable and obliging."[12]

The *History of Santa Barbara County,* published in 1883, states: "None knew him but to love the man. Whether in his church or among those of different religions, his face wore the same benevolent, cheerful feeling. With him his religion was a golden cord, which ran through every action of his life, endearing himself to all, whether Protestant or Catholic."[13]

According to Brother Joseph O'Malley, O.F.M., who was a subject of the deceased prelate and who was present at his death, González Rubio was about five feet, eleven inches in height, rather slim, his face having long, straight features, his complexion slightly dark. In appearance he was good looking and fine featured, had a dignified bearing without affectation, and a gentle gait. He was an excellent and very emphatic preacher, a man of regular religious observance, and who bore his last illness without murmuring. He was "so perfect as to prudence that all admired him. He was never prompted by the impulse of the moment. . . . By all people, nay by all who knew him, he was held in high respect, veneration and love."[14] The only observation that this writer might add to these encomiums is that of all the missionaries whose lives are recounted in this volume, González Rubio is the most consistently described by a plethora of witnesses without benefit of collusion, and this throughout his entire public career.

[1] [Patrick J. Thomas], *Our Centennial Memoir,* p. 42.

[2] Doyce B. Nunis, Jr., ed. *California Diary* (San Francisco, 1964), pp. 8-9.

[3] *Sixty Years in California* (San Francisco, 1889), pp. 73-74.

[4] Thomas C. Russell, ed. *Voyage to California Ports,* p. 82.

[5] MS in SBMA.

[6] House Chronicle in SBMA.

[7] This painting hangs in the reception room for visitors at Mission Santa Barbara. Plaza Rubio in Santa Barbara, running along the south side of Mission Park, is dedicated to his memory.

[8] Cited by Engelhardt, *Santa Barbara Mission,* p. 387.

[9] *History of California,* III, 760.

[10] Documents of the Congregation of the Propagation of the Faith, Rome. Copies in SBMA.

[11] Ibid.

[12] Bancroft Library MS.

[13] [Jesse Diamond Mason], (Oakland, Calif., 1883), p. 170.

[14] MS in SBMA.

GONZÁLEZ VIZCAÍNO, JUAN (1728-?)

Fray Juan González Vizcaíno was born in 1728 at Fromista, diocese of Palencia, Spain, and became a Franciscan in the province of Concepción, July 22, 1739. He left his friary of Villalbín, a Recollect house, in Castilla la Vieja, September 8, 1748. At the time he was described in records as of good physique, of light complexion, dark eyes and hair, tall, thin, and somewhat pallid. He sailed from Cádiz, August 31, 1749, with Junípero Serra and companions, on the *Vilasota* or *Nuestra Señora de Guadalupe*. A stop was made at San Juan, Puerto Rico, en route to Mexico, and on near arrival at Vera Cruz a severe storm threatened the ship and the lives of those on board. He landed at Vera Cruz, December 7 and arrived at San Fernando College before the end of the month.

Vizcaíno was sent to the Lower California missions, arriving at Cape San Lucas in February 1769. President Serra appointed him and Francisco Gómez as chaplains to accompany the *San Antonio* to San Diego. He embarked at the Bay of San Bernabé, February 15 and arrived at San Diego, April 11, 1769. With Juan Crespí on June 21, he explored the San Diego Valley. On July 16, he assisted Junípero Serra and Fernando Parrón in founding California's first mission. On August 15, the natives attacked the mission and during the encounter Vizcaíno received an arrow wound in the hand which had not completely healed six months after. Serra allowed him to return to Mexico. He accompanied Fernando Rivera y Moncada overland, leaving on February 11, 1770. He arrived at San Fernando College and there continued to serve the community. On June 26, 1774, he signed himself as secretary of the missions. Prior to August 24, 1777, he and Gómez had preached a mission in the diocese of Valladolid. On August 16, 1784, after a period of over thirty years spent in the service of the college, he asked for permission to return to his province, which was granted.

GUTIÉRREZ, JOSÉ MARÍA (1801-1850)

Fray José María Gutiérrez, born in 1801, was a Mexican by birth and joined the Franciscan order at the apostolic college of Zacatecas, taking his vows on December 11, 1819. After his ordination to the priesthood, he preached missions among the faithful and on August 24, 1831, was designated for the California missions. He came to California under the commissary prefect, Francisco García Diego y Moreno, sailing from San Blas on the *Catalina* as far as Cape San Lucas in Lower California. Owing to a mutiny among the sailors, the friars were stranded for a while but were able to board ship again at La Paz, where the new governor of California, José Figueroa, came aboard, and arrived at Monterey, January 15, 1833.

Gutiérrez was first assigned to Mission San Francisco Solano at Sonoma where he succeeded Buenaventura Fortuny. He baptized there from March 30, 1833, until February 24, 1834. From there he wrote several letters to the governor on the condition of the Indians and on the dangers to the country from foreigners. Mariano Vallejo had protested to the governor against Gutiérrez' practice of having the Indians flogged, but the friar contended that they had neither honor nor shame and could be controlled only by fear.

In 1834, Gutiérrez was sent to Mission San Francisco replacing Lorenzo Quijas, baptizing there between May 1, 1834, and July 2, 1839. He next served at Mission San Antonio between August 16, 1839, and November 13, 1844. Then he returned to Mexico. On March 17, 1846, he was made procurator of the missions of his college. He died of cholera at the age of forty-nine, June 29, 1850, at the Hacienda de la Quemada near Zacatecas, having received the last sacraments.

GUTIÉRREZ, ROMUALDO (ca. 1782-1845)

Fray Romualdo Gutiérrez was a native of Tequisquiapan, Mexico, born about 1782, and in 1800 was mentioned as a *corista* or cleric, preparing for the priesthood at San Fernando College, Mexico City. By December 22, 1803, he had volunteered for the California missions. He was among the group that left the college under Fray José Antonio Urrestí, arriving at Guadalajara, April 3, 1804, and in California on August 15, the same year.

President Estevan Tapis named him and José Antonio Calzada as the founders of California's nineteenth mission, Santa Ines, which was established on September 17, 1804. In ill health, Gutiérrez was transferred to San Buenaventura shortly after July 19, 1806, and there he grew worse. The doctor described his malady as an *afecto hystérico,* and in September of the same year Gutiérrez applied for his permit to retire. He left California in November with Pedro de la Cueva, probably on the *Concepción.* On September 21, 1808, he was disaffiliated from San Fernando College and was permitted to join the province of the Holy Gospel, Mexico City. He died on September 11, 1845. Details on his life between 1808 and 1845 are not available.

HORRA, ANTONIO DE LA CONCEPCIÓN (1767-?)

Fray Antonio de la Concepción Horra was born at San Martín de Rubuales, diocese of Osma, Spain, in 1767. He became a Franciscan at Abrojo in the province of Concepción, Old Castile, in 1784. With twenty-two other friars he sailed from Cádiz on the *Santiago de España* on May 8, 1795, under the commissary, Manuel Arévalo. Disembarking at Vera Cruz, Mexico, June 26, he entered San Fernando College shortly afterwards. Horra was of regular stature, light of skin, his face pock-marked, had dark brown eyes and hair, a large nose, scant beard, and a mole near his right eye. He sailed from San Blas on the frigate, *Concepción,* and arrived at San Francisco, April 17, 1797.

President Fermín Francisco de Lasuén assigned Horra together with an experienced missionary, Buenaventura Sitjar, for the founding of Mission San Miguel, which was established on July 25, 1797. In less than a month after the founding, Horra showed signs of insanity. Sitjar, who did not want to commit the case to writing, went with "incredible haste" to Mission Santa Barbara where Lasuén was staying temporarily, to give him "a perfect idea of the wild actions of said poor friar."

Lasuén sent José de Miguel to the mission. He was to attempt by gentle means to get Horra to Monterey in order to present him to Governor Diego de Borica. De Miguel was successful in his mission. Meanwhile, Lasuén apprised the governor of the reasons for the friar's removal from the mission. The soldiers of the guard were terrified and perplexed; the neophytes of San Antonio and San Luis Obispo and the pagans were horrified and frightened because he shouted and acted like a madman and showed signs of violent fury. Lasuén recommended that Horra be returned to Mexico.

Horra had fancied himself a great ruler, compelling the soldiers to fire rounds of cartridges, the Indians to discharge their arrows, and keeping the mission in general confusion. Bancroft's assertion that there was no more proof of the friar's insanity other than that he bap-tized natives without sufficient preparation and neglected to keep a proper record is meaningless in the light of the statements of Lasuén to the governor and later to the college, as well as in the subsequent action taken by physicians and Borica.

Two surgeons at Monterey examined Horra and declared him insane. Borica made it official. Horra together with José María Fernández, who was also mentally ill, was placed aboard the *Concepción* and returned to Mexico. There he unwittingly did a signal service to Cali-fornia history. He sent a memorial to the viceroy (who did not know of his mental condition) charging that he had been mistreated in California and that the missions were maladministered and the Indians mistreated. The viceroy ordered an investigation by the governor, who in turn obtained secret information from the four presidio commanders of the territory. When this information reached the viceroy, he turned it over to the guardian of San Fernando College, Fray Miguel Lull, who forwarded the presidio commanders' replies to Lasuén, also ordering an investigation. Lasuén sent the charges of Felipe Goycoechea of Santa Barbara to Estevan Tapis of the mission of the same place. The answer this missionary gave was one of the most detailed and comprehensive documents that ever emanated from a California missionary with regard to the full particulars of daily life and routine at a mission. José Señán of San Buenaventura sent in a similar document. These two replies, with Lasuén's own lengthy document, form a trilogy on mission life that is hardly surpassed anywhere. Both San Fernando and the viceregal palace were satisfied that they had been deceived, though the whole process of investigations took four years.

The guardian, Miguel Lull, notified Lasuén, May 14, 1799, that the viceroy had become convinced that Horra had a deranged mind. On May 25, the same year, Lull informed the viceroy that many of the friars had noticed that at times Horra suffered from a "disordered and disturbed imagination." A physician declared that he acted in "an extravagant manner." Lull asked the viceroy for permission to send him back to Spain. The viceroy agreed if the college would pay the expenses. At any rate Horra passed over to the college of Querétaro at the request of Lull and with permission of the viceroy. However, when the friar wished to return to San Fernando, Lull asked the viceroy not to grant the request for the "sake of peace at this college." Nevertheless, he was there in 1803 but in ill health. Horra was finally permitted to return to Spain, July 8, 1803. He arrived at Cádiz, March 20, 1804, and was incorporated in the province of Castile.

IBÁÑEZ, FLORENCIO (1740-1818)

Fray Florencio Ibáñez was born at Tarazona, Aragón, Spain, October 26, 1740, and entered the Franciscan order at the Convento de Nuestra Señora de Jesús, Zaragosa, February 8, 1757. At the *convento grande* in his province as well as at that of Calatayud he was choirmaster. On leaving Spain, he was described in records as possessing a good build, of having a light complexion, a somewhat reddish beard, and a face large and thin. He came to San Fernando College, Mexico City, May 1, 1770, together with thirty-nine other Franciscans. Besides holding the office of preacher, he was attached to the choir of San Fernando until August 16, 1774. A fine artist as well as a musician of no little ability, he spent considerable time at the college in painting large choir books, samples of which, *antiphonaria,* were brought to Mission Santa Barbara in 1882 by Fray José María de Jesús Romo.

In failing health in 1774, he obtained a transfer from the college to the province of Michoacán where he was again employed as choirmaster and professor of Latin at San Miguel de Allende until 1781, when he joined the college of Santa Cruz de Querétaro. There he became an Indian missionary serving in Sonora at Dolores del Saric in 1783, often officiating at San Francisco de Atí down to 1790, then, at Caborca in April 1796. On his journeys to Atí he traveled on foot. After seventeen years as a missionary, he returned to Querétaro and once again to San Fernando in 1800.

The next year he was on his way to California. He embarked on the frigate *Concepción* and arrived at Monterey, August 9, 1801. At Carmel mission he administered baptism on August 16 and 18. He was stationed first at Mission San Antonio from September 20, 1801, to August 17, 1803. In that same month he was transferred to Mission Soledad, where he made his first baptismal entry on October 20. He remained at that mission until November 26, 1818. However, he made no further entries in the register after July 19, 1811; for the last seven years of his life he suffered from disabling pain most of the time. He was available only for saying Mass and other duties in case of urgent necessity. Since no substitute was available, he lingered on with his equally afflicted companion, Antonio Jayme, until death came to the rescue. Ibáñez had spent a short time at Mission San Juan Bautista, August 17 to September 14, 1806, and baptized there again, August 22 and 26, 1808.

He died at Soledad, November 26, 1818, at about four o'clock in the morning, having received all of the last sacraments. Although seventy-eight years old, he had observed without dispensation all the fasts of the Church and of the Franciscan order. He was buried on the following day, November 27, 1818, under the sanctuary of the church next to the altar steps on the Gospel side.

In 1817 V. F. de Sarría wrote that he considered Ibáñez as a man of only ordinary ability. "Nor would he," recalls Sarría in his biographical sketches, "use any more footware or clothing than prescribed by the Seraphic Institute, except a single stocking which he changed from one foot to the other, accordingly as he felt the pain passing over that part of the body, which going up as it seemed to the breast, at last took away his vital spirit."

In matters connected with temporal management, Ibáñez is credited with great capability and intelligence. In person he had great strength, was tall with broad shoulders. He was very kind to the poor and lowly and loved to instruct the neophytes in their work and in music and to teach the common soldiers to read and write. On José Joaquín Arrillaga's second coming to California, Ibáñez welcomed him with music and songs, the words of which he himself had composed. He is also remembered as a dramatist of ability: his "Pastorela," a nativity play, was, it is said, a prime favorite in California.

ITURRATE, DOMINGO SANTIAGO (1770-ca. 1815)

Fray Domingo Santiago Iturrate was born in 1770 at Lugiano in the diocese of Calahorra, Spain, and entered the Franciscan order at Vitoria in 1787. On his departure for America from Cádiz in 1795, he was described as of regular stature, of light complexion, with brown hair, blue eyes, bushy eyebrows, and thick lips. He had been enlisted for service at San Fernando College, Mexico City, by the commissary, Manuel Arévalo.

Iturrate set out from the college on February 3 and arrived in California, August 22, 1800. Fermín Francisco de Lasuén sent him almost immediately to Mission San Juan Bautista, where he served until failing health compelled him to ask for retirement in 1809. His last official entry in the registers was on July 25. He sailed for Mexico in October that same year.

During Iturrate's term of service at San Juan Bautista, the final mission church was constructed, the cornerstone being laid, June 30, 1803. The edifice, however, was dedicated on June 23, 1812, after Iturrate's departure. Before he left California the missionary also officiated at Mission Santa Cruz several times in 1800 and 1803 and at San Carlos in 1801.

In 1811 Iturrate asked to be disaffiliated from San Fernando College and for incorporation into the province of Santa Elena of Cuba.

JAYME, ANTONIO (1757-1829)

Fray Antonio Jayme de Seguras was born at Palma, Majorca, in January 1757 and at baptism received the names Antonio Mariano Francisco Miguel Gaspar. He became a Franciscan at the Convento de Jesús, outside the walls of Palma, Majorca, December 7, 1774. At Barcelona, en route to America, he was appointed collector of recruits to replace the officially appointed one who had died. He sailed with this group, however, under a newly appointed collector or commissary in 1794, arriving at San Fernando College, Mexico City, August 2, the same year. In February 1795, he set out for California, arriving at Monterey on the *Aránzazu*, August 24. There he was appointed to serve at Mission San Carlos. He baptized at that mission for the first time on September 17.

He urgently asked to be changed to Mission San Antonio before January 2, 1796. A month later, Fermín Francisco de Lasuén wrote of him: "I do not know when our good Fray Antonio will make up his mind. He vacillates about everything and comes to no decision."[1]

Jayme was sent next to Mission Soledad where he baptized for the first time on May 18, 1796, and the last time on February 11, 1821. The number of baptisms at the end of 1796 was 335, but at the end of 1820 it had reached a total of 1,758. Jayme composed and signed most of the annual reports of the mission during the years of his administration and on June 20, 1814, answered the government questionnaire on the customs and habits of the local Indians. His is the shortest of all the answers given by missionaries at the time. While at Soledad, Jayme visited Mission San Carlos from time to time, baptizing there in August and October 1798, in May and August 1801, and on December 9, 1811. He baptized also at Mission San Antonio, June 11, 1798, and at San Juan Bautista once in 1798 and once again in 1803.

Sarría in his biographical sketches, 1817, stated that it appeared to him that Jayme's merit did not exceed the ordinary though he accomplished enough despite his age and infirmities. At the time when Sarría was writing, Jayme was not fully able to discharge the duties of the ministry. Since his companion, Florencio Ibáñez, was also aged and infirm, Sarría declared that Mission Soledad was "begging in justice to be relieved of its ministers."

In 1820, Mariano Payeras wrote that Jayme for many years had been a teacher in the primary schools of Majorca. "His merit is more than ordinary for tenacity and constancy in the ministry; but his aptitude is only medium; and when rheumatic pains and other grave ills attack him, in addition to his age, he is hindered very much and his work amounts to nearly nothing."

Because of his physical condition, in 1821 Jayme was sent to Mission Santa Barbara as a supernumerary where at times he ministered when he was able. There is no record of his baptizing during the first three years prior to January 6, 1824. His last baptismal entry is found on August 12, 1828. At Santa Barbara he witnessed the Chumash Indian revolt in 1824, but the Indians spared him as well as Fray Antonio Ripoll. "He was a kind-hearted, indulgent man," states Bancroft, "beloved for that reason by the neophytes."[2] Angustias de la Guerra y Ord, who lived in Santa Barbara, remembered him as an old man and noted that he walked with difficulty. Bancroft adds that in his later years he was confined to his room by the torments of rheumatism and sought alleviation on snuff and cigars. Having received the last sacraments, he died on December 1, 1829, and was buried by Fray Antonio Jimeno in the crypt of the church.

[1] Kenneally, *Writings*, I, 372.
[2] *History of California*, II, 577, n. 44.

JAYME, LUÍS (1740-1775)

Fray Luís Jayme, the son of Melchor Jayme (Jaume in the local dialect) and Margarita Vallespir, was born at San Juan, Majorca, Spain, October 18, 1740, and soon after birth was baptized, receiving the name Melchor. He obtained his early training at the convent school of San Bernardino, Petra, which Fray Junípero Serra had attended earlier. Jayme became a Franciscan at the Convento de Jesús, outside the walls of Palma, Majorca, September 27, 1760, and on making his profession the following year changed his name to Luís. He made his studies for the priesthood at San Francisco, Palma, and was ordained December 22, 1764. He became a professor of philosophy in the order. In 1770 he left Spain for America. At that time he was described as a person with a well-proportioned physique, somewhat thin, and of a darkish complexion.

In October 1770, with nine other friars he set out from San Fernando College, Mexico City, and traveled as far as Tepic, where he awaited ship passage. Embarking from San Blas January 20, 1771, the friars arrived at San Diego, March 12 and reembarked for Monterey where they arrived on May 21. There Serra assigned Jayme to San Diego. He again took passage on the *San Antonio* and took up his official duties at the southern port where Serra had founded California's first mission, July 16, 1769. It was Jayme who proposed the removal of the mission site from its original location on Presidio Hill (Old Town) to the valley where it is situated at present, and where he erected the initial mission buildings. The transfer was accomplished in August 1774. Jayme's assistant from August 30, 1773, was Fray Vicente Fuster.

The San Diego Indians of Yuman stock proved to be consistently treacherous and uncooperative, more so than in other mission areas along the coast. In the fall of 1775 some Christians absented themselves from the mission and went into the hinterland. On several occasions Jayme had been warned that trouble was brewing, but he could not bring himself to believe the information. Around midnight, November 5, 1775, about eight hundred Indians, most of whom were pagans, appeared stealthily at the mission, as later events proved, with the intention of killing all Spaniards at the mission and presidio. They set fire to the mission buildings, robbed the mission of some of its belongings, murdered Jayme and a few other Spaniards. When first aroused, the missionary had approached the Indians and said: *"Amar a Dios, hijos,"* ('Love God, my sons'), the usual greeting in early mission days, but to no avail. They clubbed Jayme to death and left his remains in the nearby arroyo. Fuster was in another part of the mission and thereby saved from death. He aided the soldiers in repelling the invaders. The battle lasted until dawn when the Indians retreated. Fuster left a vivid and detailed account of the night of terror. Jayme's remains, when they were found the next morning, were hardly recognizable.

The soldiers carried Jayme's remains to the presidio where on November 6 Fuster buried his confrere in the chapel. The registers had been burned in the fire, but Serra with the aid of Fuster was able to ascertain that up until November 5, 1775, 431 Indians had been baptized. Serra is the authority for saying that Jayme had learned the Indian language. When the new church was built in the valley by Fermín Francisco de Lasuén, the remains of Jayme were transferred there. After the dedication of the final church, November 12, 1813, the remains of Jayme, Juan Figuer, and Juan Mariner, were placed in new but separate boxes and buried in a common vault in the church between the main and the side altar. The proximate site of Jayme's murder beside the arroyo is marked by a concrete cross.

When the news of Jayme's tragic death was learned in Majorca, a portrait of the missionary was painted and hung in the Consistorial Hall of Palma, where memorials of the famous sons of the Island were kept. This painting was destroyed by a fire in modern times. In the town of San Juan, his birthplace, a painting of Jayme's martyrdom may be seen in the sacristy of the church, and a stone monument of him stands above the city hall of his native village.

JIMENO, ANTONIO (?-1876)

Fray Antonio Jimeno was a native of Mexico City, the son of José Antonio Jimeno and Gregoria Sánchez. As a youth he joined the Franciscan order at San Fernando College. He came to California as a missionary with his brother José Joaquín Jimeno and Fray Juan Moreno in September 1827. He was sent in January 1828 to Mission Santa Cruz where he began to baptize, March 21; his last entry at that mission was made on December 10, 1828. Thereupon he was assigned to Mission Santa Barbara, administering his first baptism, January 28, 1829, and his last on January 17, 1858.

Most of the Chumash of the region had been converted, and 762 of them lived at the mission at the time of his arrival; consequently, the increase in baptisms at Santa Barbara was only from 4,463 to 4,715. Jimeno, with the construction of a second tower, completed the mission church early in 1833. Secularization of the mission took place in 1834, and he signed the inventory handing the material control over to lay administrators, March 15, 1835. Later he witnessed the mission lease and sale. According to José María de Jesús González Rubio, Jimeno had learned the Chumash tongue. While at Santa Barbara, he also attended to Mission San Buenaventura between 1841 and 1843 and also baptized there at other times.

Bancroft states that Jimeno was stout and dark complexioned, amiable in disposition, kind to the neophytes, but strict in religious matters. Sir George Simpson in 1842 considered him more a man of the world than Narciso Durán, the commissary prefect. Alfred Robinson shows him in a rather hilarious mood at a festivity held in the De la Guerra home.

Mission Santa Barbara became a Franciscan hospice in 1853. The decision was reached at a meeting held at the mission attended by the resident friars, Archbishop Joseph Alemany, and the guardian of San Fernando College, Father Francisco Orruño. In the following year, July 23, 1854, the friars of the hospice opened the Apostolic College of Our Lady of Sorrows in town, of which Jimeno became a member. It appears, however, that he continued to reside at the mission to attend the remaining Indians.

It was Jimeno, according to a statement of Bishop Thaddeus Amat, who offered to exchange the property of the college for that of the mission in 1856 after his brother José Joaquín Jimeno who had been the superior and who had died shortly before on March 14 had twice declined to effect the exchange. When Jimeno succeeded his brother in office as guardian and the bishop accepted the proposal, the friars moved back to the mission about April that year. Jimeno retained the superiorship until the canonical visitation made by Francisco Caro in the late summer of 1858. González Rubio succeeded him, and Jimeno became vicar. Some of the members of the community considered him somewhat severe and not sufficiently charitable.

When a schism arose in Santa Barbara in 1858 between the partisans of the bishop and those of the friars, with the bishop preparing to leave for Rome to adjudicate matters, the mission friars, including Jimeno, were deprived of their diocesan faculties until the bishop's return in 1861. On March 19, 1858, Archbishop Alemany wrote to Rome that Jimeno was "old and not very useful" but that he believed him to be a man of good life.

Jimeno, who had permission to return to Mexico, left Santa Barbara about January 23, 1859. He again entered San Fernando College where there were still forty friars in residence. Early in April 1861, Jimeno with the other friars of the college was forced by the government to withdraw from the college and, consequently, had to live in a private home.

By June 1866, Jimeno was going blind and had to have others write letters for him. Angustias de la Guerra y Ord recalled that, in addition to his blindness, he was very poor and was living on alms. Father Joseph J. O'Keefe of Mission Santa Barbara visited him in 1874. Jimeno died on December 25, 1876.

JIMENO, JOSÉ JOAQUÍN (1804-1856)

Fray José Joaquín Jimeno, son of José Antonio Jimeno and Gregoria Sánchez, brother of Fray Antonio Jimeno, was born in Mexico City, November 30, 1804. He became a Franciscan at San Fernando College, Mexico City, in 1803, after studying at San Ildefonso College, and made his profession in the following year. Immediately after ordination in 1827, he was sent to California and arrived at San Diego in September. He was assigned to Mission San Luis Rey whose founder, Fray Antonio Peyrí, was still guiding its destinies.

Jimeno served at San Luis Rey from October 1, 1827, until April 15, 1830. When he arrived at that mission, 2,685 Christian Indians were still living there, while 22,610 cattle and 28,532 sheep and goats grazed on the mission pastures. Up until December 31, 1827, 4,821 baptisms had been administered. Mission San Luis Rey was the largest structure among the twenty-one missions of the territory. Jimeno's initial mission experience thus placed him in a highly developed missionized area. While stationed at San Luis Rey, Jimeno visited Purisima in December 1828, and presumably he visited the other missions en route.

Though Jimeno was transferred to Mission Santa Cruz in 1830, he was delayed en route at Mission San Luis Obispo for about four months, owing to the expulsion of Fray Luís Martínez by the California political authorities. When Luís Gil y Taboada arrived to take charge, Jimeno went on to Santa Cruz to replace his brother Antonio Jimeno, who was transferred to Santa Barbara. Jimeno served at Santa Cruz between October 30, 1830, and February 17, 1833. There he saw the beginnings of the secularization stir and Indian emancipation, and, though a Mexican, he pointed out the difficulties that would arise. It was his opinion that in the event of secularization, the temporalities should be distributed among the Indians but that they should be required to work lest they become vagrants. Jimeno handed the mission over to his Zacatecan successor, Fray Antonio Suárez del Real, in February 1833 and was then transferred to Mission Santa Ines as successor to Blas Ordaz and first baptized there on May 14, 1833. In 1836, 335 Indians lived at the mission. When William Hartnell, inspector of missions, arrived at Santa Ines in July 1839, he found the mission in a totally sad state.

At Santa Ines, Jimeno was involved in an unpleasant affair with Governor Mariano Chico. The governor claimed that he had sent a messenger ahead to inform Jimeno of his coming so that he could be properly received. According to Jimeno and others with him, Chico came unannounced and grew angry because no formal reception was tendered him. The case was taken to Fray Narciso Durán, who exculpated Jimeno and his associates.

On November 28, 1838, San Fernando College elected Jimeno president of the missions from San Miguel to San Diego. He announced his election to Governor Juan Bautista Alvarado on November 26. He was reelected president on April 20, 1844, and continued in that office down to the end of the mission period. On March 23, 1840, Jimeno announced his appointment as vicar forane for the bishop of Sonora.

Governor Manuel Micheltorena restored the temporal management of the missions to the Franciscans by his decree of April 18, 1843. When Bishop Francisco García Diego y Moreno of Santa Barbara obtained a large land grant from Micheltorena in the Santa Ines Valley on which to establish a seminary, the bishop appointed Jimeno its first rector. The institution opened on May 4, 1844, and was open to lay students as well as those destined for the priesthood. In addition to his other responsibilities, Jimeno taught moral theology. He soon built a two-story adobe building south of the mission which became the seminary proper. He also continued to serve the local Indians. In March 1844 the number of neophytes was 264.

Concerning the inventory of Mission Santa Ines, made prior to its being rented and sold, Jimeno declared that he was not allowed to take any part whatsoever in the transaction and considered the action therefore null and void. The mission was rented on December 5, 1845, and sold on June 15, 1846. Jimeno continued to reside there until May 7, 1850, when the seminary was surrendered to the Picpus Fathers. During his service at Santa Ines, Jimeno visited Mission Purisima on January 10, 1836, and San Luis Obispo on October 12, 1843. When Durán the commissary prefect died, June 1, 1846, Jimeno was elected to succeed him.

On leaving Santa Ines, Jimeno went to Santa Barbara for a few months. As commissary prefect he had the faculty to administer confirmation which he exercised but once, at San Juan Capistrano in August 1850 when he confirmed 133 persons. He served at Mission San Fernando from September to November 1850 and then at Mission San Gabriel from December 8, 1850, to August 18, 1852. Jimeno together with Fray Francisco Sánchez were the last Franciscans to serve that mission and the *asistencia* chapel of Our Lady of the Angels in Los Angeles. Both places were surrendered at that time to the Picpus Fathers, and Jimeno returned to Mission Santa Barbara.

In 1852 Jimeno attended the first ecclesiastical synod held in California under Bishop Joseph Alemany of Monterey, and on April 20, 1854, he was in San Francisco to testify before the U. S. Land Commission concerning the ownership of the California missions and their adjacent lands. In this testimony he stated that the Indians were considered the owners of the mission lands and that the mission churches, cemeteries, orchards, vineyards, etc., belonged to the Church. He added that a written title was not necessary according to Mexican law, but undisturbed possession alone was considered as legitimate title before the law. On October 3, 1854, Alemany ordered all books bearing the mark "College of San Fernando" to be sent to Jimeno at Santa Barbara.

In 1851 the Santa Barbara friars submitted to Alemany their plans for survival in California. As a result the latter petitioned Rome for permission to establish an apostolic college, which was granted February 28, 1852. A meeting was called at Mission Santa Barbara in January 1853, attended by the Santa Barbara friars, Alemany, and Father Francisco Orruño, guardian of San Fernando in Mexico. On January 5 it was decided that for the time being the mission should be reestablished as a hospice, and Jimeno was declared the first superior.

In the following year when plans were being laid for the establishment of the college, Alemany expressed the desire that it be founded in town, where the laity could take better advantage of the services of the friars, rather than at the mission. The Den property at State and Figueroa streets was purchased, and there the college was formally established on July 23, 1854, and, as previously arranged, with Jimeno as the first superior. On that same day four youths, destined for the priesthood, were invested with the habit of the First Order, the first investiture of Franciscans in California. They made their vows in the following year. Meanwhile, a new church, dedicated in July 1855, was built across the street — the first parish church built in the city in the American period.

According to Colonel Jonathan D. Stevenson, who on May 1, 1848, informed the ecclesiastical authorities in the East on conditions within the Church in California, Jimeno was "a young man of unsteady mind constantly urging the people of the country to resort to violent measures to rid themselves of the American authorities, but which is totally disregarded by the people and the American authorities. He has often been reproved by the Rev'd Father Gonzales for his intemperate conduct."[1]

This statement appears to be in total contradiction to an encyclical letter Jimeno had written to his Franciscan subjects, August 28, 1846, wherein he said:

As we are already under the power of the Americans, it seems to me a matter of obligation to address Your Reverences in order to admonish you tenderly to conduct yourselves with such a spirit of religion, prudence, good judgment and refinement, that we do not give them if possible, the least reason to conceive any distrust of us, and much less, of our religion. It is not my intention to advise a cowardly shame and excessive silence which would be unbecoming the Church, but rather that a very prudent conduct be observed which the existing circumstances demand: a prudence which consists in avoiding absolutely with the gentlemen who govern everything that could provoke, irritate or exasperate them and that could ill-dispose them towards our religion and its ministers.[2]

He cautioned the friars against criticism of the laws and government and urged submission to them in all things that were not contrary to their religion and good morals. He gave motives from Scripture and the church fathers and the practice of the Church in history in obeying the authorities who had effectively established themselves in an area.

This public document, formally expressing Jimeno's attitude, issued just two years before, leaves the reader baffled by Stevenson's charge — the colonel appraised the other friars and the conditions within the Church at the time fairly — particularly since Jimeno was regarded as a saint by Alemany. In the two-year interim Jimeno may have completely changed his mind.

The new bishop of Monterey, Thaddeus Amat, arrived in Santa Barbara, December 2, 1855, and made his residence at the mission. The bishop soon asked Jimeno on two separate occasions to exchange with him the college and church in town for the mission. Jimeno declined on both occasions, stating that the matter would have to be taken up with the Holy See. The exchange was effected after Jimeno's death.

Other than the fact that he suffered patiently through a long and painful infirmity, there are not available any details on Jimeno's physical condition immediately prior to his death in Santa Barbara on March 14, 1856. José María de Jesús González Rubio buried him the next day, with Amat presiding at the funeral. His remains were placed in the crypt of the church beneath the sanctuary. Jimeno was fifty-four years old and had served the Church in California for twenty-eight years.

When Alemany learned of Jimeno's death, he wrote to Santa Barbara: "I feel very much the loss of venerable Father José. He lived the life of a saint and it is evident that he closed it like a saint. I almost invoke him in heaven in behalf of the Church in California."[3]

González Rubio wrote that Jimeno "left behind him the good odor of his virtues and the memory of his example and religious life."[4]

[1] Weber, *Documents of California Catholic History*, p. 53.
[2] Original in SBMA.   [3] Ibid.   [4] Ibid.

JUNCOSA, DOMINGO (1740-?)

Fray Domingo Juncosa was born in 1740 at Cornudella, archdiocese of Tarragona, Catalonia, Spain, and became a Franciscan at the convent of Reus, November 3, 1757. He held the title of preacher when he left Reus for the Indies in 1767. At the time of his departure, Juncosa was described as of medium height, full faced, and slightly florid in complexion. One of forty Franciscans gathered together in Spain by Fray Rafael Verger, Juncosa arrived at San Fernando College, Mexico City, in 1770.

Setting out from the college with eight other Franciscans under the presidency of Antonio Paterna in October 1770, he sailed from San Blas, January 20, 1771, on the *San Antonio* and arrived at San Diego, March 12. He reembarked for Monterey on April 14 and reached the northern port on May 21. After Junípero Serra and Juan Crespí moved from Monterey to the new site of Mission San Carlos at Carmel, Juncosa together with José Cavaller remained at the Monterey presidio and served the soldiers and their families.

Serra named both to be the first missionaries of Mission San Luis Obispo which he founded September 1, 1772, though Juncosa did not arrive until some time after its establishment. He baptized there between February 3 and November 1773, when Francisco Palóu, interim president, on his way from Loreto to Carmel, took Juncosa along and placed him at Mission San Antonio. Juncosa's health was not good, and as a result his stay in California was short. Serra stated that Juncosa had repeatedly asked for permission to retire because he was shocked at the scandalous conduct of the soldiers and by other unpleasantness. He sailed for Mexico from Monterey on the *San Antonio*, June 8, 1774.

When Juncosa's health did not improve at the college, he asked for disaffiliation, May 19, 1775, and received permission to join the province of Zacatecas.

LANDAETA, MARTÍN DE (1760-1809)

Fray Martín de Landaeta was born at Cortezubi in the seignory of Vizcaya, Spain, in 1760, and became a Franciscan in the province of Cantabria in 1780. On leaving Spain for America, he was described in government records as a person with a well-formed body, with a large face, pockmarked, and having blue eyes. From San Fernando College, Mexico City, he came to California in 1791 with four other missionaries. His name appears for the first time in the registers of Mission San Francisco on August 19, where he labored until 1798, baptizing at various times at Santa Clara. He returned to Mexico after having suffered greatly from emotional disturbances. President Fermín Francisco de Lasuén gave him formal permission to leave, October 9, 1798.

While at San Francisco, Landaeta was accused of working the Indians too hard. Lasuén stated that while this charge may have been true, the matter had been corrected. There also, his two assistants, José María Fernández and Diego García, plotted with fanatical zeal to oust him from the mission. Some of the Indians and presidio officers joined in this attempt. Lasuén took a hand in the matter and the affair quieted down.

Returning to San Fernando, Landaeta petitioned for disaffiliation for reasons of health and asked permission to join the province of San Pedro y San Pablo in Michoacán. Whether he actually left the college is doubtful for in February 1800 Miguel Lull, the guardian, notified Lasuén that Landaeta's health had improved and that he had again offered his services for California. Landaeta with four others set out from the college, November 2, 1799, and from San Blas sailed on the *Concepción* for California. He arrived at San Diego, August 23, and at San Francisco, September 30, 1800. He officiated at the latter mission until October 28, 1806, when he was assigned to Mission San Fernando where he was stationed until November 3, 1809.

Already in December 1801, Landaeta was described as very ill. Early in 1803 he was suffering from rheumatic pains together with a hypochondriac condition offering little hope for recovery. He took baths at the hot springs near San Jose to obtain relief. After receiving the last sacraments, he died, most probably on November 3, 1809, at Mission San Fernando, for on the following day he was buried by Fray Marcos Antonio de Vitoria. The precise place of his burial at the mission was not noted.

When in San Francisco, Landaeta had met Captain George Vancouver in 1792, who found him to be genial, as did Dr. Georg von Langsdorff in 1806.

LASUÉN, FERMÍN FRANCISCO DE (1736-1803)

The son of Lorenzo de Lasuén and María Francisca de Arasqueta, Fray Fermín Francisco de Lasuén, was born at Vitoria, in the province of Alava, Cantabria, Spain, June 7, 1736, and was baptized on the following day by the Rev. Francisco de Elosu in the church of San Vicente Martir. His paternal grandparents were Juan de Lasuén and Magdalena Aspiunza; his maternal grandparents, Francisco Arizqueta and Agueda de Murua.

He received the Franciscan habit at the Convento de San Francisco, Vitoria, March 19, 1751, from Fray José Ramírez, the guardian. He pronounced his vows on July 7, 1752. He made some of his studies for the priesthood probably at Vitoria and definitely for a period at Aránzazu. As a deacon, which order he had already received on July 15, 1758, he volunteered for the American missions and as such was listed in passport records at the port of Cádiz, at the age of twenty-three, awaiting embarcation. He had been recruited under Pedro Pérez de Mezquía, the commissary. The records described him as a man of symmetrical build, with light, somewhat ruddy skin, a pockmarked face, with dark eyes, and dark, curly hair.

Sailing on *El Jasón,* he landed at Vera Cruz, Mexico, entered San Fernando College, Mexico City, where presumably he was ordained to the priesthood sometime before February 25, 1761, when he received faculties to preach and hear confessions. In 1762 he was sent to the Sierra Gorda missions and ministered there until 1767 when he was sent to Lower California. No details of his labors in the Sierra Gorda have come to light. With several other missionaries, including Fray Juan Crespí, he left the Sierra Gorda on July 26, 1767, and traveled directly to Tepic through Querétaro and Guadalajara, where he arrived on August 25. He stayed in the Jaliscan friary of Santa Cruz de Zacate until transportation was available to Lower California.

Under Junípero Serra as president, en route to take over the ex-Jesuit missions, Lasuén sailed from San Blas on the *Concepción,* March 14, 1768, and arrived at Loreto, Lower California, April 1. There, Serra assigned him to Misión San Francisco de Borja in the north of the peninsula. Lasuén left Loreto on April 6. On arrival at San Borjas, as the place was called, he found neither church nor house. He soon set to work to build both of adobe. Early in 1769 he traveled to Velicatá in order to minister to the soldiers of the Portolá expedition encamped there, and arrived on February 22. Subsequently returning to his mission, he remained there until it was handed over to the Dominicans in 1773.

Having been invited to serve in the new missions by Francisco Palóu, president of the Lower California missions after Serra's departure for Upper California in 1769, Lasuén awaited the arrival of the former at San Borjas and on June 23, 1773, joined Palóu on his trek to Misión Santa María where Sergeant José Francisco Ortega accompanied them as far as San Diego. They arrived on August 30. Palóu, as interim president during Serra's absence in Mexico, took Lasuén as far as Mission San Gabriel and assigned him as supernumerary. The latter arrived there on October 2, 1773, and remained until 1775. In June of that year he accompanied a packtrain to Monterey, where he arrived on June 25. Along the Santa Barbara Channel at Dos Pueblos his life became endangered when Indians attacked the packtrain. In the melee six natives were killed. At Monterey, Lasuén served as personal chaplain to Fernando Rivera y Moncada and ministered spiritually to the soldiers and their families at the presidio.

When Serra and Rivera agreed to found Mission San Juan Capistrano, the president appointed Lasuén and Gregorio Amurrió as the first missionaries. Lasuén left Monterey on August 21, 1775, and proceeded directly to San Diego, Amurrió joining him at San Luis Obispo.

Setting out from the southern port of San Diego with Lieutenant José Ortega and soldiers, Lasuén journeyed to the spot where the mission was to be founded. On October 30 he raised the cross, hung the bells, and said Mass, formally establishing the mission. Shortly after the soldiers began to construct the initial mission buildings, a messenger arrived from San Diego with the news that the Indians had burned the mission at San Diego and had murdered Fray Luís Jayme. Ortega hurried to San Diego, bidding the missionaries to follow and the soldiers to suspend the building operations at San Juan Capistrano. Lasuén was forced by these circumstances to remain at San Diego without employment.

Serra reestablished Mission San Diego in the summer of 1776 and on November 1, reestablished that of San Juan Capistrano. Lasuén accompanied Rivera north as far as San Gabriel and later went with Serra to San Luis Obispo, remaining there until 1777 when Serra appointed him as minister of Mission San Diego where he arrived by August. His first entry in the registers occurred on November 15. Lasuén served at San Diego until he received notification of his elevation to the presidency of the missions, October 11, 1785, succeeding Junípero Serra.

Lasuén's first years in Upper California were unhappy ones. He repeatedly asked to retire to San Fernando College. He stated that he had come to California only at Palóu's request and that he remained there solely because of Serra's urging. He disliked San Gabriel and was dissatisfied with his status there. Being a personal friend of Rivera, whom he greatly admired, he wished to accept the governor's offer to become presidio chaplain at Monterey. This Serra opposed because no provision had been made either by the government or by San Fernando College for such a post.

When Rivera threatened to resign if Lasuén did not become his chaplain, the latter obtained permission to go to Monterey, not disclosing the true reason for his decision. Serra allowed him the chaplaincy but with reluctance. There resulted a coolness between the two missionaries which lasted till the year 1777. Lasuén had been unaware of the friction between Rivera and President Serra, but on becoming acquainted with the true status of affairs, Lasuén made a complete *volte-face* in favor of Serra and against Rivera. He even declined to accept the personal chaplaincy after it was ratified by the college.

Both during life and after the president's death, Lasuén considered Serra a saintly man and an exemplary superior, as his writings reveal. Serra, on the other hand, praised Lasuén for his urbanity and affable manners as well as for his regular religious observance. In temperament the two men were entirely different. Lasuén was gentle and gracious and perhaps too introspective and sensitive. He found it hard to adjust himself to conditions in California. Moody and discontented, he clamored for retirement, especially from San Diego. He declared that it was only obedience that kept him in the territory. Undeniably the post at San Diego was the worst that could be offered any missionary, and Serra gave it to Lasuén precisely because he considered him the best missionary he could place there. But the crude and dangerous surroundings were hard on his refined character. The mutual correspondence between Serra and Lasuén between 1777 and 1784 shows that there was complete understanding between the two, and Serra's letters are replete with praise and encouragement.

Lasuén's feeling of inadequacy is revealed in a letter he wrote to a confrere in Mexico: "This land is for apostles only.... I am already old and all my hair is gray, and though my years have brought this about, the heavy burden of my office, particularly my five years as missionary at San Diego, has accelerated this condition greatly."[1] When Lasuén wrote those words in 1782, he was only forty-six years old. One feels that Lasuén did not realize his full potential, while others did. No one reviewing Lasuén's years in Upper California between 1773 and 1784 would dream that he was the man who would succeed Serra.

At San Diego he built a new church and enlarged the mission compound and baptized the thousandth Indian since 1769. Even after the uprising of 1775, affairs at San Diego remained unsettled, and his life was in danger for a great period of the time, owing to the nature of the local Indians.

After Serra's death, August 28, 1784, Palóu remained in California as interim president. Lasuén was subsequently appointed president by San Fernando College, February 6, 1785. He baptized at San Diego for the last time on December 5, having received news of his appointment in October the same year. Palóu embarked for Mexico from Monterey, November 13. Lasuén arrived at Monterey by January 12, 1786. For the remainder of his life, Mission San Carlos was his official headquarters.

During his presidency of eighteen years, Lasuén founded nine missions in California, just as Serra had founded an equal number before him. Moreover, he was personally present at the establishment of each. These missions were founded in the following order: Santa Barbara, December 4, 1786; Purisima Concepcion, December 8, 1787; Santa Cruz, August 28, 1791; Soledad, October 9, 1791; San Jose, June 11, 1797; San Juan Bautista, June 24, 1797; San Miguel, July 25, 1797; San Fernando, September 8, 1797, and San Luis Rey, June 13, 1798.

On March 13, 1787, San Fernando College designated Lasuén as its subject, empowered to administer confirmation on the basis of the decree of Pope Pius VI of May 4, 1785. The document, because of the circuitous channels through which it had to pass in Church and State, did not reach Lasuén until May 26, 1790, five years after it was issued, its validity good for only five remaining years. Still, Lasuén was able to confirm over one thousand persons.

On September 30, 1796, Bishop Francisco Rouset, O.F.M., of Sonora, in whose diocese California lay, granted Lasuén all his faculties with authority to delegate them to his missionaries. At the same time he made Lasuén his vicar forane and ecclesiastical judge for California, and on October 22, 1796, his military vicar. In the preceding year, 1795, Lasuén had been appointed commissioner of the Holy Office of the Inquisition.

A summary view of how the missions developed between 1785 and the end of 1803 can best be seen by comparing their statistics at the death of the two presidents. The number of missions rose from 9 to 18, the number of missionaries from 18 to 40. Baptisms increased from 6,736 to 37,976. The number of Indians living at the missions at the end of 1784 were 4,646, at the end of 1803, 18,185. Cattle increased in the same period from 5,384 to 77,578; sheep from 5,384 to 117,736. The total produce of the fields at the end of 1784 were 15,796 *fanegas,* at the end of 1803, 48,003 *fanegas.*

Under Lasuén, building operations at the missions developed apace. The mission buildings as we know them today to a very great extent date from this period. Besides the new ones which he founded, the older ones were expanded, and sturdier churches were erected, such as the present stone church at Carmel and the stone-brick church at San Gabriel. The library at Carmel under Lasuén became the first to be cataloged in California.

When the California mission system was attacked on the basis of the false charges made by the demented Antonio de la Concepción Horra, the charges were ably answered by Lasuén and his missionary associates. Lasuén, following the pattern of Serra and Palóu, defended the policy of the missionaries against the charges of Governor Pedro Fages. While Lasuén did not experience the almost constant controversies with the military and government officials that had characterized the earlier period under Serra, his presidency was not entirely devoid of differences with them. Serra had the more difficult task in laying the groundwork, and Lasuén could enjoy the fruits of the advances made. Moreover, the governors under whom he worked were more tractable. Finally, Lasuén, though firm in adhering to principles, because of his urbane character and gentle disposition developed that diplomacy in relationships which avoided heated controversies.

As president, Lasuén met a number of important personages of various nationalities who, fortunately, recorded their impression of him. When Captain George Vancouver visited Mission San Carlos in

1792, Lasuén gave him excellent hospitality. "This personage," wrote Vancouver, "was about seventy-two years of age, whose gentle manners, united to a most venerable and placid countenance, indicated that tranquilized state of mind that fitted him in an eminent degree for presiding over so benevolent an institution."[2] Vancouver named two points of the bay of San Pedro after him, Point Fermin and Point Lasuen.

When J. G. de La Pérouse, the French navigator, anchored at Monterey in 1786, he paid a visit to Mission San Carlos. Of the president he wrote that he "is one of the most worthy of esteem and respect of all the men I have ever met. His sweetness of temper, his benevolence, and his love for the Indians are beyond expression."[3]

In 1791, the Spanish voyager, Alejandro Malaspina, after visiting Monterey and Carmel, declared: "He was a man who in Christian lore, mien, and conduct was truly apostolic, and his good manners and learning were unusual. This religious had with good reason merited the esteem and friendship of both French commanders [of the La Pérouse expedition] and the majority of their subordinates."[4]

Charles Chapman said of Lasuén: "[He] worthily filled the post of the great Junípero. As a mission-founder he achieved as much; . . . he baptized a far greater number of Indians. He built up the missions economically and architecturally. He was far more successful than Serra in maintaning harmonious relations with the military. In zeal as a Christian and missionary he equalled, though he could not surpass, Father Junípero."[5]

Bancroft states that in Lasuén

were united the qualities that make up the model or ideal padre. . . . In person he was small and compact, in expression vivacious, in manners always agreeable, though dignified. He was a frank, kind-hearted old man, who made friends of all he met . . . [he had] sweetness of disposition and quiet force of character . . . no one of the Franciscans had more clearly defined opinions than he. None of them had a firmer will, or were readier on occasion to express their views. His management of the mission interests for eighteen years affords abundant evidence of his untiring zeal and of his ability as a man of business. His writings . . . prepossess the reader in favor of the author by their comparative conciseness of style. Of his fervent piety there are abundant proofs; and his piety and humility were of an agreeable type, unobtrusive, and blended with common-sense. . . . Padre Fermín — as he was everywhere known — to a remarkable degree for his time and environment based his hopes of future reward on purity of life, kindness and courtesy to all, and a zealous performance of duty as a man, a Christian, and a Franciscan.[6]

Serra called Lasuén a religious of exceptional example.

A substantial error crept into Lasuén's chronology in the matter of his age at the time of his death. Vancouver in 1792 considered the padre to be seventy-two years of age. Since he died a little over ten years after that and the death record omitted mentioning his age, historians came to the conclusion that he was about eighty-three when he died. The discovery of his birth certificate at Vitoria, Spain, in recent years, has settled the matter for all time. Lasuén at the time of his death was only sixty-seven. The fact that Lasuén in 1782 described himself as prematurely old no doubt led Vancouver ten years later to make his great misjudgment of the padre's age.

Lasuén died at Mission San Carlos, Carmel, June 26, 1803, having received the last sacraments. He was buried on the twenty-seventh by Baltasar Carnicer in the stone vault of the sanctuary closest to the main altar on the Gospel side. His remains, together with the others buried at the mission, were first discovered under heavy debris in 1856, were exhumed again in 1882, and finally in 1943. Very few of the remains survived up to this latter year. His grave has been marked with a stone slab bearing his name. A monument to Lasuén has been erected at Mission San Fernando, and Lasuén High School at San Pedro recalls his memory. His writings have been published by Father Finbar Kenneally, O.F.M., of the Academy of American Franciscan History.

[1] Lasuén to José de Jesús Vélez, O.F.M., Museo Nacional, Mexico City. Copy in SBMA.

[2] Wilbur, ed. *Vancouver in California 1792-1794*, pp. 63-64.

[3] Cited in Chapman, *A History of California*, p. 378.

[4] Ibid., pp. 380-381.

[5] Ibid., pp. 381-382.

[6] *History of California*, II, 8-9.

LÁZARO, NICOLÁS (?-1807)

Fray Nicolás Lázaro was a native of Burgos, Spain. No details of his life prior to his departure for America have been found. While at Cádiz awaiting embarkation, he switched from a group of Franciscans destined for service in San Carlos de Buenos Aires to the group going to San Fernando College, Mexico City. He sailed shortly after June 29, 1804.

He departed from the college on March 12, 1805, to serve in the California missions. Lázaro embarked at San Blas, June 2 and arrived at Monterey, August 31, 1805. From there he traveled overland south, baptizing at Mission San Antonio, September 13 and reaching Mission San Fernando, his destination, before October 5 when he administered his first baptism there. His last entry was made on June 12, 1807. In ill health, he went to San Diego to recuperate and baptized there between June 25 and August 18, the day of his death. He had received the last sacraments. He was buried by José Barona on the same day in the mission church beneath a statue of Saint Joseph. José Bernardo Sánchez entered the facts of death and burial in the register. On December 28, 1853, the Rev. John C. Holbein removed his remains with those of José Panto and Fernando Martín to the cemetery, since the church had been converted into a barracks for American soldiers.

LÓPEZ, BALDOMERO (1761-?)

Fray Baldomero López was a native of Puente in the diocese of Valladolid, born in 1761. He became a Franciscan at Domus Dei de Aguilar in 1779 in the province of Concepción. López sailed from Cádiz under the commissary, Juan de Ocón, in 1786, and then entered San Fernando College, Mexico City. He arrived in California in 1791.

With Fray Isidro Alonso Salazar he was placed in charge of Mission Santa Cruz, which had been founded by President Fermín Francisco de Lasuén, August 28, 1791. He served there until mid-summer of 1796, when he returned to Mexico. Meanwhile he baptized at Mission Soledad in September and October 1793 and at San Luis Obispo, September 3, 1796. He likewise officiated at Mission Santa Clara at various times between July 26, 1791, and July 22, 1796.

On February 27, 1793, the new mission church was abuilding, and the dedication took place, May 10, 1794. This was the third church of adobe, superseding the earlier ones of palisade and boards. By the end of 1796, 733 baptisms had been administered. Bancroft states that López was ill tempered, bickered with his companions, and received a reproof from his superior. This temper was due largely to ill health and hypochondria.

As early as August 21, 1793, López asked Lasuén to be transferred, for he did not care for temporal administration, and before February 3, 1794, he asked permission to return to Mexico. By August, Lasuén states that he had settled down but still desired to leave. While both López and Salazar declaimed loudly against temporalities, Lasuén admitted they did their work well. Still a year later, both expressed their dissatisfaction with Santa Cruz. Finally, in mid-1795 Lasuén notified both Governor Diego de Borica and Viceroy Branciforte that he had given López permission to retire because of his chronic hypochondria to which he was increasingly subject, making him unfit for the ministry.

After he returned to Mexico, it appears that López' health improved. In May 1800 he was elected vicar of San Fernando College. Early in 1802, he was selected to go to Spain as commissary to collect a number of friars to serve at San Fernando and in the missions. On July 13, 1810, he returned with fifteen recruits, meanwhile having sent still others to

Mexico from 1803 on. In the chapter of July 11, 1812, he was elected a counselor of the college and reelected on July 22, 1815.

In the chapter of August 18, 1818, he was elected guardian of the college which office he retained until July 28, 1821. He was reelected to the same office, May 23, 1824, remaining therein until May 5, 1827. After that he probably returned to Spain, for in 1827 all natives of Spain were exiled by the Mexican government.

LÓPEZ, JACINTO (1769-?)

Fray Jacinto López was born in 1796 at Toro in the diocese of Zamora, Spain. He became a Franciscan in the province of Purísima in Castile in 1783. Holding the offices of preacher and confessor, López sailed from Cádiz, June 11, 1793, for Mexico where he entered San Fernando College. At the time he was described in passport records as tall, with a swarthy complexion, chestnut-colored eyes, and dark hair.

He set out for California, arriving at Monterey, July 28, 1799. López served at Mission San Antonio from September 10, 1799, until July 27, 1800, where he complained about the discomforts of the place. He next ministered at Mission San Juan Bautista from August 13, 1800, until August 29, 1801. He was at San Luis Obispo on August 21, 1799. Twice in 1800 and again in the following year he baptized at Mission San Carlos, and at San Diego, November 28, 1801.

On October 22, 1800, Lasuén stated that López had already complained about his ailments, and on July 23, 1801, he gave him permission to return to Mexico, adding that he had served the missions in a praiseworthy manner with zeal and activity despite his infirmities. He embarked from Monterey, October 8, 1801, with Lorenzo Merelo, arriving at the college, March 21, 1802. Because of continuing poor health, he sought permission on June 21 to join the province of the Holy Gospel in Mexico City, which was subsequently granted.

LÓPEZ, JULIÁN (1761-1797)

Fray Julián López was born at Carbonero, diocese of Segovia, Spain, in 1761 and entered the Franciscan order there in 1782, thus becoming a member of the province of Concepción in Old Castile. In the company of twenty-two other friars, under the commissary, Manuel Arévalo, he left Spain for America on the *Santiago de España* which sailed on May 8, 1795, from Cádiz, and arrived at Vera Cruz, Mexico, June 26. At this period of his life, according to official records, López was described as tall, of light complexion, with a pockmarked face, and dark brown eyes and hair. He lacked the index finger of his right hand.

Through San Fernando College, he came to California, arriving at

San Francisco on the *Concepción,* April 14, 1797, and was assigned to Mission San Carlos. He was there but a short time when it became necessary for him to seek the services of a physician on May 9. Both the resident doctor and the ship surgeon diagnosed him as a very sick man, far advanced with tuberculosis. On the night of July 15-16, he died at the mission and was buried by Fray Francisco Pujol on the seventeenth in the sanctuary of the mission church on the Gospel side close to the wall. He had received the last sacraments. His remains, with those of Junípero Serra, Fermín Francisco de Lasuén, and Juan Crespí, were exhumed in 1856, 1882, and 1943.

MARINER, JUAN (1743-1800)

Fray Juan Mariner was born at Vilaplana, province of Catalonia, Spain, September 24, 1743. He made his profession at Reus, October 6, 1760, and came to Mexico in 1785 where he entered San Fernando College a short time before February 6. He arrived in California that same year at Monterey. He baptized at Mission Santa Clara, August 25 and 27, at Mission San Carlos, September 4, and at San Juan Capistrano, October 21. Mariner ministered at Mission San Diego from November 1785 until January 29, 1800. He visited San Juan Capistrano on August 30, 1789, and Santa Barbara on July 1, 1797.

On August 17, 1795, Mariner accompanied a military expedition from San Diego to San Juan Capistrano (which was reached August 26) through the interior country, exploring for a site for the future Mission San Luis Rey. This was done at the request of President Fermín Francisco de Lasuén, and Mariner kept a diary of the reconnaissance. At Mission San Diego during Mariner's term of service, Indian baptisms rose from 1,174 at the end of 1785 to 2,704 at the end of 1799 with 1,405 neophytes living at the mission at the end of the latter year.

Mariner died at Mission San Diego at 11:30 at night, January 29, 1800, and was buried in the mission church by Fray José Faura on the following day. On April 26, 1804, Mariano Payeras had the remains of Mariner, Luís Jayme, and Juan Figuer removed from the old to the new church, all being buried in the same vault. On November 12, 1813, the remains of these three again were moved to the sanctuary of the third and final church between the main and side altar, all in individual boxes but in a common vault.

MARQUÍNEZ, MARCELINO (1779-?)

Fray Marcelino Marquínez, a native of Treviño, Vizcaya, Spain, was born in May 1779 and became a Franciscan at the friary of Purísima Concepción, a Recollect house of the province of Cantabria, Vitoria,

November 22, 1798. He sailed from Cádiz shortly after April 26, 1804, and arrived at San Fernando College, Mexico City, the same year. Approximately six years later he arrived in San Francisco, California, on July 28, 1810.

Marquínez served at Mission San Luis Obispo from September 10, 1810, till October 27, 1811, and after that at Mission Santa Cruz until May 1817. He baptized at San Francisco, October 2, 1814, and at San Miguel, June 28, 1817.

Bancroft states that Marquínez "was possessed of much ability in the management of temporal affairs, and had some skill in medicine; that he was, moreover, a sensible man, and witty in his methods of expression as shown in his letters to Sola."[1] He was subject to attacks of colic which on one occasion in 1816 became serious enough to warrant his receiving the last sacraments.

Vicente Francisco de Sarría in 1817 praised him for the progress achieved at the mission during his seven-year administration, for his aid given to the sick, his practical use of medicine, and for furthering the mission's material advancement. Beyond these categories, however, his superior did not consider his merit above the average. On March 12, 1818, Sarría gave him permission to return to Mexico, declaring at the same time that Santa Cruz had "received much good from . . . [his] laborious zeal and industrious activity."

Marquínez, embarking with Fray Pedro Múñoz on March 12, 1818, on the *San Ruperto,* which touched at California on its way back from the Philippines, returned to Mexico. Having been in the service of San Fernando College for sixteen years, Marquínez asked for disaffiliation. His petition was granted, and he was accepted as a member of the province of the Holy Gospel, Mexico City.

[1] *History of California,* II, 387, n. 42.

MARTIARENA, JOSÉ MANUEL (1754-?)

Fray José Manuel Martiarena was born at Rentería, Guipuzcoa, Spain, in 1754 and became a Franciscan in the province of Cantabria. In Mexico he first entered Guadalupe College, Zacatecas, and in 1788 was transferred to San Fernando, Mexico City, entering June 2, 1790. He set out from the college about January 1794 and came to California on the *Concepción.* He served at Mission San Antonio from August 6, 1794, until June 6, 1795. It appears that President Fermín Francisco de Lasuén had some difficulty, as he did with a number of other missionaries, in finding a suitable place for Martiarena, for on August 19, 1794, he declared that San Antonio suited him quite well; still he thought that suitability would be a problem no matter where Martiarena were sent.

By mid-1795, owing to the discomforts of the climate, Martiarena had written twice to Lasuén, seeking a change. Moreover, he suffered from a profound depression and from severe headaches. Lasuén transferred him to Mission Soledad where he ministered from July 31, 1795, until March 31, 1797. When Lasuén founded Mission San Juan Bautista, June 24, 1797, he named Martiarena and Pedro Adriano Martínez as the ministers in charge. Martiarena baptized there until August 14, 1804, ministering meanwhile for a brief period at San Francisco from August 14 to December 26, 1800. At various times he also baptized at Missions Purisima, Santa Clara, San Gabriel, San Carlos, and Santa Cruz. After receiving repeated petitions to retire from the friar, President Estevan Tapis granted his wish, July 1, 1804, and commended him for his zealous labors. In 1805 he returned to San Fernando College. On July 11, 1812, he was appointed procurator of the California missions.

MARTÍN, FERNANDO (1770-1838)

Fray Fernando Martín was born at Robledillo, diocese of Ciudad Rodrigo, Old Castile, Spain, May 26, 1770, and became a Franciscan at the Convento de San Francisco, Ciudad Rodrigo, belonging to the province of San Miguel, April 29, 1787. After ordination to the priesthood, he remained for eleven years at Ciudad Rodrigo as a preacher in the surrounding area. In 1809 he volunteered for the American missions and sailed from Cádiz, March 29, 1810, on the *Neptuno,* arriving at San Fernando College, Mexico City, June 20, 1810.

In 1811 he was assigned to California, and after being delayed at Acapulco because of pestilence and insurgent activity, he reached Lower California in April. Martín traveled the length of the peninsula and reached San Diego, July 6, 1811. There his missionary service began, and there he remained for the rest of his life.

The new church was nearly complete when Martín arrived. It was blessed by Friar José Barona of San Juan Capistrano, November 12, 1813. The builder was Fray Pedro Panto, who died before its completion. In 1813 the great aqueduct at the mission was begun and finished by about 1816, and other building activity at the mission continued up to 1820. Martín baptized at the mission between July 6, 1812, and October 19, 1838. From the end of 1812 to the end of 1838, the number of baptisms rose from 4,018 to 6,906. The number of Indians at the mission in 1812 was 1,616. Martín became the senior missionary after May 16, 1820, upon the departure of José Bernardo Sánchez, who had been there since 1804.

On September 20, 1818, Martín was at Rancho Elcuaman (Santa Isabel), where preparations were being made for the establishment of a new mission. There, he celebrated Mass and baptized over one hundred Indians, after instructing them for the previous two weeks. That date is considered the official beginning of the *asistencia* of Santa Isabel. In 1822 this sub-mission had a chapel, granary, several houses, a cemetery, and an Indian population of four hundred souls. On April 20, 1822, Martín swore allegiance to the Iturbide government of Mexico. On November 19, the same year, Martín, in writing up an official account of the mission lands of San Diego, stated that he had visited Santa Isabel on a number of occasions as well as the pagans of the vicinity and that they numbered about two thousand souls.

Governor José María Echeandía called a junta of the southern padres to San Diego to assemble on April 28, 1826. Martín offered to swear allegiance to the constitution of 1824 in everything compatible with his religious conscience. He declined to solemnize the oath with religious services.

When Auguste Duhaut-Cilly visited San Diego in 1827, he met Martín and his companion missionary, Vicente Oliva. He considered San Diego the most dismal inhabited place he had encountered in California. "At a distance the place [the mission] is by no means ugly in appearance, but this diminishes the nearer one approaches, because the buildings, though well arranged, are poorly kept and in part are in ruins. A musty smell penetrates even the quarters of the fathers. Fr. Vicente [Oliva] and Fr. Fernando [Martín] are so accustomed to the disagreeable odors that they make nothing of them. Towards us, however, they showed themselves as kind as they were dirty."[1] Alfred Robinson visited the mission in 1829, and the same two missionaries welcomed him and gave him hospitality.

In 1834 the mission was secularized, the last reports being signed by Martín in 1832. On September 24, 1834, the mission was transferred by inventory from Martín to Juan José Rocha, commissioner.

The second Book of Deaths of Mission San Diego is missing, so we do not have the details of the death or burial of Martín who passed away on October 19, 1838. Bancroft states that "he was an exemplary friar," and Mariano Payeras in 1820 called him "a splendid religious." In 1817 Vicente Francisco de Sarría declared that Martín till then had rendered "full and praiseworthy service" and that his employment and merit were commendable. In 1820 Payeras wrote that "his merit is above the mediocre because of his zeal and application and his aptitude for the ministry he exercises is sufficient." He added that Martín was also fit to work among the faithful, and that he would make a good religious superior which office he would discharge with honor and edification.

When the Rev. J. C. Holbein on December 28, 1853, removed the remains of the three Franciscans from the sanctuary of the church to the mission cemetery because the mission was occupied by American soldiers, Engelhardt considered that the remains of Martín was among them. Holbein, however, was not certain of their identity.

[1] Engelhardt, *Mission San Diego*, p. 216.

MARTÍN, JUAN (1770-1824)

Fray Juan Martín was born at Villastor in the diocese of Teruel, Aragón, Spain, January 12, 1770, and became a Franciscan at Zaragosa, January 16, 1787. He studied theology at Teruel, and, having been ordained a deacon and while residing at the friary of Calatayud, he volunteered for service at San Fernando College, Mexico City. He sailed from Cádiz on the *San Nicolás*, June 11, 1793, for Vera Cruz. At the time of his departure from Spain, passport records described him as tall, light-complexioned, with blue eyes, dark hair, and a light beard. He arrived at the college, September 12, 1793. He was ordained a priest in Mexico City, saying his first Mass on January 1, 1794, but at the time had not yet finished studying his course in moral theology.

Martín set out from the college about January 1794 for California on the *Concepción*. President Fermín Francisco de Lasuén assigned him to Mission San Gabriel, where he served from March 1794 until August 7, 1796. Lasuén stated on October 27, 1794, that at that mission rather than elsewhere, Martín had better opportunities for continuing the study of moral theology with tutoring from Fray Miguel Sánchez. Martín's next assignment was to Mission Purisima between September 1796 and August 6, 1797. Thereafter, he had a long term of service at Mission San Miguel from December 3, 1797, until August 17, 1824. He learned the local language thoroughly. Martín was responsible for building the greater part of the mission compound, including the church which was begun in 1816. At the end of 1797 there had been 28 baptisms, at the end of 1824, 2,282. The number of Indians living at the mission at the end of 1824 was 904. Cattle and sheep numbered 4,092 and 11,024 respectively.

On April 15, 1814, Martín composed, at the request of the government, a document on the customs and habits of the local Indians. Some years earlier, in November 1804, he had accompanied a military expedition into the San Joaquin Valley and had found about four thousand Indians in the country which was traversed. His diary of the reconnaissance reported the fact that the Indians were eager to receive baptism, and he repeatedly and unsuccessfully proposed to Governor José Joaquín Arrillaga the founding of a mission in that vast area.

Twice Martín was chosen by commissary prefects to act as secretary on the occasion of their canonical visitations. In that capacity Martín was found at Mission San Antonio with Vicente Francisco de Sarría on June 15, 1818, and at Mission San Luis Obispo with Mariano Payeras on June 30, 1821. Missions other than his own at which he baptized, were: San Juan Capistrano, November 17, 1794; San Luis Obispo, several times between September 22, 1797, and June 11, 1811; San Antonio, a number of times between December 28, 1797, and January 23, 1808; and at Santa Barbara four times between October 5, 1794, and May 1804.

Martín was one of the several missionaries who became seriously ill in December 1800. The illness, until recent times, was considered to be the result of poisoning by Indians. Newly discovered statements by President Lasuén prove, however, that the illness was the result of drinking mescal from a copper container lined with tin.

In 1817, Sarría wrote of Martín: "His merits surpass the ordinary. With great care and amid labors and anxieties indispensably connected with a new foundation, he has advanced the mission in both the temporal and spiritual orders. He deserves to be credited, therefore, as a zealous and good laborer as well as for his knowledge of the language of said Mission San Miguel which he had administered for twenty years." Payeras in 1820 wrote of the same missionary: "His merit is great for his constant application in the ministry, though his aptitude is limited to that which he exercises and for taking charge of a religious community."

Martín died probably on August 29, 1824, at San Miguel and was buried on the thirtieth by Fray Francisco Xavier Uría. Uría in his death entry praised Martín for his indefatigable zeal in both temporal and spiritual matters. "This incessant toil was aggravated by a terrible dropsy of the breast. When it grew worse he received all the holy sacraments with great devotion."[1] His remains were interred in the sanctuary on the Gospel side of the main altar next to those of Marcelino Ciprés. Luís Martínez, Juan Sancho, and Uría assisted at the funeral.

[1] Burial Register, Mission San Miguel.

MARTÍNEZ, LUÍS ANTONIO (1771-1832)

Fray Luís Antonio Martínez was born at Briebes, diocese of Oviedo, in the principality of the Asturias, Spain, January 17, 1771, and became a Franciscan at the Convento de San Francisco, Madrid, in the province of Castile, November 10, 1785. Under the commissary, Manuel Arévalo, he embarked from Cádiz, May 8, 1795, on the *Santiago,* and entered San Fernando College, Mexico City. Passport records at the time of his departure described him as of regular stature, of light complexion, with blue eyes and dark hair, a large nose, thick lips, and a heavy beard.

Martínez arrived at Santa Barbara, May 8, 1798, and was soon sent to Mission San Luis Obispo, where he spent his entire missionary life — June 16, 1798, to February 2, 1830. The career of Martínez spans the second half of the mission's history before secularization.

The records of San Luis Obispo reveal that between the end of 1798 and the end of 1829, Indian baptisms rose from 1,486 to 2,627. Building continued at the mission down to 1820. On February 20, 1814, Martínez composed a document on the customs and habits of the local Indians at the request of the government. In May 1816, he accompanied a military expedition into the San Joaquin Valley in search of new mission sites and to secure the return of fugitive Christian Indians. He made reports on the expedition respectively to Vicente Francisco de Sarría, the commissary prefect, and to Pablo Solá, the governor.

During the Bouchard invasion of California in 1818, which coincided with Mexico's revolt against Spain, Martínez "gave evidence of remarkable courage and loyalty." Governor Solá had notified the military and the missionaries of the necessity for being on the alert. After Hipolyte Bouchard had attacked Monterey and the Rancho Ortega at Refugio, Martínez, having sent the governor twenty-five of his Indian volunteer fighters, accompanied thirty-five Indians of his mission to Santa Barbara and on as far as San Juan Capistrano to fight Bouchard if necessary and to defend the land. For these actions and for supplying medicine and supplies to the soldiers in time of need, the governor commended Martínez to the viceroy, who thanked the friar and promised to apprise the king of his services. For further aid in 1821, the governor cited Martínez to the viceroy and asked that his services to his country be written up in the *Gaceta* of Mexico City.

Martínez was on specially intimate terms with Captain José de la Guerra y Noriega of Santa Barbara, the treasurer of the California missionaries since the declaration of Mexican independence. In the De la Guerra collection there remain 119 letters addressed to the captain by the San Luis Obispo friar, wherein he commented on political affairs, and in nearly all there is evidence of his wit and sarcasm. Many of these letters were written on mere scraps of paper and were undated.

It appears that Martínez was acquainted with only some of the missions of the central area in California. He baptized once at Santa Ines, October 29, 1804, once at Purisima, July 26, 1817, three times at Santa Barbara between 1805 and 1812, and a number of times at San Miguel between 1800 and 1804.

Before 1828 Martínez had asked for his passport in order to return to Spain, but Sarría begged him to remain in California for the sake of the Indians. He complied, though he and the other Spanish missionaries were subject to expulsion under the Mexican law of 1827. Governor José María Echeandía could do little to enforce the law since the missionaries could not be replaced. However, when the Solís revolt erupted in Monterey in 1829, Martínez' position became delicate. He was accused of complicity because of his loyalty to Spain, because of hospitality given to Joaquín Solís and his men, and because of certain of his alleged remarks and actions.

On February 3, 1830, Echeandía ordered Martínez' arrest — an arrest made suddenly and obstreperously — and had Lieutenant Miguel Lobato remove him to Santa Barbara. He was first taken to the mission under the care of Fray Antonio Jimeno and then removed to the presidio where he was held incommunicado. Martínez wrote a long letter to the governor, defending his innocence and citing the violation of the Mexican constitution and the law of church immunity in his arrest and imprisonment.

A military trial was held at Santa Barbara, and despite the testimonial letters in his behalf by several other missionaries, all the judges, save one, condemned Martínez to exile. He was placed aboard the *Thomas Nowlan* under Stephen Anderson, who had to give a bond to deliver him to Peru and put him aboard the first vessel sailing from there to Spain. The ship left Santa Barbara on March 30. Martínez arrived safely in Peru and in Lima lived at the home of Antonio José Cot until he could obtain opportune passage to Europe. From Madrid he wrote to Cot, October 20, 1831: "I am in good health, less well in spirit because I cannot accommodate myself as I would like, to this climate, language and manner of life." Moreover, the Madrid he had found on his return was not the Madrid he had left as a young man. Cot relayed the news garnered from Martínez' letter to José de la Guerra y Noriega, from Lima, June 3, 1832.[1] It was in that same year that Martínez died in the Spanish capital.

Narciso Durán of Mission San Jose, May 10, 1830, wrote a long letter to President Anastasio Bustamante of Mexico, describing the deteriorating conditions in California and defending Martínez. Echeandía was soon removed from office and in a later investigation Martínez' good name was vindicated.

Before leaving California, Martínez was suffering from gout.

Concerning Martínez' character and personality much can be stated — more than for many another California missionary — because of his independence and frankness. These traits were bound to manifest themselves in words and writing. Engelhardt fully characterized him when he wrote: "[He] was noted as a confirmed wag, whose practical jokes caused much merriment among the frequently disheartened missionaries and the Spaniards generally. No one was surprised or offended at anything the jovial friar of San Luis Obispo was pleased to say or do, if we except the pompous young Californians; for the good Father in his merriest mood would never overstep the bounds of priestly dignity. Even Bancroft acknowledges that Fr. Martínez 'never scandalized his Order by irregular or immoral conduct'."[2]

Bancroft wrote of him: "Of all the padres, Martínez . . . was the most outspoken and independent in political matters, besides being well known for his smuggling propensities."[3] The latter activity, however, is seriously questioned by Engelhardt.

In 1817, his superior, Sarría, the commissary prefect, wrote of Martínez after he had been at San Luis Obispo for nineteen years: "He has in the opinion of all the most distinguished method for the administration of the mission and the control of the Indians. He had proved that the neophytes of said mission who formerly manifested signs of unrest and who even attempted to burn it down, that afterwards they behaved themselves in quietude and full subjection to the respective authorities and missionaries. To this is added a knowledge of the language of the Indians of the mission which contributes much to his success in controlling them."

Mariano Payeras, his superior in 1820, remarked: "His merit is surpassing on account of his application and for his good method of administration of the mission. His aptitude is mediocre for managing a [Franciscan] community and for holding an office [within the order]." Evidently Martínez was more of an extrovert than a mystic.

[1] The De la Guerra Collection, SBMA.

[2] Engelhardt, *Missions and Missionaries*, III, 280.

[3] *History of California*, III, 98.

MARTÍNEZ, PEDRO ADRIANO (ca. 1770-?)

Fray Pedro Adriano Martínez was born about 1770 in Spain and became a Franciscan in the province of Santiago, Galicia. He arrived at San Fernando College, Mexico City, in 1797. From San Blas he sailed on the *Concepción* and arrived at San Francisco, April 14, 1797. He then went to Mission San Carlos where he arrived on the twenty-eighth. Martínez spent a short period at Mission Santa Clara and was present at the founding of Mission San Jose, June 11, 1797. Thereupon President Fermín Francisco de Lasuén set out for Mission San Juan Bautista, which was founded on June 24, 1797. He appointed Martínez and José Martiarena as its first missionaries, the former arriving shortly after its inception. Martínez served there until November 8, 1800, baptizing meanwhile on a number of occasions at Mission Santa Clara.

He became terrified by the earthquakes at San Juan Bautista in 1800. Lasuén later declared that the missionary had not slept inside since their occurrence and had asked to be changed to another mission. The president sent him temporarily to Santa Clara. Martínez took a dislike, however, to California and its people and began to suffer from headaches and indigestion.

Lasuén next assigned him to San Miguel where he served from January 6, 1801, until June 8, 1804, baptizing on occasions at Missions San Luis Obispo and Purisima. As early as 1801, he asked to be retired because of illness and a lack of patience with the Indians, and his pleas for retirement continued. Finally President Estevan Tapis under date of July 1, 1804, granted the desired permission. Martínez was credited with working with apostolic zeal despite his viewpoints and illness.

At the college in the chapter of July 8, 1809, Martínez was elected vicar of the institution and shortly afterward, July 11, 1812, was appointed procurator of the California missions. On December 14 the same year, however, he requested and was granted disaffiliation from the college. He returned to Spain and arrived at San Juan de Zerdedo by January 2, 1816.

MARTÍNEZ DE ARENAZA, PASCUAL (ca. 1762-1799)

Fray Pascual Martínez de Arenaza was born in the Basque province of Alava, Spain, not later than 1762, and became a Franciscan in the province of Cantabria. He arrived at San Fernando College, Mexico City, in 1785. Recommended for missionary work among the Indians, he was characterized as having a good reputation but lacking in experience. He came to California probably in 1787 and served as supernumerary for a short time. He was then sent by President Fermín Francisco de Lasuén to Mission San Carlos where he served for the next ten years until 1797.

Lasuén had offered him the ministry of the newly established mission of San Jose in 1797, but Martínez declined. The last trace of his activity in California was found at Mission Soledad on October 3, 1797. The only other mission where records of his visits exist is Santa Clara. After he had asked for retirement a number of times because of physical ailments, Lasuén, on July 8, 1797, presented the request to Governor Diego de Borica, who granted it the same day.

Martínez returned to Mexico on the *Concepción* with Friars Antonio Horra, Diego García, and José María Fernández, and he died there of consumption sometime before May 14, 1799. In mission documents he is referred to generally as Arenaza rather than Martínez de Arenaza, his full name.

MERELO, LORENZO (1756-1801)

Fray Lorenzo Merelo was born in 1756 on the Caribbean island which the Spaniards originally called Hispaniola and which today comprises the countries of Santo Domingo and Haiti. In later life he refers to his homeland as Santo Domingo yet he states that the island had been ceded to France, which would indicate Haiti as his birthplace. Hence the exact area of his birth remains uncertain. Had he stated that part of the island was given to France, the matter would be entirely clear.

Merelo became a Franciscan in the province of the Holy Cross which comprised the Caribbean area. Later he joined the Colegio de Jesús Crucificado in Guatemala and on September 5, 1798, was incorporated into San Fernando College, Mexico City. He arrived at Monterey, July 28, 1799, and served at Mission San Francisco from mid-August 1799 until October 1800. Unable to stand the fog and winds of the area, he was transferred to Mission San Antonio where he ministered from June 21 to August 9, 1801. Even there his health did not improve. On one occasion it was feared that he would die.

On March 31, 1800, Merelo wrote to San Fernando College giving an account of his health, stating that he wished to return to his friary on the island of Santo Domingo. But the island had been given to France, and though he then preferred to go to Yucatan, was unable to do so, owing to war conditions. He expressed the wish to return to San Fernando College for permanent incorporation.

Lasuén admitted that Merelo was in poor health but recognized that he had a good disposition for work. He had treated everyone well, had been active and devoted to what he could do, and would have accomplished a great deal had he enjoyed better health. His health had improved over a two-month stay at Mission San Carlos early in 1801. But in spite of taking baths at the hot springs near San Miguel, he remained generally in a poor state. Given permission to return to Mexico, Merelo embarked at Monterey, October 8, 1801, and died at sea December 4, en route to San Fernando College.

MERINO, AGUSTÍN (1769-?)

Fray Agustín Merino was born at Briones, in the diocese of Calahorra, Spain, in 1769. He became a Franciscan at Vitoria in the province of Cantabria in 1788. Volunteering for the American missions, he joined a band of future missionaries gathered by the commissary, Manuel Arévalo, and sailed from Cádiz in 1795. On leaving Spain, he was described in records as of regular stature, with dark hair, brown eyes, a thick nose, and a scar above his upper lip on the left side.

In Mexico City he entered San Fernando College and from there set out for California, arriving on the *Concepción* at San Francisco,

April 14, 1797. President Fermín Francisco de Lasuén appointed Merino together with Isidro Barcenilla as the first two missionaries to be in charge of the newly founded Mission San Jose. Both missionaries became ill early in their period of service. Merino's malady threatened his reason. José Viader informed Lasuén that Merino was "completely deranged" and brought him to Mission San Carlos where he was in an "upset" condition. Lasuén informed Governor Diego de Borica that Merino had asked for permission to return to Mexico, that he was afflicted with "a great disorder of mind," and that it was impossible to effect a cure in California. On August 13, 1799, Lasuén gave Merino his formal permission to leave. In January 1800, he and three other missionaries boarded a vessel at Monterey and returned to San Fernando College.

MIGUEL, JOSÉ DE (1761-1813)

Fray José de Miguel, a native of Zarbitu, Navarre, Spain, was born in 1761, and became a Franciscan at Vitoria, in the province of Cantabria in 1780. He left his province as a deacon about September 1786. Passport records described him as a man possessing a well-formed body, a large, thick nose, and blue eyes which were somewhat recessed. He sailed under the commissary, Juan de Ocón, and upon arrival in Mexico, entered San Fernando College. He eventually came to California, arriving at Monterey, August 2, 1790.

President Fermín Francisco de Lasuén assigned De Miguel to Mission Santa Barbara. Traveling overland, he baptized at San Luis Obispo, August 19, and at Purisima, August 25. At Santa Barbara he baptized for the first time on September 13, 1790, and continued to do so until September 13, 1798, meanwhile ministering at Mission Purisima from time to time.

De Miguel was in charge of Mission Santa Barbara when Captain George Vancouver visited the settlement in 1793. He entertained the captain at the mission and was invited to dine aboard ship. Vancouver praised the friar for his hospitality and generosity. It was De Miguel who was entrusted by Lasuén in 1797 with the responsibility of taking the insane friar, Antonio Horra de la Concepción, from San Miguel to Monterey, in which he was successful.

De Miguel petitioned for retirement as early as October 1794 and repeated his requests for the next four years. Lasuén finally granted the petition on October 26, 1798, and notified Governor Diego de Borica to that effect. Upon his return to San Fernando College, he asked to be disaffiliated and for permission to join the province of Michoacán; and this request was granted. However, when his health was restored, he rejoined the college, realizing that he had made a mistake in leaving.

Again he volunteered for California, arriving there in August 1800. He was assigned to Mission San Luis Obispo where he ministered from September 18, 1800, until September 26, 1803. He was then transferred to Mission San Gabriel where he labored from November 8, 1803, until January 27, 1813. He was present at the dedication of the stone church of Mission San Juan Capistrano, September 7, 1806. He baptized at Mission San Fernando, June 13, 1807. In 1813, because of illness, he returned there and died on June 1. Fray Ramón Olbés buried him on June 2 in the mission church, the friar having received the last sacraments. Baldomero López, writing to José Señán on July 1, 1813, reported that "he died as a true son of our Seraphic Patriarch."

MORENO, JOSEPH MATÍAS (1744-1781)

Fray Joseph Matías Moreno, according to Juan Domingo Arricivita, author of the *Crónica Apostólica,* was born at Almorza in the jurisdiction of Soria, diocese of Osma, Spain, in 1744, and was baptized on May 24. He was the son of Matías Moreno and María Catalina Gil. Moreno became a Franciscan at the Convento de San Francisco, Logroño, in the province of Burgos, June 22, 1762. After ordination, he held the title of preacher. He was a man of talent and was endowed with a lively spirit. Had he remained in Spain, he would probably have been destined to hold a chair of philosophy or theology.

Enlisting under the commissary, Arricivita, for the college of Santa Cruz de Querétaro, Moreno traveled from Madrid to the port of Santa María near Cádiz. There, between March and November 1769, he awaited embarkation for America.

From Querétaro, Moreno was sent to the missions of Sonora as a supernumerary. When the Colorado River missions were to be founded among the Yumas, Moreno was designated as a companion to Fray Juan Díaz at Misión San Pedro y San Pablo de Bicuñer, established north of present-day Fort Yuma in 1780. In July 1781, the Yumas rose in revolt against the Spaniards, and both missionaries at Bicuñer were killed, July 17. Moreno's remains were found five months later and when discovered gave evidence that he had been decapitated. With those of his murdered confreres his remains were first taken to Misión San Pedro y San Pablo at Tubutama, Sonora, and finally interred at the college of Santa Cruz de Querétaro in 1794.

MORENO, JUAN (1799-1845)

Fray Juan Moreno was born on January 27, 1799, at Montenegro, Old Castile, Spain, and became a Franciscan in Mexico, where he first joined the province of the Holy Gospel, Mexico City, but as a theologian, on November 8, 1825, petitioned for admission to San Fernando College in the same city. He was admitted there on October 24, 1826, and came to California with Antonio Jimeno in the following year. Moreno and the two Jimeno brothers were the last recruits the California missions received from the college.

Moreno first baptized at Mission San Carlos in December 1827. He was stationed at Mission Santa Barbara between January 26, 1828, and February 2, 1829. He baptized at Mission Santa Ines on February 11; was at Mission Santa Cruz from August 8, 1829, until October 30, 1830; then at Mission San Juan Bautista from November 22, 1830, until May 14, 1833; then at Mission San Miguel from October 2, 1835, until October 24, 1840. While there he officiated a few times at Missions Santa Ines and Purisima. Moreno was next stationed at Mission Santa Ines as a missionary from April 10, 1842, on and, beginning with May 4, 1844, was a professor in the diocesan seminary at the mission, where he was in charge of primary education. He died at Santa Ines, December 27, 1845, and was buried at the mission by Fray Francisco Sánchez. For some unexplained reason his death record is incomplete.

Asisara, an Indian at Mission Santa Cruz, stated that Moreno was very skillful in throwing a riata and proud of his success in lassoing bears. "Except that he was a quiet, patient man, well liked by all, we know very little about him,"[1] states Bancroft laconically.

Angustias de la Guerra y Ord said that Moreno was of an ordinary build but quite thin and had a fine face. He was completely innocent in character. "I never saw him ill at ease."[2]

[1] *History of California*, IV, 645, n. 25.
[2] Price and Ellison, tr. *Occurrences in Hispanic California*, p. 35.

MORENO, RAFAEL DE JESÚS (1795-1839)

Fray Rafael de Jesús Moreno was born in 1795 in Mexico and became a Franciscan at the college of Guadalupe, Zacatecas, May 16, 1817. He made his profession on May 17, the following year. Subsequently, he was ordained to the priesthood, December 23, 1820, by Bishop Juan Francisco Castiñeza at Durango. He received faculties to preach and to hear confessions, April 28, 1821. His college's estimate of him is contained in the statement that he was a man of very fervent religious spirit, zealous in the ministry, and an obedient subject. Moreno was named novice master, July 30, 1828, which office he held for three years. He was one of the friars designated on August 24, 1831, to take over the northern Fernandino missions in California.

On July 17, 1832, the newly appointed governor of California, José Figueroa, sailed on the *Catalina* from Acapulco to San Blas to take aboard the Zacatecan missionaries going to California. Among them was Fray Francisco García Diego y Moreno, the commissary prefect, and Fray Rafael Moreno, the president. They arrived at the end of July at Cape San Lucas, where, because of a mutiny among the sailors, Figueroa and the friars were stranded. The friars decided to proceed to Upper California overland, but upon reaching San José del Cabo they returned south, and later were able to board ship at La Paz, arriving at Monterey, January 15, 1833.

Moreno was both president and vice-commissary prefect and resided with García Diego y Moreno at Mission Santa Clara. When he changed his residence to Mission San Rafael, he became involved politically and ecclesiastically with General Mariano Vallejo on November 20, 1833, when the latter held him responsible for an unprovoked attack on a band of friendly Indians, twenty-one of whom were killed and twenty wounded. The general demanded that García Diego investigate the matter and punish Moreno. The commissary prefect suspended him and summoned him from San Rafael to Santa Clara with the announced intention of sending him back to the college for trial. García Diego y Moreno soon learned that he had acted too hastily. The two friars, Bernardino Pérez and Lorenzo Quijas, who had been sent to San Rafael to investigate the charges, found Moreno innocent; he was restored to his office and duties.

He held the office of vice-commissary prefect until 1838, visiting the missions in 1837 and administering confirmation at Santa Clara, San Jose, San Antonio, and San Francisco at various times. Faxon Dean Atherton, who met Moreno at Mission Santa Clara on May 8, 1836, wrote in his diary: "The Padre of this Mision, Padre Moreno, is a devilish shrewd kind of character, and understands buying and selling as well as most anyone I have fallen in with."[1]

He called on Moreno again in July 1837 and stated on July 21:

The Padre is a great advocate in favour of Indian civilization, stating that from his own experience of them he was certain they possessed abilities equal to the whites and would make as respectable appearance in the world if they could be made to forget the vicious habits of their fathers.... Although the good Padre advocates the Indians cause, he acknowledges that he believes it utterly impossible that their condition should be bettered, that they must and will die off and disappear before the more morally educated white man. ... The Padre says he is greatly pleased that they have taken the Mision from him as it leaves him more leisure to attend to his spiritual concerns.[2]

Toward the end of his life he resided at Mission San Jose to regain his health. He suffered from dysentery for three months before his death and died there between midnight and three o'clock in the morning on the night of June 8, 1839. He was buried in the mission church on the ninth by Fray José María González Rubio. His death record is found in the registers of San Jose and Santa Clara.

González Rubio, who entered the facts into the Mission San Jose register, wrote of Moreno that he "was a man of religious virtues and gifted with zeal for the house of God for which he suffered much because of an unfounded accusation which really weakened and changed much of his character which was one of the strongest. As a result of this sad experience he died."[3] Manuel Jimeno, administrator of customs at Monterey, stated that Moreno's illness was brought on by a fit of anger and that his death was caused by a mercurial potion prescribed for him by an English doctor.

[1] Doyce B. Nunis, Jr., ed. *The California Diary* (San Francisco, 1964), p. 8.
[2] Ibid., p. 58.
[3] Burial Register, Mission San Jose.

MUGÁRTEGUI, PABLO JOSEPH (1736-?)

Fray Pablo Joseph Mugártegui, the son of Pedro Joseph Mugártegui and María Antonia de Ormoza, was born at Marquina, diocese of Calahorra, Spain, and was baptized October 31, 1736, by the Rev. Miguel Adorriaga in the parish church of Santa María de Xemeín. Mugártegui's paternal grandparents were Pedro Fernández de Mugártegui and María de Oca; his maternal grandparents, Agustín de Ormoza and María Josefa de Torrezar. Mugártegui became a Franciscan at the Convento de San Francisco, Bilbao, April 26, 1757, and having been ordained a priest, was appointed preacher and confessor in 1765. In 1768 he became a professor of philosophy.

As a member of the province of Cantabria, he left the friary of Bilbao and traveled to Cádiz, bound for the American missions in 1769. At the time, he was described in passport records as having a good physique, a large face, which was pockmarked, and dark brown hair. He traveled to Mexico with thirty-nine other Franciscans and arrived at San Fernando College in 1770 under the commissary, Fray Rafael Verger.

When President Junípero Serra left Mexico City in August 1773, his negotiations with Viceroy Antonio María Bucareli y Ursúa in favor of the California missions finished, Mugártegui was given to him as a companion. He accompanied Serra in a coach as far as Guadalajara, where they took ship together at San Blas, sailing on the *Nueva Galicia* or *Santiago,* January 24, 1774, arriving at San Diego, March 13. Because Mugártegui was ill, he remained at the southern port until September, when he was sent north, baptizing at Mission San Gabriel, September 27, and at Mission San Luis Obispo, November 11. He was stationed at Mission San Antonio from January 8 till August 7, 1775, and at Mission San Luis Obispo, August 20, 1775, till November 12, 1776.

From there Mugártegui proceeded to San Juan Capistrano, to which Serra appointed him as cofounder together with Gregorio Amurrió. Mugártegui baptized there for the first time, December 25, 1776, and remained there until his retirement to Mexico in 1789.

When Fermín Francisco de Lasuén was named president of the missions, February 6, 1785, Mugártegui was named vice-president of the southern missions from Santa Barbara to San Diego, a jurisdictional innovation. At the same time he was named president in the case of Lasuén's death or incapacity.

In the chapter held in Mexico City, May 23, 1789, Mugártegui was elected guardian, which position he held until the chapter of May 26, 1792, when he was made professor of philosophy and theology at San Fernando College. He was made visitor-general of his own college on May 23, 1795. On February 19, 1798, he asked for disaffiliation from the college and for permission to return to his province of Cantabria. However, he joined the province of the Holy Gospel and became its *custos*. On July 17, 1802, he asked to be restored to San Fernando College. The request was granted, but he had to renounce his accumulated rights as a former prelate with regard to voting and other privileges.

MÚÑOZ, PEDRO (1773-1818)

Fray Pedro Múñoz was born on June 19, 1773, at Puerto de Baños, diocese of Placencia, Estremadura, Spain, and entered the Franciscan order, January 10, 1793, at the Convento de Santa María de Gracia, a Recollect house of the province of San Miguel. He had difficulty overcoming the reluctance of his superiors in allowing him to become a missionary since it was the policy of the province not to provide missionaries for the Indians. He finally left Cádiz for Mexico shortly after June 20, 1803, on the *San Miguel* alias *Sagrada Familia*. He arrived at Vera Cruz in August and on September 9 entered San Fernando College. When he left Spain, passport records described him as a person of regular stature, with hazel hair, gray eyes, and a regular nose.

In December 1803 Múñoz volunteered for the California missions. He arrived at San Francisco, August 14, 1804. There he was assigned to Mission San Miguel where he administered his first baptism, October 13, 1804, and where he continued to officiate until May 22, 1807. After that he was transferred to Mission San Fernando where he baptized between July 12, 1807, and October 7, 1817. During his first two years there he administered the mission alone. He also baptized at Mission San Juan Bautista, May 19, 1805, at Mission San Luis Obispo, February 9, 1806, and at Mission San Antonio, April 4, 1806.

Múñoz took part in two military expeditions in California. The first occurred in 1806 when he and Ensign Gabriel Moraga set out from San Juan Bautista, September 21 to search for localities suitable for missions. He kept a diary of the reconnaissance which is dated at San Miguel, November 6, 1806. The explorers crossed the San Joaquin River and subsequently forded a stream called Nuestra Señora de la Merced. Múñoz pronounced the area suitable for a mission. Thereafter the party crossed the Dolores, Guadalupe, and San Francisco rivers and reached El Rio de la Pasión; the San Joaquin area was widely explored. Moraga led the party to the Río de los Santos Reyes, or Kings River. The region of present-day Visalia was declared acceptable as a mission site. Probably the areas along the banks of the Tulare and Kern rivers were reached, and Mission San Fernando through the Tejon Pass, November 2. En route, Múñoz had baptized 149 very aged or dying Indians. The second expedition, of which Vicente Francisco de Sarría speaks in 1817, is not recorded with regard to time and place, though it was undertaken from Mission San Miguel and was the longer journey of the two.

While at Mission San Fernando, a boy of the *gente de razón* whom the friars of the mission were teaching to read and write, three times placed something in Múñoz' food that each time brought him close to death's door. This information Múñoz himself communicated to Fray Estevan Tapis, who revealed the fact to Fray Pedro Martínez from Santa Cruz, on November 28, 1812.

The commissary prefect, Sarría, wrote of Múñoz: "His merit has not been small in the activity with which in his first zeal and spirit, he labors more than could be expected from the serious attacks of illness he suffered and the little robustness of health he enjoys." Because of this condition, Sarría, on February 18, 1818, granted him permission to retire to Mexico, commending him for "apostolic zeal and unflagging industry." Múñoz returned with Marcelino Marquínez on the *San Ruperto,* embarking at Monterey, March 12, 1818. However, Múñoz died at Tepic about May 18 while en route to the college.

MURGUÍA, JOSÉ (1715-1784)

Fray José Murguía was born on December 10, 1715, at Domayguia, Alava, Spain. He came to Mexico as a layman and became a Franciscan at San Fernando College, June 28, 1736, and was ordained a priest in 1744, and subsequently held the office of preacher. In 1748 he was sent to the Sierra Gorda missions northeast of Querétaro, where he labored for nineteen years "with great example." As minister of Misión San Miguel de Concá under the presidency of Junípero Serra, he built the present stone church which was finished on September 17, 1754.

In 1767 he was named as one of the missionaries who were to accompany Serra to Lower California to take over the ex-Jesuit missions there. He traveled directly from the Sierra Gorda to Tepic to await with Serra and his companions available passage from San Blas. They sailed on the *Concepción,* March 14, 1768, and arrived at Loreto, April 1. On the third, Serra assigned him as missionary at Santiago de las Coras for which he started out on the sixth. He baptized there from May 4, 1768, until May 17, 1769, when Serra appointed him as chaplain for the *San José* bound for Upper California.

However, in May 1769, a pestilence broke out at San José del Cabo. Murguía hastened to the afflicted mission, where he eventually fell ill. He went on to Misión Todos Santos half dead to replace Ramos de Lora whom Francisco Palóu had sent with an important message to Visitor-General José de Gálvez in Sonora. Upon the latter's return, Palóu recalled Murguía to Loreto in May 1770. He then served at Misión San Xavier until 1772. Meanwhile the *San José* had sailed and was lost at sea.

In August 1772, Murguía received orders to proceed to San Fernando de Velicatá. From there, on August 3, 1773, he set out with Palóu and several other friars for San Diego under escort of Sergeant José Francisco Ortega, arriving August 30. Continuing the journey northward, Murguía came to San Luis Obispo where Palóu placed him as supernumerary and where he baptized from November 13, 1773, to February 7, 1774. Serra, returning from Mexico City, found him at Mission San Antonio and took him along to Mission San Carlos. They arrived at Carmel on May 6 where Murguía remained until he was appointed cofounder with Tomás de la Peña of Mission Santa Clara, January 12, 1777. At Monterey Murguía attended the departure ceremonies of the Pérez expedition to the northwest in 1774 and witnessed the arrival of the Anza expedition in 1776 on its way to establish San Francisco.

Murguía was not actually present when Mission Santa Clara was founded but came a little later with cattle and supplies from Monterey. Except for a visit to San Carlos in 1782 and others to San Francisco, October 3, 1781, and April 26, 1782, he remained at Santa Clara until his death. Murguía started a new church at the mission, and the cornerstone was blessed by Serra on November 19, 1781. In the spring of 1784, Serra set out from Monterey for the northern missions. Having confirmed at Santa Clara, he continued on to San Francisco and while there received the news that Murguía had died at 9:15 in the morning of May 11 and that he was buried the next day in the church he had just finished constructing. The church was dedicated on the fifteenth by Serra, who considered it the "prettiest" of the nine existing mission churches. At the time of Murguía's death, 647 Indians had been baptized at Santa Clara since 1777.

Palóu called Murguía "a perfect religious and a magnificent laborer in the vineyard of the Lord."[1] Serra wrote, "I have grieved over and will continue to lament for a long time over the loss of a missionary who was so good that perhaps no one else can replace him."[2]

[1] Geiger, tr. *Palóu's Life of . . . Serra*, p. 240.
[2] Serra to the missionaries, San Francisco, May 11, 1784. Biblioteca Nacional, Mexico. Copy in SBMA.

MURO, MIGUEL (1790-1848)

Fray Miguel Muro was a native of Mexico. He became a Franciscan in the province of Zacatecas in 1807. As a cleric, prior to ordination, he joined the college of Guadalupe at Zacatecas and received all the orders from tonsure to the diaconate included, May 29, 30, and 31, 1814, and the priesthood, March 25, 1816, from the hands of the Most Rev. Dr. Juan Cruz Ruiz de Cabañas, bishop of Guadalajara. On September 16, the same year, he received the faculties to preach and hear confessions. Muro was appointed novice master on July 22, 1822, which position he held until July 9, 1825, and again from August 9, 1834, to June 17, 1837. He also gave some missions as a home missionary, one such at Monclova in Coahuila in 1817. In that same year Muro was sent to Texas and was placed in charge of Misión Espíritu Santo. In the summer of 1819 he was transferred to Mission San Jose, now in the city of San Antonio. In the fall of 1820, Muro began to exercise the ministry at Misión Refugio, where he remained until that mission was secularized in February 1830. For a period of three years he acted as chaplain of the presidio of La Bahía (the later Goliad) as well as pastor of the townspeople. At the end of this time he was recalled to the college at Zacatecas where he held the offices of novice master and community counselor.

Muro was one of a group of friars who came to California with Bishop Francisco García Diego y Moreno on the *Rosalind,* arriving at San Diego, December 10, 1841. He was assigned to Mission San Jose from 1842 until May 1845 and to Mission San Francisco, June 14 to October 1845. William H. Davis, the merchant, who met him at Mission San Jose, recalls in his *Sixty Years in California* that Muro was a friar of exemplary life and adds that he was intimately acquainted with him. "Fr. Muro while I was visiting him along in 1843-1844 . . . mentioned to me his knowledge of the existence of gold in the Sacramento Valley as a great secret, requesting me to promise not to divulge it. I have never mentioned it to this day to anyone."[1] Muro's statement was corroborated by Fray Jesús María Vasquez del Mercado of Santa Clara. Presumably the padres obtained their knowledge from the Indians.

Muro returned to Mexico before the American occupation of California. He died at the college of Zacatecas, June 20, 1848, as a result of an internal fistula from which he had patiently suffered intense pain for six years. Gangrene developed, and eventually his mind became affected. Before death he received only extreme unction. His college record characterized him as a man of "irreprehensible life."

[1] Page 233.

NOBOA, DIEGO (1742-?)

Fray Diego Noboa was born in 1742 at Santiago de Compostela, Galicia, Spain, and became a Franciscan on February 27, 1760, at Coria. He left the friary at Salamanca in 1769 for Cádiz, bound for the American missions. According to passport records, he possessed a good physique, a longish face, and dark brown hair. He entered San Fernando College, Mexico City, in 1770, with the title of preacher.

Noboa came to California with Juan García Riobó, arriving at San Francisco on the *Favorita,* June 2, 1783. At first he was stationed at Mission San Carlos, but upon the death of José Murguía at Santa Clara in May 1784, President Junípero Serra sent him there as a replacement. Noboa served under Tomás de la Peña for ten years, until his retirement to Mexico on August 11, 1794, during the presidency of Fermín Francisco de Lasuén. He had also baptized at San Francisco a number of times.

Noboa had become very despondent and depressed, according to Lasuén. He sailed from Monterey on the *Concepción* in company with De la Peña and Bartolomé Gilí. He received credit from Tomás de Pangua, guardian, in 1793, with having served in the missions with exemplary zeal and edifying conduct. Miguel Lull, a later guardian, notified Lasuén on June 6, 1798, that Noboa had died.

NORIEGA, MATÍAS DE SANTA CATALINA (1736-?)

Fray Matías de Santa Catalina Noriega was born in 1736 at Andinas in the area of Oviedo, Spain, and became a Franciscan at San Fernando College, Mexico City, November 8, 1767, and was ordained a priest sometime after September 9, 1772.

In 1778 he was assigned by the college as a chaplain for a sea voyage to the Pacific Northwest. Noriega arrived at San Blas by January 20, 1779. Together with Juan García Riobó he embarked on *La Princesa* or *Nuestra Señora del Rosario,* which sailed from San Blas, February 12, 1779, and anchored at San Francisco, September 15, having sailed on a reconnaissance voyage as far north as Alaska within sight of Mount St. Elias, which was sighted on August 2. The cross was planted, Mass was sung, and a sermon preached.

Noriega remained in California as a missionary, taking Pedro Benito

Cambón's place at Mission San Francisco. He baptized there from April 11, 1780, until July 14, 1781. Then he was transferred to Mission San Carlos as assistant to President Junípero Serra at whose death he was present on August 28, 1784. Noriega visited Mission Santa Clara during August 1781 and Mission San Antonio, September 28, 1781. He was at San Carlos until October 1787 and returned to Mexico in 1789.

In the chapter of May 26, 1792, Noriega was elected a counselor of the college, which office he retained until May 23, 1795. On June 6, 1798, Fray Miguel Lull, guardian of the college, informed President Fermín Francisco de Lasuén that Noriega had died.

NUEZ, JOAQUÍN PASCUAL (1785-1821)

Fray Joaquín Pascual Nuez was born at Luco, in the district of Daroca, archdiocese of Zaragosa, Spain, February 20, 1785, and became a Franciscan at the Convento de San Francisco, Calatayud, September 24, 1800. He sailed from Cádiz, March 29, 1810, and arrived at San Fernando College, Mexico City, June 20, the same year.

On July 1, 1811, Nuez received notification that he was accepted for the California missions. He set out with five other friars. At Acapulco he and his companions were delayed by pestilence. They finally sailed for Lower California, arriving at Loreto, April 23, 1812, and after more delay made their way overland to San Diego, which they reached on July 6. Nuez first served at Mission San Fernando from August 8, 1812, to June 17, 1814, then at Mission San Gabriel from August 24, 1814, to December 30, 1821. He visited Mission San Juan Capistrano where he baptized on December 9, 1814. Nuez also acted as secretary for the commissary prefect of the missions, Vicente Francisco de Sarría, on his canonical visitations, accompanying him to San Diego, August 16, and San Juan Capistrano, October 16, 1816, and to San Fernando, August 11, 1818.

While at San Gabriel, Nuez accompanied a military expedition sent out on November 22, 1819, to punish Mojave Indians from the Colorado who had killed several San Gabriel neophytes. Nuez kept a diary of the expedition, which returned on December 14.

Sarría wrote of him in 1817: "He distinguished himself by his constant industry and his corresponding merit is marked for attention chiefly to the spiritual affairs which a mission of 1,650 neophytes demands besides a numerous population in the pueblo [of Los Angeles] and other inhabitants three leagues distant from the mission and various ranchos situated in different directions." In 1820, Mariano Payeras, commissary prefect, stated that Nuez' merit was above average as was his aptitude and that in time he would be worthy of receiving an assignment of any trust.

Bancroft wrote of him: "He was a good man, loved by all; and though young he was regarded by his prelate as a missionary of more than ordinary ability and promise. . . . In his last years his piety verged upon asceticism, and he expressed a strong desire to pass the rest of his days as a recluse."[1] After an illness of twenty-four days and having received the last sacraments, he died at Mission San Gabriel, December 30, 1821, and was buried on the following day in the church by Fray Vicente Pascual Oliva. Eulalia Pérez in her "Recuerdos" described him as "tall, thin, light-skinned, with black hair and [he] was very good to all."[2]

[1] *History of California*, II, 567, n. 25.
[2] Bancroft Library MS.

OLBÉS, RAMÓN (1786-?)

Fray Ramón Olbés was born at Ateca, in the district of Calatayud, archdiocese of Zaragosa, Aragón, Spain, February 8, 1786, and became a Franciscan at Zaragosa, January 1, 1802. As a deacon he sailed from Cádiz on the *Neptuno*, March 29, 1810, and arrived at San Fernando College, Mexico City, June 20, the same year. Already on July 13, he was assigned to the California missions but was impeded from arriving there before 1812, owing to revolution in Mexico and pestilence at Acapulco. From the latter port he obtained passage to La Paz, Lower California, where he arrived on April 23, 1811, and there he was detained by fever. From Loreto he sailed to the port of San Luís and traveled overland to San Diego where he arrived July 6, 1812.

Olbés served at Mission Santa Ines from November 20, 1812, to March 1813, and at Mission Santa Barbara from September 8, 1813, to April 26, 1816. While at the latter mission, he composed the document on the customs and habits of the local Indians, requested by the government, December 31, 1813. Olbés was stationed at Mission San Luis Rey from May 1816 to June 1818 and at Mission Santa Cruz from 1818 till November 1821. He baptized at Mission San Gabriel in April and on August 6, 1813.

Bancroft states that his usefulness was impaired seriously by his fitful and eccentric moods, amounting at times almost to insanity, a condition which perhaps resulted from poor health. He often scolded the inhabitants of nearby Branciforte, as well as the provincial authorities. Olbés was at Santa Cruz when Hipolyte Bouchard threatened to attack the place in 1818, but the pirate did not appear.

Vicente Francisco de Sarría stated in 1817 that Olbés served the missions in a regular manner and promised even greater things because of his zeal. In 1820 Mariano Payeras declared that his merit was laudable and his aptitude very sufficient for a complete and effective missionary either among the faithful or the pagans. At the time, however, Olbés was ill, and for that reason he sought permission to return to Mexico. He sailed from San Diego, November 15, 1821. Having arrived at the college, on April 11, 1822, Olbés asked for disaffiliation from San Fernando and for permission to return to his native province.

OLIVA, VICENTE PASCUAL (1780-1848)

Fray Vicente Pascual Oliva was born at Martín del Río, Aragón, Spain, July 3, 1780, and became a Franciscan at the Convento de Nuestra Señora de Jesús, Zaragosa, February 1, 1799. He sailed from Cádiz, March 29, 1810, on the *Neptuno* and arrived at San Fernando College, Mexico City, July 20, 1810, departing for California in 1811. However, revolution in Mexico caused delays, and a pestilence at Acapulco prevented Oliva from continuing the journey with his fellow companions when he was laid low by the fever. Finally, he obtained passage on the *Tagle* or *Santa Catalina* and arrived at Monterey, August 4, 1813.

Oliva served at Mission San Carlos as supernumerary between October 28, 1813, to late in the year 1814. Next he is found at Mission San Fernando from September 9, 1814, until July 26, 1815, followed by a term of service at Mission San Francisco between November 26, 1815, and September 18, 1818. He then served at Mission San Miguel from February 26, 1819, till February 25, 1820. Oliva's longest years of service were at Mission San Diego between 1820 and 1846 with two intervening years (1832-1834) at Mission San Luis Rey and the two final years of his life at Mission San Juan Capistrano. His name appears likewise in the registers of Mission San Antonio, December 30, 1813, San Miguel, November 8, 1815, San Francisco, November 26, 1815, San Juan Bautista, June 24, 1816, Santa Cruz, July 13, November 15, 1818, Santa Ines, April and May 1819, Mission Purisima, April 13-14, and May 2-7, 1820, and at Mission San Gabriel at various times in 1831-1832 and between December 31, 1832, and March 8, 1833.

Concerning Oliva's labors at San Francisco, Vicente Francisco de Sarría wrote in 1817: "In this great vineyard which the Lord has prepared for Himself at that mission and at the adjacent pueblo, he labors with zealous intrepidity for its success becoming in my opinion the hands and feet, as it were, of his good companion [Ramón Abella] in as much as he goes and labors where the other, owing to other occupations and greater age, is unable to go."

In 1820 Mariano Payeras wrote of Oliva: "His merit is ordinary and his aptitude is sufficient for its exercise and with good application he could also be a good preacher among the faithful." On May 20, of the same year, however, Payeras wrote a significant paragraph to the guardian of San Fernando College. In ordinary matters Oliva was very fine, but unfortunately he became inebriated at times. Oliva made spiritual retreats, made promises of amendment, and even shed tears of repentance. As a last recourse Payeras sent him to San Diego under the direction of Fray Fernando Martín, "a splendid religious" who, he hoped, would get Oliva out of his moral difficulty. "If he succeeds in this, we will have one missionary more; but I have never seen any drinker show lasting amendment; if he does not succeed, then he is close by the port whence he can embark [for Mexico]."[1] Evidently Martín was able to reform Oliva, for the latter remained in California until 1848. Perhaps it was to this weakness that Bancroft referred when he wrote: "Oliva's moral character was not in all respects above suspicion, though there is no definite evidence against him."[2]

Oliva did not take the oath in favor of the Mexican constitution in 1826 for reasons of conscience with the result that Governor José María Echeandía proposed him as a candidate for expulsion from the territory.

At San Diego Oliva met Auguste Duhaut-Cilly in 1827 and Alfred Robinson in 1829 and 1831, Bishop Francisco García Diego y Moreno in 1841, and Eugène Duflot de Mofras in 1842. After the death of Martín, October 19, 1838, Oliva was alone at San Diego. Thus he experienced the decline of the mission from the time of its secularization, September 20, 1834.

In 1832 Oliva was called to Mission San Luis Rey to manage the temporalities of the huge establishment, leaving the spiritual affairs to José Antonio Anzar. When the latter left for the north early in 1833, Oliva grew despondent, allegedly, so Narciso Durán stated to Governor José Figueroa, because of the insubordination of the Indians, and fell into a deep melancholy. In consequence, Durán reassigned him to San Diego.

Duhaut-Cilly mentioned the poor quality of the food and the untidy service at the padres' table and the fact that the padres were surprised that no one wanted to eat with them. Robinson as well as Mofras described the decadence of San Diego in the early forties where Oliva carried on with a small number of Indians. Oliva resumed temporal management of the mission as a result of Governor Manuel Micheltorena's decree of March 23, 1843, restoring the management to the missionaries.

Whereas there were 3,000 head of cattle and 10,000 sheep nine years before, all that was left at San Diego were four cows, four calves, and a bull. Durán wrote of the situation on February 29, 1844: "This mission has always been a poor one which hardly ever had enough for the support of its Indians; but to-day it has nothing. Fr. Vicente Oliva is in charge of a population that may number one hundred souls."[3] On October 28, 1845, Pío Pico decreed the sale of the mission. Oliva's last entry in the register was on June 14, 1846. On leaving for San Juan Capistrano, Oliva named José Antonio Estudillo as administrator. On July 29, 1846, the flag of the United States was raised in the plaza of Old Town.

Mission San Juan Capistrano had been without a priest since the departure of José María Zalvidea in November 1842, though a priest visited it from time to time. Oliva baptized there from September 6, 1846, until July 11, 1847. At the mission Oliva died alone without the assistance of a priest at one o'clock in the morning of January 2, 1848. His illness had been brief. Fray Blas Ordaz of San Gabriel had been called, but he himself was ill and was prevented from traveling because of floods. Ordaz was assured by eyewitnesses that Oliva had commended himself to God in his last moments. Ordaz buried Oliva on January 29 on the Epistle side of the sanctuary. In December 1912, the Rev. St. John O'Sullivan, pastor of the mission, made excavations to locate Oliva's remains. They were discovered under a double layer of large-sized floor tiles at a spot designated in the Burial Register. The remains had been buried in priestly vestments.

[1] Payeras to the guardian, Purisima, May 20, [1820?], Archivo General de la Nación, Mexico City.

[2] *History of California*, V, 623 n.

[3] Engelhardt, *Missions and Missionaries*, IV, 323.

ORAMAS, CRISTÓBAL (ca. 1759-?)

Fray Cristóbal Oramas was a native of Icod on the island of Tenerife. He became a Franciscan at San Fernando College, Mexico City, being listed as a student cleric there in 1785. On April 1, 1786, Fray Juan Sancho, the guardian, stated that Oramas was scarcely one year professed, but before entering the order at San Fernando, he had been a curate for five years, hence was already an ordained priest, a member of an undisclosed diocese. "He is a thorough religious, a man of noble disposition and of exemplary conduct." Oramas left the college for California with five other missionaries in April 1786 and arrived probably at Monterey during that same year.

President Fermín Francisco de Lasuén appointed Oramas together with Antonio Paterna as cofounders of Mission Santa Barbara, which was established December 4, 1786. All three had already arrived at Santa Barbara in October and stayed at the presidio both before and after the founding until about April 1787. Oramas baptized at San Buenaventura, December 8, 1786, and again April 2-22, 1787. He commenced to baptize at Santa Barbara, January 4, 1787, and continued to do so until August 20, 1790.

Oramas was next sent to Mission Purisima, where he baptized from December 28, 1789 until November 2, 1792. He at times also visited Mission San Luis Obispo, where he baptized. After asking for a change, he was next assigned to Mission San Gabriel where he ministered from November 17, 1792, until September 23, 1793. Lasuén, on February 22, 1793, stated that in his work he was restricted to a supernumerary position because of depression and hypochondria.

Oramas petitioned to return to Mexico, and his request was granted. En route, he baptized at Mission San Diego, October 13-14, 1794. He arrived in Mexico most probably early in 1795. On August 8, 1795, he was made novice master at San Fernando College. On September 5, 1798, he requested to be transferred to the college of Santa Cruz de Querétaro for reasons of health, and his petition was granted.

ORDAZ, BLAS (1792-1850)

Fray Blas Ordaz was born in 1792 at Corvero de Río Alamo, six leagues from Calahorra in the province of Burgos, Spain. He left Cádiz shortly after June 14, 1819, on *El Relámpago,* and subsequently entered San Fernando College, Mexico City, that same year. He came to California in the following year, landing at Monterey about August 8 and baptized at Mission San Carlos on the thirteenth. Mariano Payeras, the commissary prefect, said of the newcomer in 1820: "Experience will reveal his merits; but he manifests a laudable disposition." Ordaz' first appointment was to Mission San Francisco, where he first baptized on September 28, 1820. His last baptism there was administered on September 22, 1821.

While at San Francisco, Ordaz accompanied a military expedition to the north under Captain Luís Argüello. It had been rumored that some English or American immigrants had established themselves about forty or fifty leagues north of San Francisco Bay, and the purpose of the expedition was to ascertain the facts. It started out on October 18, 1821, first by water to the vicinity of San Rafael and Carquinez Strait, then overland along the Sacramento River which on this occasion was called the Jesús María. The expedition crossed the Coast Ranges to the west and returned on November 15 to the starting point through the area where today the cities of Ukiah, Santa Rosa, and San Rafael are located. It is impossible to determine the most northerly point reached, for Narciso Durán, who also was a member of the party, failed to give distances in the diary which he kept. Bancroft is of the opinion that the expedition may have gone as far north as the latitude of Shasta.

Ordaz baptized at Soledad, December 21, 1821, and was then stationed at Mission San Miguel where he officiated between January 19 and

September 15, 1822. He was at Mission Purisima between April 13, 1823, and March 25, 1824, baptizing meanwhile at Mission Santa Ines, June 2 and 9, 1823; at Mission San Buenaventura, July 13-25, 1823; and at Santa Barbara, August 14, 1824. Ordaz' next lengthy period of service was at Mission Santa Ines from March 25, 1824, to April 3, 1833. He was then assigned to Mission San Buenaventura, where he labored from May 11, 1833, to July 5, 1837, and following that, Mission San Fernando from May 20, 1837, to June 30, 1847. He had declined the pastorate of Los Angeles, April 27, 1836, for reasons of health. After San Fernando he was stationed at Mission San Gabriel until his death. He baptized there for the last time on November 21, 1849. While at San Gabriel, he also had charge of Mission San Juan Capistrano. Other missions at which he had baptized were San Carlos, twice, in 1820 and 1821, and San Luis Obispo several times in 1823.

In 1823 he was present when the president of the missions, José Señán, died at San Buenaventura. In 1824 he was at Purisima when the Chumash Indian revolt broke out, February 21. Ordaz and his companion, Antonio Rodríguez, together with soldiers and their families, took refuge in the mission compound, and, after a truce had been effected, he accompanied the families to Mission Santa Ines. When Alfred Robinson visited Santa Ines in 1829, he stated that Ordaz received him with the accustomed hospitality of the mission padres, the living quarters clean, and the gardens filled with fruit trees, and the storehouses well filled with grain.

According to Engelhardt, Ordaz was piqued over his transfer from Santa Ines to San Buenaventura. There "his pent-up anger exploded to the extent that he would endeavor to annoy Fr. Durán, his superior, when there was a chance, especially by joining politicians and other worldly people to divert himself on visiting Santa Barbara town. This went on for about two years unknown to the public, save that Fr. Durán made Governor Figueroa a confidant of the facts, in consequence of which Fr. Ordaz recovered his moorings, and a great calm ensued."[1]

In 1834 letters written by Ordaz, Angel Ramírez, and Antonio M. Lugo reached Monterey which accused Captain José de la Guerra y Noriega, Sergeant José A. Pico, Fray Narciso Durán, and Fray Tomás Esténaga, "those irreconcilable foes of our country," of plotting against the government. When the matter was thoroughly examined by José Figueroa, he learned that the four men had merely gotten together on a legitimate business deal.

The question of Ordaz' immorality was ventilated early in this century by opposing schools of thought represented by Bancroft and Engelhardt. Bancroft wrote: "Padre Blas was a lively and good-natured man, but his fondness for women involved him occasionally in scandal and reprimand from his superiors."[2] When Bancroft offered no proofs for his assertions, Engelhardt called him an "unscrupulous prevaricator." In a long defense of Ordaz in his *History of Mission Santa Inés,* the Franciscan historian outlined his reasons favoring Ordaz' innocence.[3]

On September 18, 1832, Durán issued a long circular letter in Latin to the friars of all the missions which they were to copy in the *Libro de Patentes.* He warned them to live worthy of their vocation, to avoid scandal, and to pay particular attention to the Franciscan Rule which forbade suspicious dealings with women. The letter stated that one friar, who was not named, was not conducting himself worthily as a priest and Franciscan. In Engelhardt's opinion the statement was pointed at Ordaz, who, he said, was a victim of rumors circulated by discontented Indians of the mission, and the letter under these circumstances should not have been issued. Instead Ordaz should have been called in to explain the matter.

Bancroft probably lacked the necessary documents to prove his accusation, while Engelhardt lacked the means to make his defense water tight. Bancroft perhaps knew more than Engelhardt gave him credit for. The plain fact is that Ordaz' bad reputation perdured down to the early days of the American occupation.

When Colonel Jonathan D. Stevenson of the First New York Regiment was in Los Angeles on May 1, 1848, he wrote to the church authorities in the East, describing religious conditions in California, a letter that was forwarded to the Congregation of the Propagation of the Faith in Rome. Since the abandonment of the missions, he declared, of the few priests who remained, some were aged, sick, and infirm, while there were others who "by careless and dissolute life have forfeited the respect of their parishioners." Stevenson stated that he received his information from the respectable people of the country. Then he added: "There are but three Priests for the entire Southern District of California embracing a coast of some 500 miles. Of these there is but one who appears to render any service whatever, and his character is so notoriously profligate that his influence and respect is entirely gone; he is a Spaniard, old and somewhat infirm and has been 29 years in this country, his name is Blaz Ordaz."[4]

Ordaz was the last of the Fernandinos to die in California. He received the last sacraments and died at Mission San Gabriel where he was buried by Fray José Joaquín Jimeno, November 11, 1850, in the church on the Gospel side. Four other priests were present at the interment.

During the heated controversy in Santa Barbara between Bishop Thaddeus Amat and the Franciscans of the Apostolic College of Santa Barbara (1856-1861), which brought about a schism in the town, the bishop taking the case to Rome, the name of Ordaz came up again in the documentation sent to Rome. The bishop charged that the prevailing immorality in his diocese was owing, in part at least, to the immoral behavior of some missionary friars toward the end of the Mexican regime. Señor U. Yndart of Santa Ines, in his letter of October 11, 1859, which was certified by the pastor Cipriano Rubio, a Spaniard, stated that he had *heard* of Ordaz' immorality, that he was present at his funeral at San Gabriel, and that upon inquiring as to who was in charge of his funeral, he was told that it was Ordaz' daughter and his son-in-law.

The Rev. Cipriano Rubio is more explicit in his letter of October 20, 1859, written at Santa Ines and forwarded to Rome. He declared that Ordaz' incontinence was notorious, that *it was said* that he had had illicit relations with various women and that it was beyond doubt that he had had various children from a single woman, one of whom he knew — Vicente Ordaz — whom the padre himself had baptized and whose baptism he had recorded in the church register, Entry No. 1,311, folio 101, and which Ordaz himself signed.[5] Vicente Ordaz later had a notorious reputation in Santa Barbara, where he at one time was held for murder but was subsequently released.

Finally, Bishop Joseph Alemany of Monterey adverted to the fact of Ordaz' immorality in his diary on December 29, 1850, stating that the latter was the father of three children, the youngest of which was eight years old.

[1] Engelhardt, *Mission Santa Ines*, p. 182.

[2] *History of California*, IV, 759.

[3] Engelhardt, op. cit., pp. 179-183.

[4] Weber, *Documents of California Catholic History*, p. 53.

[5] Entry No. 1,311 of the Santa Ines Baptismal Register does not say explicitly that the child baptized was that of Blas Ordaz but strongly leads to that suspicion. On Dec. 19, 1830, Fray Ordaz baptized a child whom he named Vicente and whom he described as the "legitimate son" of María Soledad Ortega and of "an unknown father" [sic!]. Entry No. 1,326, fol. 103, contains the baptism of Lorenza Manuela Juana by Ordaz, on June 2, 1832, who is called the "legitimate daughter" of María Soledad and of "an unknown father" [sic!]. The third descendant spoken of by Alemany is not accounted for.

PALÓU, FRANCISCO (1723-1789)

Fray Francisco Palóu, the son of Sebastián Palóu and Miquela Amengual, was born at Palma, Majorca, Spain, January 22, 1723. His parents were members of the parish of Santa Eulalia. Palóu was baptized on the day following his birth at the cathedral by the Rev. Dr. Antoni Ribat, a canon, and received the names Francisco Miguel Joseph Joachim. On March 6, 1724, Palóu was confirmed at the cathedral by the Most Rev. Juan Fernández Zabate, bishop of Majorca.

Having completed his primary schooling in the city of Palma, Palóu entered the Franciscan order, November 10, 1739, at the Convento de Santa María de los Angeles de Jesús, outside the walls of Palma, receiving the habit from the Very Rev. Antonio Perelló. Palóu made his solemn profession on November 11, 1740. Thereupon he was sent to the Convento de San Francisco, Palma, to study the three-year course in philosophy which he took under Fray Junípero Serra from 1740 to 1743, followed by the course in theology, 1743-1746. Having been elevated to the priesthood in 1743, he took competitive examinations in February 1749 for the lectorate in philosophy, which he successfully passed, and consequently received the commission to teach philosophy, beginning in the fall of 1750. However, Palóu never taught, for, meanwhile, he had decided to become a missionary among the Indians of America.

It was Serra who invited Palóu to join him in the missionary enterprise, an invitation Palóu gladly accepted. He received the formal permission for himself and Serra on Palm Sunday, 1749, from the commissary general in Madrid. That very day Palóu hastened to the nearby town of Petra, where Serra was preaching a mission, to communicate the news, shortly returning to Palma to make arrangements for transportation. With Serra he left Palma on April 13, 1749, on an English vessel for Málaga, and from there on a Spanish vessel for Cádiz. At Cádiz, Palóu was described in passport records as a person of medium height, swarthy in complexion, with dark eyes and hair.

Palóu, Serra, and eighteen other friars set sail at the end of August, stopped at San Juan, Puerto Rico, in October, then on to Vera Cruz, Mexico, where they landed on December 7, after weathering a storm that nearly brought disaster to the ship and passengers. At Vera Cruz, Palóu fell deathly ill. He recovered, however, in time to join his fellow friars for the ride on horseback to Mexico City, where they arrived sometime before January 1, 1750, and there entered San Fernando College.

Palóu was among those who volunteered for the Sierra Gorda missions early that same year. With Serra he walked the entire distance and arrived at Jalpan, mission headquarters, on June 16. Palóu remained there at Misión Santiago with Serra for at least eight years, receiving high praise from the college authorities for his missionary ability. When Serra was recalled to Mexico City late in September 1758, Palóu remained at the mission for some time afterward, though both he and Serra were destined to be sent to the San Saba missions in Texas where two missionaries had been killed and a third wounded by the Apaches. At one period Palóu was president of the Sierra Gorda missions, but the years are unknown.

Palóu served the college in various capacities between the years of his missionary career in the Sierra Gorda and that of the Californias.

He was vicar of the institution from November 28, 1761, until December 1, 1764. He was a counselor of the college from December 1, 1764, until his departure for Lower California in July 1767. Before the end of 1766 he was made a commissioner of the Holy Office of the Inquisition for the period of the Huasteca mission of six months, of which no doubt he was actually a member.

When the king of Spain, Carlos III, expelled the Jesuits from his dominions in 1767, their missions in Mexico to a great extent were taken over by the Franciscans, a matter regulated by the government. The Fernandinos were assigned to Lower California, the Queretarans to the Pimería, and the members of the province of Jalisco to Nayarit. Serra, Palóu, and others rode to Tepic through Querétaro and Guadalajara between July 14 and August 21, 1767, and found hospitality at the Convento de Santa Cruz de Zacate.

As a result of political maneuvering on the part of the Jaliscans, the original assignments were reversed so that the Fernandinos were to be sent to the Pimería. Palóu notified Serra at Matanchel who, in consequence, returned to Tepic. Palóu and a number of his confreres had notified the college that they had volunteered for Lower California and preferred to return to the college unless arrangements were again reversed. To insure success to this end, Serra sent Palóu and Miguel de la Campa y Cos back to Mexico City. They set out from Tepic on October 19 and arrived at Guanajuato, November 1, where José de Gálvez, the king's visitor-general, happened to be. He urged Palóu to continue on to Mexico City, where the latter arrived on November 9. After consultation between the college authorities and the viceroy, the Fernandinos were restored to the field originally allotted to them. Palóu and De la Campa returned to Tepic on December 31, bringing along two additional missionaries, Dionisio Basterra and Juan de Medina Veitía.

Until proper shipping could be obtained, the friars gave missions to the faithful in and about Tepic. Palóu and two others preached in the ancient settlement of Compostela. Ultimately, Palóu and the rest of the company sailed from San Blas on the *Concepción*, March 14, 1768, and arrived at the roadstead of Loreto, April 1. Palóu was assigned to Misión San Xavier, located at a distance of about twenty-two miles southwest of Loreto, leaving on April 6. There he remained until Serra set out for Upper California in the spring of 1769. When Serra reached the last mission in the north, Palóu was notified that from then on he was to be president of the Lower California missions. This office he held until 1773 when the mission field was handed over to the Dominicans. As president, Palóu resided at Loreto.

At that time, instead of returning to the college, Palóu elected to serve in the new missionary field of Upper California. He left Loreto by ship on May 24, 1773, and sailed as far as Misión Santa Rosalía de Mulegé, thence traveled overland to San Fernando de Velicatá where he joined five other friars who were to be conducted to San Diego by Sergeant José Francisco Ortega. The party arrived at the port, August 30. Meanwhile, on August 19, Palóu determined the boundary line between the Franciscan missions to the north and those of the Dominicans to the south.

Since Serra at the time of Palóu's arrival in San Diego was in Mexico City, and Antonio Paterna was only temporarily in charge, the jurisdiction of the new missions fell into the hands of Palóu until Serra's return to San Diego, March 13, 1774. Palóu journeyed overland from San Diego to Monterey and Carmel, placing friars and mission helpers at various missions along the route. Also Palóu collected historical data on the five missions which he later included in his *Noticias de la Nueva California*. The then existing missions were San Diego, San Gabriel, San Luis Obispo, San Antonio, and San Carlos. On December 10, 1773, Palóu finished his report on the status of the missions and sent it to Antonio María Bucareli y Ursúa, the new viceroy, who declared it a masterly presentation — the best that he had received to date on the new territory. Palóu with the other friars and the lay Spaniards on the Monterey peninsula were in a state of quasi-starvation until relief came with the arrival of Serra at San Carlos, May 11, 1774, and of the supply ships that had been sent through his intervention. And during the weeks while Palóu was awaiting assignment at Mission San Carlos, he aided in mission work and planted a garden.

Serra sent him as a diarist on two expeditions to San Francisco, both under Captain Fernando Rivera y Moncada. The first left Monterey, November 23 and returned December 4, 1774. At San Francisco, Palóu planted a cross on what is known today as Sutro Heights. In 1775 Palóu was sent to San Francisco a second time, accompanied by Bruno de Heceta, to select a site for a future mission. The expedition left Monterey, September 4 and returned October 1, 1775.

The San Francisco Bay area having been reconnoitered by members of the Anza expedition and colonists having been brought in from Mexico, Palóu and Fray Pedro Cambón were assigned to establish California's sixth mission at San Francisco. Under Lieutenant José Joaquín Moraga, the two padres, sixteen soldiers, and seven colonists set out from Monterey, June 17, 1776, and arrived at the proposed mission site beside Dolores Lake, June 27. On June 29 Palóu celebrated Mass there in an *enramada* and a month later joined the new military camping site several miles to the north. He signed the initial pages of the mission registers, August 1, when building commenced, but this was not the official date of the mission's establishment, which did not take place until October 9. On September 17, he attended the formal establishment of the presidio.

Mission progress was slow in the beginning because of the poor soil of the area, and baptisms had to be limited to the number that could be fed, clothed, and housed, except of course persons in danger of death. Meanwhile, Palóu and Cambón also had to attend to the spiritual needs of the presidials. When Palóu left San Francisco for Mexico City in 1785, 447 Indians had been baptized and 250 were living in the Christian village adjacent to the mission. It was Palóu who laid the cornerstone of the present Mission Dolores, as it is popularly called, April 25, 1782.

Palóu was at Mission Santa Clara with officers of *La Princesa,* which had put into San Francisco in November 1779, when Serra unexpectedly arrived from Carmel. Together they traveled to San Francisco where confirmation was administered. Palóu was again at Santa Clara in May 1784 when hurriedly called there to attend the dying Fray José Murguía, who passed away on the eleventh, and remained there for the dedication of the new church which Murguía had built and which Serra dedicated on May 16.

Besides these visits to Santa Clara and two visits to Carmel in 1779 and 1782, there is no record of Palóu being absent from San Francisco after the founding of the mission in 1776. Early in August 1784, he received a missive from Serra to come down to Carmel in order to talk over the possible expulsion of the Franciscans from these missions and their replacement by the Dominicans as well as to help Serra prepare for death. Palóu traveled overland via Santa Clara and arrived at Carmel on August 18. There followed some days of conferences. When Serra's health grew worse, Palóu notified the missionaries of San Antonio and San Luis Obispo. He prepared Serra for death by administering to him the last sacraments. Palóu had been Serra's confessor since 1750.

Serra died on the afternoon of August 28, 1784, and Palóu buried him, as Serra had requested, close to the remains of Fray Juan Crespí. Once more Palóu became acting president of the California missions. His health had been failing for some years, and he had asked for retirement as early as 1778. He had actually obtained permission to retire some years before Serra's death. Only that event detained him longer in California. He returned to San Francisco, though during the next year he spent considerable time at Santa Clara. He also founded a sub-mission or *asistencia,* which he called San Pedro y San Pablo, at present-day San Mateo, where the soil was better than at San Francisco.

After Serra's death, Palóu began writing the president's biography, finishing all except the last chapter in California. Thus he became

California's and San Francisco's first author. The last entries which Palóu made in the mission registers are found for July 1785.

Palóu once more went south to Monterey and sailed on *La Favorita*, November 13, bound for Mexico. With him he had the manuscripts which have since become famous, *Noticias de la Nueva California* and the *Relación histórica* or biography of Serra.

Upon arrival at San Blas, Palóu continued his journey through Tepic, Guadalajara, and Querétaro, suffering from fever at the latter place, and reached San Fernando College, February 21, 1786. For a sore leg he took baths at El Peñon, east of the capital, and was restored to health by April. At the request of his superior, he set to work answering charges made against the California missionaries by Governor Pedro Fages. The finished document was presented to the viceroy. In Mexico City, Palóu also completed the *Relación histórica* by adding the long chapter on Serra's virtues after consulting the extensive library of San Fernando for appropriate passages from the fathers and doctors of the Church. Through benefactors the book was published by the firm of Zuñiga y Ontiveros, Mexico City. When it appeared in 1787, copies were sent to the royal palace in Madrid, to Majorca, and to the missions of Sonora and California. Responses from all these areas were full of highest praise for the work. The *Noticias* was not published until the middle of the nineteenth century.

In the summer of 1786, the triennial chapter was held at San Fernando. Palóu, despite his protests and resignation, was elected guardian and was confirmed in office. He died in office, April 6, 1789, at the college of Santa Cruz de Querétaro, and there he is presumably buried. At the time of his death, he was sixty-seven years old. Palóu's last years at San Fernando were saddened by the presence there of two psychopaths who had come from Spain respectively in 1786 and 1788 — Mariano Rubí and Bartolomé Gilí — whom neither the guardian nor the viceroy could control. Concerning this period, Fray Tomás de Pangua, guardian, on September 13, 1793, wrote to the viceroy, stating that it was unfortunate that the guidance of the community fell to a superior who was not only advanced in years but who had already arrived at his second childhood and who could do nothing but cry like a child and lock himself in his cell out of fear. This could refer only to Palóu, since Pablo de Mugártegui was guardian from 1789 to 1792, under whom Rubí and Gilí went to California in 1790 and 1791 respectively and who, upon his elevation, was only fifty-three years old.

Palóu, though an able missionary and excellent administrator, is best remembered as California's first historian and biographer. Through his writings much that would have been lost is now preserved. He was an eyewitness of most of what he wrote and moreover collected many documents relating to history as it was being made. His facts are considered dependable.

Between Serra and Palóu there had been mutual admiration and respect ever since the two had met in the classroom of San Francisco de Palma in 1740. It appears that Palóu saw eye to eye with Serra in the conduct of mission affairs. It was through the pen of Palóu that the portrait of Serra has been preserved better than that of any of the other early friars of California. He considered Serra a saintly man and a zealous missionary.

Professor Herbert E. Bolton, formerly of the University of California, Berkeley, declared that if Palóu were to be given an honorary degree it would read as follows: "Fray Francisco Palóu, diligent student, devout Christian, loyal disciple, tireless traveller, zealous missionary, firm defender of the faith, resourceful pioneer, successful mission builder, able administrator, and fair-minded historian of California."[1]

[1] Palóu, *Historical Memoirs of New California*, I, xc.

PANELLA, JOSÉ (1761-?)

Fray José Panella was a native of Barcelona, Catalonia, Spain, born on February 11, 1761. He became a professed member of the Franciscan order at Barcelona on March 28, 1776. As a member of San Fernando College, Mexico City, he came to California, arriving at San Francisco, April 14, 1797, on the *Concepción*. Panella served at Mission San Diego from June 2, 1797, until January 20, 1803, and for a short time within that period at Mission San Luis Rey in 1798.

At San Diego Panella became unpopular because of alleged harsh treatment of the natives so that President Fermín Francisco de Lasuén was forced to send him away for a period. The military commander at San Diego notified the president prior to September 30, 1798, that the Indians were dissatisfied and discontented with the missionary to such an extent that he feared an uprising. Lasuén commented that Panella, through no fault of his own, was useless for the ministry, for he had periods of emotional imbalance. He had been annoying to all, and the missionaries found him hard to associate with.

Later, however, after a personal investigation, Lasuén informed Governor Diego de Borica that there was little foundation to the charges of cruelty. Panella himself explained to the governor that on a certain festive occasion he merely had not allowed the Indians to have their own way. In 1801, Lasuén declared that Panella's attacks were noticeably increasing and with them his bad disposition. At the same time he declared that military officers were prompt to report everything that could defame a missionary. As a result of his continuing illness, Panella was given permission to return to Mexico. He sailed on October 4, 1803.

In 1809 he returned to his native Catalonia, having made application already in 1804.

PANTO, JOSÉ PEDRO (1778-1812)

Fray José Pedro Panto was born in 1778 at Balberde del Fresno, diocese of Coria, Estremadura, Spain, and became a Franciscan in the province of San Miguel. He enlisted for the American missions in 1803, sailing from Cádiz shortly after June 20 on the *Sagrada Familia*. At the time he was a preacher and confessor and was described in passport records as tall, thin, light-complexioned, with dark hair, and with a scar near the lachrymal of the left eye. Also he had a large nose which was slightly twisted. He arrived at Vera Cruz, Mexico, in August 1803, entered San Fernando College, Mexico City, sailed for California and arrived at San Francisco, July 28, 1810. He served at San Diego until his untimely death on June 30, 1812.

Bancroft states that Panto was "a rigorous disciplinarian and severe in his punishments. One evening in November 1811 his soup was poisoned, causing vomiting. His cook Nazario was arrested and admitted having put the 'yerba,' powdered *cuchasquelaai,* in the soup with a view to escape the father's intolerable floggings, having received in succession fifty, twenty-five, twenty-four, and twenty-five lashes in the twenty-four hours preceding his attempted revenge. There is much reason to suppose that the friar's death on June 30th of the next year was attributable to the poisoning."[1]

Engelhardt states that the poisoning had occurred seven months before Panto's death, and an attack of violent vomiting appears to have brought on a lingering disease from which the friar died. Suspicion fell on Nazario, the cook, who being apprehended, acknowledged his guilt. It appears that Panto did not want to prosecute or even testify against the Indian.

Domingo Carrillo, acting commander of the presidio, however, wrote to President Narciso Durán for permission for Panto to testify, which was given with the proviso that if found guilty the Indian was not to receive capital punishment. Engelhardt considers the Indian's statement with regard to the number of lashes he was given as too absurd to need disproval. Sergeant José María Pico, the appointed defender of Nazario, stated that his crime was justifiable in view of Panto's excesses, which fact Engelhardt states "was not proved." Nazario, however, was sentenced to eight months labor at the presidio as a lesson to others. The limit allowed for the castigation of an Indian was from twelve to twenty-five lashes and then only once. Engelhardt states that this was a regulation no missionary would have dared to disregard.

Panto baptized for the last time at San Diego, June 21, 1812, and died on June 30. He had received the last sacraments except the Viaticum because of his continuous vomiting. He passed away at seven o'clock in the evening, and, as the notation in the register states: "He died from food poisoned by the cook according to opinions." Panto was buried in the mission church by Gerónimo Boscana, Fray Tomás Ahumeda, O.P., from Lower California, being present. His remains were probably among those moved from the church to the cemetery by the Rev. John C. Holbein, December 28, 1853, when the mission was converted into a military barracks by American soldiers.

[1] *History of California*, II, 345.

PARRÓN, FERNANDO (ca. 1728-?)

Fray Fernando Parrón was born about 1728 at Arroyo del Puerco in the diocese of Coria, Estremadura, Spain, and became a Franciscan on June 11, 1746. He was a preacher at the friary of Trujillo in the province of San Miguel when recruited for the American missions by Pedro Pérez de Mezquía. On leaving Spain, he was described in passport records as thin, with swarthy skin, pallid complexion, a heavy beard, and dark eyes and hair. He sailed from Cádiz on *El Jasón,* September 5, 1759.

In Mexico he entered San Fernando College and eight years later became one of the group of missionaries under Junípero Serra who took over the ex-Jesuit missions in Lower California. He left the college on July 16, 1767, and arrived at Tepic on August 21. He sailed from San Blas on the *Concepción,* March 14, 1768, and arrived at Loreto, April 1. On the third, Serra assigned Parrón as his assistant at Misión Loreto.

When Visitor-General José de Gálvez decided on the conquest of Upper California, Serra appointed Parrón as one of the naval chaplains for the maritime expeditions going to San Diego. Parrón left Loreto, May 25, 1768, for La Paz, whence he sailed on the *San Carlos* alias *El Toyson,* January 9, 1769. The northern harbor was reached on April 29.

He was present at the founding of California's first mission by Serra at San Diego, July 16, 1769. Parrón and Francisco Gómez were appointed as its first ministers. In the early period, though ill himself, he labored with "inflexible intrepidity" in administering to the sick and experienced the first difficult years at the mission, witnessing hostility, insurrection, and discouraging lack of growth. After ten new friars were sent to California in the spring of 1771, Parrón was relieved of his post and returned to Mexico, most probably overland through Lower California. On December 2, 1772, he sailed from Loreto to San Blas on the *Lauretana.* In 1779 he was listed as novice master at San Fernando College, and on June 17, 1780, he was elected a counselor of the same institution.

PATERNA, ANTONIO (1721-1793)

Fray Antonio Paterna was born in 1721 at Seville, Andalusia, Spain, and became a Franciscan in the same province in 1743. Before leaving his native country, he resided at the Convento de San Francisco, Seville, and held the title of preacher. He was described as a man of good physique, thin, light-complexioned, with scant beard, blue eyes, and dark hair. Paterna sailed from Cádiz, December 29, 1749, on the *Nuestra Señora de Begoña* with twelve other friars under the leadership of Fray Pedro Pérez de Mezquía. After entering San Fernando College, Mexico City, about April 1750, he was sent to the Sierra Gorda missions which he served for twenty years. His name appears in the registers of Misión Nuestra Señora de la Luz, Tancoyol, on October 25, 1751, again in 1754, while his last entry is found on October 9, 1770.

In the latter year Paterna was sent to California as the leader of nine other friars. He sailed from San Blas on the *San Antonio,* January 20, 1771, and arrived at San Diego, March 12 and at Monterey, May 21. There, Junípero Serra appointed him and Antonio Cruzado to be the founders of Mission San Buenaventura. He sailed back to San Diego, July 14 and set out from the southern port with Governor Pedro Fages and soldiers for the north, August 6, 1771. However, on arriving at Mission San Gabriel and learning of Indian troubles there, Fages suspended the founding of San Buenaventura. Paterna and Cruzado shortly thereafter took charge of Mission San Gabriel instead, since the founding fathers, Pedro Cambón and Ángel Fernández Somera y Balbuena, were returning to Mexico.

Paterna administered his first baptism at San Gabriel, November 2, 1772, and his last in January 1777. For a short period he was acting president of the California missions between the time that Serra returned to Mexico in October 1772 and Palóu arrived at San Diego from Lower California, August 30, 1773. He was host to the Anza expedition at San Gabriel between January 4 and February 21, 1776, while Anza went to San Diego to aid Fernando Rivera y Moncada in the Indian revolt there. Early in 1777 Paterna received permission to return to Mexico, but he was only able to reach San Diego the day after the ship left (he baptized at San Diego, February 22, 1777), so he wrote to Serra for assignment.

Serra sent him to Mission San Luis Obispo where he baptized between October 1, 1777, and December 8, 1785. He had traveled posthaste to see Serra before he died but arrived too late and fell seriously ill at Carmel where he remained to recuperate. He baptized at Mission San Carlos between October 3, 1784, and May 23, 1785.

President Fermín Francisco de Lasuén chose Paterna together with Cristóbal Oramas, a newcomer from the college, to become the founders of California's tenth mission, Santa Barbara. Paterna left San Luis Obispo with Lasuén and arrived in Santa Barbara as early as October 1786. The mission was founded December 4. Before and after the founding, Paterna lived at the nearby presidio for about six months. He remained at Santa Barbara until his death in 1793. While there, he was also in charge of the Spaniards of Santa Barbara presidio. The number of Indians baptized at Mission Santa Barbara until the end of 1792 was 729, the number of whites, 98. Christianized Indians to the number of 504 were living at the mission at the time of his death. Paterna built the first two churches of adobe and gave the present mission buildings their orientation.

Paterna received the last sacraments before his death, which occurred on February 13, 1793. Francisco Dumetz of San Buenaventura buried him in the church on the following day. On February 24, Lasuén wrote to San Fernando College: "During all these years he conducted himself like a good old man and till his death, he labored like one in robust health and distinguished himself in the judgment and in the view of all by his zealous discharge of the apostolic ministry."[1]

In 1820 when the fourth (the present) church of stone was dedicated, Paterna's remains were transferred by President José Señán from their original resting place to the new vault beneath the sanctuary. His remains, however, could not be identified in 1911 when the vault was opened for repairs. Paterna Road on Santa Barbara's Riviera recalls the first missionary "pastor" of mission and presidio.

[1] MS in SBMA.

PAYERAS, MARIANO (1769-1823)

Fray Mariano Payeras, son of Antonio Payeras and Gerónima Borras, was born at Inca, Majorca, Spain, October 10, 1769. In baptism he received the names Pedro Antonio. He became a Franciscan at Palma, October 6, 1784, and made his profession at San Francisco el Grande, Palma, October 11, the following year. While a member of the friary of Alcudia, he volunteered for service at San Fernando College, leaving his abode on February 19, 1793. He sailed from Cádiz, June 11 on the *San Nicolás* and arrived at the college on September 12, the same year. On leaving Spain, he was described in passport records as being of medium stature, of swarthy complexion, with chestnut-colored eyes, dark hair, and a light beard. When, after two years at the college, he applied to be sent to California, the guardian, Antonio Nogueyra, declared that he was a person of approved conduct and entirely satisfactory to the college membership.

Payeras sailed for California on the *Aránzazu* and arrived at San

Francisco, June 18, 1796. His name appears first in the registers of Mission San Carlos, July 10, the same year. He served there until September 7, 1798. As early as January 26, in the same year, Fermín Francisco de Lasuén conferred upon him by subdelegation all the faculties he had received from the bishop of Sonora. Payeras' faculties extended over Missions San Carlos, including the Monterey presidio, San Juan Bautista, San Antonio, and Soledad. Payeras next served at Mission Soledad from November 1798 until July 23, 1803, then at San Diego between December 11, 1803, and September 30, 1804. While at Soledad, he visited Mission San Miguel in December 1800 and Santa Clara in July 1801. For the final period of his life Payeras was missionary at Purisima between 1804 and 1823, serving briefly at Soledad again in 1817.

At Mission Purisima Payeras completed the irrigation system and on January 1, 1811, reported the building of a new and shorter road for public service from Santa Ines to Purisima and from there to San Luis Obispo. This is the first-known section of a California road for which exact measurements were given as to width and length. On January 13, 1810, Payeras sent to President Estevan Tapis "the longest communication of its kind extant between two missionaries in the field."[1] It is a comprehensive record of Payeras' first five years as missionary in the area of Purisima. Paganism had practically ceased to exist, and there were abundant cattle for food and sheep for wool.

The earthquake of December 12, 1812, destroyed the greater part of the mission structures at Purisima. This was followed by a season of heavy rainfall which caused further deterioration. Payeras chose a new site for the mission at Los Berros, which is the present location of the restored mission northeast of Lompoc. The official transfer took place on April 29, 1813. Both the president of the missions, José Señán, and the governor, José Joaquín Arrillaga, gave their approval on March 30. At the new site an entirely new establishment was built, and during that period Payeras composed a catechism in the native language. The number of Indians baptized at Purisima between the years 1805 and 1823 was 893.

When the fourth president of the missions, José Señán (1812-1815) asked to be relieved of his office, San Fernando College named Payeras to succeed him on July 24, 1815. Payeras took over his duties on November 22 and continued to live at Purisima. The mission system was still running smoothly, and Payeras had thirty-seven missionaries working under him. However, the Mexican revolution against Spain had broken out in 1810, and the annual ships with supplies and pay for the soldiers no longer arrived in California. As a result the missions were called upon to support the presidios and pueblos. Payeras approved this request in a circular letter, December 19, 1819. In time the government owed the missions nearly 500,000 pesos, which were never paid nor did the friars receive their annual stipends.

During the Bouchard invasion in 1818, Payeras was an active participant in the defense of the country. He kept close watch over the insurgents' movements and notified other missionaries and the Santa Barbara presidio. He sent forty armed neophytes to Mission Santa Ines. Governor Pablo Solá praised Payeras' actions and notified the viceroy accordingly. Because of the increase in number of an inferior type of soldier in California, Payeras on October 9, 1819, ordered the missions to construct separate buildings for them away from the mission compounds.

Payeras concerned himself with Russian affairs in the northern part of the territory. He addressed a letter to the king on the subject, May 2, 1817. When the imperial commissioner, Rev. Agustín Fernández de San Vicente, arrived in California in 1822, he went to Fort Ross for a personal inspection of the Russian settlement. He was accompanied by Luís Antonio Argüello, commander of the San Francisco presidio, and Payeras. The latter kept a diary of the journey which shows that he left Monterey, October 11, 1822, and reached Fort Ross on October 21. Payeras drew up a long description of the fort and vicinity. He left there on the twenty-fourth and visited Missions San Rafael, San Jose, Santa Clara, and San Juan Bautista on his return.

It was during Payeras' term as president that California's twentieth mission, San Rafael, was founded, December 14, 1817, in the presence of Friars Vicente Francisco de Sarría, Narciso Durán, Ramón Abella, and Luís Gil y Taboada. It was first established as an *asistencia* of Mission San Francisco, since it was considered a better place of residence for the sick Indians of the region. Payeras visited the mission again in 1818 in the company of Commander Argüello.

In his biennial report of 1815-1816, Payeras strongly recommended the occupation of the interior valley, the San Joaquin, with the establishment of a presidio and one or more missions. There were practically no more missions to be built along the coast, and there were at least about four thousand pagan Indians in the interior. He made a similar recommendation in the report of 1817-1818. On July 2, 1820, when there arose a question of fewer missionaries being sent to California, Payeras proposed that the southern missions be retained by the Fernandinos while those of the north be handed over to another college.

On August 8, 1818, Payeras was reelected president, despite the fact that he had asked to be relieved of the office. Since the office of commissary prefect had become vacant and no successor to Sarría was appointed, all the former powers of the president once again came into the hands of Payeras. However, after a year and some months the office of commissary prefect was revived and this time conferred upon Payeras, October 9, 1819, while Señán was chosen to be president a second time. Official notice of these changes was received in California on April 1, 1820, when the two padres embarked upon their official duties. Payeras made Señán his vice-prefect and remained commissary prefect until his death.

On December 31, 1820, Payeras finished writing his biographical sketches of the missionaries serving under him in California which together with Sarría's of 1817 comprise an invaluable source of data on the men who manned the missions. From June to October 1820, Payeras made his canonical visitation of the missions of the north and in the following year those of the south. On September 21, 1821, Payeras set out with Fray José Bernardo Sánchez from San Diego to explore the interior country between there and San Gabriel to select future mission sites. He arrived at San Gabriel on October 1. En route Payeras dedicated the new chapel of San Antonio at Pala, an *asistencia* of Mission San Luis Rey, and authorized Mass to be said at the site of Santa Isabel. En route he found five sites suitable for future missions. In 1821 Payeras fostered the building of the chapel of Our Lady of the Angels (the Plaza church) at Los Angeles whose cornerstone had been laid already in 1814. He asked the missions to help toward finishing the building. The church was dedicated on December 8, 1822.

When news arrived that the California missions should be handed over to the diocesan clergy in 1821, Payeras was agreeable. Nothing, however, came of the proposal. On June 18, the same year, Payeras sent a lengthy memorial to the viceroy, complaining about the dictatorial attitude of Governor Solá in assuming temporal authority over the missionaries.

Upon Mexico's successful revolt against Spain, General Agustín Iturbide became emperor of Mexico, and California was officially notified of the change in 1822. Solá called to Monterey the military commanders of the territory as well as Friars Payeras and Señán to consider the effects of this change on California. Sessions opened there on April 9. An oath was taken to support the new government on the eleventh. Payeras delivered an appropriate address in the presidio church. In the previous year Payeras had taken the oath to support the Spanish constitution of 1812. When Canon Agustín Fernández de San Vicente came to California to inquire concerning the loyalty of the missionaries to the Mexican government, he called for a detailed commitment from each missionary. Payeras ordered his friars to comply. On November 9, 1822, when the California electors met at Monterey for the purpose of choosing the first members of the territorial legislative assembly, Payeras celebrated a solemn high Mass and delivered a sermon.

Payeras enjoyed, like all the presidents since Lasuén, the powers of vicar forane of the bishop of Sonora. However, unlike Serra and Lasuén, but like Tapis and Señán, he did not have the faculty to administer the sacrament of confirmation.

The commissary prefect suffered considerably during the last year of his life. He had an abscess on the back of his head and was forced to keep it bandaged. One leg became infected from a scratch sustained while on a journey. His health failed, and he administered his last baptism on March 5, 1823. He received the last sacraments at Purisima, which, it will be recalled, he had reestablished in 1813, and he died on April 28, 1823. He was buried the following day by Fray Antonio Rodríguez in the sanctuary of the church on the Epistle side near the pulpit. At his demise, Payeras was fifty-three years, seven months, and eighteen days old. He had been a Franciscan for thirty-eight years and had lived in California for twenty-seven.

Friar Rodríguez stated in his death entry that Payeras had disposed himself for death "with religious and exemplary edification." When Señán issued his circular announcing the commissary prefect's death, he stated that Payeras "left us an edifying example of his love for God, piety, attachment to religion, conformity to the divine will, and of all virtues. His death is, therefore, very much felt by all, especially by me."[2]

In 1817, Sarría in his biographical sketches characterized Payeras as follows: "I consider his merit as exceptional and distinguished for his genius as a religious as well as an industrious and successful manager. . . . His disposition fits him for other offices especially such as are somewhat analagous to the ministry that has been entrusted to him." Payeras was president at the time those lines were written.

Engelhardt considered Payeras an unusually capable man and in zeal for the welfare of the Indians unsurpassed. Bancroft wrote of him:

There was no missionary with whose public life and character for the past eight years the reader is better acquainted than with that of Payeras. . . . There was no friar of better or more even balanced ability in the province. He was personally a popular man on account of his affable manners, kindness of heart, and unselfish devotion to the welfare of all. It was impossible to quarrel with him, and even Governor Solá's peevish and annoying complaints never ruffled his temper. Yet he had extraordinary business ability, was a clear and forcible as well as a voluminous writer, and withal a man of great strength of mind and firmness of character. He was called to rule the friars during a trying period, when it would have required but a trifle to involve the padres and soldiers in a quarrel fatal to the missions. . . . With much of Lasuén's suavity and none of Serra's bigotry, he had all the zeal of the latter and more than the shrewdness of the former. His death just at this time, in the prime of life, must be considered as a great misfortune.[3]

Angustias de la Guerra y Ord said of him: "I remember him as a man of good color and a most sympathetic face. Many times I heard my father [José Antonio de la Guerra y Noriega] and others talk of the virtues, good qualities, talents and energy of this missionary."[4]

Mission Purisima was restored by the United States government, its dedication taking place on December 7, 1941. It is now a state park. Payeras' remains were uncovered on July 27, 1936, in the presence of this writer and other witnesses and definitely identified.

[1] Engelhardt, *Mission La Concepcion Purisima*, p. 21.
[2] April 29, 1823, MS in SBMA.
[3] *History of California*, II, 489-490.
[4] Price and Ellison, tr. *Occurrences in Hispanic California*, p. 35.

PEÑA SARAVIA, TOMÁS DE LA (1743-1806)

Fray Tomás de la Peña Saravia was born in 1743 at Brizuela, diocese of Burgos, Spain, and became a Franciscan at Santander, November 13, 1762, in the province of Cantabria. He was a member of the community of Vitoria when he set out for the American missions in 1769. In passport records at the time he was described as a person of medium height with a large face that was pockmarked. De la Peña, one of a group of forty friars under Fray Rafael Verger, left from Cádiz for San Fernando College, Mexico City, where he arrived in 1770. He held the office of preacher.

He set out from the college in October 1770 and sailed from San Blas in February 1771, but having been driven south by a storm to Manzanillo, he went overland up the coast of Sinaloa and from there reached Loreto, Lower California, November 24, 1771. President Francisco Palóu assigned him to Misión San José del Comundú. He came to Upper California with Francisco Dumetz in September 1772. (The latter had come down to obtain provisions for Mission San Gabriel.) De la Peña served as a missionary at San Diego until September 26, 1773. He joined Palóu, who had delivered his missions to the Dominicans, and accompanied him as far as Mission San Luis Obispo where Palóu placed him, in Serra's absence, as a supernumerary. However, when Serra returned from Mexico, he assigned De la Peña and Juan Crespí as chaplains of the *Santiago* under Captain Juan Pérez, who was to make a reconnaissance of northwestern waters. The ship sailed from Monterey, June 11 and returned August 24, 1774, having penetrated as far north as the present Queen Charlotte Islands in western Canada. De la Peña kept a log of the voyage.

De la Peña was still at Mission San Carlos when the members of the Anza expedition arrived at Monterey in 1776. President Serra chose him and José Murguía to be the cofounders of Mission Santa Clara. De la Peña was present at the founding of Presidio San Francisco, September

17, 1776, and at the formal founding of the mission on October 9, the same year. He then returned to Monterey and set out with Captain Fernando Rivera y Moncada for San Francisco where he arrived on November 26, selecting en route the site of the future mission of Santa Clara. This latter mission was founded on January 12, 1777, at Thamien along the shore of the Río Guadalupe. De la Peña was later joined by Murguía, who came up from Monterey with cattle and supplies. De la Peña served at the mission until January 1794, and after the death of Murguía in May 1784 he was in charge. He baptized at San Francisco from time to time between 1777 and 1793 and at Mission San Carlos on August 14, 1790.

At the time of De la Peña's departure from California, 2,923 baptisms had been administered at Santa Clara, while the number of cattle increased to 4,200 and sheep to 1,000 head. The missionary experienced a season of flood conditions in 1779 when the mission had to be relocated closer to the present site of the university at a place called Socoistraka. The cornerstone of that church was blessed by Serra in 1781 and the church dedicated by him in May 1784.

The civilian pueblo of San Jose had been founded (November 29, 1777) too close to the mission of Santa Clara in clear violation of Spanish laws. The resultant complaints on the part of the Indians and the padres led Murguía and De la Peña to protest to Governor Felipe de Neve through Serra in a long *representación* which Serra praised for its apt and cogent reasoning. In November 1782, Governor Pedro Fages, who succeeded Neve, held a conference with the Santa Clara padres concerning the boundary lines between mission and pueblo. The result was quite unsatisfactory to the mission. While Serra continued to fight the case with the government, no decision was made in his lifetime, and De la Peña, after his retirement to Mexico, was occasionally called upon to give testimony on the case.

A quite lengthy document was drawn up in 1790 centering on De la Peña for his alleged mistreatment of several Indians, two of whom, it was claimed, died as a result of their injuries. A full investigation, into which President Fermín Francisco de Lasuén entered, disclosed the fact that the charges were based on a calumny by one commandant, González, whom De la Peña had reprimanded for misbehavior. On January 2, 1787, Fages wrote to Palóu that "the father comes out innocent of the calumny, with his credit and reputation clear."[1] De la Peña interceded with the authorities to mitigate the punishment of his accuser, who was released after giving a public apology. The viceregal government had taken cognizance of the matter and upon investigation declared De la Peña "innocent" and "his conduct both good and religious."

Lasuén, in defending De la Peña before the civil authorities, declared that he was "a good priest, an experienced missionary, and one who upholds the honor of his apostolic calling. He carries out his duties punctually."[2] Joaquín de Castro, a soldier, attached to Mission Santa Clara, who had often accompanied De la Peña on journeys and on investigations concerning Indians, declared that "he had noticed nothing but a love for them that was too trustful, an extreme good humor, and a degree of patience and courtesy that was unusual."[3]

Early in 1793 De la Peña's condition was in a physically precarious state, and in May 1794 Lasuén found "Father Peña so ill that one could not help feeling the greatest pity and compassion for him. He is dejected and very apprehensive, ceaselessly fretting, and talking to himself, and completely in the grip of a profound melancholia."[4] A little later he said that De la Peña was at Santa Cruz in a "completely demented condition." Lasuén asked José Joaquín Arrillaga for permission to send him back to Mexico on the *Concepción,* then at anchor in Monterey. De la Peña sailed from there on August 12, 1794. He arrived at San Fernando College on December 21. On May 23, 1795, he was elected a counselor of the college, an office which he held for three years. For a period he was procurator of the California missions. He died in Mexico sometime prior to February 1806.

[1] Palóu, *Historical Memoirs*, IV, 380.
[2] Kenneally, *Writings*, I, 119.
[3] Ibid., I, 130.
[4] Ibid., I, 306.

PÉREZ, JOSÉ BERNARDINO DE JESÚS (?-1873)

A native of Mexico, Fray José Bernardino de Jesús Pérez became a Franciscan at the college of Guadalupe, Zacatecas, and in course of time became well known in other sections of the country. The history of his college describes him as most respected for his well-known virtues of humility, charity, joviality and lovableness. He was one of the grandest prelates of the college.

Pérez accompanied Fray Francisco García Diego y Moreno to California in 1833 to take over the northern missions of the Fernandinos. He set sail from San Blas for Lower California on the *Catalina,* but he and his companions became stranded when the sailors mutinied and took over the ship. The friars tried to reach Upper California overland but turned back after getting as far as San José del Cabo. They finally obtained passage at La Paz on the ship which was taking Governor José Figueroa to Monterey, at which port they arrived January 15, 1833.

As commissary prefect, García Diego y Moreno chose Santa Clara as his place of residence and retained Pérez as his secretary. Pérez was one of the two friars whom he sent to Mission San Rafael to investigate the charges against Fray Rafael Moreno who had been accused of instigating an unprovoked attack on friendly Indians, a number of whom were killed and injured. The investigation cleared the friar of the charges. Pérez accompanied García Diego y Moreno in the visitation he made through the Zacatecan missions in 1835.

After García Diego y Moreno had consulted the Fernandino president Narciso Durán at Santa Barbara on concerted action in mission affairs, he went to Mexico to deal directly with the federal government. He took Pérez along with him, sailing November 17, 1835.

Pérez did not return to California. In the chapter of July 6, 1840, he was elected a counselor of the college and at the same time was appointed vicar of the institution. He was elected guardian probably in 1843.

Owing to the anticlerical legislation in Mexico, Pérez was exclaustrated with the rest of the community in 1859. The friars betook themselves to San Fernando College, Mexico City. There Pérez was elected guardian of the Zacatecan group, November 28, 1860. In a subsequent chapter, November 12, 1863, José María de Jesús Romo was elected guardian, but since he soon went to the Holy Land to establish a foundation, Pérez as vicar ruled the community for a period. He never returned to Zacatecas but died at Tepozotlán, June 15, 1873, and was buried in the chapel of Nuestra Señora del Refugio.

PEYRÍ, ANTONIO (1769-?)

Fray Antonio Peyrí is one of the few California missionaries who left to posterity a brief autobiographical account of his early life which he wrote out on the second page of the front flyleaf of a book in vellum covers, entitled *Directorio Moral por Fr. Frco. Echarri, O.F.M.* (Madrid, 1790), Volume II, and which was discovered by Engelhardt at Mission San Luis Rey on October 9, 1912.

Peyrí was born on January 8, 1769, at Porrera, archdiocese of Tarragona, Catalonia, Spain, and was baptized the same day. He was confirmed on October 30, 1772. He lived at Porrera until 1775 when he went to Vinols in the same archdiocese and there remained for a year. Then, returning to Porrera, the lad remained there until 1778 when he departed for Lleysa, staying there until 1781, once more returning to Porrera. He stayed there until 1784. The next move was to Cornudella where he made his abode until 1787. Finally, he went to Reus where he entered the Franciscan order, October 21, 1787. He made his profession there, October 22, the following year. Peyrí does not give the names of his parents, nor does he enlarge upon the reasons for his frequent changes of residence in his early years.

After his novitiate, Peyrí was sent to Escornalbu to study for a year, then to Gerona where he remained until 1794. At the latter place he received all the orders leading to the priesthood as well as the priesthood itself, the latter on March 16, 1793, and he said his first Mass on April 1. At Gerona he received his commission to become a missionary in America. He started out from the monastery with Fray José Viader, September 14, 1794, reached Barcelona on the twenty-fourth, went on to Madrid which he left on October 25 for the port of Santa María near Cádiz where he was detained until passage was available. He sailed from Cádiz, May 8, 1795, with twenty other friars. In passport records at the time of his departure, he was described as a man of regular stature, light-skinned, with red hair, blue eyes, large temples, a roundish nose, and a scar above the left eye.

Peyrí arrived at Vera Cruz, Mexico, July 26 and at San Fernando College, Mexico City, August 23. He remained there until March 1, 1796, when he set out with four companions for California. At the time of his leaving, Father Antonio Nogueyra, the guardian, stated that Peyrí was a religious of accepted conduct and a person of entire satisfaction to the superiors of the college. Peyrí sailed from San Blas, April 5, 1796, and disembarked at San Francisco, June 18, 1796. His first assignment was to Mission San Luis Obispo where he arrived on July 19. While stationed there, he baptized once at Mission San Antonio on April 15, 1798, at Purisima once in 1797 and in 1798, and once at Santa Barbara, June 3, 1797, and once at Soledad, April 2, 1798.

On April 15, 1798, Peyrí was destined by President Fermín Francisco de Lasuén for the founding of California's eighteenth mission, San Luis Rey, which was actually established on June 13. En route Peyrí baptized at Mission San Gabriel, May 31. Fray José Faura was given to him as an assistant. For the rest of his life in the territory, Peyrí was associated with San Luis Rey. The fact that he built up the entire mission from a brush hut to the largest establishment in California makes the story of Peyrí and the mission one and the same. The registers of the mission are lost, but the annual and biennial reports remain, and these enable one to follow the work of this able and industrious missionary from year to year.

Between 1798 and December 1831, 5,295 Indians were baptized, and when Peyrí left the institution, 2,819 Christianized Indians called San Luis Rey their home. The mission started with 162 head of cattle and 600 sheep, but at the end of 1831 it had 26,000 head of cattle and 25,500 head of sheep. Spiritually and materially the mission was built up in thirty-four years by Peyrí and his twelve successive Franciscan assistant missionaries.

Peyrí composed and signed the answers to the government questionnaire on the habits and customs of the local Indians, December 12, 1814. On November 22, 1822, and again on October 8, 1827, he composed documents describing the mission lands and their assets. To San Luis Rey belonged the San Juan, Santa Margarita, San Jacinto, and Las Flores ranches, the latter with its own chapel. The present mission church was dedicated, October 4, 1815, and the *asistencia* chapel of San Antonio, Pala, was established, June 13, 1816. Peyrí was present also at the dedication of the stone church at San Juan Capistrano, September 7, 1806. On June 8, 1827, he was chosen by San Fernando College to succeed Fray José Bernardo Sánchez as president of the missions should Sánchez die or become incapacitated.

When Auguste Duhaut-Cilly visited San Luis Rey in 1827, he considered the plant a superb structure. Peyrí greeted him with the "affability and politeness he possessed in so great measure. He had us served at once with chocolate, and ordered beds prepared for us, that we might lie down until the dinner hour. At noon we were again together, and we enjoyed this excellent man's pleasant and lively conversation."[1] The next day, the Feast of St. Anthony (June 13) was celebrated religiously and socially. The Frenchman added that the buildings were planned on a grand scale after the ideas of the friar. For many years it was thought that Peyrí himself was the actual builder and master mason. This, however, is incorrect. Peyrí himself explicitly stated in the document which he placed in the mission's cornerstone that the master mason of the church was José Antonio Ramírez. Duhaut-Cilly recorded that San Luis Rey produced the best grape wine in California and that the mission's olives were exquisite in flavor. Concerning the Indians, he declared that they were the best treated of all the missions. In 1829, Peyrí received the trapper, James Ohio Pattie, and hospitably received Alfred Robinson.

Vicente Francisco de Sarría, the commissary prefect, in 1817, said of Peyrí: "He not only merits the title of founder of the mission . . . but also has served it for the lengthy period of nineteen years having advanced it greatly by his personal activity and diligence." He praised him also for establishing Pala. Mariano Payeras wrote in 1820: "His merit is distinguished as founder and builder of a beautiful mission in the spiritual and temporal matters which it enjoys. His aptitude is limited to the ministry he exercises and for the common governing of a community." In 1813, Peyrí was chosen by Sarría as secretary for the canonical visitation he made at Mission San Diego, November 3, 1813.

In the matter of political loyalty, Peyrí was less attached by Spanish ties than were most of the missionaries, and he took the oath required in 1826 to support the Mexican constitution. He likewise adopted the phrase of the Mexican republicans: "Dios y Libertad." He was even enthusiastic about the national cause. When news of the expulsion of the Spaniards from Mexico came in 1827, however, he demanded his passport, even though Governor José María Echeandía asked President Guadalupe Victoria of Mexico to allow the friar to remain. Peyrí insisted that he was growing old and no longer fit for service. He finally obtained his passport from the government authorities together with the full payment of his stipends which were in arrears. Engelhardt says of him that he was "the zealous and most practical of the missionaries. . . . Fr. Peyrí erected and successfully managed the largest and most populous Indian mission in both Americas."[2]

Stories vary as to how Peyrí finally quit his mission. He left it in the hands of Fray José Antonio Anzar, the Zacatecan, and secretly went to San Diego where he boarded the *Pocahontas* which sailed on January 17, 1832, for Mazatlán. With him he took two Indian youths of San Luis Rey, Pablo Tac and Agapito Amamix, both of whom were destined for the priesthood. He went on to Mexico City, staying at San Fernando College, where as a counselor of the institution he signed the official books between November 12, 1832, and January 15, 1834. No doubt the purpose of his long stay there was to give the two Indian boys some necessary scholastic training before they would enter their higher seminary training in Rome.

After the Englishman, Alexander Forbes, had met Peyrí, during the latter's journey to Mexico, he wrote of him:

At his mission, strangers of all countries and modes of faith, as well as his fellow subjects, found always a hearty welcome, and the utmost hospitality. Many of my countrymen and personal friends have related to me, with enthusiasm, the kindness and protection which they have received at his hands, boons which are doubly valuable where places of entertainment do not exist, and where security is not very firmly established.

I had the pleasure of seeing the Father Peyri on his way to Mexico; and although I had heard much of him before, yet his prepossessing appearance, his activity and knowledge of the world, far above what could have been expected under the circumstances, gave me even a higher opinion of his worth than I before entertained. The excellent climate from which he had come, and his constant employment in the open air, made him look like a robust man of fifty years of age, although he was then sixty-seven; and although his general character and manners were, necessarily, very different from what could be expected from a mere cloistered monk, yet in his grey Franciscan habit, which he always wore, with his jolly figure, bald head, and white locks, he looked the very *beau ideal* of a friar of the olden time. This worthy man having now entered the cloisters of a convent, may be considered as dead to the world; but he will live long in the memory of the inhabitants of California; and of those numerous strangers who have been entertained at his hospitable board at San Luis Rey.[3]

Peyrí and the Indian boys left Mexico in February 1834 for Europe by way of New York and France and arrived at Barcelona on June 21. Owing to the turbulent conditions in Spain, Peyrí could not reach his native town of Porrera for some time. To a friend, Don Estevan Anderson in Scotland, he wrote: "I confess that I have been very much disappointed at having left my California in order to come to my country."[4] He looked for peace and found only confusion. Moreover, the government had exclaustrated all religious orders so that there was no longer any Franciscan home to which he could go. Religious either had to become diocesan priests or go to live privately in some home. Peyrí expressed his desire to return to California, for he was an exile in his homeland. The Mexican government had given him permission to return, but his passport was good only for two years. His doctors, however, forbade him to travel, for he was sixty-five years of age and ill. Meanwhile he had placed his Indian seminarians in the College of the Propaganda in Rome. Unfortunately both died before reaching the priesthood. There is no record of Peyrí's death or burial. The drawing of Peyrí in Forbes's *California* was said by old Californians to be a good likeness of the padre. Peyrí is the only missionary whose labors and whose monument were described in detail by one of his Indian neophytes, Pablo Tac. Eulalia Pérez remembered Peyrí as of "a good build, stout, light-complected, a Catalán, very amiable and endearing."[5]

[1] "Duhaut-Cilly's Account," p. 226.
[2] Engelhardt, *San Luis Rey Mission*, p. 205. On what basis and from what source Engelhardt made this statement is unknown.
[3] *California: A History of Upper and Lower California* (London, 1839), pp. 229-230.
[4] *San Luis Rey Mission*, p. 84.
[5] Bancroft Library MS.

PIERAS, MIGUEL (1741-1795)

Fray Miguel Pieras was born in 1741 at Palma, Majorca, Spain, and became a Franciscan at the Convento de San Francisco, Palma, February 3, 1757. As a member of the community of San Bernardino, Petra, Majorca, he left for the American missions in 1769. At the time of his departure from Cádiz, he was described in passport records as a person of medium height, with a face that was pockmarked, scant beard, and chestnut-colored hair. He held the office of preacher. With thirty-nine other Franciscans he came to San Fernando College, Mexico City, under Fray Rafael Verger.

In October 1770, he set out for California, sailing from San Blas, January 20, 1771, on the *San Antonio* and arriving at San Diego, March 12. He continued on to Monterey by sea where he arrived on May 21. President Junípero Serra appointed him and his fellow Majorcan, Buenaventura Sitjar, as cofounders of Mission San Antonio, Pieras being in charge. The mission was established, July 14, 1771. Except for brief intervals Pieras served at San Antonio until he left California in 1794. He officiated at Mission San Carlos, Carmel, at various times between September 1772 and June 1788, at Mission San Luis Obispo between August 1773 and November 1793, and at Santa Clara on August 21, 1785. His last baptism at San Antonio was on April 27, 1794.

By the end of 1793, 2,021 Indians had been baptized at San Antonio, and 1,142 were living at the mission. The cattle numbered 1,300 head, the sheep 1,554. Pieras selected the present site of the mission, which lies half a league or so farther north from the original site. The roof of the church was the first one in California to be covered with tile. On December 8, 1781, Serra wrote: "Thus far San Antonio conquers and more so with its roofing of tiles."[1]

Owing to recurrent illness in 1793, Pieras asked permission to retire to the college, which was granted on December 24. The governor gave his permission on May 28, 1794. Pieras probably boarded the *Concepción* at Monterey and stopped at Santa Barbara where he baptized on July 16 and August 14 and at San Diego, September 17 and 19. Sailing for Mexico, again on the *Concepción,* he eventually arrived at the college on December 21. By Tomás de Pangua, the guardian, Pieras was called a religious of "irreprehensible life" and the viceroy was informed that he had labored with "indefatigable zeal." Pieras died at the college, April 14, 1795.

[1] Junípero Serra Section in SBMA.

PRESTAMERO, JUAN (1736-?)

Fray Juan Prestamero was born in 1736 at Labastida, in the archdiocese of Calahorra, Spain, and became a Franciscan at the Convento de San Francisco in Vitoria, June 29, 1751, where he became a fellow novice with Fermín Francisco de Lasuén. He had been ordained a deacon by July 15, 1758. At the time of his recruitment for San Fernando College, he was a member of the friary of San Francisco de Ebro. He sailed from Cádiz on *El Jasón,* September 5, 1759. He was described in passport records as of good stature, light-complexioned, with a heavy beard, dark, sleek hair, dark eyes, and with the scar of a wound above the right eyebrow.

Having entered the college probably in 1759, he was ordained a priest there sometime before March 16, 1760. On January 4, 1764, because of illness and consequent inability to follow the strict religious life of the college, he asked permission to return to Spain. He had served in the Sierra Gorda missions for a period, his name appearing in the registers of Tancoyol for June 10, 1763.

On June 26, 1769, he was in Madrid asking to return to the college and to serve in the California missions. He stated that he had made a mistake in returning to Spain, his decision having been based on apprehension and melancholy. Permission was given him to return to the Indies on July 24. Again he sailed from Cádiz under Fray Rafael Verger as commissary. At the college he was commissioned to serve first in Lower California and was made superior of the group sent out in October 1770. In February 1771, he sailed from San Blas on the *San Carlos* with nineteen other missionaries. A storm blew the ship south to Manzanillo, and the friars were forced to travel overland up the coast to Tamasula in Sinaloa where the *Concepción* took them aboard. They arrived at Loreto on November 24, 1771.

President Francisco Palóu assigned Prestamero together with Tomás de la Peña and Vicente Imas to Misión San José del Comundú. When the Franciscans handed over the missions of Lower California to the Dominicans in 1773, Prestamero was one of the eight destined for service in Upper California. With Palóu and four others he left San Fernando de Velicatá, August 3, 1773, and arrived at San Diego, August 30. Again with Palóu he continued north as far as Mission San Luis Obispo, arriving on October 25. There, Palóu stationed him as a supernumerary. However, it was not long before he started to suffer from severe stomach trouble. When Junípero Serra returned from Mexico in 1774, he gave Prestamero permission to return to San Fernando College. He remained at San Luis Obispo until July 1774, then went to Mission San Carlos, Carmel, embarked on the *San Antonio,* July 7, and stopping at San Diego, he left there on August 4. At San Fernando College he asked for disaffiliation because of ill health, May 4, 1775. He petitioned for permission to join the province of Jalisco.

PUJOL, FRANCISCO (1762-1801)

Fray Francisco Pujol, son of Juan Pujol y Soulie and Josefa Pujol y Derans, was baptized at Alos, diocese of Urgel, Spain, March 7, 1762, and became a Franciscan, February 13, 1787. He left Spain for Mexico but did not reach San Fernando College until August 19, 1793, owing to the war between Spain and France. He fell into enemy hands while en route and during this period suffered "terrible imprisonments." At San Fernando College he went out on a mission tour among the faithful, though the locale is unknown.

Pujol arrived at San Francisco on the *Concepción,* April 14, 1797, and arrived at Carmel on the twenty-eighth. He served at Mission San Carlos from 1797 till 1800. He assisted at Mission San Antonio from December 27, 1800, until January 17, 1801, when he went to Mission San Miguel where several of the missionaries of that mission and of

San Antonio were ill. He himself became ill and was brought back to San Antonio on February 27 and died, March 15, 1801. He had baptized at Mission San Juan Bautista, March 14, 1798.

Bancroft states:

Here [at San Miguel] he [Pujol] was attacked with the same malady that had prostrated the others, and was brought back suffering terribly to San Antonio. . . . His death was witnessed by Ciprés, Sitjar, and Merelo, by Sergt. Roca, Cadet Fernando Toba and Surgeon Morelos. It was intended to make a post-mortem examination but the body was in such condition that it was not practicable. There seems to have been no doubt in the minds of the people that his death was the result of poisoning by the Indians. His body was buried . . . with military honors, rarely accorded in the case of a simple missionary; but it is not unlikely that he was the company chaplain at Monterey. On June 14, 1813, Pujol's body was transferred with that of Sitjar to a grave in the presbytery of the new church at San Antonio on the gospel side. He was generally regarded as a martyr, or a victim to his own zeal and enthusiasm for missionary duty. . . . According to the last authority ["Monterey, Diario"] an examination was made and the intestines found to be black and putrid.[1]

President Fermín Francisco de Lasuén on March 30, 1801, wrote to the guardian of San Fernando, José Gasol, that Pujol died at 8:00 in the morning, March 15, 1801, having received all the sacraments. He had suffered terrible pains, convulsions, and spasms, all of which he endured with great patience. The surgeon, Juan Morelos, held an autopsy at three o'clock in the afternoon and found that all his interior was decomposed and gangrened. The news was published that without doubt the missionary was poisoned.

Concerning the untimely death and its peculiar circumstances, Engelhardt wrote:

While active there [at Mission San Carlos] with Father José Viñals, end of December, 1800, the missionaries of San Miguel, Fathers Baltasar Carnicer and Juan Martín, and Father Marcelino Cipres of San Antonio visiting there suddenly fell gravely ill. Father Pujol volunteered to serve at Mission San Miguel during their illness which was attributed to poisoning at the hands of some malevolent Indians. His offer was accepted by Father Presidente Lasuén, who was distressed for having no Father to send there. Father Pujol hastened to San Antonio taking nothing along but his habit. He reached there on December 27th, and nursed Father Carnicer back to health till January 17, 1801. Thereupon he hurried to succor the two Fathers at San Miguel and nursed them back to comparative health; but he himself became the victim of his charity. He contracted the same malady, but with greater violence. His companion, Father Pedro Martinez also fell sick, but recovered. Father Pujol suffered excruciating pains in the intestines. In order to relieve him, Father Cipres had him taken to Mission San Antonio, leaving alone Father Pedro Martinez at San Miguel, who was now in good health. Father Pujol arrived at San Antonio on February 27, 1801, just two months after he had hastened to San Miguel. Fathers Sitjar and Cipres saw, however, that the malady had become acute, and therefore they administered the Holy Viaticum.[2]

Friar Lorenzo Merelo, who on account of ill health had been permitted to go from San Francisco to San Antonio, wrote the following account: "I was for a time at Mission San Carlos, and this news which we received on February 27 made it necessary for me to return to this Mission of San Antonio, although I had not yet recovered from an attack which prevented me from returning earlier." Merelo came to San Antonio, March 5. Pujol appeared not to be as ill as was feared but his malady was aggravated, and on March 12, "the force of the fever drove him unconscious nor did he recover consciousness, convulsions and horrible spasms shaking the body all over with pains, especially in the intestines which caused him to cry out aloud."[3]

Merelo testified that the autopsy took place that afternoon in the presence of witnesses to determine, if possible, if poison was the cause of death. "They could only verify that the inside was entirely rotten and gangrened, for the stench that came out left no room for more investigation. When this operation had been done the body was shrouded."[4] The remains were buried in the sanctuary of the mission on the Gospel side between the main altar and the wall of the church. Burial took place at ten o'clock the next morning.

New evidence obtained in recent years from a letter of Lasuén to Fray José Gasol explains the illness of Friars Martín, Ciprés, and Isidro Barcenilla. The poisoning of the three missionaries at San Miguel was not caused by the Indians but rather because of the fact that they had drunk some mescal from a copper container lined with tin. Is it possible that Pujol, like the other missionaries, was ignorant of the cause of their poisoning and had also drunk the same substance?

[1] *History of California*, II, 147, n. 54.
[2] Engelhardt, *San Antonio . . . Mission*, p. 105.
[3] Ibid., pp. 105-106.
[4] Ibid., p. 106.

QUIJAS, JOSÉ LORENZO DE LA CONCEPCIÓN (?-?)

Bancroft states that Fray José Lorenzo de la Concepción Quijas was an Indian, probably a native of Ecuador, who had been a muleteer and trader before becoming a friar in Mexico. The Franciscan records there show that Quijas made his profession at the college of Guadalupe, Zacatecas, January 12, 1830, that he was presented to the discretory as a candidate for the priesthood, November 12, 1831, and that he was ordained by the Most Rev. José Antonio Zuburía, bishop of Durango, in the parish of Sombrerete, December 4, 1831. He was assigned to the California missions, February 16, 1832.

Quijas was one of the group of Zacatecans who came to California with

Fray Francisco García Diego y Moreno in 1833 to take over the northern missions from the Fernandinos. He arrived at Monterey, January 15, 1833, in the company of Governor José Figueroa. Quijas was assigned to Mission San Francisco where he remained until the following year; then he was stationed at Mission San Francisco Solano at Sonoma and San Rafael until 1843 and finally at Mission San Jose until 1844. He also baptized at times at Mission Santa Clara in 1835 and 1843.

Together with Fray Bernardino Pérez he was sent to San Rafael by García Diego y Moreno in 1833 to investigate the charges made against Fray Rafael Moreno that he had unjustly provoked an attack against peaceful Indians with the result that a number of them had been killed and injured. The investigation proved that Moreno was innocent.

On April 8, 1843, the college of Guadalupe appointed Fray José Antonio Anzar president of the Zacatecan missions and Quijas as vice-commissary prefect. On October 15, Quijas notified Bishop García Diego y Moreno of his appointment, at which the bishop registered surprise. He asked Quijas not to exercise his powers and added that if he did, his actions would be null and void. Quijas answered that if he did not act according to his powers, granted by his legitimate superiors, he would be considered insubordinate. The friar held that until the bishop formally accepted the missions as parish churches and appointed curates to administer them, his powers as vice-commissary prefect remained. The bishop complained to the discretory of the college, where a meeting was held to consider the matter, July 2, 1844.

Quijas issued a circular letter to the friars of his jurisdiction stating that he was soon leaving for Mexico, the purpose of which journey was to lay the matter of the dispute before his superiors and that, meanwhile, the friars were not to show the bishop the official books of the missions should the bishop appear at them on a canonical visitation. The bishop had written to Quijas that he had received instructions from Rome as to the manner in which the diocese was to be governed and that he had shown these instructions to Narciso Durán at Santa Barbara, who was the commissary prefect of the Fernandinos and who had agreed not to do anything without consulting the bishop.

After Quijas left California, the bishop asked Governor Figueroa to prevent the friar from entering any California port should he attempt to return. He also ordered the friars not to allow him to function as a priest should he appear at any of the missions. Meanwhile, the discretory of the college rejected the claims of the bishop and sent them to Fray Rafael Soría, the commissary prefect, stating that the matter should have been referred to him in the first place as the proper channel of communications. Quijas remained in Mexico.

On April 15, 1846, Quijas asked for and obtained disaffiliation from his college and passed over to the province of San Diego, whose headquarters were in Mexico City, February 22, 1847. On January 4, 1847, however, he had asked for reinstatement in his college, but his request was unanimously denied. He was later accepted as a member of the college of Zapopan, and when he again applied for affiliation into Zacatecas, September 9, 1849, his request was denied a second time.

There remains to be considered Quijas' character and reputation in California. Bancroft states:

> He was a large, fine-looking man, of more than ordinary natural abilities and education; kind-hearted and popular when sober; but from about 1836 he gave himself up to strong drink. He made no enemies, and all speak well of his natural abilities, but all testify to his drunkenness, and fondness for dancing and debauchery. Peirce, Simpson, Phelps, and other foreign visitors were witnesses of his drunken pranks, as well as many Californians.
> Unfortunately Quijas and two or three other black sheep of the Zacatecan flock were so situated as to come much in contact with foreigners, and this fact did much to discredit all the friars in the opinion of the immigrants. Dr. Sandels found him in 1834 a reformed man at S. José, and the same year came his appointment as vice-president [should read vice-commissary prefect]; but we have no means of knowing how long his reformation lasted, as he disappears from the record in April 1844, nothing being known of the circumstances of his departure. Charles Brown claimed to have met him in Mexico in 1857, when he was curate at Ometepec.[1]

Af Sandels, to whom Bancroft refers, had this to say: "The Mission of San Jose was still in a tolerable state of economy. A couple hundred Indians were still there.... Padre Liges [sic!] had then the management of the Mission. He was brought up in rural pursuits, and was a powerful, active man, although, in the depressed and despised state in which the friars had been kept for some years he had taken to drink. But he was now himself again, returned to active life and honor."[2]

William Heath Davis who visited Quijas in San Francisco in 1833 wrote: "I visited the Mission Dolores frequently during our stay in port here, was always kindly received by the Padre, and drank as fine red wine as I ever have since, manufactured ... from grapes brought from the Missions of Santa Clara and San Jose."[3]

Sir George Simpson described Quijas in 1842 as follows: "Father Quijas is one of those jovial souls who show that, in the New World as in the Old, power and wealth are more than a match for monastic austerities; nor has the removal of the corrupting influences rendered his reverence a more rigid observer of his vows, excepting always (thanks to Murphy and Vallejo) the single article of poverty."[4]

Henry A. Peirce recalls in his journal, December 5, 1841, that he met Quijas (he spelled the name Kijos) at Mission San Rafael where he found the padre "quite drunk," though he gave him an "affectionate" embrace after the Spanish manner. In a conversation he "continued to rave like a mad man" and accused the Reed family of not showing him the proper respect. He pulled a penknife on Mr. Reed, threatening him, but Reed merely remonstrated with him gently. On cooling down, Quijas burst into tears, gave Reed the knife and asked him to plunge it into his breast, for he deserved the punishment. Reed paid no attention but went away. It was in the course of the evening that Quijas told Peirce that he had been born in Quito of Indian parents, that he had been a muleteer and merchant before becoming a priest. He boasted of his Indian heritage, abused the Spaniards, and complained of the government of California. "The priest possessed fine features, [was] highly intellectual and bore the character of a learned man. His knowledge of the Indian languages of California was said to be very extensive. His private character in point of chastity and temperance is of the worst kind."[5]

José Arnaz in his "Recuerdos" relates that when the Russian ship *Petr* under Kostromitinov visited San Francisco in 1840, a dance was held aboard. Quijas participated in it, changing clothes with Arnaz, the latter putting on Quijas' *levita* while the padre wore the clothes of Arnaz. Both danced the quadrille "while the girls slit their sides with laughter." The "Recuerdos" gives this sketch of the friar: "Quijas who was a very good friend of mine told me once that he had been a muleteer in Mexico — I do not know why he told me this — and that he abandoned that way of life and became a friar. He was a man of very liberal outlook."[6]

Faxon Dean Atherton in his diary states that he met Quijas at Mission San Jose and notes that the padre had been a muleteer, then a soldier. He reports further Juan Bautista Alvarado's statement that Quijas "was outstanding in oratorical and high-sounding phrases" but "was a malignant person, perhaps outstandingly evil, but he was not a fool. Religion to him . . . was nothing more than a Sunday thing."[7]

[1] *History of California*, IV, 681, n. 18.

[2] G. M. Waseurtz af Sandels, *A Sojourn in California by the King's Orphan* (San Francisco, 1945), p. 77.

[3] *Sixty Years in California*, p. 9.

[4] Thomas C. Russell, ed. *Narrative of a Voyage to California Ports in 1841-42* (San Francisco, 1930), p. 57.

[5] Bancroft Library MS.

[6] Bancroft Library MS.

[7] Doyce B. Nunis, Jr., ed. *The California Diary* (San Francisco, 1964), p. 163, n. 27.

QUINTANA, ANDRÉS (1777-1812)

Fray Andrés Quintana was born on November 27, 1777, at Antonorra, in the diocese of Calahorra, province of Alava, Spain, and was baptized on the thirtieth by the Rev. Andrés Ochoa de Alda in the church of San Vicente Martir. He was the son of Ramón de Quintana and Josefa Ruiz de Alda. His paternal grandparents were Jacinto de Quintana and Teresa Pérez de Arenaza; his maternal grandparents, Antonio Ruiz de Alda and María Martínez de Laydalga. He entered the Franciscan order at the age of seventeen and had finished his studies for the priesthood in the province of Cantabria by 1804. Shortly after April 26 of that year, he sailed from Cádiz for Mexico and was described in passport records as of regular stature, of florid complexion, with dark hair, blue eyes, and thick eyebrows.

Having entered San Fernando College, Mexico City, he volunteered for the California missions, leaving the college in January 1805. He sailed from San Blas, June 2 and arrived at Monterey, August 31, the same year. In California he served at a single mission, Santa Cruz, from 1805 until his tragic death on October 12, 1812. On that morning he was found dead in bed and was buried on the following day. The only other mission where Quintana baptized was at San Juan Bautista, September 6, 1805, and in June and July 1800.

Quintana had been ill and had gone to Monterey for treatment when his companion at Mission Santa Cruz, Marcelino Marquínez, also became ill during his absence. Quintana then returned to the mission even before he was quite well himself. A superficial investigation after his death satisfied those at the mission that death was due to natural causes and that there had been no violence. However, Lieutenant José María Estudillo, on orders from Governor Pablo Solá, wrote to Marquínez that it was indispensable that the surgeon, Don Manuel Quijano, examine the remains, for his death appeared suspicious to the civil authorities. Marquínez was asked to give access to Quintana's sepulcher. The surgeon made his investigation during the following week and arrived at the conclusion that no violence had occurred and that the padre, who had been ill and unable to dress himself without aid, had died a natural death.

About two years later, however, great suspicion was aroused when some Indians of the mission were overheard, speaking about the manner of Quintana's death. Eight were arrested and questioned. The Indians acknowledged their guilt and gave as their motive for killing the missionary, Quintana's cruelty. They alleged that he had had the Indians beaten, and in one instance, two were so mistreated, they almost died. In order to take revenge they had recourse to strategem.

During the night they feigned a sick call. Quintana was described as a powerful man hence the Indians did not dare attack him during the day. The missionary answered their call, but instead of asking one of the guards to accompany him as he was required to do, he went alone. When

204

he was safely away from the mission area, the Indians attacked him and "dispatched him in a most revolting and diabolical manner." President Estevan Tapis stated that it would be indecent to describe the manner in which he was killed. After the padre was dead, the Indians brought him back to the mission and laid him in his bed so as to make his death appear a natural one.

On October 2, 1814, writing to Fray Norberto de Santiago from Mission San José, Fray Narciso Durán declared: "I believe Your Reverence has already been apprized concerning the horrible assassination of the deceased Father, Andrés Quintana, minister of the Mission of Santa Cruz during the night of October 11-12, in 1812, going to hear a confession in the garden. Those of the house murdered him in so barbarous a manner that I doubt if such cruelty has ever been resorted to in the most barbarous nations for they tortured him *in pudendis* and suffocated him at the same time with the cloths used in administering extreme unction. All those guilty are now prisoners."[1]

Governor Solá was extremely interested in the case and conducted a careful investigation both with regard to the methods of punishment of Indians at the missions and with regard to the character of Quintana. The resulting evidence showed that punishment with the lash was considered light (usually twelve to fifteen strokes from a lash made of two ropes) in dealing with transgressors against chastity and theft, which "whipping is more adapted to children of six years than to men, most of whom received it without an exclamation of pain."[2]

Concerning the character of Quintana, the governor reported:

[From] the conduct of the late Fr. Andrés Quintana, I have learned that he was a very pious missionary, and that while seriously ill himself his complying with the duties of his ministry was rather the cause of his premature death. . . . I also know that this good Father went to excess, not in punishing his Indians but in the love with which he ever regarded them. He strained all his faculties as far as zeal and industry carried him in order to improve and advance them. He distinguished himself among many for the solicitude and tenderness of his paternal care to relieve his neophytes of whatever savored of troublesome vexation. For this he would not hesitate to sacrifice his own tranquility. It may even be said that this good disposition of mind, or call it zeal peculiar to his ministry, was consuming him internally, as is very well known here.[3]

Solá was happy to state that not only the good reputation of Quintana but of the other missionaries of the province was vindicated by his investigations. Vicente Francisco de Sarría, the commissary prefect, on April 3, 1816, answered this letter of Solá stating that it appeared to him "good and satisfactory" and added that "you describe well the distinctive characteristics of said Fr. Quintana in what you say about him."[4]

Solá referred the case to the viceroy. Five of the criminals were sentenced to receive two hundred lashes each and were made to work in chains for from two to ten years. The others involved, died, meanwhile, in prison.

Despite this careful examination made by Solá and the vindication of Quintana by his contemporaries, Sir George Simpson as late as 1842 in his *Narrative* blackened Quintana's character in the following paragraph:

In 1823 [sic!] one Quintana, then a priest of Santa Cruz, forgot one of his vows in the society of a certain squaw, who, through penitence, or indignation, or vanity, or some other motive, let her husband into the secret of her conquest. After watching his opportunity, the man at length succeeded in mutilating the lover in the most brutal manner, leaving him insensible, but was himself dragged to the calabozo, whence, according to common rumor, he was soon afterwards carried off by the Devil for his impiety. Quintana, on the contrary, died with the fame of a martyr, for a long time elapsed before the truth was known through the confessions of a woman who had been privy to the injured savage's fatal revenge."[5]

Here no doubt Simpson is voicing a popular rumor over thirty years after the event. With an unfavorable opinion of more than one padre's unclerical behavior at the time of his visit, he could be easily led to believe a similar situation existed in an earlier period. The Indians of the earlier period, however, did not allege immorality but cruelty.

The case of Quintana leaves certain other questions unanswered, however. If the missionary was murdered in a way that was "revolting" and "indecent" even to describe, how is it that not even upon a careful examination of the remains there were to be found no bruises nor traces of blood or mutilation? The guard situation at the mission must, moreover, have been deplorable. Mission gates were locked at night, and a guard was required always to be on the *qui vive*. It is difficult to understand how one or several Indians could enter the mission compound, rouse the padre, take him to a village, murder him, bring him back dead and mutilated, place him in bed, and make it appear as if he had merely died in his sleep, and then return home quietly and safely. Was there a guard on duty at all? Quintana disobeyed regulations or at least ignored custom in not having at least one soldier guard accompany him outside the mission. Yet, if he did this, he showed the innate kindness credited to him in not wishing to disturb anyone, even a guard. Was he so kind and naïve as to trust the Indians? Naïveté is possible. Luís Jayme at San Diego had shown a similar but fateful trustfulness.

[1] Private collection, Santa Barbara.

[2] Engelhardt, *Missions and Missionaries*, III, 14.

[3] Ibid., 14-15.

[4] Ibid., 15-16.

[5] Thomas C. Russell, ed. *Narrative of a Voyage to California Ports in 1841-42* (San Francisco, 1930), pp. 105-106.

RIPOLL, ANTONIO (1785-?)

Fray Antonio Ripoll was born on March 27, 1785, at Palma, Majorca, Spain, and became a Franciscan at the Convento de San Francisco, Palma, September 19, 1799. He sailed from Cádiz shortly after March 29, 1810, on the *Neptuno* and reached San Fernando College, Mexico City, in July 1810. In July, the following year, he was sent to the California missions, but since the roads were infested with insurgents he was delayed in reaching his destination. He did not arrive in Lower California until April 1812, and presumably from Loreto he reached San Diego overland on July 7.

Ripoll's first assignment was at Mission Purisima where he baptized between September 14, 1812, and May 1, 1815. He was then transferred to Mission Santa Barbara where he officiated between June 14, 1815, and January 23, 1828. Ripoll baptized at Santa Ines in 1815 and 1822 and at San Miguel in 1824. At Santa Barbara he was responsible for building the present stone church, which took five years to construct, between 1815 and 1820, and which was solemnly dedicated on September 10 in the latter year.

During the Bouchard invasion of 1818 Ripoll trained a company of local Indians prepared to fight the enemy. These he called *Compañia de Urbanistas Realistas*. Ripoll accompanied the white population of Santa Barbara to Mission Santa Ines when the invader threatened, but Santa Barbara was left unmolested. Ripoll was at Santa Barbara when the Chumash revolt took place in 1824, which had originated at Santa Ines. On this occasion the Santa Barbara Indians fled over the mountains into the San Joaquin Valley. Ripoll accompanied the commissary prefect, Vicente Francisco de Sarría, and a military expedition thither to bring them back. His account of the event, Bancroft states, is the best document on the subject.

When there was talk of handing over some of the missions to the college of Orizaba, among them Santa Barbara, Ripoll, on January 1, 1819, wrote to the guardian of San Fernando College that he would be willing to join that of Orizaba in order to remain working at Santa Barbara, since he had a knowledge of the Chumash language. Concerning Mariano Payeras and Ripoll, Engelhardt wrote that both were unusually capable men, and in zeal for the spiritual welfare of the Indians, they were not surpassed by any of the friars. Angustias de la Guerra y Ord, who in her youth knew Ripoll, stated in her memoirs: "Padre Ripoll loved his neophytes as a devoted mother."[1]

Sarría wrote of him in 1817: "After [Purisima] he entered the service at Santa Barbara in whose ministry and its immediate presidio he is occupied, his diligent and zealous activity merits some commendation in the discharge of his duties and obligations." In 1820 Payeras declared:

"His merit is above the ordinary and in proportion I consider also his aptitude for the ministry among the faithful and the pagans, and no less for one or the other commission of office [in the order]."

Fearing that he would be exiled from California because of the Mexican law of 1827 banishing all Spaniards, Ripoll with José Altimira of San Buenaventura secretly left Santa Barbara on January 23, 1828, on the *Harbinger* under Captain Joseph Steele and eventually returned to Spain. In 1832, according to Bancroft, he was living at Palma and was in good health. What happened to him after the secularization of religious houses in his homeland in 1834 is not known.

The flight of the two padres right under the nose of Governor José María Echeandía, who at the time was in Santa Barbara, caused consternation. The runaways were accused of taking large sums of money with them. While Angustias de la Guerra y Ord states that "they carried no money or supplies for the voyage," a better explanation is given by Auguste Duhaut-Cilly on his return to Santa Barbara in 1828:

> This circumstance [of Ripoll's leaving] made clear to me why, at my former stop here [in 1827], Fray Antonio, knowing I was the bearer of a draft for seven thousand franks on the English government, begged me earnestly to give it to him for piasters, an offer which I accepted. He had undoubtedly already conceived the plan of leaving California. On buying from me this bill of exchange, he had declared to me that this money belonged to him, and that it came from the stipends of four hundred piasters a year granted to each missionary by the Spanish government. I had too high an opinion of this religious to believe it otherwise; but when some persons told me that, on leaving, he had carried away large sums, I did not give credit to these injurious assertions.[2]

[1] Price and Ellison, tr. *Occurrences in Hispanic California*, p. 9.
[2] Carter, "Duhaut-Cilly's Account of California," p. 328.

RODRÍGUEZ, ANTONIO CATARINO (1777-1824)

Fray Antonio Catarino Rodríguez was born in 1777 at San Luís Potosí, Mexico, and became a Franciscan at the Convento de San Francisco, San Luís Potosí, in the province of Zacatecas, January 1, 1794. In course of time, he held the offices of preacher, professor of moral theology, vicar of the convent, and master of novices. He entered San Fernando College, Mexico City, August 15, 1808, and came to California in the following year, disembarking at Monterey on June 22.

In the register of Franciscan missionaries who came to the port of Santa María near Cádiz between 1803 and 1868 there is mention of a Fray Antonio Rodríguez, who arrived there, March 22, 1805. According to the register he was a son of the province of Mexico and had come there as chaplain of the merchant ship, *San Miguel,* which the English had captured on the previous February 16. The records state that Rodríguez had returned to the Indies. Whether this Rodríguez was the subject of our biography is uncertain, since both Antonio and Rodríguez are very common names. The "province of Mexico" would also have been that of Santo Evangelio. Our Rodríguez belonged to the province of Zacatecas. However, the two provinces may have easily been confused, or the record may have referred to Mexico in general.

Rodríguez was first sent to Mission Santa Cruz where he baptized between August 18, 1809, and November 19, 1811, exercising the same function at San Juan Bautista on November 12 and 18, 1809, and at San Francisco, August 19, 1811. He was next assigned to Mission San Luis Obispo where he baptized from February 12, 1812, to April 13, 1821, and then at Mission Purisima from March 2, 1821, to September 20, 1824. He was sent to San Luis Obispo a second time, and there he died, November 25, 1824, at 2:00 in the morning, having received the sacraments. He was buried in the church near the sanctuary by Luís Antonio Martínez.

Rodríguez experienced trying days during the Chumash revolt in 1824 at Purisima at a time when he was already infirm. Bancroft states: "He was taken by the rebel neophytes and kept for some weeks a prisoner; but was treated with great respect, and worked faithfully for the interests of his flock at the time of their surrender." Furthermore, according to Bancroft: "His virtues and kindness of disposition caused him to be well liked by the Indians."[1] At the time, Rodríguez was very corpulent, with prominent eyes and a large face.

In 1817 Vicente Francisco de Sarría, the commissary prefect, evaluated Rodríguez as follows:

If I must say the truth, . . . I cannot determine the merit of this father with regard to the disposition or special qualifications which I recognize in a missionary. Moreover, I well understand, and must assure, that he could display some brightness in the pulpit of the respectable communities of the kingdom, which does not include the simple functions of a missionary and the mechanisms of their hardships. Nevertheless I shall not take from him the merit of having been a missionary. . . . It is not little that he has adapted himself to either in what pertains to the mere administration of the sacraments, in preaching the word of God to the *gente de razón* also; and though it were no more than to be an associate to his companion, and to care for the vehicles and shops, all of which he did, and is doing, in addition to whatever has been indicated about the father on whom this report is made.

Evidently, while there was nothing against Rodríguez as a man and a priest, he seemed somewhat miscast in the role of a complete missionary.

Mariano Payeras in 1820 could say something more favorable of him. "His worth is from mediocre to a higher degree and his aptitude for our ministry is complete and for the offices that are similar to those he exercised in his mother province." Fray Luís Antonio Martínez, who was his superior at San Luis Obispo and one of the best missionary administrators in the territory, wrote in the death record that Rodríguez had been "energetic in the apostolic work to instruct and to care for the neophytes that were entrusted to him."[2] Rodríguez accompanied Sarría in 1818 and Payeras in 1821 to Mission Purisima as secretary when they made their canonical visitations.

Angustias de la Guerra y Ord wrote that Rodríguez was "a man of ordinary size, but very gray and with a large face. He had large eyes. He was most agreeable with everyone, and his manners were very good."[3]

[1] *History of California*, II, 580-581, n. 48.
[2] Burial Register, Mission San Luis Obispo.
[3] Price and Ellison, tr. *Occurrences of Hispanic California*, p. 34.

RUBÍ, MARIANO (1756-?)

Fray Mariano Rubí, the son of Mateo Rubí and Margarita Durán, was born on March 26, 1756, at Lluchmayor, Majorca, Spain, and was baptized by the Rev. Julio Salvá and was given the name Mateo. Rubí was confirmed by the Most Rev. Llorens Despuig y Cotoner. He became a Franciscan at the Convento de San Francisco, Palma, and made his profession on March 26, 1772. In 1786 he held the titles of preacher and professor and at the time was described as of regular stature, light-complexioned, with large blue eyes, dark hair, and heavy beard. He sailed for Vera Cruz, Mexico, about September 1786.

Rubí's advent to the New World brought him only unhappiness and frustration to his superiors in Church and State. According to the guardian of San Fernando College, Tomás de Pangua, Rubí joined another malcontent, Bartolomé Gilí, and the two caused considerable consternation in the community. Rubí regretted having come to America, manifested disgust for the regular observance of religious life and repugnance for the customs of the college. No doubt the superiors of San Fernando would have been glad to send him back to Spain. But they were not free to do so, for Rubí had come to Mexico at the king's expense and was expected to serve the college for ten years, regardless of the damage he would cause to religion by his presence in an area he loathed.

As early as April 28, 1788, Rubí petitioned the viceroy to be transferred to the missions of Tampico, then governed by the province of the Holy Gospel. On June 30 the same year he wrote to the viceroy again stating that, owing to headaches and stomach trouble, he could not follow the regular life as lived at San Fernando, especially the choir and meditation from midnight until 2:15 in the morning. Nor could he fulfill the office of frequently preaching to the people. He asked for permission to join some province. This petition was sent back to the discretory, which also refused to act on it.

The discretory replied that Rubí was healthy enough to perform the duties required of him. He appeared in the refectory of the infirmary only for the noon-day meal, for afternoon lemonade, and for supper. He used to stay out at night, "a thing unheard of at San Fernando." Nor did he apply the Mass intention, according to the mind of the guardian. To the discretory Rubí's professed inability to preach or hear confessions was not borne out by fact. When he was sent out to give missions, he did well. But as soon as he came home, he became "ill." The superiors tried to bring him around to conformity but without success.

Unfortunately in 1790 the viceroy ordered that both Rubí and Gilí be sent to California, which the superiors did reluctantly. Rubí arrived at Monterey, August 2, 1790, and was stationed at Mission San Antonio where he baptized between November 29, 1790, and July 12, 1791. Shortly after Mission Soledad was established, October 9, 1791, he was sent there as an associate to Diego García. There were dissensions and disagreements between the two. On one occasion García had to call the corporal of the guard to restrain Rubí, for he feared that the latter might lay violent hands on him. García notified President Fermín Francisco de Lasuén that Rubí carried side arms on his person. Rubí continued to baptize at Soledad from February 12, to August 19, 1792.

Toward the end of the year Rubí went to Monterey to receive treatments from the presidio physician because of various ailments. Lasuén considered him to be seriously ill. On January 10, 1793, Dr. Pablo Soler declared that Rubí needed protracted treatment and that his condition would only deteriorate if he remained in California. The president notified the guardian of San Fernando College that Rubí was sick and incapable of giving any service, and Governor José Joaquín Arrillaga permitted him to return to Mexico. Rubí left Monterey early in the year, sailing on the *Aránzazu*, and was at San Blas February 6.

In October 1793 and again in February 1794, the guardian of the college wrote to Lasuén for a detailed report on Rubí's conduct and excesses as well as for an official certificate on the nature of his illness which, states Bancroft, was doubtless venereal. The guardian declared that Rubí was to be expelled for the honor of the college. The guardian stated, September 13, 1793, that Rubí had returned from California with the disease commonly called *morbo gálico* and that he had been treated by doctors at San Fernando for two months. They suggested application of mercurial unction, for which the infirmary of San Francisco, Mexico City, was better adapted. When this was done, Rubí then returned to San Fernando. On September 10, 1793, Licenciado Manuel Moreno certified that the nature of Rubí's illness was a matter of doubt, since both the *escorbuto* (scurvy) and the *gálico* (syphilis) had the same symptoms. However, he treated him for both. When Rubí once more applied to the viceroy in 1794 for permission to go to the missions of Tampico, the petition was refused. The council of the college also gave him a negative answer.

The end of Rubí's life story is not known. It is clear that he was in need of psychiatric aid. It is just as clear that government interference in the religious realm for financial reasons and for legal requirements did a disservice to religion in general and to the Franciscan order in particular.

SAINZ DE LUCIO, JUAN (1771-?)

Fray Juan Sainz de Lucio was born in 1771 at Guadareya, archdiocese of Burgos, Spain, and entered the Franciscan order, probably in the province of Cantabria. He left Cádiz as superior of eight other friars shortly after June 20, 1803, on the *San Miguel* or *Sagrada Familia* and arrived at Vera Cruz, Mexico, in August of the same year. He held the offices of preacher and confessor and was described as a man of regular height, white-complexioned, with hazel-colored hair, blue eyes, and with a dimple on his chin.

After having spent three years at San Fernando College, Mexico City, he sailed for California and arrived at Monterey, June 6, 1806. There he was assigned to Mission San Francisco, where he baptized from October 1, 1806, to January 13, 1816, meanwhile serving for a short time (July to September 2, 1808) at Mission San Juan Bautista. He was back at San Juan Bautista as a supernumerary toward the close of his California career when he had become ill. His name appears in the registers there only once, March 20, 1816. Soon afterward he went to Mission San Carlos, Carmel, where he baptized from June 24 to November 11, 1816. Though he had already been granted permission by Vicente Francisco de Sarría to leave on November 6, 1815, he did not depart until November 1816. Mariano Payeras on October 1 stated that Sainz de Lucio was very ill. At the college on May 12, 1817, he petitioned for incorporation into the province of Jalisco because of illness. The petition was granted.

SAIZAR DE VITORIA Y ODRIOZOLA,
MARCOS ANTONIO (1760-1836)

Fray Marcos Antonio Vitoria, whose full name was Marcos Antonio Saizar de Vitoria y Odriozola, was born in 1760 at Vitoria, province of Alava, diocese of Calahorra, Spain, the son of Miguel Saizar de Vitoria and María Andrea Odriozola. He became a Franciscan at San Francisco el Grande, Vitoria, in the Franciscan province of Cantabria, September 11, 1776, and was ordained a priest at Zaragosa in 1784. In his province he was stationed at Bilbao, Aránzazu, Piedrola, and in the Recollect friary of Concepción, where he held the position of novice master for ten and a half years. From there he set out for the New World to become an Indian missionary. For four and a half years he was visitor for the Third Order of his province.

Vitoria sailed from Cádiz on approximately June 20, 1803, on the *San Miguel* or *Sagrada Familia,* arrived at Vera Cruz, Mexico, in August, and at San Fernando College, Mexico City, September 9. At this period he was described as of regular height, of a swarthy complexion, pockmarked, with dark hair and eyes and with a mole on the right side of his nose.

He left the college, March 12, 1805, embarked at San Blas, June 2, and arrived at San Francisco, August 31, 1805. In California he was stationed at Mission Santa Barbara, October 20, 1805, to June 30, 1807, at San Buenaventura, July 12, 1807, to October 13, 1817, at San Fernando, December 1817, to April 11, 1820, at San Buenaventura again, 1820 to 1824, at Purisima, December 18, 1824, to June 19, 1835, and finally at Mission Santa Ines until his death, July 25, 1836. He assisted at the dedication of the stone church of Mission San Juan Capistrano, September 7, 1806. He made two visits to Santa Barbara, baptizing there in March 1808 and on August 28, 1824.

With regard to his political affiliations, it is known that at first he agreed to take the oath of loyalty to the Mexican constitution of 1824 but then retracted, limiting his adherence to obedience to the constituted authorities. It appears that his reputation for holiness and virtue was greater than his ability as a missionary. Bancroft says of him: "Padre Vitoria was a most virtuous and exemplary man, always in feeble health, not accredited by his superiors with great ability, but beloved by his neophytes."[1] Angustias de la Guerra y Ord wrote of him that he "was truly an angel — he was child-like."[2]

Vicente Francisco de Sarría in 1817 declared concerning him: "Because of his innocence and candidness, which it appears constitutes his true character, and by the general edification which results from these qualities, his merit should not be placed among the lowest category even though he may not do as much as many others [with regard to missionary labors]. He himself believed that he could not fulfill all the duties of a missionary because of his various infirmities." Once, when close to death, he asked for retirement, but when his superior, Sarría, pointed out that there was no one to replace him, he remained in California and tried to do what he was able.

Mariano Payeras said of him in 1820: "His most revealing merit is his distinguished virtue and happy simplicity, but his aptitude [as a missionary] is mediocre and what aptitude he has is more for work among the faithful." Upon his death, his companions, Felipe Arroyo de la Cuesta and José J. Jimeno, wrote: "In all places he exercised his apostolic ministry with great zeal for souls and with exemplary edification of the neophytes, soldiers, people of the country and foreigners who knew him. He merited for himself the respect, attention, appreciation and the eulogies of everyone, even the enemies of Catholicism on account of his virtues, charity, supreme and continual mortification and religious affability. He is indeed worthy of everlasting memory."[3]

Narciso Durán, on receiving a notification of his death, July 25, 1836, memorialized him in glowing words:

> The Lord has been pleased to take from us the principal column of the seraphic edifice in this California. He has taken from us an angel in the flesh or a man without flesh, the venerable and holy Father, Fray Marcos Antonio de Vitoria, of whose holy, religious and evangelical life, all of us are witnesses. All we are witnesses of that most profound humility and evangelical simplicity and seraphic spirit of religion which so greatly adorned the venerable deceased and with these and all the other virtues proper to a religious, he has adorned so much this California that his memory here will last forever.[4]

Durán questioned whether Vitoria needed the friars' prayers.

These testimonies, unvarying in their praise and made without collusion, point to Vitoria as one of the "saints" of the California conquest yet who, though successful in the domain of Christian virtues, was less useful as a missionary in the performance of the daily mission routine of chores and charges. Having received the last sacraments, he died at Mission Santa Ines, July 25, 1836, and was interred below the sanctuary on the Epistle side close to the communion railing. Ramón Abella, Arroyo de la Cuesta, and J. J. Jimeno were present at his funeral.

[1] *History of California*, V, 764.

[2] Price and Ellison, tr. *Occurrences in Hispanic California*, p. 33.

[3] Engelhardt, *Mission Santa Ines*, p. 108.

[4] Doc. No. 3614, California Mission Section, SBMA.

SALAZAR, ISIDRO ALONSO (ca. 1758-?)

Fray Isidro Alonso Salazar was born in the region of Cantabria, Spain, about 1758, and joined the Franciscan order in the same province. He sailed from Cádiz for Mexico where he joined San Fernando College in 1784. In 1791 he arrived in California. Together with Baldomero López he was one of the first two missionaries to be in charge of Mission Santa Cruz, which was founded by President Lasuén, August 28, 1791. Prior to that Salazar had baptized at San Francisco, August 9.

Salazar served Santa Cruz until 1795. He did not harmonize too well with López, became dissatisfied with California, and told Lasuén so in a "torrent of comments, obscure, confused and extreme." In 1793 he asked to be transferred because of his dislike for temporal administration. This was impossible, for such administration was attached to every mission. Having obtained permission from the viceroy to leave, January 23, 1795, even before fully serving ten years, he left California from San Francisco, September 14, and arrived at San Fernando College, March 22, 1796. In California he had baptized at Santa Clara several times in 1791 and 1794.

In Mexico City the viceroy asked Salazar to give an account of the California missions, which he did in a document entitled "Condición actual de California." He recommended a site between Santa Cruz and San Francisco for the future location of Branciforte. He stated that California was rich in minerals but that they were not being developed for fear of foreigners coming in. He declared also that the pueblos were given preference over the missions in the matter of commercial sales.

Miguel Lull, the guardian, on October 1, 1798, gave Salazar a recommendation to his province in Spain, stating that he had served the college for fourteen years, five of them in California, and that he had given missions to the faithful in the archdiocese of Mexico and in the diocese of Puebla and in Mexico City itself in the years 1786 and 1789. At the college he had been faithful in attending its religious exercises and in regular Franciscan observance. On October 25, 1798, Salazar obtained disaffiliation from the college, and before May 14, 1799, he passed over to the province of Michoacán.

SÁNCHEZ, FRANCISCO (1813-1884)

Fray Francisco Sánchez was born in August 1813 at León, in the state of Guanajuato, Mexico. He studied for the diocesan priesthood and received all the orders including the diaconate from the bishop of Morelia. On deciding to become a Franciscan, Sánchez entered the college of Guadalupe, Zacatecas, in February 1837 and made his profession the following year. He was ordained a priest in 1838 by Bishop Diego Aranda y Carpintero of Guadalajara. In 1840 Sánchez with other missionaries preached a mission in Puebla.

When Bishop Francisco García Diego y Moreno sought recruits for the diocese of Both Californias, Sánchez was among those who volunteered. He sailed with the bishop's entourage on the *Rosalind,* which arrived at San Diego, December 11, 1841, and finally at Santa Barbara, January 11, 1842. Sánchez made his home with the bishop at the mission and was a member there of his seminary staff until May 4, 1844, when the new seminary opened at Mission Santa Ines. At that mission Sánchez was vice-rector and taught philosophy and Latin. He remained there until 1850. Other assignments for this period were: Mission San Buenaventura from May 15, 1842, to February 11, 1843, and again later in 1852 and 1853. From September 30, 1850, to August 15, 1852, he was at Mission San Gabriel. Thereafter, he returned to Mission Santa Barbara.

On April 20, 1854, Sánchez was in San Francisco testifying before the U. S. Land Commission concerning the ownership of the missions and mission lands. Among other things he stated that no deed was necessary to prove the existence of church property and that Mexico respected canon law and the conciliar legislation of the Church.

He became a member of the formal hospice at the mission, beginning with the month of January 1853 and was one of the original members of the College of Our Lady of Sorrows in the town of Santa Barbara in July 1854. Sánchez was novice master and taught Latin. He moved back to the mission in April 1856 with the rest of the college members when, at the request of the new bishop of Monterey, Thaddeus Amat, the college property was exchanged for the mission. His faculties were rescinded as were those of José María de Jesús González Rubio and Antonio Jimeno in 1858, owing to the schism that had arisen in town between the factions favorable to the bishop and to the friars, but were restored in 1861 upon the bishop's return from Europe.

As a member of the apostolic college in Santa Barbara, Sánchez gave many missions among the faithful throughout California. A notable one occurred in 1872 which he described in a document and which took him to Sacramento, Stockton, San Jose, San Francisco, San Quentin Prison, San Rafael, Healdsburg, and other places. In 1874 and 1875 he was stationed at St. Francis Orphanage and at Immaculate Heart parish in the Pajaro Valley near Watsonville.

Archbishop Joseph Alemany of San Francisco declared that while Sánchez was less learned than González Rubio, he was nevertheless a man of virtue and zeal and was greatly esteemed. Engelhardt calls him "an indefatigable missionary," with the whole of California as his field. Many interesting stories concerning his activity and personality, years after his death, survived among the descendants of the people amidst whom he labored. In 1910 when Brother Joseph O'Malley, who had been one of Sánchez' confreres at Santa Barbara, gave testimony on Sánchez' life and activity, he stated that the padre was "a very zealous preacher and missionary. He was impulsive but otherwise a holy man; he never found fault with the eating or drinking."[1] Sánchez was immortalized by Helen Hunt Jackson in her novel *Ramona,* in which he was given the name, Salvierderra.[2]

For a period of ten months before his death, Sánchez could not say

Mass because of a fall. He slept on a bed of rawhide in one of the rooms of the mission at Santa Barbara fronting the corridor. On April 17, 1884, Father Joseph J. O'Keefe found him in the throes of death, and he died in his arms. His remains were placed in the crypt of the church. Together with those of González Rubio, they were removed to a vault in the mission cemetery in 1899. At the time, through the glass covering the upper portion of the coffin, the padre's features were still recognizable.

José María de Jesús Romo, O.F.M., who inscribed his death record into the "Libro de Difuntos" of the College of Our Lady of Sorrows, wrote of him: "His virtues as priest, religious and missionary are well known in California. Most rare was it when he did not celebrate Mass. He was constant in prayer. Daily he went to confession. His poverty was extreme for he never had more with him than his poor habit in conformity with the Franciscan rule, his breviary and a very few books. The journeys he took were always in the apostolic manner without staff and scrip. His love toward poor sinners was such that he not only never sent anyone away unconsoled who came repentant to his feet, but also the most obstinate he sought out and in a thousand ways invited them to do penance. His love toward the Blessed Virgin and his devotion to her, with special emphasis on her sorrows at the foot of the cross, was most fervent, praying to her daily once or twice or more often in reciting the most pious devotion of the Holy Rosary and always the fifteen mysteries. In summary, he was a model in all things and a man of admirable simplicity. The Lord tried him for eight long months with a most painful illness in which he suffered a veritable martyrdom and comforted at various times by the reception of all the sacraments he gave his soul to his Creator placidly on April 1, 1884."[3]

[1] MS in SBMA.
[2] See Davis and Alderson, *True Story of "Ramona,"* passim.
[3] In SBMA.

SÁNCHEZ, JOSÉ BERNARDO (1778-1833)

Fray José Bernardo Sánchez was born at Robledillo, diocese of Ciudad Rodrigo, Old Castile, Spain, September 7, 1778. He received the Franciscan habit in the convent of Santa María de Gracia, a Recollect friary, in the province of San Miguel Estremadura, October 9, 1794. In February 1803, he sailed from Cádiz and arrived at Vera Cruz, Mexico, in July and at San Fernando College, Mexico City, in August. Shortly before December 22, 1803, he volunteered for the California missions. With nine other friars, of whom José Antonio Urrestí was the superior, he set out from Mexico and arrived at San Francisco, August 14, 1804.

Sánchez' missionary life in California is easily compartmentalized by his years of service in San Diego (1804-1820), at Purisima (1820-1821), and at San Gabriel (1821-1833). He served under Presidents Estevan Tapis, José Señán, Mariano Payeras, and Narciso Durán, and under the commissary prefects, Vicente Francisco de Sarría and Payeras. He himself was president of the missions between 1827 and 1831. En route to San Diego, he stopped at Santa Barbara, leaving on October 1, 1804. His first entry in the San Diego registers appeared in October 1804, his last on May 16, 1820.

Mission San Diego had been established for thirty-five years when Sánchez arrived there, and 3,204 baptisms had been administered. By December 31, 1820, they had increased to 5,359. Fray José Barona was in charge until January 24, 1811, when Sánchez succeeded him. A new church, begun on September 29, 1808, was dedicated on November 12, 1813. In this latter year work was begun on the dam and aqueduct both of which were completed in 1816. Sánchez composed and signed the answers to the government questionnaire on the customs and habits of the Indians, December 23, 1814.

Out of San Diego Sánchez accompanied a military expedition through the rancherias of the interior country within a radius of thirty leagues. This was on orders of Governor José Joaquín Arrillaga, May 6, 1806. The expedition set out on June 20 and returned on July 14. During that same year Sánchez interposed in a quarrel between Lieutenant José de la Guerra y Noriega and Lieutenant Francisco María Ruiz, preventing bloodshed. In September 1806, he was present at the dedication of the stone mission church at San Juan Capistrano. Appeal was made to Governor Pablo Solá in 1816, 1818, and 1819 (the last by Payeras) for permission to establish an *asistencia* at Santa Isabel, and authority was finally granted. The first Mass, however, was said there in a temporary chapel, September 20, 1818. Sánchez visited Mission San Luis Obispo, baptizing there December 19, 1810.

The missionary's first signature at Purisima is that of July 2, 1820, his last, November 28, 1821. While stationed there, he baptized on a few occasions also at Santa Ines. In the closing months of 1821 the commissary prefect, Payeras, chose him as secretary for the canonical visitation of the southern missions from Purisima to San Diego. From the latter port he accompanied Payeras on a reconnaissance of the interior country between San Diego and San Gabriel between September 10 and October 1. Sánchez kept a diary of this trek, which he entitled "Diario de la Caminata."

Sánchez spent the rest of his life at Mission San Gabriel, his first entry occurring there on October 8, 1821, his last on January 15, 1833. During the first six years he served under José María Zalvidea, and when the latter was transferred to San Juan Capistrano in January 1827, Sánchez was placed in charge, and in that position he remained until death.

Baptisms increased from 6,785 at the end of 1821 to 7,823 at the end of 1832.

Mission San Gabriel had been established in 1771 and had been in existence for fifty years when Sánchez arrived. The mission plant had long been perfected, though in 1828 the stone church required some reconstruction. In the following year he could write: "The church is beautifully adorned with everything for divine worship." It was during Sánchez' term of office at San Gabriel that the *asistencia* church of Our Lady of the Angels (the Plaza church of today) was completed, its dedication taking place on December 8, 1822.

When Jedediah Smith and his company of fur hunters arrived at San Gabriel in 1827, they were hospitably received by Sánchez. Referring to the padre and his associate, Harrison S. Rogers, of the Smith party, wrote: "They all appear friendly and treat us well, although they are Catholics by profession, they allow us the liberty of conscience, and treat us as they do their own countrymen, or brethren."[1] Rogers left a detailed account of the mission and the manner of life led there.

Concerning Sánchez personally, Rogers wrote: "Old Father Sanchus (Sanchez) has been the greatest friend I ever met with in all my travels, he is worthy of being called a Christian, as he possesses charity in the highest degree, and a friend to the poor and distressed. I ever shall hold him as a man of God, taking us when in distress, feeding, and clothing us. . . ."[2]

Sánchez was also a great admirer of Joseph Chapman, who had been captured during the Bouchard invasion of California in 1818. Chapman spent a number of years at San Gabriel, improving the mission with his mechanical skills, and he edified Sánchez with genuine Catholic life. Early in 1831, the William Wolfskill and George Yount party stayed for two weeks at Mission San Gabriel, enjoying the hospitality of Sánchez.

When Sánchez spoke satirically about the "imaginary" *ayuntamiento* of Monterey, he received a reprimand from Governor Luís Antonio Argüello, August 31, 1823. It appears that Sánchez was also opposed to the granting of mission lands by the governor to private individuals. When Governor José María Echeandía came to California in 1826, he called upon the inhabitants to take the oath of loyalty to the constitution of October 4, 1824. Sánchez, who with the other friars met the governor at San Diego, April 28, 1826, opined that he could not take the oath except "in so far as may be compatible with our religion and profession."

When Durán's first term as president of the missions came to an end, the Mexican government informed San Fernando College that it considered Durán *persona non grata* for the office. Consequently, at the chapter held on June 9, 1827, Sánchez was unanimously elected president. When he received the news of his elevation in November that year, he was thrown into consternation, and on expressing his dismay to Durán, was told on November 24 that he had no choice but to accept. His three-year administration is not noteworthy for any outstanding events. Most of the controversial issues of the day were handled by the commissary prefect, Sarría. Sánchez was of course vicar forane for the bishop of Sonora.

When, in 1828, certain letters of his were opened by government officials, Sánchez demanded his passport. But he was subsequently mollified by Echeandía. Sánchez was at San Gabriel when Governor Manuel Victoria was wounded in a nearby battle by the forces of Echeandía and who was brought to Mission San Gabriel. Sánchez as ecclesiastical judge for the bishop of Sonora handled the famous Fitch-Carrillo marriage case. Henry Fitch and Josefa Carrillo had eloped to Chile to be married there and had later returned to California. Sánchez rendered a decision on December 28, 1828, declaring the marriage valid but irregular. Because of the scandal, certain penances were imposed, one of which was the donation of a fifty-pound bell to the Plaza church of Los Angeles.

When the new Mexican constitution of 1828 was promulgated in California and the declaration made that those refusing to support it were to be banished, Sánchez was among the first to demand his passport. However, it was not issued, and Sánchez declared himself willing to take only a conditional oath. He was among those recommended by Echeandía to the central government who were to be retained in California.

An embarrassing jurisdictional question in church matters arose in 1831 when Fray Mariano Sosa and several friars of the college of Guadalupe, Zacatecas, appeared at Mission San Gabriel to prepare the way for their college to take over the northern missions. Sánchez was surprised that Sosa came with the title of vicar forane and with the power to confirm. The affair was reported to San Fernando College, and, when an investigation was made, it was discovered that the administrator of the diocese of Sonora was not acquainted with the fact that the president of the California missions was ex-officio the vicar forane of the bishop. Sosa consequently resigned his vicar foraneship, but he was allowed to administer confirmation since that faculty emanated from another source. Meanwhile, Sánchez' term as president expired, and, as he had repeatedly requested, he was relieved of the burden. On June 16, 1831, Durán, no longer *persona non grata,* was reelected. For the remainder of his life Sánchez continued as a simple missionary at San Gabriel.

As far as the proposed secularization of the missions was concerned, Sánchez on September 7, 1831, declared that he would welcome it for personal reasons, but that he feared that it would spell the ruination of the missions. When Echeandía issued his *Reglamento* on November 18, 1832, Sánchez replied in critical tone, declaring that the method would be ruinous.

Nothing is known of Sánchez' last illness and death or even of its exact time. It had probably occurred on January 15, 1833, for records show that on the following day, as was the custom, Fray Vicente Pascual Oliva buried Sánchez in the sanctuary of the mission church. He was fifty-five years old.

Concerning his character and abilities, Sarría wrote in 1817: "His merit consists in a praiseworthy and regular exercise of his duties. At present he is resting from the ministry, not without poor health." In 1820 Payeras considered his "merit as distinguished for his good services in these missions and more than medium in his aptitude for our entire ministry, for our prelacies, and for whatever else may occur in the cloister." In a letter of April 22, the same year, Payeras spoke of Sánchez as a man "of talent and religious spirit." Engelhardt opined that Sánchez was a very pious, zealous, and energetic missionary and an excellent religious who nonetheless dreaded the office of superior. Bancroft considered him "an able manager of temporal affairs . . . [who] took great pride in the prosperity of his mission, being greatly disappointed and perhaps soured by the disastrous results of secularization, against which he had struggled in vain, even to the extent of slaughtering the mission cattle at the last."[3]

Alfred Robinson, who met him in 1829, wrote the following: "Possessing a kind, generous and lively disposition, he had acquired, in consequence, a multitude of friends, who constantly flocked around him; whilst through his liberality the needy wanderer, of whatever nation or creed, found a home and protection in the mission."[4]

The Scotsman, Hugo Reid, who married an Indian and who lived for many years at Mission San Gabriel, has left a most detailed description of Sánchez. He was of a cheerful disposition, frank and generous in nature. At times he lost his temper. He was a great sportsman and capital shot with rifle and fowling piece. In ecclesiastical affairs he was solemn, in trade, formal, in the government of the mission, active, lively, and strict. In social intercourse, he was friendly, full of anecdote, fond of a joke, even a practical one. He was more lenient than Zalvidea with the neophytes. He created a better morale among the Indians and provided better clothing for them.[5] "He died in 1833 regretted by all the community, and leaving everyone who knew him sad at his loss. His course was a good one."[6]

When Auguste Duhaut-Cilly visited Mission San Gabriel in 1827, he wrote that Sánchez gave him a kind welcome, so much so that he would have liked to prolong his stay there.

Eulalia Pérez, who lived at San Gabriel, said that Sánchez was of medium height, stout, light-complexioned, very good and kind, and that he and his companion, Zalvidea, treated the Indians very well and that both were loved by the whites, the Indians of the mission, and other Indians.

Michael C. White, who came to California in 1828, states that he knew Fray Sánchez of San Diego intimately and that he was "an uncle of the Father Sanchez of San Gabriel; he told me so himself. He was a very old man, doubled up a great deal (in 1832). He was of a very nice, affable manner, very attentive to his duties. He died in San Diego."[7] In those statements White opens up a confusing labyrinth. There was no "Father Sanchez" at San Diego in White's time. José Bernardo Sánchez had been there from 1804 to 1820 but was at San Gabriel where White correctly puts him. Miguel Sánchez had died in 1803, so White could not have known him. White should have said that he knew Fray Fernando Martín of San Diego, who served there from 1811 to 1838. The matter is cleared up in a letter that Martín wrote to Sánchez, undated[8] from San Diego, wherein the former calls the latter "Father President and my nephew" and refers to himself as "your old uncle." Hence the encomium applied by White to "Father Sanchez" in San Diego should be applied to Fernando Martín, who was the uncle of José Bernardo Sánchez of San Gabriel.

[1] Cited in Engelhardt, *San Gabriel Mission*, p. 149.

[2] Ibid., p. 153.

[3] *History of California*, III, 642, n. 8.

[4] *Life in California*, p. 44.

[5] Dakin, *A Scotch Paisano*, pp. 16-17.

[6] Ibid., p. 280.

[7] *California All the Way Back to 1828*, p. 92.

[8] The original is in the Honnold Library, Claremont, Calif. A photostatic copy is in SBMA, No. 3382a in the California Mission Section.

SÁNCHEZ, MIGUEL FRANCISCO (1738-1803)

Fray Miguel Francisco Sánchez was born in 1738 at Baguera, archdiocese of Zaragosa, Spain, and became a Franciscan at Calatayud, December 4, 1757, in the province of Aragón. In 1769 he volunteered for the American missions and left his friary at Teruel for Cádiz. Under the leadership of Fray Rafael Verger and in the company of twenty-nine other Franciscans, he sailed for Mexico, where he arrived in 1770. Records at this period describe him as having a good physique, a roundish face, and a florid complexion.

In February 1771 Sánchez and nineteen other friars set out for the mission field of Lower California. From San Blas his ship was driven south to Manzanillo. He was forced to travel overland to Tamasula in

Sinaloa where another ship picked him and his companions up and took them to Loreto, at which port they arrived on November 24.

Together with Marcelino Senra, Sánchez was appointed by President Francisco Palóu to Misión Todos Santos, where he remained until the missions were handed over to the Dominicans in 1773. Palóu left him and Pedro Cambón at San Fernando de Velicatá to take charge of the goods of the Fernandinos being collected there. Owing to restrictions of red tape on the part of the governor and the Dominican mission president, Sánchez was obliged to stay at Velicatá for a whole year. He left on August 23, under escort of José Francisco Ortega and arrived at San Diego, September 26, finally reaching Monterey, October 28, 1774. He began and ended his missionary career in Upper California at Mission San Gabriel. Between his assignments there, it is somewhat difficult to follow his course.

Sánchez commenced to baptize at San Gabriel, September 1, 1775, and continued to do so until about the middle of 1792, baptizing meanwhile at San Juan Capistrano and San Diego on two occasions in 1779. In July 1792 he arrived at Monterey, according to Fermín Francisco de Lasuén, "healthy, strong and robust." He served at Santa Clara from July 22, 1792, until October 17, 1797. From there he went at various times to San Luis Obispo, San Carlos, Santa Cruz, Soledad, San Antonio, San Jose, and San Francisco and even San Gabriel, baptizing on occasion.

He returned to San Gabriel in October 1797, and there he remained until his death on January 27, 1803. Lasuén subdelegated to him his powers of vicar foraneship on January 26, 1798, to be exercised over Los Angeles, San Gabriel, San Juan Capistrano, and San Fernando. Already in 1796 Sánchez had asked to retire but agreed to remain another year. He was buried on January 28 by Fray Norberto de Santiago on the Epistle side of the main altar. He had received all of the last sacraments. By some historians he is mistaken for two different persons, being called either Francisco or Miguel Sánchez. He was only one — Miguel Francisco Sánchez.

SANCHO, JUAN BAUTISTA (1772-1830)

Fray Juan Bautista Sancho, the son of Pedro Sancho and Margarita Lliteras, was born at Artá, Majorca, Spain, December 1, 1772, and was baptized on the same day. He was confirmed on May 17, 1779. Sancho received the Franciscan habit at the Convento de San Francisco, Palma, February 9, 1791, and made his profession on February 10, the following year. After ordination to the priesthood, he became a preacher and choirmaster. Sancho was blest with a strong and agreeable voice and taught music, both the Gregorian plain chant and figured music.

Sancho volunteered for the Indian missions of America and sailed from Cádiz, June 20, 1802, on the *San Miguel* or *Sagrada Familia* and arrived at Vera Cruz in August. Passport records at the time described him as tall, swarthy, with dark hair, gray eyes, a large, thick nose, thick beard, and bushy eyebrows. By December 22, 1803, he had volunteered for the California missions. He set out from San Fernando College, Mexico City, in February 1804 and arrived at Monterey, August 4. His only ministry in California was at Mission San Antonio, where he remained until his death in 1830.

Mission San Antonio was fortunate in that it had a succession of able missionaries, all of whom served for lengthy periods in one place: Buenaventura Sitjar, 1771-1808, Pedro Cabot, 1804-1834, and Sancho, 1804 till 1830. Sancho and Pedro Cabot built the new mission church (the present restored one) which was finished in 1813.

Both Vicente Francisco de Sarría in 1817, and Mariano Payeras in 1820, Sancho's superiors, had high praise for his missionary qualities. The former wrote of him: "In its [San Antonio's] spiritual development he is justly considered as one of the best among the missionaries because of his constancy, zeal, application, activity, industry in the development of buildings together with his knowledge of the language of the mission." The latter stated: "His merit corresponds with his great application and efficiency in every branch of the ministry, and his aptitude is for a complete missionary and for one or the other offices in the Order." For eight months before those lines were written, Sancho had been suffering from severe rheumatic inflammation complicated by other ailments.

Pedro Cabot, his companion of many years at San Antonio, entered a long biographical sketch into the Death Register of the mission in 1830, a praiseworthy model of recording which unfortunately was not followed by most of the missionaries who buried their confreres. He declared:

Man may be praised after death hence what I say serves for the edification of those in the future. ... Father Sancho was animated by a good spirit, and he had a sound intention in his deliberations. He labored much as well in the spiritual as in the temporal line.

In particular his constancy stands out. By means of this the good Religious and Model of missionaries knew how to combine both occupations. He would be seen at labor in the shops and in the field enduring the greatest heat and the extreme cold weather with the same patience. He would not forget the sick, and how to cure their afflictions; and he administered the holy Sacraments to the infirm most punctually. He saw that the neophytes never lacked the spiritual instructions, or remained idle. Vices he would reprehend and all would be encouraged to practice virtue.

The rest he took on days when on account of bad weather he could not leave the house consisted in composing catechetical instructions. In this he was greatly aided by the good knowledge which he possessed of the idiom of these natives. In this occupation he many times would forget the hour of dinner or supper. When he observed that I would lend him a hand, it seemed to him that he did nothing, since he had not done it all alone."[1]

On one occasion when Cabot suggested to Sancho that he allow a certain chore go, Sancho answered: "If I eat, I must work." This is proof that he was a declared enemy of idleness.

Cabot continued: "These last ten years he lived full of pains, caused doubtless by his labors and hardships." Since November 1829 he suffered from inflammation of the thigh "which years before had formed a tumor and at last burst at the knee, accompanied by a constant fever. He surrendered himself to great suffering and bore them with all patience for more than two months."[2]

Having received the last sacraments, Sancho died at three in the morning, February 8, 1830, conscious to the end. Cabot buried him on the Gospel side of the sanctuary in the tomb closest to the center. In final tribute Cabot wrote of his confrere: "We may judge his death as happy, as well on account of his poverty, as for the detachment from everything in the world, ardent zeal for Religion, and the increase of the Catholic Faith, as he devoted his whole life to it in word and deed."[3]

In political matters Sancho was staunchly pro-Spanish and anti-republican. He upheld Fernando VII and refused to take the oath upholding the constitution of Mexico. In 1829, Governor José María Echeandía recommended that Sancho be sent out of the province.

While stationed at Mission San Antonio, Sancho baptized at Mission Soledad between 1819 and 1829 and at Mission San Miguel in 1808, 1824, and 1829.

In appreciation of Sancho's musical ability, Father Owen Da Silva, O.F.M., has written: "It seems that the Northern Missions were more blessed with good musicians. Neighbor to Padre Ibañez, again to the Southwest, was Padre Juan Sancho of Mission San Antonio. When a cleric in Spain, Padre Sancho copied down much of the music sung by the monastery choir. Many of his small, closely written pages, dated Mayorca 1795-96, have been preserved in the Stanford Museum. One page bears the interesting footnote: 'I have just finished writing this, the 21st of May, about 11 o'clock at night.'"[4]

[1] "Libro de Difuntos," Mission San Antonio, Entry No. 3499, cited in Engelhardt, *San Antonio*, pp. 109-110.
[2] Ibid., p. 110-111.
[3] Ibid., p. 111.
[4] *Mission Music of California*, p. 23a.

SANTA MARÍA, VICENTE DE (1742-1806)

Fray Vicente de Santa María was born in 1742 at Haras, diocese of Calahorra, Spain, and became a Franciscan at San Francisco de Estella, October 17, 1759. He left his friary of Burgos in 1769 for Cádiz, where he joined thirty-nine other Franciscans under the leadership of Fray Rafael Verger, and sailed for Mexico, the destination being San Fernando College, Mexico City. In passport records at the time of his departure, Santa María was described as having a good physique, dark hair, and a florid countenance. He held the office of preacher.

Santa María was among the twenty friars sent to Lower California from San Fernando College in October 1770. They sailed from San Blas on the *San Carlos*, February 1771 and arrived at Loreto, November 24. President Francisco Palóu assigned Santa María as assistant to himself at Loreto and in December 1772 appointed him to Misión San Xavier. When the missions were handed over to the Dominicans, Santa María returned to San Fernando College, sailing from Loreto on the *Concepción*, May 24, 1773.

Late in 1774 Santa María was appointed chaplain for the *San Carlos*. The captain, Juan Bautista de Ayala, had orders to reconnoiter San Francisco Bay in preparation for the settlements to be established by Juan Bautista Anza. The *San Carlos* arrived at Monterey, June 27, 1775, and left there, July 27, entering the bay of San Francisco, August 2, the first ship in history to go through the Golden Gate. The party explored San Francisco and San Pablo bays as well as the mouth of the San Joaquin River. The *San Carlos* remained anchored in the bay for forty days, awaiting the return of the land expedition. And when it did not appear, Ayala decided to return to Monterey. Santa María buried two letters for the men of the expedition at the foot of the cross, which Palóu had erected on Point Lobos the year before. The *San Carlos* reached Monterey, September 22, 1775.

Santa María returned to San Blas with the ship, but he came back to California in the following year on the *San Carlos*, which reached Monterey on June 3, 1776, having sailed from San Blas, March 3. At the request of President Junípero Serra, Santa María sailed with him to San Diego on the *San Antonio*. They left the northern port on June 30 and reached San Diego on July 11. There Serra asked Santa María to take the place of Vicente Fuster, who had gone through the Indian revolt of November 1775 and who had a revulsion for the local Indians. Santa María declined indignantly, stating that he had come to California as a ship chaplain and not as a missionary. Serra, moreover, had previously assured him that he would not be given an assignment.

Serra left Santa María at San Diego as the missionary later complained, "as a bird in the air." Evidently Santa María finally agreed to serve as a missionary in California, for he was assigned to Mission San Francisco shortly after January 1777 and remained there until June 11, 1782. He also baptized at Mission San Antonio, October 22, 1777.

When Serra founded Mission San Buenaventura, March 31, 1782, he appointed Santa María to that mission soon afterward. He served there with Francisco Dumetz and José Señán until 1806. Santa María helped out at times at Presidio Santa Barbara before the founding of the mission, December 4, 1786, and in 1785 had reconnoitered the area of Montecito with Governor Pedro Fages, looking for a proper site for the mission. In August 1795, Santa María accompanied an expedition which explored the interior country between San Buenaventura and San Gabriel, taking the route through present Simi, Santa Susana, and San Fernando. The expedition, led by Ensign Pablo Cota, set out on August 16, and Santa María kept a diary of the trek.

Santa María dealt with Captain George Vancouver both at Santa Barbara and at San Buenaventura in 1793. Of Santa María, Vancouver wrote:

> The pleasing society of our good friends at the mission and Presidio [at Santa Barbara] was this day augmented by the arrival of Friar Vicente Santa Maria, one of the Rev. Fathers of the mission of San Buena Ventura.... The motives that induced this respectable priest to favor us with his company, evidently manifested his christian-like benevolence. Having crossed the ocean more than once himself, he was well aware how valuable the fresh productions of the shores were to persons in our situation; under this impression he had brought with him, for our service, half a score sheep, and twenty mules laden with the various roots and vegetables from the garden of his mission. This excellently-good man earnestly intreated that I would accompany him by land back to Buenaventura.[1]

Santa María was invited to dine aboard Vancouver's ship, and the captain accepted the padre's invitation to visit San Buenaventura, which he did by ship, Santa María accompanying him. Vancouver stated that Santa María spoke the native language "very fluently," called him "our hospitable friend," and named the point near San Pedro, Point Vicente, in memory of him.

Between 1782 and 1806 the number of baptisms effected at San Buenaventura was 2,306, while in the latter year, 1,159 Christian Indians were living in the mission village. After receiving the sacraments, Santa María died on July 16, 1806, and was buried on the following day by Marcos Antonio de Vitoria, assisted by Señán, in the mission church. His remains were transferred to the new church (the present one) on September 10, 1809, by Señán and placed above the floor in a niche which entered the wall on the Gospel side. According to Señán, Santa María died of dropsy.

[1] Wilbur, ed. *Vancouver in California 1792-1794*, pp. 157-158.

SANTIAGO, NORBERTO DE (ca. 1760-ca. 1818)

Fray Norberto de Santiago was born at Samiano in the district of Treviño, León, Spain, and became a Franciscan in the province of Cantabria. He came to Mexico in 1785 and entered San Fernando College, Mexico City. He arrived in San Francisco in the fall of 1786 and served the mission of that port between December 27, 1786, and August 13, 1787. He baptized at Mission Santa Clara in September and December of 1786 and again on September 6, 1787. Santiago served next at Mission San Juan Capistrano between January 20, 1788, and August 4, 1810. Meanwhile he baptized at Mission San Diego, December 17, 1788, and in May and July 1797 and at Mission San Gabriel, August 3, 1803.

Santiago was present at the founding of Mission San Luis Rey together with Antonio Peyrí and José Faura, June 13, 1798. With Vicente Fuster he planned and built the stone church of Mission San Juan Capistrano, which was dedicated on September 7, 1806, and he was present at the death of Fuster in 1800, whom he succeeded.

Late in 1810, with Fray Domingo Carranza and Captain José de la Guerra y Noriega, he sailed for Mexico on the *San Carlos* from San Diego as far as San Blas. The latter port was in the hands of insurgents. All on board were made prisoners. The friars were condemned to death, but the sentence was not carried out. Santiago notified the guardian of the college of these events, April 10, 1811, from Guadalajara. At the college, January 8, 1813, Santiago was named procurator of the California missions, and on July 22, 1815, he was elected a counselor of the college and continued serving as procurator. He died sometime before January 2, 1819.

SARRÍA, VICENTE FRANCISCO DE (1767-1835)

Fray Vicente Francisco de Sarría was born in November 1767 at San Esteban de Echébarri, Vizcaya, Spain. In 1783, he became a Franciscan at Bilbao. After ordination to the priesthood, he became a professor of philosophy for lay students and prefect of studies and professor of arts for the Franciscan clerics at Bilbao. In June 1804, he sailed from Cádiz for the American missions, entered San Fernando College, Mexico City, and in 1809 was sent to California. He arrived on *La Princesa* at Monterey, June 22, 1809. Sarría was assigned to Mission San Carlos, Carmel, and made his first entry in the registers there on September 10.

After only three years in California Sarría was chosen the first commissary prefect of the territory, an office created by the commissary general in Madrid. The commissary prefect of the missions, according to this new arrangement, relieved the president of the missions of some of his responsibilities, especially dealings with the territorial government and the general supervision of the friars. The president represented the bishop of Sonora. Thus, as a Franciscan, Sarría outranked the president. He was elected to this office by the discretory of San Fernando College, July 13, 1812, and held it until Christmas 1818. While Sarría was commissary prefect, José Señán was elected president and was followed by Mariano Payeras after three years. Notice of Sarría's election arrived in California only toward the end of December 1812, and he waited another six months before announcing it to the missionaries.

When Sarría's election as prefect became known, Estevan Tapis, writing to Fray Pedro Martínez from Santa Cruz, November 28, 1812, declared: "Who will dispute Padre Lector Sarría's merit for the office of prefect, who (aside from his transcendant abilities) in his missionary activity among the neophytes accomplished so much in so short a time. And who will likewise dispute the fitness of Father Señán for the office of president, who besides being the dean of the missions, is well known for his zeal, prudence, virtue and knowledge as well as having many other qualifications which also the Father Lector Sarría has in abundance."[1]

Meanwhile Sarría composed a Pastoral Letter which he issued at Mission San Carlos, July 2, 1813, comprising seventeen closely written pages and embracing forty-eight articles exhorting the missionaries on the Franciscan Rule and covering matters that refer to the Indians and missions. From September until November that year he conducted his first canonical visitation of the territory, interviewing the friars and inspecting the mission registers. For part of this visitation he engaged the services of ex-president Tapis as secretary.

When the presidios began to suffer want because of the nonappearance of the relief ships from Mexico in consequence of the outbreak of the revolution against Spain, the acting governor, Luís Argüello, appealed to the missions for economic assistance. Sarría issued circulars to the missionaries on the subject, June 6, October 12, and November 19, 1814. The missions responded liberally. Other circulars followed on February 16, 1815, and on January 5, 1816. Though Sarría was liberal and cooperative in this matter, at a later period, when he considered the demands excessive and unreasonable, he did not hesitate to inform the governors to that effect.

When it became known that the death rate of the Indians was increasing, with the implied suggestion of neglect on the part of the missionaries, Sarría promptly conducted an investigation. He concurred with the missionaries' belief that the increasing number of deaths were the result of *mal gálico*, contracted through immoral relations with presidial soldiers, which brought about debilitation of the native race. Sarría flatly declared this to be so to the governor, Pablo Solá, June 28, 1815, saying that at some of the missions for a person to marry was tantamount to dispatching the same to the cemetery.

On the question of runaway Indians, Sarría wrote to the same governor, June 10, 1816, to the effect that while soldiers were necessary for accompanying expeditions into the interior for purposes of exploration, they were not necessary for preaching the gospel. He maintained that the Indians would gladly receive the friars if they came alone.

During the second half of 1816, Sarría made his second canonical visitation, using several of the friars as secretaries. Upon his return to San Carlos, January 25, 1817, he issued his second Pastoral Letter containing twenty-seven articles. He insisted on Franciscan simplicity and poverty, urged the friars to cultivate a taste for study and reading, an example of which he set, and ordered the custom of ringing the church bell at three o'clock in the afternoon for the Holy Souls. There followed a third letter, September 3, 1817, in which he recognized that Franciscan observance was in the main good, and in no small number of cases, very good, but that there still existed certain imperfections in individual cases. He made subsequent visitations in 1818 and in 1825.

When California's twentieth mission, San Rafael, was established with Sarría's approval and was founded on December 14, 1817, he was himself present to celebrate the Mass. Present with him were Friars Narciso Durán, Ramón Abella, and Luís Gil y Taboada.

On May 6, 1816, the Franciscan commissary general of the Indies called for a detailed report concerning all the friars in California. Sarría responded by writing his biographical sketches, the document being dated November 5, 1817. These are invaluable for information on the vital statistics and capabilities of the missionaries then laboring in California.

When San Fernando College was no longer able to supply a sufficient number of friars to maintain all the missions adequately, the guardian and counselors of that institution suggested that the nine missions in the southern area be entrusted to the Franciscans of the college of Orizaba. Sarría was in favor of the plan. In this he differed from Mariano Payeras who preferred the relinquishing of the northern missions. Sarría also suggested that lay brothers might be sent to California with advantage, especially in those missions where there was only one missionary priest. However, neither of these plans materialized.

When the chapter met at San Fernando College, August 8, 1818, Payeras was continued as president, but since the commissary general had authorized no election for commissary prefect, that office became vacant. When the news arrived in California, Sarría resigned his office, December 25, 1818.

Sarría and Payeras, the former as representative of the president of the missions, and José Señán, together with the presidio commanders, attended the junta, called by Governor Solá at Monterey, April 9, 1822, to consider their attitude toward the new regime in Mexico instituted by the imperial regency under Iturbide. It was agreed that all should take the oath of loyalty. Moreover, the bishop of Sonora and San Fernando College had given orders to the friars to comply. Sarría also took an active part in the proceedings of the junta respecting the selection of a deputy to Mexico from California. Later, when Mexico sent the canon Agustín Fernández de San Vicente to California to assure the new regime of the territory's loyalty, Sarría, Payeras, and Tapis attended a meeting at Monterey which planned for self-government in the territory, including that of the Indians — the relationship between the friars and the Indians to remain as before.

Not long before President Señán died at Mission San Buenaventura, August 24, 1823, he dictated a letter to Sarría naming him president ad interim. At the same time, the latter become vice-prefect. Sarría received this letter on September 5, but until May 24, 1824, however, he merely referred to himself as vice-prefect of the missions. At the college chapter, May 24, 1824, Sarría was again appointed commissary prefect to fill the vacancy created by the death of Payeras, which occurred April 28, 1823. Instead of appointing a new president, the college sent the official patent to Sarría, asking him to name a padre of his choice, which he did, selecting Narciso Durán of Mission San Jose. The latter notified Governor Argüello of his appointment, April 2, 1825.

Señán had little more time before his death than to express disapproval of José Altimira's unauthorized founding of Mission San Francisco Solano. It was Sarría who addressed a severe reprimand to the young, independent missionary. Although Altimira was allowed to remain at his post, his action caused complications between Sarría and the governor.

In 1824, Sarría became involved in the Chumash Indian revolt along the Santa Barbara Channel coast. The revolt had been caused by the excessive demands made by the military upon the missions in the form of services and aid which entailed more work for the Indians but for which they received no pay. Proximately, the revolt was triggered by the excessive flogging of an Indian at Santa Ines by the local corporal. The Santa Barbara Indians, after a battle with the presidio troops, fled over the mountains into the San Joaquin Valley. The first military expedition sent against them failed in its objective to bring them back. A second one which Friars Sarría and Antonio Ripoll accompanied was successful. Sarría had urged Governor Argüello to grant the Indians full pardon and offered to go in person to persuade them to return, and by

June 1824, this had been accomplished. Antonio María Osio declared that "only the high esteem in which the California inhabitants . . . held the Rev. Fr. Vicente de Sarría and likewise the veneration of the Indians for him on account of his many virtues, dispelled their fear when he reassured them."[2]

A break on political matters between Sarría and the government of Mexico and California occurred after the overthrow of Iturbide when the Mexicans promulgated on October 4, 1824, a new constitution providing for a republican form of government. Governor Argüello summoned the legislative assembly to Monterey in February 1825 and notified Sarría that he was expected to take the oath of loyalty to the new constitution. Sarría declined, stating that he could not do so without violating prior obligations of justice and charity. Nor would he sing a High Mass or a *Te Deum* as Argüello had ordered for the occasion. Sarría acted as he did as a matter of conscience though he realized that he might be banished for his noncompliance. However, he allowed the friars under his jurisdiction to make up their own minds as to whether or not they would take the oath.

While the assembly, soldiers, and citizens took the oath on March 26, Sarría remained aloof. On April 7 Argüello convoked the assembly to consider what action should be taken against Sarría. The situation was reported to Mexico. On April 23, Sarría in a long letter to Durán expressed his views on the oath in detail, having sent a similar letter to Argüello on the fourteenth. He stated that he would be willing to take an oath of fidelity to the government and promised not to act against the established government. President Guadalupe Victoria of Mexico in June 1825 ordered Argüello to arrest Sarría and to deport him to Mexico without delay, though his person was to be respected. This order was partially carried out in October, but Sarría's arrest appeared to be only nominal. His name does not appear in the San Carlos registers for a period of about a year, but he suffered no interference in his personal movements or liberty. Sarría continued to hold the office of commissary prefect until midyear 1830.

On August 7, 1826, Sarría in a long letter to his friars reminded them of their duties in political matters, while he defended his own attitudes. He offered to leave California and go to the Sandwich Islands as a missionary, but the government would not allow this. And though José María Echeandía had been repeatedly told to exile Sarría to Mexico, he declined to do so for fear of the resulting chaos that would come to the missions. Echeandía continued to deal with him as a lawful ecclesiastic.

Auguste Duhaut-Cilly in 1827 visited Mission San Carlos and there met Ramón Abella, Altimira, and Sarría, the latter "a man of distinguished merit and great virtue." At the time of his visit, Sarría "was in utter disgrace among the Mexicans, for having refused to take the oath to the constitution, and prevented his subordinates [not so] from consenting to it: he was also, in a manner, held as prisoner and kept in sight at San Carlos. The agents of the Mexican government considering him, therefore, as the main obstacle to the submission of all the other missionaries, would have liked to send him back to Mexico." Duhaut-Cilly was approached concerning that possibility. He declared: "And he [Sarría] showed me the liveliest gratitude when I disclosed to him my sentiments in this regard."[3]

On February 17, 1828, Sarría left Mission San Carlos for Soledad to replace Fray Francisco Xavier Uría who had been sent to San Buenaventura after the flight of Altimira. There he remained until his death seven years later. In 1830 Sarría was appointed vice-prefect, the commissary prefectship being retained at San Fernando College.

Soledad was always a poor mission, but Sarría carried on the work there to keep it going. In 1832 he completed a provisional church when an earlier one collapsed during a flood. When Alfred Robinson visited Soledad in 1829, he described Sarría as "a pious old man [who] controls its concerns, and pours out to his guests with free hospitality the abundance thereof. His charities, his goodness, and meekness of character are proverbial; and to have known old Pádre Seria was a happiness indeed."[4] Even when the northern missions were transferred to the Zacatecan missionaries in 1833, Sarría remained at Soledad, since no Zacatecan was appointed to administer it. Hence he was the last Fernandino at any of the northern missions.

While at Soledad, Sarría composed and sent to the missionaries his treatise on Caesarean operations, "Descripción de la Operación Cesaria," a copy of which is in the Santa Barbara Mission Archives. It was translated by Sherburne F. Cook in *California and Western Medicine* (San Francisco, 1937). In the foreword Cook states:

> The two documents which are here presented as translations offer an insight into a medical problem which at one era in the history of the state attained considerable significance. This problem involved the extraction of fetuses from pregnant mothers when the latter died for various reasons, in order that baptism might be given. What rendered the situation unusually perplexing was that practically no competent medical men, or even midwives, existed who were capable of performing what is here called the caesarean operation. The only individuals with the requisite intelligence and interest in the matter were the missionaries. They encountered the situation mentioned very frequently among their neophytes, the converted Indians, of which there were many thousands. Furthermore, it was also to their interest that the spiritual needs of the white population be properly cared for.[5]

Speaking of Sarría's contribution, Cook continues:

Although himself by no means versed in medicine, he read what literature he had available, utilized a wide personal experience, and wrote out a treatise on the caesarian operation for the benefit and guidance of his followers. This treatise, which occupies itself as much with theologic as with strictly medical matters, represents the serious attempt of an intelligent man to contribute to the existing knowledge of his place and time. As such it may be regarded as the first original contribution ever offered by a resident of California in the field of medicine.[6]

The Caesarean operation described by Sarría did not involve the removal of the fetus from a living mother but from one who had died in order that the fetus might be baptized. Sarría addressed his letter to the missionaries, July 26, 1830, and sent along a copy of his treatise, asking that it be retained at all the missions.

Sarría died at Soledad alone, May 24, 1835, at the age of sixty-eight. Various conflicting reports are given concerning his death. Bancroft states that he "died suddenly, perhaps fell while saying mass at the altar." Padre Jesús María Vásquez del Mercado declared that his violent death was a result of a "scarcity of food." A similar story was heard by Angustias de la Guerra y Ord and was given credence by Eugène Duflot de Mofras. General Mariano Vallejo states that his death was caused by the neglect of the Mexican friars. Finally Bancroft opines: "The truth is, probably, that the aged friar, childishly insisting upon remaining alone with his Indians, overtaxed his strength and shortened his life, circumstances rendering suitable care impossible. I do not credit Mercado's charges, or believe that there was an administrator in Cal. who would have maltreated a missionary so widely known and loved."[7] Padre Sarría's remains were carried to Mission San Antonio and buried in the mission church on the Epistle side of the sanctuary in the sepulcher nearest to the wall, May 27, 1835, by Fray Mercado, who also made the long entry into the Burial Register.

In Mercado's words, Sarría was a "well-deserving and venerable Religious, model and example of apostolic missionaries, animated with ardent charity" for the conversion of the pagans. His missionary life was characterized by energy in evangelical preaching and in his practice of "sublime virtues," especially those of religious perfection. Sarría was a special devotee of poverty in his detachment from earthly things, was mortified in his senses, chaste, spending much time in prayer even through the greater part of the night. He was indefatigable in study, most observant in obedience, zeal, patience, charity, and humility.

Mercado stated that Sarría died between four and five o'clock on a Sunday afternoon, having, on the preceding Saturday night, suffered severe cramps in the legs, accompanied by evacuation and vomiting. Sarría sent a messenger to call Mercado, who hastily arrived just a little after the padre had expired. Nicolás Alviso had remained with Sarría and testified that Sarría died an edifying death — that "of a truly just man."[8]

In March 1949, the burial vaults of the padres interred in the sanctuary of Mission San Antonio were opened. Individual remains were not identified beyond the recognition of their presence in the vaults according to the original burial records. In the vault closest to the wall on the Epistle side was a redwood coffin, at a depth of about three and a half feet, in which a skeleton and a well-preserved skull were found. All appeared to be in a fair state of preservation, but no remnants of clothing were found.

[1] Private collection, Santa Barbara.
[2] Engelhardt, *Santa Barbara Mission,* p. 136.
[3] "Duhaut-Cilly's Account," pp. 151-152.
[4] *Life in California,* p. 90.
[5] Page 107.
[6] Ibid., pp. 107-108.
[7] *History of California,* III, 689n.
[8] Engelhardt, *Mission Nuestra Senora de la Soledad,* pp. 64-67.

SEÑÁN, JOSÉ FRANCISCO DE PAULA (1760-1823)

Fray José Francisco de Paula Señán (Señant in Catalonian) was born at Barcelona, Catalonia, Spain, March 3, 1760, and became a Franciscan at San Francisco el Grande in the same city, January 6, 1774. He left his native city for the American missions, April 10, 1784, and arrived at San Fernando College, Mexico City, about mid-September, the same year. Señán remained at the college for about three years before setting out for California.

He arrived at Monterey early in October and remained as missionary at Mission San Carlos, Carmel, until 1795, during the presidency of Fermín Francisco de Lasuén. Señán was present when Captain George Vancouver visited there in 1793. He himself visited Mission San Antonio where he baptized at various times and Santa Clara where he officiated on September 16 and 23, 1787. Having been employed in the service of the college for ten years and worn out by his labors, Señán requested permission to return to Mexico; among other difficulties, he could no longer ride horseback. Lasuén had been reluctant to lose him, for, when Señán first indicated his desire to return, the president wrote to the guardian of the college: "He is a good religious, a good worker, well-fitted to serve as a missionary here — in one word, he is a very good apostolic missionary."[1]

He sailed from San Francisco, September 14, 1795, stopped over for a short time at San Diego, where he baptized on November 1, and continued on to San Blas. At Tepic he became gravely ill but recovered and arrived at San Fernando College, March 22, 1796.

Señán remained at the college for three years. Shortly after his arrival, Viceroy Branciforte asked him to make a report on the reasons why the colonization of California was progressing so slowly. Señán finished his report on May 4, 1796. This document gives considerable light on conditions in the territory.

In 1798, with six other friars, Señán set out for California a second time, sailed on the *Concepción,* and arrived at Santa Barbara on May 8. Señán's next period of service lasted twenty-seven years, all of which were spent at Mission San Buenaventura. Baptisms at that mission numbered 1,823 at the end of 1798 but rose to 3,648 by the end of 1825. Señán lived to see the mission reach its completion during his tenure of office. Fray Vicente de Santa María, who had preceded him at San Buenaventura, was with him till the former died on July 16, 1806. After that Señán had as his assistant Marcos Antonio de Vitoria, who remained with him till Señán himself passed away.

The new mission church was completed in 1809 and was dedicated on September 9. It was badly damaged in the earthquake of 1812 but was repaired, and a new tower was built. The rededication ceremony was held July 14, 1814. In 1816 the small *asistencia* chapel of San Miguel which had been destroyed in the earthquake was rebuilt.

On August 11, 1815, Señán wrote a detailed account of the customs and habits of the Ventureño Chumash in response to a questionnaire of the Spanish government. This was done at all the missions, but Señán's account is longer and more detailed than those of other missions, and, as in his other writings, Señán displayed a very neat, readable handwriting. In the Santa Barbara Mission Archives is a "Confesionario" in the hand of Señán, with questions and answers in Chumash and Spanish, giving evidence of his familiarity with the native language. This has been edited together with an English translation by Madison S. Beeler.

In 1818 Señán and his neophytes had a bad scare when the revolutionary, Hipolyte Bouchard, invaded the California coast and threatened to destroy the missions. Señán, with the Indians, church goods, and cattle, traveled nine miles into the interior to a place called Purisima Nueva and remained there for a month, suffering hardships in the cold of November. He witnessed some Indian trouble at the mission in 1819 when a number of Mojave Indians visiting there were imprudently mishandled by the soldiers and some of them killed. Señán explained the affair in letters to Governor Pablo Solá on June 3 and to Captain José de la Guerra y Noriega of Santa Barbara, June 1, 1819.

While residing at San Buenaventura, Señán served both as missionary and president of the missions. As early as March 18, 1807, San Fernando College had named Señán president in the event of Estevan Tapis' incapacity or death. He actually became president only after Tapis resigned at the end of three terms, July 11, 1812. Notification of the fact did not reach him, however, until November of that year. At the same time, ecclesiastical authority in California was split between the office of president and that of commissary prefect, a new office instituted by the commissary general of the Franciscans in Madrid. The official in this position was required to transact mission matters with the territorial government and to act as a permanent visitor-general of the missionaries, and in this respect outranked the president. The president, however, more or less retained the authority of a commissary provincial and was the vicar forane and ecclesiastical judge of the bishop of Sonora. Thus the president was the highest ecclesiastical personage in the territory and as such outranked the commissary prefect. While Señán was president, Vicente Francisco de Sarría held the office.

Shortly before Señán assumed office as fourth president of the California missions, December 8, 1812, Fray Estevan Tapis, writing to Fray Pedro Martínez, November 28, 1812, declared: "Who will dispute the fitness of Father Señán for the office of president who besides being the dean of the missions, is well known for his zeal, prudence, virtue and knowledge as well as having many other qualifications."[2] At his own request, he retired from office after three years, for he disliked to exercise authority, and was succeeded by Mariano Payeras. However, on April 1, 1820, Señán was re-appointed president and held the office until his death in 1823. Because of his preference for private as against official life, or perhaps because of his unruffled disposition, Señán was known as "Padre Calma."

Señán founded no new missions, but under his administration Fray José Altimira established California's twenty-first mission at Sonoma, July 4, 1823, without proper authority. Señán authorized the establishment of the *asistencias* of San Antonio de Pala in 1815 and that of Santa Isabel in 1821. Likewise ground was broken for the establishment of the *asistencia* of Our Lady of the Angels (the Plaza church) at Los Angeles. Señán laid the cornerstone, August 13, 1814.

The series of earthquakes in 1812 caused damage to a number of missions in southern California. Thus Señán's first term as president may be looked upon as a period of reconstruction. Mission Purisima was completely destroyed. It had been built where Lompoc is now situated, and Señán gave permission for its relocation at the present site. The stone church at San Juan Capistrano was damaged beyond repair and has never been restored.

Tapis' church at Santa Barbara (built in 1794) was damaged and repaired, but the present stone church was built between 1815 and 1820 and was dedicated by Señán in the presence of Governor Solá, September 10, 1820. Señán and his neophytes took the oath at San Buenaventura, May 16, 1822, to uphold the constitution of the Mexican regency.

While Señán was assigned to San Buenaventura, he also baptized upon various occasions at Santa Barbara and much earlier, on May 27, 1801, at San Fernando.

He died at San Buenaventura at seven o'clock in the morning, August 24, 1823, after a long and painful illness, which he bore with patience and resignation, and after having received the last sacraments. He was placed by Francisco Suñer in a vault of masonry on the Epistle side of the altar on August 25, after his remains had been carried in procession around the patio of the mission. Present at his death and burial were Friars Suñer, Marcos Antonio de Vitoria, and Blas Ordaz. He was buried "not without the tears of those who knew well what a loss was his edifying conduct, fervor and zeal for the salvation of souls."[3]

Señán was described as a man who "had made good studies and was uncommonly gifted. He possessed a remarkably retentive memory; and as he had the Gift of Counsel, he was consulted not only by his brethren, but also by the Superiors themselves and by the officials in the greatest difficulties; and as he was pious and possessed an active mind combined with indefatigable zeal, he was twice elected Presidente of these Missions."[4]

Concerning his character and abilities, Sarría on November 5, 1817, wrote: "His character is excellent as also the qualifications he manifests as missionary; wherefore his merit during the long years of his career is supremely eminent, not only for the management of his Mission and his knowledge of the language of its Indians, but also for his being the Presidente of the Missions.... His aptitude is not limited to the office of missionary; in my opinion, it extends to many other positions, to which in or out of the College he could be appointed."[5] Sarría considered him especially fit to write the history of the California missions and urged him to do so, but he declined because the work would interfere with the spiritual and temporal progress of his mission.

Payeras on December 31, 1820, stated that Señán's "merit is most worthy of any distinction and office that might be given him." He referred to Señán's "well-known aversion to every office," however. "I consider him very capable of compiling a historical narrative of these missions, at which he is already working, by direction of the Most Rev. Commissary General."[6] Whatever happened to this manuscript no one knows.

José Ramón Antonio Váldes, a soldier stationed at San Buenaventura in Señán's last days, recalls that the padre was short and stout, with rather fair complexion, and appeared younger than he actually was. At the time of his death he was sixty-five. In this final period of his life, he is also reported to have suffered from failing eyesight.

Lesley Byrd Simpson, who edited Señán's letters, characterized him as "humble and self-effacing ... with no ambition other than to serve God, his Order, and his College. He was, above all, a human and humane man, not always wise, not always strong, but always faithful to his charge. He was a tremendous patriot and came close to hating the French when they invaded his *patria*."[7]

[1] Lasuén to Tomás de Pangua, Oct. 20, 1792, Kenneally, *Writings*, I, 258.

[2] Private collection, Santa Barbara.

[3] Engelhardt, *San Buenaventura ... Mission*, p. 124.

[4] Ibid.

[5] Ibid., p. 121.

[6] Ibid., pp. 121-123.

[7] Nathan and Simpson, tr. and ed. *Letters*, p. ii.

SERRA, JUNÍPERO (1713-1784)

Born at Petra, Majorca, Spain, November 24, 1713, a son of Antonio Nadal Serra and Margarita Rosa Ferrer, farmers, Junípero Serra was baptized on the same day at St. Peter's Church by the Rev. Bartolomé Lladó and was given the names Miguel José. His paternal grandparents were Miguel Serra and Juana Abraham, his maternal grandparents, Bartolomé Ferrer and Martina Fornés. At the age of two he was confirmed by the Most Rev. Atanasio Esterripa y Tranajaúregui, bishop of Palma. In Petra, Serra attended the primary school of the Franciscans conducted at the friary of San Bernardino. At the age of fifteen he was taken by his parents to Palma to be placed in the charge of a cathedral canon, and he began to assist at classes in philosophy held in the Franciscan monastery of San Francisco.

At the age of sixteen Serra was admitted as a novice at the Convento de Jesús outside the walls of Palma, September 14, 1730, and made his profession on September 15, the following year, into the hands of the Very Rev. Antonio Perelló. On this occasion he chose the name, Junípero, in memory of the brother companion of St. Francis.

From 1731 to 1734 Serra studied philosophy and from 1734 to 1737 theology at the Convento de San Francisco. The date of his ordination to the priesthood is not known, though it probably occurred during the Ember Days of December 1738. Sometime before, he entered competitive examinations for the lectorate of philosophy in his province. This title he received with the unanimous consent of his examiners.

Serra's first appointment was that of librarian of his friary, a position he held for a little over a year from 1739 until the fall of 1740. For the next three years he conducted the course of philosophy at San Francisco, which was offered to students for the priesthood, Franciscan and secular, and to laymen in his province. Among his students were Francisco Palóu and Juan Crespí. In the meantime, Serra obtained his doctorate in theology in 1742 from the Lullian University, Palma. He was called to the Scotistic chair of theology at the same university as primary professor in January 1744, a position he retained until he resigned in January 1749 to become an Indian missionary in America. During his teaching career Serra was frequently called upon to preach in Palma and in various parts of the island, both to religious and to the laity. He was considered an able teacher and a forceful and zealous preacher.

On April 13, 1749, in company with his former pupil, Francisco Palóu, Serra sailed from Palma for America by way of Málaga and Cádiz. He departed from the latter at the end of August and after a sea voyage of ninety-nine days landed at Vera Cruz, Mexico, December 7, 1749, having preached a mission en route at San Juan, Puerto Rico. He nearly lost his life in a storm off the coast of Vera Cruz.

Despite the fact that horses were supplied for the friars at the port, Serra and an unnamed companion elected to walk the distance of 250 miles between Vera Cruz and Mexico City. They reached San Fernando College, January 1, 1750, spending the previous night at the shrine of Our Lady of Guadalupe.

Within six months after his arrival at the college, an urgent call came for volunteers for the Sierra Gorda missions. Serra and Palóu were among the group that volunteered, and both walked the distance to Jalpan, the central mission, about 175 miles distant. These missions had been placed under the college in 1744 and were located among the Pame Indians. They were new Christians, many with just a veneer of Christianity, while still others were pagans. At Jalpan, which possessed an adobe church, Serra had 1,000 parishioners. The natives lived in primitive huts.

During his apostolate in the Sierra Gorda between 1750 and 1758, Serra not only built a beautiful church, which is still in use, but developed his mission in both religious and economic directions. Under his presidency of the missions (1751-1754), the missionaries of the other four towns, Concá, Landa, Tilaco, and Tancoyol, also built mission churches similar to the one at Jalpan, all of stone and richly ornamented. They remain in service today. In 1752 Serra was appointed a commissioner of the Holy Office of the Inquisition for the Sierra Gorda district and for all parts of New Spain where he happened to be preaching and where there was no other resident commissioner.

Serra learned the Otomí language of the natives and put into force the traditional mission methods successfully used by the Franciscans in Texas. Zealous in preaching and in promoting both liturgical and popular devotions, he succeeded in bringing the Pames to practice the faith in an exemplary way. Serra used a visual method of teaching religion. Economically his mission prospered through the introduction of domestic animals, the fostering of agriculture, and the development of commerce. He also defended Indian rights against white settlers in a protracted contest over the valley of Tancama. During building operations on his church, he worked as an ordinary day laborer.

While successfully guiding the destinies of Jalpan, Serra was hurriedly called to the college, where he arrived September 26, 1758. The Apaches had destroyed the mission of San Sabá in Texas killing two missionaries and wounding a third. Serra and Palóu were to be sent as replacements. However, the plan never matured, owing to unsettled conditions and government delay. Thus Serra remained at the college as a home missionary until 1767. There he was made choir director, master of novices from 1761 to 1764, college counselor (discreet) from 1758 to 1761, and a confessor within and without the college. He likewise continued to function as commissioner of the Holy Office.

As a home missionary Serra preached missions twice in Mexico City as well as in the districts of Mezquital and Zimapan. In an unknown year he preached missions in the Río Verde area belonging to the diocese of Morelia. With five companions he conducted missions for six months in the dioceses of Puebla and Oaxaca from 1762 to 1763, proceeding first to Puebla itself. He continued his way to the coastal plains about Tuxpam, thence south to the area of Acayucan, inland by canoe, and by mountain trail to the Mijes country in central Oaxaca, preaching at Villalta and finally in Oaxaca itself, then called Antequera.

Another large area missionized by Serra and his companions was the Huasteca in the eastern mountain area of Mexico as far north as Valles. This mission tour took place in the years 1766-1767. While engaged in giving a mission in the Mesquital in 1767, Serra was summoned to the college and there learned that he was to assume the presidency of the ex-Jesuit missions of Baja California. He set out in mid-July and reached Tepic, in the area of which he gave missions, eventually setting sail from San Blas, March 14, 1768, and reaching Loreto on April 1. Serra resided at the former Jesuit headquarters and assigned missionaries to the fifteen missions between San José del Cabo in the south and Santa María in the north. At first the missionaries were in charge of spiritual affairs only, but in August they were also entrusted with the temporalities.

When José de Gálvez, visitor-general of New Spain, arrived in the peninsula in midsummer of 1768 and announced the forthcoming spiritual and temporal conquest of Upper California, Serra enthusiastically volunteered at once to join him, and to enlist other volunteers, he visited the northern missions as far as Guadalupe. Later, he traveled south to the mining town of Santa Ana to confer with Gálvez, where the two worked out the details of the northern conquest. Before returning to Loreto, Serra visited the southern missions. At La Paz, on January 6, 1769, Serra blessed the flagship, *San Carlos,* and sped it on its way for the occupation of San Diego.

Finally, on March 28, 1769, Serra left the mission at Loreto on muleback, rode north to join the Portolá expedition, and in company with it arrived at San Diego, July 1. En route, he founded his first mission among pagans at San Fernando de Velicatá, May 14. Serra kept a diary of this journey during which, especially in its upper reaches, he suffered greatly from an infirmity in his legs and feet and had to be carried on a stretcher. Only when a muleteer prepared an ointment for his relief was the pain finally alleviated. Gaspar de Portolá suggested that Serra return to Loreto and abandon the attempt to reach San Diego and Monterey. But he refused, declaring that he preferred to die on the road rather than give up his objective to reach those harbors.

Serra devoted the next fifteen years of his life to the Upper California apostolate. During that period he founded the following nine missions: San Diego, July 16, 1769; San Carlos, Monterey-Carmel, June 3, 1770; San Antonio, July 14, 1771; San Gabriel, September 8, 1771; San Luis Obispo, September 1, 1772; San Francisco, October 9, 1776; San Juan Capistrano, November 1, 1776; Santa Clara, January 12, 1777; and San Buenaventura, March 31, 1782. He was present at the founding of Presidio Santa Barbara, April 21, 1782. During his presidency the civilian pueblos of San Jose (November 29, 1777) and Los Angeles (September 4, 1781) were founded by Governor Felipe de Neve, but their spiritual administration was subject, as was that of the four presidios of San Diego, Monterey, San Francisco, and Santa Barbara, to Serra and his missionaries.

Serra remained at San Diego until April 14, 1770, when he embarked for Monterey. From June 3, 1770, until his death, he maintained his headquarters at Mission San Carlos. During his California career Serra made four round trips between Carmel and San Francisco, always through Santa Clara. The distance between Carmel and San Diego was traversed overland five times, with a number of side trips also to the intervening missions. In 1772 Serra went to Mexico to deal with Viceroy Antonio María Bucareli y Ursúa concerning mission development. He returned to California early in 1774. Four times he traveled by ship between Monterey and San Diego. From 1778 until 1784, Serra administered confirmation when visiting the missions, a privilege he had by apostolic indult.

The close union of Church and State in the Spanish colonial regime, the double aspect of the conquest, military and religious, the distance of California from the home bases in Mexico, the low cultural level of the California Indians offered the president vexatious problems throughout his administration. His many letters and reports are replete with the difficulties encountered in these early years. Serra insisted that the missions be founded in the tried and traditional system used in Texas and the Sierra Gorda. He and his missionaries were in charge of spiritualities and temporalities. Domestic animals were introduced into the land; agriculture was started; trades were taught. Six totally different languages prevailed in the mission territory. By the time of Serra's death, ex-governor Neve declared that the California missions were the best in the entire Provincias Internas, and, a few years after Serra's death, Governor Pedro Fages declared that the perfection of the California missions was due to the indefatigable zeal of those who founded them. By the end of 1784, Indian baptisms at the first nine missions reached the number 6,736, while 4,646 Christianized Indians were living in them. By 1833, when twenty-one missions had been founded, nearly one hundred thousand Indians had been baptized.

Serra died at Mission San Carlos, August 28, 1784, at the age of seventy, attended by his one-time pupil and collaborator, Francisco Palóu. The next day he was buried in the floor of the sanctuary of the church he had built, on the Gospel side.

Serra was small of stature, five feet two inches in height. He had a sonorous voice, had swarthy skin, dark hair and eyes. Though it appears that he had a fundamentally robust constitution, he suffered a great deal during the latter part of his life from 1750 on and doubly so after 1758. His first affliction was the swelling and painful itching of his feet and legs from mosquito bites sustained on his trek from Vera Cruz to Mexico City. Scratching caused varicose ulcers. At times he could neither stand nor walk. After 1758 he began to suffer from asthma, and the ailment remained with him to his dying hours. Serra's zeal and dynamism prevented these physical ailments from substantially arresting the progress of his apostolate.

In character Serra was eager, optimistic, zealous, dynamic, even adamantine. Strength of character and undeviating purposefulness marked his entire life. Primarily a man of action, he preferred the active apostolate to the classroom or to writing. He remained a model religious despite his distractions and activity — a man of prayer and mortification. He had a consuming love for the Indian and ever defended him. His obedience to his religious superiors was a marked characteristic. Considered a man of saintly qualities during his life by such men as Palóu, Fermín Francisco de Lasuén, Juan Sancho, Pablo Font, and others, he has been thought so unbrokenly since his death.

In the nature of his work and in the milieu of his times he was called upon to exercise the so-called militant virtues. In the politico-ecclesiastical regime in which he had to labor there were many occasions for disagreement and controversy, and Serra had his differences with three successive governors, Pedro Fages, Fernando Rivera y Moncada, and Felipe de Neve. By some Serra was considered too aggressive, zealous, and demanding. Serra fought for the freedom of the Church in the confirmation controversy against royal infringement. Though he fought for the Indians, he believed in and practiced corporal punishment when their misdeeds called for it. He had the qualities of a fine administrator. The mystic and the man of affairs were harmoniously blended in him.

A legend sprang up in California that Serra always walked between the missions despite his illnesses and the prohibition from traveling without a military escort. This legend arose because of faulty translations of Palóu's *Life,* which did not distinguish the fine nuances of the expression *andar.* Serra walked only once between two missions — in 1779 between Carmel and Santa Clara. Frequently his riding is positively mentioned.

The cause for Serra's beatification was commenced in the diocese of Monterey-Fresno in 1934, and the diocesan process was finished in 1949. At present the case is in the hands of the Sacred Congregation of Rites. As of today Serra's writings have been approved. His virtues are being studied. Serra's remains at Carmel were exhumed in 1856, 1882, and in 1943, in which last year they were scientifically examined and identified by physical anthropologists. This writer was present at the exhumation of 1943.

Serra monuments and memorials dot his Camino Real from Majorca to California. He is the subject of several dozen biographies in various languages. His writings with translation have been published in four volumes by the Rev. Antonine Tibesar, O.F.M. He is known as the Apostle of California. Serra International was established in his honor. His life and his mission system are studied in California schools. Few missionaries have achieved such an enduring widespread fame.

Fray Pablo Font, O.F.M., a brother of Fray Pedro Font, O.F.M., a member of San Fernando College while Serra was there between February and September 1773, wrote to a confrere in Spain in August 1773 the following appraisal of Serra:

The Father-President Junípero Serra is a religious of the Observant order, a man of very venerable age, formerly professor at the University at Palma,

244

who during twenty-four years, since he has been a missionary of this college, has never spared himself in toiling for the conversion of the faithful and the unfaithful. Notwithstanding his many and laborious years, he has the qualities of a lion, which surrenders only to fever. Neither the habitual indispositions from which he suffers, especially in the chest and in difficulty of breathing, nor the wounds in his feet and legs have been able to detain him for a moment from his apostolic tasks. He has astonished us during his recent sojourn, for, although very sick, he never failed, day or night, to take part in the choir, much less when he had fever. We have seen him apparently dead, only to be almost immediately revived. If now and then he attended to the needs of bodily health at the infirmary, it was only because he was ordered to go there. . . .

In very truth, on account of these things, and because of the austerity of his life, his humility, charity, and other virtues, he is worthy to be counted among the imitators of the apostles. And now he is returning, as if it were nothing, to Monterey, a distance of a thousand leagues by sea and land, to visit those missions and rejoice them by his presence and by the measures which he has procured, and to preside over them and found other missions until he shall die. . . . Much more could I say of this holy man.[1]

When Palóu concluded his life of Serra, the *Relación Histórica,* he wrote:

His memory shall not fail, because the works he performed when alive shall be impressed in the minds of the dwellers of this New California; despite the ravages of time, they shall not be forgotten.

He who performs actions of glory — even though he himself as a mortal is subject to Time, which consumes him — is not subject to Time as respects his deeds of glory. For these enjoy as it were an immunity of immortality; they are exempt from the jurisdiction of Time. Father Junípero ended his life as subject to Time, having lived seventy years, nine months and four days, having labored in the apostolic ministry one half of his life, and in these Californias sixteen years, leaving behind him in Old California (where he lived a year) a mission he founded; and in this Upper California, . . . previously inhabited only by pagans, he left fifteen settlements, six inhabited by Spaniards or whites, and nine by full-blooded native neophytes baptized by His Reverence and his missionary companions.[2]

[1] Chapman, *History of California,* p. 358.
[2] Geiger, *Palóu's Life of Fray Junípero Serra,* pp. 256-257.

SITJAR, BUENAVENTURA (1739-1808)

Fray Buenaventura Sitjar was baptized Antonio, December 9, 1739, at Porreras, the place of his birth, Majorca, Spain. He was the son of Antonio Sitjar and Juana Ana Pastor. He became a Franciscan at the Convento de Jesús, Palma, April 20, 1758, and on the occasion of his profession assumed the name Buenaventura. He left the Convento de San Francisco, Palma, in 1769, and with thirty-nine other Franciscans under the leadership of Fray Rafael Verger, sailed from Cádiz for Vera Cruz, Mexico. At the time of his departure, Sitjar was described in passport records as of medium height, with a florid complexion, and a scant beard. He held the office of preacher.

Sitjar was one of the group of thirty friars who left San Fernando College, Mexico City, in October 1770, bound for service in the Indian missions of Upper and Lower California. Ten of these, including Sitjar, sailed on the *San Antonio* from San Blas, January 20, 1771, arriving at San Diego, March 12, and at Monterey, May 21. President Junípero Serra appointed Sitjar and Miguel Pieras as the cofounders of Mission San Antonio, which was established July 14, 1771, with Pieras as the superior. Sitjar remained at San Antonio for the rest of his life except for one year in 1797-1798 at Mission San Miguel when he was also the cofounder and senior missionary. In August 1795, he set out with Sergeant Mariano Castro, Corporal Ignacio Vallejo, and soldiers for a survey of the Nacimiento River, selecting the site of Las Pozas as the proper place for the founding of the Mission San Miguel. He kept a diary of the trek which terminated on August 27. At San Antonio he had received Captain Juan Bautista Anza and his expedition on March 6, 1776. Sitjar was present at the funeral of the first president of the missions, Junípero Serra, at Mission San Carlos, August 29, 1784, and at the death of Francisco Pujol at San Antonio. Sitjar succeeded Pieras as senior missionary when the latter returned to Mexico in 1794.

At Sitjar's death in 1808, 3,400 Indians had been baptized. The mission at the end of that year had 4,000 head of cattle and 10,500 sheep. All the buildings put up at San Antonio prior to 1794 were at the instigation of Pieras; after that all those prior to 1808 were constructed by Sitjar. Sitjar proved to be an able linguist of the Mutsun language of his mission. His dictionary, the "Vocabulario de la lengua de los Naturales de la Misión de San Antonio, Alta California," was printed in 1861.

Sitjar baptized at Mission San Carlos, August 29-30, 1784, and at San Luis Obispo, August 19-21, 1792, and August 23, 1786. On August 29, 1808, he said Mass as usual and then accompanied some Indians to their work. "Neither the ice of the winter nor the heat of the summer would prevent him from performing his duty in this line. . . . A little after ten o'clock he retired to the house writhing with continuous cries of pain which excited grief and compassion in all who saw him, since he found no relief in any posture. In this condition he passed the five days that the illness lasted. The Surgeon called from the presidio of Monterey pronounced the malady inflamation of the bowels and the bladder. It was accompanied by continuous vomiting so that he could not receive holy Viaticum."[1] Friar Pedro Cabot and Juan Bautista Sancho assisted him spiritually in his last moments while the corporal of the guard and various Indians prayed at his bedside. He died on September 3, 1808, about eleven o'clock in the morning.

On the fourth, funeral services were held, and the remains were buried in the sanctuary on the Gospel side. Besides the padres mentioned, Antonio Jayme of Soledad and Juan Martín of San Miguel assisted at the funeral. On June 14, 1813, the remains of Sitjar were removed to the new (present but restored) mission church. Fermín Francisco de Lasuén, June 19, 1801, wrote of Sitjar that he was "above reproach as a religious and missionary," that he knew the local dialect, and was a painstaking teacher to the Indians.[2]

[1] Engelhardt, *San Antonio*, p. 108.
[2] Kenneally, *Writings*, II, 199-200.

SOLÁ, FAUSTINO (ca. 1760-1820)

Fray Faustino Solá, a brother of Governor Pablo Solá, was born probably at Mondragón, Vizcaya, Spain. He was a member of San Fernando College, Mexico City, and came to California in 1786. He served at Mission San Luis Obispo from September 29, 1786, to February 14, 1787, and at Mission San Francisco from October 11, 1787, until April 21, 1790. He had baptized at Mission Santa Clara in April and June of 1788 and at Mission San Carlos, Carmel, in July 1790, prior to his return to Mexico. The guardian of the college, Tomás de Pangua, had already informed the viceroy on September 5, 1792, that Solá had become incapacitated for work both within and without the college. When he died at the college in 1820, he had been out of his mind for thirty years.

SUÁREZ DEL REAL, ANTONIO DE LA CONCEPCIÓN
(1804-1850)

Fray Antonio de la Concepción Suárez del Real was born in Mexico in 1804 and made his novitiate and profession as a Franciscan at the college of Guadalupe, Zacatecas, May 17, 1825. He was ordained a priest by the bishop of Puebla, December 22, 1827, and received faculties to preach and hear confessions respectively on May 7 and June 12, 1830. On August 24, 1831, he was assigned to serve in the missions of California. He sailed from La Paz late in November with Governor José Figueroa and in the company of his Zacatecan fellow missionaries under the leadership of Francisco García Diego y Moreno, arriving at Monterey, January 15, 1833.

Suárez del Real replaced the Fernandino, José Joaquín Jimeno, at Mission Santa Cruz in 1833 and remained in charge until 1844. According to Bancroft, he also assisted at times at Mission San Francisco. That he had succeeded his brother, Fray José Suárez del Real, at Monterey by August 18, 1844, is revealed in a letter addressed to the

247

town council protesting the fact that no house had been provided for him and that he was obliged to live with a private family. On November 16 of that year he stated that he had received orders to return to his college.

Concerning the character of Suárez del Real, Bancroft wrote: "Padre Real was a dissolute man addicted to more than one vice, and even accused of theft, but credited with having been kind and indulgent to his neophytes. Sir Geo. Simpson, Laplace the French voyager, and Josiah Belden have something to say of the friar's character."[1]

Cyrille P. T. Laplace wrote of him:

[The sight of him] was really something to be startled at; for it would be difficult to meet an individual with a more insolent look, of more arrogant countenance, of more disheveled appearance than this Mexican padre with his sun-scorched face, his large black eyes against a yellow background, his head covered with a broad-brimmed hat, his otherwise white [gray] Franciscan robe now soiled with a thousand spots, without capouche and tucked up to his cincture to allow full liberty to his lower members; and finally with a blunder-buss slung across his back, which gave a picturesque touch to his garb.[2]

The Rev. Doroteo Ambris, secular pastor of Mission San Antonio, stated in a letter to Rome, dated July 16, 1859, at the time of the Bishop Amat-Franciscan college controversy, that Antonio Suárez del Real had replaced his brother at Monterey and there caused a scandal particularly by his intemperance and resulting disorders. He frequently drank to excess even in public taverns, joined the lowest type of people in their fiestas, and took part in their dances and riotousness. Ambris further claimed that Suárez del Real, in order to live in the town of Monterey where he could devote himself more fully to dissipation, exchanged for a very miserable house the whole mission establishment of Carmel together with its orchard, and this arbitrarily with the permission of his superior. Ambris finally complained that when he later tried to rescind the contract (in which action he was successful), Fray José María de Jesús González Rubio was opposed to the action "because he wished to favor one of his brethren."[3]

The Scotch navigator, Sir George Simpson, in his *Narrative of a Voyage to California Ports in 1841-42*, having maligned Andrés Quintana on information undoubtedly picked up in local gossip, related of Suárez del Real that he followed in the footsteps of Quintana "though with more caution and greater success" and that he found "pleasant relaxation, to say nothing of his bottle, in a seraglio of native beauties, which is said to be, in general, more numerously garrisoned than the castle of Monterey. I need hardly add that the mission in question is in the usual state of decay and dilapidation."[4]

The charge of robbery mentioned by Bancroft is that of Josiah Belden,

248

owner of a store located in the mission buildings which he rented from the priest. He was robbed of goods amounting to one hundred and fifty dollars on one occasion when he was absent in the country, circumstantial evidence pointing to Padre Real. Doyce B. Nunis, Jr., however, who edited the Belden memoir, where this charge appears, is of the opinion that the robbery may have actually been committed by Indians. In this passage Belden also refers to Real's gambling and drinking.[5]

Subsequently returning to the college of Zacatecas, Suárez del Real was eventually elected novice master, August 26, 1848, from which office he resigned, May 1, 1849, though his resignation was not accepted. When cholera broke out in the surrounding neighborhood, the superior sent him to San José de la Isla near Zacatecas to assist the pastor, Juan Felipe Arriaga, who had fallen ill. Unfortunately, Suárez del Real himself contracted the disease. While attempting to return to the college on an unbroken horse, he was thrown and was forced to lie by the roadside until a passerby picked him up and brought him to Zacatecas. During his convalescence he developed pneumonia and, having received the last sacraments, died at five o'clock in the morning, June 3, 1850. He was buried in the vault of the church. The college record characterized him as a man of "full obedience."[6]

[1] *History of California*, V, 689.

[2] Bancroft Library MS, cited in French in *History of California*, III, 695n.

[3] Archives of the Propaganda, Rome. Copy in SBMA.

[4] San Francisco, 1930, p. 106.

[5] *Josiah Belden 1841 California Overland Pioneer: His Memoir and Early Letters* (Georgetown, Calif., 1962), pp. 61 and 83.

[6] Data from the archives of the former college of Zacatecas in SBMA.

SUÁREZ DEL REAL, JOSÉ MARÍA DEL REFUGIO
(ca. 1804-?)

Fray José María del Refugio Suárez del Real, brother of Antonio, was born in Mexico about 1804. He made his profession as a Franciscan at the college of Zacatecas, May 13, 1828, and was ordained to the priesthood on December 4, 1831, at Sombrerete by Bishop José Antonio Zubiría of Durango. Selected to serve in the California missions, February 16, 1831, he subsequently sailed from La Paz, accompanied by his Zacatecan brethren under the commissary prefect, Francisco García Diego y Moreno, with the governor, José Figueroa, arriving at Monterey, January 15, 1833. He was assigned until 1843 to Mission San Carlos, Carmel, and was also responsible for the care of Monterey where he lived most of the time, buying a house there in 1837. In 1844 he was at Santa Clara with the town of San José under his ministration. During these years he baptized at Soledad (June 1839) and at Santa Cruz (1839), at San Rafael (December 1833), and at San Francisco (May 1845).

Suárez del Real was present at Figueroa's deathbed and administered the last rites to him, September 29, 1835. On April 3, 1840, he informed Governor Juan Bautista Alvarado of a plot against the government by a group of Americans under Isaac Graham, and, as a result, they were arrested and sent to Mexico. Between the years 1846 and 1851 he had trouble with the political authorities. In 1851, the guardian of the college called upon José María de Jesús González Rubio to suspend Suárez del Real if the latter could not be induced to leave California voluntarily.

Thus persuaded, Suárez del Real, upon his return to Mexico, was offered the post of army chaplain by the government, but on November 18, 1851, the college refused to grant him permission. He became secularized from the order, the notice of his incorporation into the diocese of Sonora being read at Zacatecas, May 14, 1855. He was at San José del Cabo in Lower California in 1853 and in 1855 was serving as parish priest at Mazatlán.

Concerning Suárez del Real, Bancroft wrote: "Padre José María somewhat resembled his brother in character, though an abler man, with more skill in concealing his irregularities. It is most unfortunate for the general reputation of the Cal. padres — a most excellent body of men, as is fully shown in these volumes — that the Real brothers, Quijas, Mercado, and a few other black sheep of the fold were the friars whose conduct was best known to the foreign immig., and on whom many pioneers have founded their estimate of the missionaries."[1]

The Rev. Doroteo Ambris, in his letter to Rome, July 16, 1859, included an indictment against Suárez del Real similar to the uncomplimentary account of Antonio Real. He reported that the former, while in charge of Carmel and Monterey, caused a scandal by living almost publicly with three women, two of whom were single, one a widow. They were known as the "women" of Real and their children by him known as the "Real" children. In 1859 one of the single women was living at San Antonio. Her son was called José María del Real. The widow and the other single woman resided at Monterey in houses built for them by Real and which he had left to them upon his return to Mexico.

When Real was sent to Santa Clara to replace Jesús María Vásquez del Mercado "to succeed him in everything," he took care of the woman and children of Mercado, according to Ambris, "and continued increasing the family with some other children." (The mother of those children was living at the time of Ambris' writing.) "Some of these children are known by the name Real, and others by Mercado." While serving at Santa Clara, Real sent aid to his women and offspring in Monterey and at times visited them. "This padre who did not lack money, left [California] and according to news received, he got mixed up in political matters in Mexico, was taken prisoner to Mexico [City] and there he secularized and joined the diocese of Sonora."[2]

James Alonzo Forbes, son of James Alexander Forbes, a Scotsman who first came to California in 1831 and who was a sort of majordomo for Fray José Viader at Santa Clara in 1832 and who later became British vice-consul at Monterey, was baptized by Real at Santa Clara, October 7, 1850. In a letter to the historian, Engelhardt, Jolon, December 30, 1905, Forbes wrote concerning Real:

He was in Monterey before Ambriz, was a boon companion of Alvarado set and with them led beastly lives reeking with concupiscence. He kept several concubines at Monterey [the] most noted of them was one Guadalupe Castillo and Rosa Linares or Abila. The latter also lived promiscuously with several loose characters. At Santa Clara [the] padre had the woman he lived with and from who he had several children (I knew two boys and one girl). The woman lived across the street from the Mission church. The girl died and he buried her in the body of the church, placed a plate with inscription on the wall. Rev. John Nobili removed the plate and I think, had the remains exhumed and buried in the grave yard. From here Padre Real went to Mexico and there joined some gamblers — and I believe afterwards was reconstucted. He was a man of fine appearance and very popular with the fast set. The woman the padre kept at Santa Clara was a Silveria Pacheco. People who ought to know accused the padre of being accessory before the fact to the poisoning of two men, one a Frenchman, and one Avila or Abila, who had been ordained a priest and went to Santa Clara to celebrate his first Mass, and then retain the parish, Real to be sent away. The motive attributed [to] his real reluctance, Santa Clara and the woman. I will say, however, that the last seemed only as rumor.[3]

Antonio Coronel in his "Cosas de California" wrote that he had met Padre Real at the San Joaquin and there showed him a bag of gold which he claimed to have brought from the Stanislaus camp [Sonora] which had recently been discovered. That was in August 1848.[4]

[1] *History of California*, V, 689-690.

[2] Archives of the Propaganda, Rome. Copy in SBMA.

[3] Original in SBMA. The Rev. José de los Santos Avila came to California with the first bishop, Francisco García Diego y Moreno, as a student for the priesthood, studied at Santa Barbara and Santa Ines, and was ordained at Mission Santa Barbara, Jan. 1, 1846. On Feb. 1, 1846, he was appointed to the pastorate of Santa Clara and San Jose to succeed Real. He died at Santa Clara on the night of March 25, 1846, "the night before he was to celebrate his first holy Mass" (Engelhardt, *Missions and Missionaries of California*, III, 343, n. 28). The statements of Forbes and Engelhardt regarding Avila's first Mass must refer to Avila's first Mass at Santa Clara and not to his first Mass in the absolute sense.

[4] Bancroft Library MS.

SUÑER, FRANCISCO (1764-1831)

Fray Francisco Suñer was born in 1764 at Olat, Catalonia, Spain, and became a Franciscan in the province of Catalonia, at the Convento de San Francisco, Barcelona, April 14, 1779. After ordination to the priesthood, he served his community as preacher for twelve consecutive years and for six years held the office of visitor-general to the members of the Third Order in his province.

At the age of forty, in 1804, he volunteered for the American missions and left Cádiz in April of that year for Mexico. He arrived at San Fernando College, Mexico City, on July 14. At the time, he was described in government records as of regular stature, his face notably pock-marked, as having a divided beard, frizzled hair, and hazel-colored eyes. He disembarked at Monterey, August 13, 1808.

In California he served at Mission San Carlos, Carmel, from 1808 to 1809; at San Juan Capistrano, March 4, 1810, to April 23, 1814; at Mission San Luis Rey, May 1814 to September 1816; at Mission Santa Barbara, October 27, 1816, to December 23, 1823; and at Mission San Buenaventura, where he died, from 1823 until 1831.

Suñer was one of the few Spanish missionaries who took the unqualified oath of allegiance to the Mexican constitution because of the stipulation in Articles 3 and 4 that the Catholic, Apostolic, and Roman religion is and will be the only and permanent one.

Suñer was at Santa Barbara during the years when the present stone mission church was built, and, though he was the senior missionary, responsibility for most of the work devolved upon Antonio Ripoll, his assistant, because of the former's illness. Suñer gave a lengthy description of the dedication of the completed church in the Baptismal Register, September 13, 1820.

After his transfer to San Buenaventura in 1823, Suñer wrote to Fray Juan Cortés in Mexico, under date of October 16, 1824: "Nothing but the Divine Will has persuaded me to take over as Minister of this Mission to fill the vacancy left by the Reverend Father President Fray José Señán."[1]

Suñer became blind in 1825; his last baptismal entry was August 2, 1825. José Altimira in the second Book of Burials states that Suñer, because he officiated at the funerals, should have signed the Entry Numbers 85 to 112 in 1825, but was unable to do so because of his affliction. The friar lived on, however, until January 17, 1831, when he passed away after having received the sacraments. Francisco Xavier Uría buried him in the mission church on the Gospel side of the sanctuary.

Bancroft states that Suñer was a preacher of more than ordinary eloquence but that his influence as a missionary was seriously impaired because of his broken health. On this account he had made repeated attempts to obtain his passport for retirement. His situation probably had much to do with his brusque manners and irritable temper which made him generally unpopular.

Angustias de la Guerra y Ord expressed a similar opinion: "I knew him at Santa Bárbara as a companion to Padre Ripoll. He was a man of violent character and very ill natured. He was thin, of good figure, more short than tall, a little heavy in the shoulders. He was self-important. His manners were very brusque. I remember that we children did not like him at all."[2]

[1] Nathan and Simpson, tr. and ed. *Letters*, p. 174.
[2] Price and Ellison, tr. *Occurrences in Hispanic California*, p. 35.

TAPIS, ESTEVAN (ca. 1756-1825)

Fray Estevan Tapis was born at Coloma de Farnes, Catalonia, Spain, about 1756. Though Bancroft gives the year and date of his birth as August 25, 1754, and in this is followed by Engelhardt, neither giving a source, Tapis' death record in 1825 states that he was sixty-nine years old, which would place his birth in the year 1756. A document dated 1786 in the Archivo General de la Nación records his age as twenty-eight, which would place his birth in the year 1758.

Tapis entered the Franciscan order at Gerona, January 27, 1778. He received his sailing permit on May 31, 1786, and embarked on June 4, arriving in Mexico on the *Bendición de Dios* in the company of Fray Jayme Cañals. At this period of his life, according to passport records, Tapis was of regular stature, thin, with dark eyes and hair. Having entered San Fernando College, Mexico City, he was commissioned to serve as a California missionary, December 10, 1789, and arrived at Monterey, August 2, 1790.

At mission headquarters, San Carlos, Carmel, where he was met by President Fermín Francisco de Lasuén, he remained for about four months. Eventually assigned to Mission San Luis Obispo, he arrived there, December 20, 1790, and served at the mission until March 24, 1793.

The next ten years found Tapis at Mission Santa Barbara, and he left his mark on its spiritual and material progress. When he arrived, José de Miguel was the superior, upon whose departure in September 1798, Tapis succeeded him. Tapis' records in the registers of Mission Santa Barbara are models of neat, regular chirography.

The number of Indians that had been converted at Santa Barbara by the end of 1793 was 775. By November 24, 1804, when Tapis relinquished his position to become president of the missions, 3,092 had become Christians, 1,783 of them living at the mission. The third church constructed at the mission, of adobe, with six side chapels, was dedicated on March 19, 1794. Tapis had a hand in the painting and embellishing of the interior of this building, unfortunately partially destroyed by the earthquake of December 21, 1812. The original quadrangle of the mission was finished in 1796 and a second one started the following year. He was responsible for the erecting of other buildings and workshops and for creating in 1798 the model Christian Indian village to the west of the mission. When completed in 1807, the village numbered 252 homes. The mission chapel dedicated to San Miguel at Cieneguitas, situated between Santa Barbara and Goleta, was built by Tapis in 1803. He also made plans for a mission reservoir and irrigation system in 1799, but these were not constructed until the years 1806-1808 by his successors.

Tapis at one time considered the possibility of establishing a mission on populous Santa Cruz Island. He did undertake the founding of the nineteenth mission in California, at Santa Ines. He accompanied Commander Felipe de Goycoechea in the fall of 1798 on a reconnaissance of the Santa Ines Valley and chose the site of Alajulapu as the proper location for the mission which was later founded there on September 17, 1804, by Tapis himself.

The friar was at Santa Barbara when Captain George Vancouver visited the port in 1793. The extant accounts of the expedition are most laudatory of the friars and the military for their hospitality and friendship.

While Tapis was at Santa Barbara, he received from President Lasuén subdelegated faculties for the mission, the presidio, and Mission San Buenaventura which the president himself had received as vicar forane and ecclesiastical judge of the bishop of Sonora. At the request of Lasuén, he composed in 1800 a masterly document on the mission system, as it obtained at Santa Barbara, in answer to certain misrepresentations made by the local commander, De Goycoechea. Its detailed description of methods and practices makes it one of the finest and most comprehensive documents written during the mission period.

San Fernando College had already nominated Tapis on January 26, 1798, to succeed Lasuén as president of the California missions in the event of the latter's death or incapacity to govern. Indeed, Lasuén had proposed him as a possible successor. Very shortly after Lasuén died, on June 26, 1803, Tapis was informed of his new position by special dispatch from Carmel. He did not move to Carmel immediately, remaining at Santa Barbara until September 24, 1804. This office he retained until 1812.

During his term as president he spent various periods of time at Missions Santa Barbara, Santa Cruz, San Luis Rey, Santa Ines, and

Purisima. He baptized at San Fernando, April 21, 1805; San Juan Capistrano, July 22, 1808; and San Jose, April 26, 1809. The new mission church at San Gabriel was blessed, February 21, 1805; he dedicated the large stone church at San Juan Capistrano, September 7, 1806, later demolished by the earthquake of 1812; he dedicated the mission church of San Jose on April 23, 1809.

Bishop Francisco Rouset extended to Tapis the same faculties of vicar forane and ecclesiastical judge that had been the prerogative of his predecessor. Though he actually founded only one mission — Santa Ines — Tapis fostered, with the aid of military governors, several expeditions into the interior country to explore for possible mission sites. Such explorations were undertaken out of Santa Barbara, San Diego, San Juan Bautista, and San Francisco, with Tapis supplying the chaplains and diarists.

The era was one of general peace. The mission system which had been founded by Serra and perfected by Lasuén continued to develop smoothly. Tapis' duties were mainly administrative. During his incumbency, the number of Indians living at the missions increased from 18,185 to 20,002, while the number of baptisms rose from 37,976 to 55,865.

In general, historians agree that Tapis was a truly evangelical priest and a fervent preacher who was remarkably wise in his relations with his fellowmen and who had a personality characterized by sweetness and gentleness. He was held in high esteem for his learning and piety. He performed his duties ably and ruled the missions with zeal and wisdom, though Bancroft states that Tapis left less of his individuality in the records than any other president.

As early as September 1810, Tapis had petitioned the college to be relieved of the presidency. Fray José Señán was elected as his successor, July 13, 1812. Notification of this fact, however, did not reach California until November. Tapis thereafter joined the ranks of the ordinary missionaries in the territory. He served at Mission Purisima from September 4, 1811, to August 14, 1812, while still president, and afterward, for about a year each, at San Carlos and Santa Ines. While serving at San Carlos, as secretary he accompanied Vicente Francisco de Sarría, the commissary prefect, on an official tour of visitation of the missions. Tapis was finally stationed at San Juan Bautista, under Felipe Arroyo de la Cuesta, between February 13, 1815, and November 3, 1825. It was there that he took the oath on April 21, 1822, to support Mexican independence.

Tapis died at San Juan Bautista, November 3, 1825, and was buried on the following day in the sanctuary on the Gospel side. He had received the Viaticum from Sarría and extreme unction from De la Cuesta.

Present at the funeral were Friars José Viader of Santa Clara, Buenaventura Fortuny of San Jose, and Luís Gil y Taboada, who conducted the funeral services and made the entry into the Burial Register.

Concerning Tapis, he wrote:

In all these [missions] he conducted himself as a man truly apostolic giving examples in the whole territory of all the virtues especially in prudence in his dealings with the Superiors and with the governors living at the time. In consequence he was much loved by the Religious, the military, the settlers and Indians. He preached continually with fervor. When he could he would teach the boys the rudiments of ordinary schooling; he would write the music for the singers in the church . . . by which means he endeavored to elevate the festivities and solemnities so as to attract devotion, worship, and veneration in the solemnities not only among the Indians, but also among all others. In this way he would see that they made their confessions on the major feasts. In truth, Fr. Tápis exercised his apostolic ministry to edify all. Hence it is that he was a blameless Religious, worthy of the highest praise, and honor to this territory, and particularly to the College of San Fernando de Mexico. . . . He lived filled with the spirit of the Lord.[1]

On the margin Gil y Taboada added that Tapis was sixty-nine years old at his death, a Franciscan forty-eight years, a priest forty-four, and for forty years had lived in the New World, thirty-five of which were spent in California.

[1] Engelhardt, *Mission San Juan Bautista*, p. 101.

TORRENT, HILARIO (ca. 1740-1799)

Fray Hilario Torrent was born about 1740 at San Hilario, Catalonia, Spain, and became a professed Franciscan at Barcelona, June 24, 1761. After ordination to the priesthood, he was active as a preacher for a long period, was guardian of a friary for three years, and vicar for a longer time. He is described as a man of talent and accomplishments. Having joined San Fernando College, Mexico City, he was sent to California in 1786 with high recommendations for general ability and experience.

His one place of service in the mission territory was at San Diego. He arrived there on *La Princesa,* ministering from November 11, 1786, until September 27, 1798. Beyond the faithful performance of his missionary duties, there is little to distinguish his term of service. The number of baptisms grew from 1,229 at the end of 1786 to 2,615 at the end of 1798. He visited Missions San Juan Capistrano and San Gabriel, baptizing there respectively in 1785 and 1793.

President Fermín Francisco de Lasuén, when asked by San Fernando College in September 1796 to suggest candidates for the presidency of the missions to succeed him, named Vicente Fuster, Estevan Tapis, and Torrent. The last choice is difficult to understand, for on July 21 Lasuén had described Torrent's condition as follows: "(For months past) [he] has been suffering from acute depression which causes him to spend almost all the time weeping. He went to San Capistrano, and it seems he is beginning to recover."[1]

When Torrent retired from California, Lasuen could say of him no more than that he was "half paralyzed, very forgetful, disturbed in mind, partially blind, and suffering from an impediment in speech. He sometimes weeps and laughs like a child, and according to the settled conviction of everyone he is incapable of discharging the duties of this ministry."[2]

Torrent sailed for Mexico from San Diego on *La Princesa,* November 8, 1798, and died sometime before May 14, 1799, of a convulsion, presumably at San Fernando College.

[1] Kennealy, *Writings,* I, 388.
[2] Ibid., II, 58.

URÍA, FRANCISCO XAVIER DE LA CONCEPCIÓN (1770-1834)

Fray Francisco Xavier de la Concepción Uría, the son of Antonio de Uría and María Polonia de Arruti, was born in 1770 at Ayzarna, in the jurisdiction of Certona, diocese of Pamplona, Spain. He became a Franciscan at San Sebastión, January 13, 1789. In 1795, while still a student of theology, he left his native country for San Fernando College, Mexico City, where he was ordained to the priesthood. He sailed from Cádiz on May 8, 1796, and disembarked at Vera Cruz, June 26. He was of regular height, with a pallid complexion, hazel-colored eyes and hair, a thin nose, bushy eyebrows, and a scar below a dimpled chin. Uría was sent to the California missions on December 14, 1796, and arrived at San Francisco on the *Concepción,* April 14, 1797. He "labored with zeal in them until his retirement to said college [San Fernando] in 1805." After two years he returned to California.

In his first period of service, Uría was stationed at Mission Santa Barbara from June till September 1797, at Mission Purisima from October 2, 1797, to July 26, 1798, and at Mission San Fernando until he returned to Mexico. He had baptized at San Juan Capistrano, March 1, San Gabriel, October 19-31, and San Diego, December 18, 1799. Upon his return to California, where he arrived, August 13, 1808, at Monterey, he was stationed at Mission Santa Cruz for a short period, at Mission Santa Ines from December 12, 1808, to January 29, 1824, when the Chumash revolt broke out, and for a time at Mission Santa Barbara. While en route to Mission Soledad, where he baptized between December

26, 1824, and February 1828, he baptized at Mission San Miguel in September and October. He was finally stationed at Mission San Buenaventura from early February 1828 until April 12, 1834. Uría refused to take the oath of allegiance to the Mexican constitution of 1824.

Vicente Francisco de Sarría wrote in 1817 that Mission Santa Ines "has received plenty of improvement because of his [Uría's] evangelical labors, industry and work." In that year, because of his health, he had received permission again to return to Mexico. Mariano Payeras stated in 1820: "His merit is distinguished because of his good endeavors and efficiency in this ministry and his aptitude is not limited to it, for it can be used also in behalf of the faithful and for some commission and employment in the cloister."

Bancroft writes that he "was stout in physique, jolly in manner, addicted to pleasantries and jokes, indulging sometimes in coarse language, kind-hearted and well liked though at times very quick-tempered. He was an excellent manager of temporal affairs, and was noted for his generosity, especially to the Indians."[1] Angustias de la Guerra y Ord recalled that Uría was "a very generous man."[2] Alfred Robinson testified to his hospitality as well as to his practical jokes. Uría also had his eccentricities, a few of which are described by Robinson: "At dinner the fare was sumptuous, and I was much amused at the eccentricity of the old Pádre, who kept constantly annoying four large cats, his daily companions; or with a long stick thumped upon the heads of his Indian boys, and seemed delighted thus to gratify his singular propensities."[3]

In 1833, Uría became so ill that it was necessary to remove him from San Buenaventura to Santa Barbara for medical treatment. As early as February 6, 1830, Dr. Stephen Anderson, then in Santa Barbara, described the padre's condition in a formal statement:

> I certify that the Rev. Fr. Francisco Xavier de Uría . . . has suffered for the last twelve months from the *Piedra de Variga,* and to all appearances his infirmity is daily getting worse. He suffers also from spasms on one side of the face which is very much aggravated at the Mission. For some time he has had dropsical swellings on the legs which increased to such an extent as to deprive him of their use. In order to alleviate his infirmities somewhat, it is absolutely necessary that he give up the management of the Mission entirely; for if he retains that office, his maladies will soon be incurable.[4]

In time he was permanently removed to Santa Barbara and stayed at the house of Captain José Antonio de la Guerra y Noriega where, after receiving the last sacraments, he died, November 5, 1834. He was buried at the mission on the following day by Antonio Jimeno, and his remains were placed in the crypt beneath the sanctuary of the church.

Nowhere has the writer found evidence that Francisco Xavier Uría and José Antonio Uría were brothers or in any way related, though both were born in the same general area.

[1] *History of California*, III, 659, n. 8.

[2] Price and Ellison, tr. *Occurrences in Hispanic California*, p. 33.

[3] *Life in California*, p. 61.

[4] Engelhardt, *San Buenaventura ... Mission*, p. 68.

URÍA, JOSÉ ANTONIO (1769-1815)

Fray José Antonio Uría was born in 1769 at Azcoitia, diocese of Pamplona, Spain, and became a Franciscan in the province of Cantabria at Aránzazu in 1789. In 1792 he was a member of the friary of Mondragón. Enlisted for service at San Fernando College by the commissary, Manuel Arévalo, in 1796, he sailed in that year from Cádiz, bound for Vera Cruz. At the time of his departure, he was described in passport records as tall and thin, light-complexioned, with hazel-colored eyes, brown hair, a long nose, having a chin scar, and a wart on his face.

He arrived at Monterey, July 28, 1799. President Fermín Francisco de Lasuén first assigned him to Mission San Jose where he served from August 1799 until July 1806, followed by service at Mission San Fernando between October 31, 1806, and November 1808. Thereafter he was stationed at Mission San Juan Capistrano until October 1812. He had meanwhile baptized at San Francisco, February-March 1801, at San Carlos in July 1801, at San Juan Bautista in June and July 1801, and again in October 1803.

In 1802, Uría was already suffering from urinary disturbances and from severe attacks of hemorrhoids and on this account wished to retire. He disclosed to José Viñals in 1807 that his appointment to Mission San Fernando was the high-water mark of his miseries and sufferings, despite the fact that he had obtained permission to retire.

At San Fernando he succumbed to melancholy until Pedro Múñoz, "an agreeable companion" arrived. Georg von Langsdorff, who met Uría at San Francisco in 1806, considered him a very intelligent but very serious person. By November 19, 1812, he had received permission to return to the college. Fray Pedro Adriano Martínez stated that Uría died in Mexico in 1815.

URRESTÍ, JOSÉ ANTONIO (1775-1812)

Fray José Antonio Urrestí was born in 1775 at Mañaria, diocese of Calahorra, Spain, and became a Franciscan in the province of Cantabria. He set out for the missions in the New World on the *Sagrada Familia* from Cádiz, shortly after June 20, 1802, having the offices of preacher and confessor. At the time of embarcation, he was described in passport records as of regular stature, light-skinned, with hazel-colored eyes, and with a heavy beard. He arrived at Vera Cruz, Mexico, in August and subsequently entered San Fernando College.

Urrestí acted as president of a group of ten missionaries who set out from the college for California. They left Guadalajara, April 23, 1804, for Tepic and San Blas, and eventually arrived at Monterey, August 15, 1804. In California, Urrestí served at Mission San Gabriel from October 16, 1804, until September 12, 1806, during which period he baptized on one occasion at San Juan Capistrano. At Mission Santa Barbara he officiated between December 22, 1806, and October 8, 1808. He then served at Mission San Fernando from December 6, 1808, until his death on January 4, 1812. He baptized at Santa Barbara on September 9, 1809, and he had attended the dedication of the church at San Juan Capistrano, September 7, 1806. Before his death, Urrestí received the last sacraments except, because of vomiting, the Viaticum. He was buried at Mission San Fernando by Pedro Múñoz on January 5.

There appear to be no particular characterizations of Urrestí by his contemporaries.

USÓN, RAMÓN (1737-?)

Fray Ramón Usón was born in 1737 at Caspe, archdiocese of Zaragosa, Spain, and became a Franciscan at San Francisco de Zaragosa in the province of Aragón, November 9, 1752. In 1769 he left the friary at Mora for the missions in the New World. He sailed with thirty-nine other Franciscans under the leadership of Fray Rafael Verger and arrived at San Fernando College in 1770. At the time he was described in records as of medium height, with an aquiline face, pockmarked, with a somewhat reddish beard.

Usón left San Fernando College, Mexico City, in October 1770 and sailed from San Blas on the *San Carlos,* February 1771 for Loreto in Lower California. Shortly after arrival, he was appointed by President Francisco Palóu to Misión San Xavier. In 1772 he was sent to Upper California, going overland by way of Velicatá and arriving at San Diego in November 1772. He was at Mission San Gabriel from December 3, 1772, till January 16, 1773, and for short periods at Missions San Luis Obispo and San Antonio, at the latter, November 6, 1773. On July 7, 1774, he sailed from Monterey for San Diego and then to Mexico on *El Príncipe* to seek a remedy for a disease of the eyes from which he was suffering. He left San Diego, August 4. On November 10, 1774, the guardian, Francisco Pangua, appointed him chaplain of the *San Antonio.* Usón made the round trip from San Blas to San Diego, June 1775, but later that year he was unable to continue his service as chaplain.

On November 26, 1777, Viceroy Antonio María Bucareli y Ursúa wrote to the Council of the Indies that Usón had been ill since 1770 and had been given permission to go from San Fernando College to the province of Zacatecas by the Franciscan commissary general on condition that the viceroy also gave his permission. This the latter was unable to do. However, Usón continued to remain at Zacatecas without being officially transferred there. Bucareli left the final judgment to the king.

VÁZQUEZ DEL MERCADO, JESÚS MARÍA (ca. 1808-?)

His full name was Jesús María y José Guadalupe de la Trinidad Vázquez del Mercado. He was a native of Mexico, born about 1808, and became a Franciscan at the college of Guadalupe, Zacatecas, making his profession, January 14, 1829. He was ordained a priest at Sombrerete, December 4, 1831, by the Most Rev. José Antonio Zubiría, bishop of Durango. In the discretorial meeting of February 16, 1832, he was proposed as one of the missionaries who were to go to California for the purpose of taking over the northern missions from the Fernandinos and was definitely assigned on April 7.

Vázquez del Mercado arrived at Monterey, January 15, 1833, with Governor José Figueroa, Fray Francisco García Diego y Moreno, and companions. During his stay in California, he served at Mission San Rafael, 1833 to 1834, at San Antonio, December 9, 1834, to October 16, 1839, at Santa Clara, 1839 to 1844, and had care of Soledad also between June 18, 1834, and October 2, 1839. He baptized at San Francisco in 1833 and on August 22 and October 13, 1840; at San Juan Bautista, January 12, 1834; at Mission San Jose, January 8, signing at the latter place the official books; he also baptized at Santa Cruz in May and June of the same year.

In 1833 he notified the governor that the Russians were enticing neophytes away from San Rafael, were buying stolen cattle, and were invading Mexican rights in various ways. In 1834 he made a bitter complaint against a Mexican commander, Angel Ramírez, for his treatment of the Indians. The alcalde, A. M. Pico, February 24, 1844, charged Mercado with illicit use of mission property, insubordination, and calumny, and cited him to appear before him, which the latter refused to do. Jesús Pico states that he was sent to Santa Clara to arrest the padre, that he put him aboard a vessel in San Francisco which took him to Monterey and from there to Mexico after the writing of abusive letters to Governor Juan Bautista Alvarado and Joaquín Castro. Bishop García Diego y Moreno, José María de Jesús González Rubio, and José Anzar, president of the Zacatecans, investigated the charges and found no cause for censuring Mercado. The college of Guadalupe resented the treatment given him and as a result recalled three of its subjects in

California, Miguel Muro, José María Gutiérrez, and Antonio Suárez del Real.

William Heath Davis, who met him at Mission Santa Clara, writes concerning him:

He confided to me his knowledge of the existence of gold in the same locality [the Sacramento Valley]. . . . Father Mercado was a brilliant conversationalist, and talked with the greatest fluency, in a steady stream of discourse, hour after hour; and I greatly enjoyed hearing him. . . . I would . . . suggest that it would be better to make the matter [of gold] known to induce Americans and others to come . . . develop the country, build towns, . . . He would answer that the immigration would be dangerous; that they would pour in . . . overrun the country; . . . [the] work of the Missions would be interferred with, . . . I never heard from any one, except the two priests [Mercado and Muro] of gold in Northern California prior to its discovery in 1848 at Sutter's mill.[1]

The friars had received the information from Indians.

Bancroft wrote of him:

Though a man of good abilities and education, of fine presence and engaging manners, he was an intriguer, arbitrary in his acts, and always ready to quarrel with any one who would not accept his views. Especially did he deem it his mission to quarrel with the secular authorities, and on the few occasions where there was no real cause for complaint he had no scruples about inventing pretexts. He was engaged with Angel Ramírez in political plottings against Alvarado's government; and though often appearing as a defender of the Indians' rights, he did much more harm than good by his injudicious acts. He is represented as a hard drinker, a gambler, and a libertine — the father of many half-breed children at each of the missions where he served; and all that can be said in mitigation of this bad reputation is that much of the testimony, though not all, comes from men who were not friendly to the padre, being directly or indirectly parties to some of his many controversies.[2]

There is a letter in the archives of the Propagation of the Faith in Rome written by the Rev. Doroteo Ambris from Mission San Antonio, July 16, 1859, concerning the immorality of Mercado at Santa Clara. He stated that when Fray José María Suárez del Real was sent to Santa Clara to take Mercado's place, Real took care of the woman and children of Mercado and had some children of his own by her, some of whom went by the name of Real, others by the name of Mercado.

After Mercado returned to Mexico, the college of Zacatecas — doubtless not knowing of his irregularities in California — elected him novice master, November 29, 1845, from which office he resigned on June 30, 1846. He became disaffiliated from the college, July 10, 1846, and passed over to San Fernando College, Mexico City.

[1] *Sixty Years in California,* pp. 233-234.
[2] *History of California,* IV, 682, n. 20.

VIADER, JOSÉ (1765-?)

Fray José Viader was born on August 27, 1765, at Gallines, diocese of Gerona, Catalonia, Spain, and entered the Franciscan order at Gerona in May 1788 in his native town. He left Spain on the *Santiago de España* with twenty-two other friars on May 8, 1795, under the leadership of Manuel Arévalo. They disembarked at Vera Cruz, Mexico, June 26, 1795, and proceeded to San Fernando College, Mexico City. At this period Viader was described as tall, light-complexioned, with hazel-colored hair and eyes, and a thick nose. In later life he was described as a large man of fine physique, with great physical strength and courage. He was somewhat reserved and stern in manner with strangers but well liked by his acquaintances with whom his manner was always frank and courteous. He was a diligent and effective man of business, greatly devoted to the temporal prosperity of his mission but, as Bancroft says, "not always impressed with the sanctity of the revenue laws."[1] In a letter of the guardian of the college, Antonio Nogueyra, February 23, 1796, the viceroy was informed that Viader was a religious of "proven conduct and of entire satisfaction" to the rulers of the college.

Viader arrived on the *Aránzazu* at San Francisco, June 18, 1796. He was promptly assigned to Mission Santa Clara, setting out for his destination on June 30. There he remained for thirty-seven years until his retirement from California. When Viader arrived, Miguel Sánchez was superior, a position he retained until transferred to Mission San Gabriel in 1797. Magín Matías Catalá became superior, and he retained this position until his death in 1830, after which Viader succeeded him and held the position until 1833.

Early in his career at Santa Clara, Catalá was afflicted with inflammatory rheumatism to such an extent that he found it extremely difficult to go about, with the result that the management of the temporalities of the mission fell chiefly to the lot of Viader, who was an extremely capable administrator. By the end of 1832, 8,536 baptisms had taken place at Santa Clara, while the number of neophytes living at the mission was 1,125. By the end of 1832 Santa Clara had had the greatest number of baptisms of any California mission.

The padres of Santa Clara had had charge also of the civilian pueblo of San Jose since 1777. The cornerstone of the church was laid there, July 12, 1803, Viader being among those present.

Viader accompanied two military expeditions in 1810, sent out by the governor to look for new mission sites. The first expedition departed from Mission San Jose, August 15 and proceeded into the San Joaquin Valley to the mouth of the river of the same name, then, continued along it for a distance of about eighty or ninety miles, crossed the Coast Ranges, and came into Mission San Juan Bautista on August 27.

The second expedition left Mission San Jose, October 19, penetrated into the San Joaquin Valley as far as the Merced River, and returned to Mission Santa Clara on October 28. Viader kept diaries of both expeditions.

Despite his activities and success, Viader was not an entirely happy man in his California service, for on April 14, 1820, he asked for permission to return to Mexico. Continuing illness and mental distress, he stated, made him habitually unattuned to the ministry in California, disliking in particular the burdens connected with managing the temporalities. On May 3, 1820, he wrote a second time: "For the love of God, let my permission arrive." Whether the permission arrived or not is unknown. Others had received permission for similar reasons — men who had served fewer years than Viader. He remained long after the requests were made and can only be regarded as the object of admiration and respect in making the sacrifice of extending his service and in continuing labors that were distasteful to him.

After 1811, supply ships for some period of time no longer arrived from Mexico, and successive governors demanded increased productivity from the missions in order to obtain sufficient provisions for the presidios. Viader was the only missionary who protested. On May 3, 1820, with Catalá he addressed a lengthy appeal to the governor for relief from some of the demands made upon the mission, and on December 21, 1821, he wrote to Mariano Payeras, bitterly complaining that the soldiers were inconsiderate and often coupled their demands with threats.

Viader took the oath of loyalty to the Iturbide regency under orders from the college and the bishop of Sonora. However, after its downfall, he consistently declined to accept the subsequent constitution of 1824, but promised obedience to the constituted authorities. On June 16, 1829, after all Spaniards in Mexico had been banished and San Fernando College was reduced to a handful of friars, Viader, Antonio Peyrí, and Juan Amorós, all three of whom were in California, were elected as counselors of the college, probably to keep up the semblance of a full college regime. But this gave them title and honor without effective participation in government.

When all the missions north of San Miguel were handed over to the Zacatecan missionaries in 1833 on February 13, the commissary prefect, Francisco García Diego y Moreno, chose Santa Clara as his abode, and Viader accordingly assigned Santa Clara over to him, remaining with him, however, for several months.

Though Viader administered only one mission, he had the opportunity of visiting most of the others between Sonoma and San Diego. He was at San Carlos, May 19, 1799, and June 28, 1803, when Fermín

Francisco de Lasuén died. He was at Mission San Jose in June 1800 and again, as secretary to Vicente Francisco de Sarría, for the visitations made in 1816 and 1818. Viader visited Mission Santa Cruz together with Narciso Durán and was there when Andrés Quintana was murdered by the Indians in October 1812. He was at Mission San Juan Bautista, June 13, 1803, June 22-24, 1820, and on February 19, 1821. In 1818 he was secretary to Sarría for the canonical visitation to San Francisco and San Rafael. In 1833 he spent the summer and fall at Mission San Juan Capistrano, an indication that he had come south overland and in this case would have visited all the missions en route. He baptized at San Diego, November 17 and 22, 1833, and sailed from that port for Mexico. Henry Virmond, a German merchant in Mexico, reported Viader's safe arrival in Havana, Cuba, and it may be assumed from this that he was returning to his native Spain.

Sarría in 1817 wrote concerning Viader: "Santa Clara is the only mission together with the neighboring town of San Jose which has been the scene of his apostolic labors ... which I classify as a regular performance of duty. However, the many years he has served and the added fact that he continued to serve there when he had requested to retire and made the sacrifice of remaining when it was pointed out that he could not be spared, makes his merit worthy of some consideration." Payeras in 1820 was more generous in his appraisal of Viader: "His merit is above the ordinary and I consider equally his aptitude for whatever might be offered him in the ministry and for some office in the Order."

When Auguste Duhaut-Cilly met Viader at Santa Clara, the latter gave the traveler a cordial welcome. The Frenchman stated that Viader was "a modest and truthful man," who revealed to him that he had killed a hundred bears by shooting them after he had ensnared them with other dead animals. Viader often signed the documents he wrote, "Padre de las Gallinas," possibly because of similarity in sound to the name of the town in which he was born.

[1] *History of California*, III, 726, n. 22.

VIÑALS, JOSÉ (1759-?)

Fray José Viñals was born at Villafranca, Catalonia, Spain, August 14, 1759, and was professed as a Franciscan in the same province, October 14, 1776. With a number of confreres he set out from his province, June 26, 1778, to enter the college of Tarifa, Spain. There he remained until July 22, 1787, when chosen to live at the college of Moquegua. Next, he entered the service of San Fernando College, Mexico City, and volunteering for the Indian missions, he arrived at Santa Barbara on the

Concepción, May 8, 1798. President Fermín Francisco de Lasuén appointed him to Mission San Carlos where he served from August of that year until 1804. Viñals also baptized at San Luis Obispo on June 31, 1798, at Santa Clara in July and September of the same year and again in February 1799, and at Mission San Jose on March 11, 1799.

Having repeatedly asked to retire, declaring that it was impossible to continue without losing his health or his mind, Viñals was permitted to leave California in the latter part of 1804. In Mexico, at San Fernando College, on July 12, 1806, he was appointed procurator of the California missions, an office he held for about two years. In 1809 he wrote to Captain José de la Guerra y Noriega in Santa Barbara, asking for traveling money and for alms to aid his aging parents, since he intended to return to Spain. On March 16, 1811, he asked for disaffiliation from the college and for permission to join the province of the Holy Gospel which was granted.

Angustias de la Guerra y Ord said of Viñals that he played the guitar and sang very well, all of which was very pleasant and diverting. One day when he was playing, he put his instrument aside and said to her father, José de la Guerra: "Countryman, this is not for a friar, I am going to become a Carthusian." Later, according to the same informant, he entered a Carthusian monastery in France or at least somewhere in Europe. He wrote to De la Guerra at that time and thus gave him his farewell message.[1]

Bancroft writes of him: "He was of an ardent, gay temperament while in California, being a fine singer and performer on the guitar. It is necessary to add that the moral character of Viñals was not wholly above suspicion, for he was at one time accused before the alcalde of San José of having been the father of three children brought into the world by a certain señora of that locality."[2]

[1] Price and Ellison, tr. *Occurrences in Hispanic California,* pp. 35-36.
[2] *History of California,* II, 147, n. 55.

ZALVIDEA, JOSÉ MARÍA (1780-1846)

Fray José María Zalvidea was born on March 2, 1780, at Bilbao, Vizcaya, Spain, and entered the Franciscan order, December 13, 1798, in the province of Cantabria. He sailed from Cádiz shortly after June 29, 1804, and subsequently arrived at San Fernando College, Mexico City. He left the college on March 15, 1805, for San Blas, whence he sailed on June 2 for San Francisco, arriving at the latter port on August 31. In California, Zalvidea was stationed first at Mission San Fernando from February 1 to August 31, 1806, an appointment he found "totally repugnant." Then he was sent to Mission San Gabriel where he served from December 19, 1806, to January 15, 1827. During this period he visited San Fernando, December 8 to 29, 1815, April 29 to May 1, 1821, and again between November 27, 1825, and February 1, 1826. He was assigned to Mission San Juan Capistrano where he labored between March 4, 1826, and November 26, 1842. And, finally, he was at Mission San Luis Rey until his death in 1846.

Zalvidea baptized at Mission San Juan Bautista, October 10, 1805, and at Santa Barbara in October and November 1806 and again on December 21, 1807. He was at San Buenaventura for the dedication of the church, September 9, 1809.

Zalvidea took no part in political controversies, and when California became a part of Mexico, he was willing to swear allegiance to the republic in so far as it was consistent with his religious profession. In 1806 he accompanied a military expedition that started from Santa Barbara. Crossing the mountain ranges of the interior country, the trek terminated at Mission San Fernando. He kept a diary of the journey and baptized a number of old and dying Indians en route.

Bancroft states that from the first Zalvidea was rated by his superiors as one of the best and most zealous of the friars as priest, teacher, and manager of temporalities. In their judgment, his great field of labor was at San Gabriel where for twenty years he worked incessantly, building up its temporal interests without neglecting the spiritual or losing the esteem of his neophytes or of others who came in contact with him. "He was doubtless in those days a model missionary, and then and later was regarded by the common people as a saint. He gave much attention to viticulture at S. Gabriel, being the first to introduce this industry on a large scale, and taking the greatest pride in his immense vineyard."[1]

Vicente Francisco de Sarría in 1817 praised Zalvidea in these precise terms:

In my judgment he is one of the best missionaries in this land and his merit is shown by his untiring tenacity in his teaching, instructing and in the spiritual formation of his neophytes, not leaving them even until the last moment of their lives; also this is seen in the great number of Christians which constitute his mission which is notable and singular; also in consideration of his assiduity and in his knowledge of the language, his efforts and consistency in the fulfillment of other obligations not only those which refer to personal religious ones, but also to those of the ministry which bind him to the people of the pueblo three leagues away [Los Angeles] and others in various ranches and districts.

Mariano Payeras in 1820 added these observations: "His merit is distinguished by his activity and application in all the branches connected with his ministry. His aptitude, provided full health were his, is extended for the same degree of activity among the faithful and the pagans as well as for some offices that the superiors might wish to confer upon him. However, he is now experiencing reversals in his health."

In his later years Zalvidea showed some eccentricities such as mixing all foods at table and eating them in this manner; his habit of saying, "Vamos, si señor," when one met him and, then, turning his eyes away; and when walking about, at times stopping to make strange gestures and exclaiming, "Vete, Satanás," as if in conflict with the devil or driving away temptations in thought. He was known to practice mortifications such as wearing a belt of iron points and using the scourge on himself. Still he always retained a clear head for practical matters. He was a tall person, was light-complexioned, of fine presence, was courteous in his manners, with a smile and a kind word for all. He was skilled in the use of the Gabrieliño tongue.

He died at Mission San Luis Rey apparently early in 1846 as he was being prepared to be taken to San Juan Capistrano in a cart. He was buried in the mission church to the left of the altar. As early as 1831 Zalvidea had spoken of the fact that he suffered attacks of asthma.

Zalvidea, whom Michael C. White knew intimately, was described by him as "a tall, rawboned, stout man, very industrious and intelligent, constantly at his work, spiritual, but also in developing the resources of San Gabriel mission and subsequently of San Juan Capistrano. He was in the full sense of the word a saint. He planted fruit trees in the ravines and in many places distant from the missions, for the benefit of the bronco Indians."[2] He might be termed the Franciscan Johnny Appleseed.

Eulalia Pérez, who knew him at San Gabriel, asserted that Zalvidea was always very considerate with the Indians, was loved by them as well as by the whites. He greatly improved the mission and provided well for the neophytes and even for the pagans. Angustias de la Guerra y Ord did not know him personally but only from reputation and declared that he was considered a "most virtuous and wise priest," ever active and industrious.

Don Agustín Janssens recalled that "Padre Zalvidea was a man of great talent and of saintly repute because of his upright virtue. Many attributes were credited to him which were incomprehensible, and for them to be true one must believe that he had second sight or was inspired. I was inclined to think that many of these reports were exaggerated, or never happened, but this does not detract from the fact that Padre Zalvidea has been a great figure in the historic scene of California."[3]

Again he declared: "The padre experienced religious exaltations and sometimes twitched as he undertook to drive away the devil, but otherwise he was of sane mind. He carried on conversations perfectly and one could take advice from him about any matter, as he gave the impression that whatever was said to him would be well considered. The goodness of his heart had no limit."[4]

[1] *History of California,* V, 621-622 *n.*

[2] *California All the Way Back to 1828,* p. 92.

[3] ... Ellison and ... Price, tr. *The Life and Adventures in California of Don Agustín Janssens* (San Marino, 1953), p. 22.

[4] Ibid., p. 109.

⋙ APPENDIX I ⋘

Franciscans Who Visited California
Between 1769 and 1848

CAMPA Y COS, MIGUEL DE LA CONCEPCIÓN (1719-1792)

Fray Miguel de la Concepción Campa y Cos was born in 1719 at Nombre de Dios, Durango, Mexico, and entered San Fernando College, Mexico City, December 7, 1742. After ordination to the priesthood, he served as a missionary in the Sierra Gorda missions for about twenty years, remaining there until 1767 when he was recalled to serve in the missions of Lower California. His name is found in the registers of Misión Tilaco for July 20, 1748, and October 3, 1758, and of Misión Landa for February 1763 and in 1764.

With five other confreres, among whom was Juan Crespí, Campa y Cos went directly from the Sierra Gorda to Tepic to join the group of missionaries who had set out under the leadership of Junípero Serra from Mexico City in July 1767. Owing to the machinations of the Jaliscan friars, who had been destined originally for Nayarit, the Fernandinos were reassigned to Nayarit and the Jaliscans to Lower California. Serra sent Francisco Palóu and Campa to the visitor-general, José de Gálvez, then at Guanajuato, and on to Mexico City to vice-regal headquarters to protest the change in plans. Palóu and Campa left Tepic, October 19, 1767, returning on December 31, their mission successful.

With fifteen other friars under Serra, Campa sailed on the *Concepción* from San Blas, March 14, 1768, and arrived at Loreto, Lower California, April 1. On the third, Serra appointed Campa y Cos as minister of Misión San Ignacio de Cadegomó near the center of the peninsula. He started out for his destination on April 6. In March 1769 a land expedition led by Gaspar de Portolá left Loreto for the occupation of Upper California. On Serra's instructions, Campa joined Portolá and his men on March 27 at Cadegomó and marched with them to the last Christian outpost in the north, Santa María de los Angeles. There he awaited the arrival of Serra, who came on May 5. The expedition set out again on the eleventh and came to Velicatá where Serra founded Misión San Fernando on May 14 and appointed Campa y Cos as its first minister.

Campa was made substitute president of the Lower California missions in the event of Palóu's inability to function. When the Franciscans relinquished the Lower California missions to the Dominicans in 1773, Campa was left at Velicatá to surrender the northern missions into the newcomers' hands. Thus he was the last of the Fernandino missionaries to leave the territory. Completing his assignment, he went to Loreto and from there returned to San Fernando College sometime after April 14, 1774.

In the spring of 1775 a fleet of four vessels was dispatched by Viceroy Antonio María Bucareli y Ursúa for the purpose of exploring the northwest Pacific. San Fernando College was called upon to supply chaplains. The guardian, Fray Tomás de Pangua, assigned Campa y Cos to the *San Carlos,* then to the *Santiago* or *Nueva Galicia,* with Fray Benito de la Sierra as companion. Campa kept a log of the voyage along the Pacific coast.

The ships were under the command of Bruno de Heceta. They sailed from San Blas, March 16, 1775, directly north to a point now known as Trinidad in northern California. On June 11, Heceta took possession in the name of Spain. Campa raised the cross on Trinidad Head, sang the High Mass, and preached. The place was so named because the celebration took place on Trinity Sunday.

Leaving Trinidad on June 19, the explorers continued northward and by July 14 reached Grenville Harbor, halfway up the coast of the present state of Washington. Campa did not go ashore, though a cross was raised there. On the return voyage the explorers named the mouth of the present-day Columbia River, La Asunción de Nuestra Señora. They arrived at Monterey, August 29, 1775. Heceta decided to go overland to visit the site of the future San Francisco. Palóu and Campa were assigned to accompany him. The expedition set out on September 4 and reached the area of present-day Sutro Heights on the twenty-second; it left the San Francisco area, September 24, returning to Monterey, October 1.

When the *Santiago* returned to San Blas at the end of October, Campa y Cos begged his superiors to be relieved of his chaplaincy. Because of his age — fifty-six — his request was granted.

In the chapter of May 24, 1777, Campa was elected a counselor of the college, a position he retained until 1779. For the chapter of May 24, 1783, Campa was named official visitor and commissary for San Fernando College. On July 23, 1783, he was elected novice master at the age of sixty-four. He died in 1792.

CUCULLA, FRANCISCO (?-?)

Fray Francisco Cuculla, a native of Mexico, was one of the group of missionaries of the college of Guadalupe, Zacatecas, who came to California in 1831 to arrange with the Fernandino missionaries there to take over the northern missions between Soledad and Sonoma. With Fray Mariano Sosa and two others, he traveled by way of Lower California and arrived at Mission San Gabriel in April 1831. There the missionaries were guests of the president, José Bernardo Sánchez. Cuculla and his companions baptized at times at the mission as well as at the Plaza church in Los Angeles. The register of Mission San Buenaventura shows that Cuculla was also there on July 24, 1831. He returned to Mexico probably on January 17, the following year.

EIXARCH, TOMÁS (1742-?)

Though his name was spelled in various ways by others, Eyxarch, Eixarth, Ezyarch, Eciarc, Esiare, etc., he himself wrote his name, Eixarch. He was born at Liria, archdiocese of Valencia, in 1742. He came to the college of Santa Cruz de Querétaro together with Fray Juan Domingo Arricivita on the *San Francisco* or *Matamoras* in 1767. At the time he was described in passport records as a person with lemon-colored skin, dark eyes and hair.

Eixarch was missionary at San José de Tumacácori (in present-day Arizona) in 1775 when he received orders from the guardian of his college to associate himself with Fray Francisco Garcés and accompany the Anza expedition as far as the Colorado River. Both missionaries were to feel out the Yumas concerning the establishment of a Spanish settlement and missions among them. The Anza expedition set out from San Miguel de Horcasitas, Sonora, September 29, 1775, Eixarch joining it at Tubac, near Tumacácori, October 21. At the Colorado it was welcomed by Chief Palma on November 30.

Eixarch remained among the Yumas on the California side of the river until May 11, 1776, excepting a short trip to Caborca, and interested Palma in making a trip later to Mexico City to see Viceroy Antonio María Bucareli y Ursúa. He taught the Yumas the elements of Catholic doctrine and succeeded in having some of them attend devotions. He described the soil and some of the Indian customs in the diary he kept between December 4, 1775, and May 11, 1776. While living in the area of present Fort Yuma, he planted a small fruit and vegetable garden and built a primitive house. When Captain Juan Bautista Anza, Pedro Font, and soldiers returned to Fort Yuma after successfully leading their expedition to San Francisco, Eixarch accompanied them to Sonora, reaching Horcasitas, June 1. Chief Palma who was with them continued on to Mexico City with Anza.

Shortly after, Eixarch became missionary at Oquitoa, attending at the same time the presidio church at Altar in Upper Sonora. His name appears in the Oquitoa Baptismal Register from September 11, 1776, until February 1, 1781.

FARNESIO, FRANCESCO ANTONIO (ca. 1746-?)

Fray Francesco Antonio Farnesio was born in Italy about 1746. He arrived at Monterey on the *Concepción* in December 1804 from China, where he had been a missionary. Ill health compelled him to leave his field of labor, and with the permission of his superiors, he came to California in the hope that the milder climate would improve his health. From Monterey he proceeded to Mission Purisima where the records show him on October 1, 1805. At that time he was supposed to be on his way to Mexico City. He had requested Fray Mariano Payeras to make financial arrangements for him with the procurator in Mexico. However, he had expressed the hope that he might be allowed to stay in California to end his days with the missionary padres of his order.

While the Spanish padres received him with great kindness and informed Fray President Estevan Tapis of his desire, the latter had to reply, after consulting the guardian of San Fernando College: "I should gladly grant you faculties if I could, but since you have been sent to the Chinese Empire by the Sacred Congregation of the Propagation of the Faith to serve as missionary, *you ought to be sent here by our Catholic Spanish King, who in virtue of the authority which he possesses and which is committed to him by the Holy See, as Delegate of the same Supreme See, can and is bound to approve those missionaries who are to be sent hither and elsewhere in the two Americas subject to him.*"[1] Evidently, Farnesio was unacquainted with the provisions of the *patronato real* which controlled the sending of missionaries to Spanish overseas possessions.

Meanwhile Farnesio was permitted to say Mass and perform such functions as needed no special faculties, pending a reply from Mexico. On June 10, 1805, the viceroy wrote that Farnesio could not remain in California and was directed to return to Italy. In accordance with this command, he sailed from San Diego on *La Princesa,* November 6, 1805.

Bancroft erroneously states that Farnesio was not a friar. Mariano Payeras definitely states that he was and that he was a good religious.

[1] Engelhardt, *Missions and Missionaries*, II, 616.

FONT, PEDRO (1738-1781)

Fray Pedro Font, a brother of Fray Pablo Font of San Fernando College, was a native of Catalonia, born in 1738 at Gerona, who came to the college of Santa Cruz de Querétaro with the mission of 1763 and in 1773 became an Indian missionary in Sonora. He had an excellent voice and was attached to the college choir for which he made many choir books. His special abilities and interests extended beyond music, to include mathematics and geography. Font's chief fame lies in his connection with the second Anza expedition of 1775-1776 as chaplain and diarist. He was serving at Misión San José de los Pimas when the guardian of the college, Romualdo Cartagena, requested him to join the expedition, which was to lead settlers and soldiers into California and to establish San Francisco as a frontier settlement.

Font started out with the expedition from San Miguel de Horcasitas, Sonora, September 29, 1775, and arrived at Tubac, Arizona, October

21. Proceeding from the latter place on the twenty-third by way of San Xavier del Bac (near present-day Tucson), he crossed the Colorado, November 30 and reached Mission San Gabriel, January 4, 1776. On the tenth, Font journeyed to San Diego with a group of soldiers to investigate the Indian uprising which occurred there on November 5, 1775, and which resulted in the death of Fray Luís Jayme and the burning of the mission.

Font returned to San Gabriel and, rejoining the expedition, February 21, traveled along the Santa Barbara Channel coast, through Missions San Luis Obispo (where he baptized on March 3) and San Antonio, reaching Monterey, March 10. The next day, Friars Junípero Serra, Francisco Palóu, José Murguía, Pedro Cambón, and Tomás de la Peña came over from Mission San Carlos, Carmel. They joyfully embraced Fray Font and cordially welcomed Juan Bautista Anza and his people. Font sang a High Mass and preached a fervent sermon reviewing the vicissitudes of the great trek. On March 22, he left with Anza for the proposed site of San Francisco and eventually returned to Monterey, April 8. The return journey began from there, April 14, and the original starting point, Horcasitas, was reached, June 1, 1776. Font wrote two diaries of the expedition, a short and a long one. Both have been translated in *Anza's California Expeditions* by Herbert E. Bolton. Font concluded the latter diary at Tubutama, Sonora, May 11, 1777.

Concerning Font's diary, Bolton has written:

Of all the diarists of the Anza expeditions Font was the master. His observations were keen. He had a sharp eye for landmarks, and a canny knack of telling what he saw. His record of distances and directions is so accurate and his description of natural features is so graphic that nothing surprises the explorer of his trail. The remarkable diary tells him just what to expect. Font was a man of liberal education, which is reflected in the richness of his allusions and the clarity of his expression. He had a mathematical turn of mind which he carried even to his sermons. He had a reputation for knowledge of latitudes and map making which he sustained by the performance of his difficult task with Anza.

Font is entitled to all the more credit from the fact that he was ill during most of the expedition. He was under the weather when he left Horcasitas. . . . It is not strange, therefore, that Font was pessimistic and irritable, that he found the Indians disgusting, that he was not always pleased with the weather or the country over which he traveled, or even that he sometimes complained of Anza. But in spite of his illness and his temperament, or because of them, he wrote a superb diary — one of the best in all Western Hemisphere history, it is safe to say. In his official journal he faithfully described the itinerary, the natural features of the country, the Indians, and the Spanish establishments passed through. And then, in the private diary, he added to these official things all the gossip of the trail.[1]

On the road, Font used the compass and quadrant, an astrolabe, graphometer, and level. He was likewise a skillful performer on the psaltery — similar to a triangular zither or table harp — which he played many times along the trail. At San Diego he gave performances on a bad spinet which he found there. He encouraged singing by the soldiers and their families in the church services. His fame, however, will ever be connected with his diary.

According to the Death Register of the apostolic college of Santa Cruz de Quéretaro, Font died on September 6, 1781, at Misión Pitic, Sonora.

[1] *Anza's California Expeditions,* IV, v-vi.

MARTÍNEZ, JESÚS MARÍA (?-?)

Fray Jesús María Martínez was a member of the college of Zacatecas and was one of the small group of missionaries who came to California in 1831 to prepare the way for the Zacatecan friars to take over from the Fernandinos the northern missions from Soledad to Sonoma. He was at Mission San Gabriel from April to December 31, 1831, and baptized there from time to time. He returned to Mexico in 1832.

NOCEDAL, JOSÉ (1746-1778)

Fray José Nocedal was a native of Chalco, Mexico, born in 1746. He became a Franciscan at San Fernando College, Mexico City, April 23, 1764, and had Fray Junípero Serra as his novice master. In 1776, together with Vicente de Santa María, he was assigned by the college as a ship chaplain on the Pacific. Both friars sailed on the *San Carlos,* leaving San Blas on March 9 and arriving at Monterey June 3. He baptized at Mission San Carlos, June 23, 1776. Nocedal continued on to San Francisco, entering the harbor on August 18. He was present for the dedication of the presidio, September 17, 1776, and saw the beginning of the mission, started by Francisco Palóu.

Upon his return to Mexico, Nocedal next became chaplain on the *Santiago,* which sailed out of San Blas, March 1, 1777, and arrived at San Francisco, May 12. The *Santiago* left that port on May 27, stopped at Monterey from May 28 to June 8, and returned to San Blas. Nocedal sailed a third time on the *Santiago* out of San Blas, leaving March 6, 1778, and arriving at San Francisco, June 17. He returned to San Blas on the same ship, and, while on his way to the college, he died at the hospice of Santa Cruz, Tepic, and was buried there.

SIERRA, BENITO DE LA (1729-1778)

Fray Benito de la Sierra was born in 1729 at Cervera de Pisuegra, León, Spain, and became a Franciscan at San Fernando College, Mexico

City, January 11, 1756. He sailed from La Paz, Lower California, with José de Gálvez and Fray Juan de Escudero, April 14, 1769, and arrived at Loreto, April 22. President Francisco Palóu assigned him to Misión Santa Rosalía de Mulegé on May 1. When the missions of Lower California were turned over to the Dominicans in 1773, Sierra sailed from Loreto on the *Concepción,* June 15, 1773, and returned to the college.

On May 13, 1774, Sierra was appointed full-time librarian at the college, but before the end of the year, November 18, he was assigned to a ship chaplaincy out of San Blas. With Fray Miguel de la Campa y Cos, he sailed on the *Santiago* or *Nueva Galicia* under Captain Bruno de Heceta, leaving San Blas, March 16, 1775. The ship sailed to the waters of northern California, and at Trinidad Head the cross was planted, a Mass and *Te Deum* sung, June 11. On July 14, Grenville Harbor, on the coast of the present state of Washington, was reached and a cross erected by De la Sierra and Heceta. On the return voyage the mouth of present-day Columbia River was named La Asunción de Nuestra Señora, August 15. The *Santiago* arrived at Monterey, August 29.

Having returned to Mexico, Sierra embarked on a second maritime voyage as chaplain on *El Príncipe* or *San Antonio,* captained by Diego Choquet, and which sailed from San Blas, March 9, 1776. It arrived at Monterey, May 21. With Junípero Serra and Vicente de Santa María, Sierra sailed to San Diego, leaving Monterey, June 30 and arriving at San Diego, July 11. Sierra returned to Mexico and subsequently sailed out of San Blas a third time again on the *San Antonio,* February 28, 1777, arriving at San Diego, May 4. From there he returned to San Blas and died at that port in 1778.

SOSA, MARIANO (?-?)

A native of Mexico and a member of the college of Guadalupe, Zacatecas, Fray Mariano Sosa was one of the group of friars sent to California in 1831 by Fray Francisco García Diego y Moreno to prepare the way for the Zacatecans to take over from the Fernandinos the northern missions from Soledad to Sonoma. Sosa was at Mission San Gabriel as the guest of Fray José Bernardo Sánchez, Fernandino president, in 1831 and in the early part of 1832. Sosa had come to California with the title of vicar forane of the bishop of Sonora and claimed as vice-commissary prefect the faculty of administering confirmation. Sánchez had the same delegated authority of vicar forane and considered it peculiar that Sosa held the identical faculties.

Sánchez wrote to the guardian of San Fernando College, Ildefonso Arreguín, who at the same time was commissary prefect of the Fernandinos. Sánchez was informed that Sosa by virtue of his office as vice-commissary prefect could confirm, but his status as vicar forane would have to be confirmed by the bishop of Sonora. There was no bishop at the time but only an administrator who had conferred the title of vicar forane on him through an error committed probably in ignorance of the fact that this faculty always accompanied the office of president of the missions.

Sosa resigned his office as vicar forane when he learned that Narciso Durán had succeeded Sánchez as president in June 1831, and upon whom the administrator of Sonora officially conferred the office of vicar forane. Durán, however, allowed Sosa to confirm. He administered confirmation at Mission San Gabriel and Los Angeles, November 3-17, 1831, to as many as 704 persons, among whom was the convert William Hartnell. This was the first time in twenty-eight years that confirmation had been administered in California, since no one had been empowered to do so after the time of Fermín Francisco de Lasuén. Sosa also confirmed at San Diego and probably at San Luis Rey and baptized at San Luis Obispo, August 29, 1831. He and his companions left California for Mexico with Governor Manuel Victoria in January 1832 from the port of San Diego. He died on February 20, 1841.

❧ APPENDIX II ☙

List of Franciscan Missionaries
who served in Upper California, 1769-1848

Name	Date of Birth	Place of Birth	Province-Diocese	Country	Franciscan Province Membership	College	Arrival in America	Arrival in California	Years of Service in California	Date of Departure	Date of Death	Place of Death	Missions Served in California
ABELLA, JOSE RAMON	May 28, 1764	Monforte	Zaragosa	Spain	Aragon	San Fernando	June 26, 1795	May, 1798 Santa Barbara	44		May 24, 1842	Santa Ines	San Francisco, San Carlos, San Luis Obispo, San Miguel, Purisima, and Santa Ines
ALTIMIRA, JOSE	1787	Barcelona	Catalonia	Spain	Catalonia	San Fernando	1819	Aug. 18, 1820 Monterey	7 years 5 months	Jan. 23, 1828			San Francisco, San Francisco Solano, and San Buenaventura
AMESTOY, MARCOS	1778	Trevino	Calahorra	Spain	Catalonia	San Fernando	Aug, 1803	Aug. 14, 1804 S. Francisco	11 years 1 month	Sept. 22, 1815			Santa Barbara
AMOROS, JUAN	Oct. 10, 1773	Porrera	Catalonia	Spain	Catalonia	San Fernando	July, 1803	Aug. 15, 1804	27 years 2½ mo.		July 14, 1832	San Rafael	San Carlos and San Rafael
AMURRIO, GREGORIO	1744	Bastida	Calahorra	Spain	Cantabria	San Fernando	1770	Aug. 30, 1773 S. Diego	6	Autumn of 1779			San Luis Obispo and San Juan Capistrano
ANZAR, JOSE ANTONIO	Before 1793			Mexico	Jalisco	Zacatecas		Early in 1831 S. Diego	23	Late in 1854	Dec., 1874	Colima, Mexico	San Luis Rey and San Juan Bautista
ARROITA, FRANCISCO JOSE	Before 1762			Spain	Cantabria	San Fernando	1785	Sept. 1786	c. 10	1797	March 5, 1821	Mexico City	San Luis Obispo and Purisima
ARROYO DE LA CUESTA, FELIPE	Apr. 29, 1780	Cubo	Burgos	Spain	Burgos	San Fernando	1804	Aug. 13, 1808 Monterey	32 years 1 month		Sept. 20, 1840	Santa Ines	San Juan Bautista, San Luis Obispo, San Miguel, Purisima, and Santa Ines
BARCENILLA, ISIDRO	1766	San Manes	Palencia	Spain	Concepcion	San Fernando	June 26, 1795	Apr. 14, 1797 S. Francisco	7 years 6 months	October, 1804			San Jose, San Francisco, and San Gabriel
BARONA, JOSE	Mar. 24, 1764	Villanueva del Conde	Burgos	Spain	Burgos	San Fernando	June 26, 1795	May 8, 1798 Santa Barbara	33 years 2 months		Aug. 4, 1831	San Juan Capistrano	San Diego, San Gabriel, San Juan Capistrano, and San Luis Rey
BARRENECHE, JUAN ANTONIO	1749	Lecaroz	Navarre	Spain	Santa Elena, Cuba	Queretaro		1779 Fort Yuma	1		July 19, 1781 Ft. Yuma	Fort Yuma	Concepcion
BOSCANA, GERONIMO	May 23, 1776	Lluchmayor	Majorca	Spain	Majorca	San Fernando	Oct. 24, 1803	June 6, 1806 Monterey	25 years 1 month		July 5, (6), 1831	San Gabriel	Soledad, Purisima, San Luis Rey, San Juan Capistrano, and San Gabriel

*California Historical Society Quarterly, XLIV (1965), 297-308. Reprinted by permission of the publisher. Amended by the author.

FOLIO 2

Name	Date of Birth	Place of Birth	Province-Diocese	Country	Franciscan Province Membership	College	Arrival in America	Arrival in California	Years of Service in California	Date of Departure	Date of Death	Place of Death	Missions Served in California
CABOT, JUAN VICENTE	March 9, 1781	Bunola	Majorca	Spain	Majorca	San Fernando	c. Oct, 1804	Aug. 31, 1805 Monterey	30	1835			Purisima, San Miguel, San Francisco, and Soledad
CABOT, PEDRO	Oct. 3, 1777	Bunola	Majorca	Spain	Majorca	San Fernando	Aug, 1803	Aug. 15, 1804	32 years 2 months		Oct. 11, 1836	San Fernando	San Antonio, San Miguel, and San Fernando
CALZADA, JOSE ANTONIO	Nov. 24, 1760	Trinidad		Cuba	Santa Elena	San Fernando		Oct. 1787 and May 8, 1798 Santa Barbara Monterey	25 years 5 months	Summer of 1796	Dec. 23, 1814	Santa Ines	San Gabriel, Santa Barbara, San Luis Obispo, Purisima, and Santa Ines
CAMBON, PEDRO BENITO	1738	Leaya	Galicia	Spain	Galicia	San Fernando	May, 1770	March 12, 1771 and Dec. 9, 1781 S. Diego	19	1779 and 1792			San Gabriel, San Francisco, and San Buenaventura
CARNICER, BALTASAR	1770			Spain	Aragon	San Fernando	1793	Apr. 14, 1797 S. Francisco	11	1808			San Miguel and San Carlos
CARRANZA, DOMINGO	1770			Spain	Cantabria	San Fernando		May 8, 1798 Santa Barbara	12 years 7 months	Late in 1810			Santa Cruz, San Luis Rey
CATALA, MAGIN MATIAS	Jan.29, 1761	Mont-blanch	Catalonia	Spain	Catalonia	San Fernando	1786	July, 1793 Monterey	37 years 5 months		Nov. 22, 1830	Santa Clara	Santa Clara
CATALAN, BENITO	1766	Alzola	Catalonia	Spain	Aragon	San Fernando	1795–1796	Apr. 14, 1797 S. Francisco	3 years 6 months	Jan., 1800			San Antonio
CAVALLER, JOSE	1740	Falcet	Catalonia	Spain	Catalonia	San Fernando	1769–1770	Mar. 12, 1771 S. Diego	18 years 9 months		Dec. 9, 1789	San Luis Obispo	San Carlos and San Luis Obispo
CIPRES, MARCELINO	c. 1769	Huesca	Aragon	Spain	Aragon	San Fernando	c. 1794	Aug. 24, 1795 Monterey	14 years 5 months		Jan. 31, 1810	San Miguel	San Antonio and San Luis Obispo
CORTES, JUAN LOPE	1772	Torrejon de Ardoz	Toledo	Spain	Castile	San Fernando	July 26, 1795	June 18, 1796	9 years 4 months	Nov. 5, 1805			San Gabriel, San Fernando, and Santa Barbara

Name	Date of Birth	Place of Birth	Province-Diocese	Country	Franciscan Province Membership	College	Arrival in America	Arrival in California	Years of Service in California	Date of Departure	Date of Death	Place of Death	Missions Served in California
CRESPI, JUAN	March 1, 1721	Palma	Majorca	Spain	Majorca	San Fernando	Apr., 1750	May 14, 1769 S. Diego	12 years 7 months		Jan. 1, 1782	San Carlos	San Diego and San Carlos
CRUZADO, ANTONIO	1724	Alcarazejo	Andalusia	Spain	Los Angeles	San Fernando	Apr., 1750	March 12, 1771 S. Diego	33 years 7 months		Oct. 11, 1804	San Gabriel	San Gabriel
CUEVA, PEDRO DE LA	1776	Hornachos	Estremadura	Spain	Estremadura	San Fernando	1803	Aug. 14, 1804 S. Francisco	2 years 3 months	Nov., 1806			San Jose
DANTI, ANTONIO	1760	Sampedor	Catalonia	Spain	Catalonia	San Fernando	1786	July, 1790 Monterey	6 years 4 months	Nov., 1796			San Francisco
DIAZ, JUAN	May, 1736	Alazar	Andalusia	Spain	Estremadura	Queretaro	1763	1780 Ft. Yuma	c. 1		July 17, 1781	San Pedro y San Pablo de Bicuner	San Pedro y San Pablo
DULANTO, ANDRES	1774	Suzarra	Burgos	Spain	Cantabria	San Fernando	Aug., 1803	Aug. 15, 1804 Monterey	4 years 1 month		Sept. 11, 1808	Santa Barbara	San Juan Bautista and Santa Barbara
DUMETZ, FRANCISCO	1734	Palma	Majorca	Spain	Majorca	San Fernando	1770	Mar. 12, 1771 S. Diego	39 years 10 months		Jan. 14, 1811	San Gabriel	San Diego, San Carlos, San Buenaventura, San Fernando, and San Gabriel
DURAN, NARCISO	Dec. 16, 1776	Castellon de Ampurias	Catalonia	Spain	Catalonia	San Fernando	1803	June 6, 1806 Monterey	40		June 1, 1846	Santa Barbara	San Jose and Santa Barbara
ESCUDE, JAYME	July, 1779	Gandesa	Catalonia	Spain	Catalonia	San Fernando	July, 1810	July 15, 1812 S. Diego	10 years 5 months	c. Dec., 1822			San Luis Rey and Santa Cruz
ESPI DE VALENCIA, JOSE DE LA CRUZ	Jan. 3, 1763	Turis	Valencia	Spain	Valencia	San Fernando	c. Sept., 1786	July, 1793 Monterey	6½		Jan. 16, 1800	Cuba	San Antonio, Soledad, Santa Clara, and San Francisco
ESTENEGA, TOMAS ELEUTERIO	1790	Anzuola	Vizcaya	Spain	Cantabria	San Fernando	1810	Aug., 1820 Monterey	c. 26		Early in 1847	San Fernando	San Carlos, San Miguel, San Francisco, San Rafael, San Gabriel, and San Fernando
ESTEVAN, PEDRO DE SAN JOSE	1751		Castile	Spain	Santa Elena, Cuba	San Fernando		Jan., 1795 Monterey	c. 8½	Nov. 4, 1802			San Antonio, San Diego, and San Gabriel

Name	Date of Birth	Place of Birth	Province-Diocese	Country	Franciscan Province Membership	College	Arrival in America	Arrival in California	Years of Service in California	Date of Departure	Date of Death	Place of Death	Missions Served in California
FAURA, JOSE	c. 1773	Barcelona	Catalonia	Spain	Catalonia	San Fernando	1798	May 8, 1798 Santa Barbara	c. 11 years 6 months	End of 1809			San Luis Rey and San Juan Capistrano
FERNANDEZ, GREGORIO	c. 1754	Burgos	Burgos	Spain	Burgos	San Fernando	1785	c. June, 1794	11 years 5 months	Nov. 6, 1805			San Luis Obispo and Purisima
FERNANDEZ, JOSE MARIA	Before 1773	Madrid	Toledo	Spain	Castile	San Fernando	1795	Sept., 1796 S. Francisco	1 year 3 months	Sept., 1797			San Francisco
FERNANDEZ, MANUEL	1767	Villar	Tuy Galicia	Spain	Galicia	San Fernando	1793	1794	c. 4	Late in 1798			Santa Clara, San Francisco, and Santa Cruz
FERNANDEZ DE ULIBARRI, ROMAN	Feb. 28, 1773	Ali	Calahorra	Spain	Cantabria	San Fernando	Aug., 1803	June 22, 1809 Monterey	11 years 11 months		June 16, 1821	San Gabriel	San Juan Bautista, Santa Ines, Purisima, and San Fernando
FIGUER, JUAN	c. 1742	Anento	Aragon	Spain	Aragon	San Fernando	1770	Nov., 1772 S. Diego	12 years 1 month		Dec. 18, 1784	San Diego	San Gabriel, San Luis Obispo, and San Diego
FORTUNY, BUENAVENTURA	1774	Moster	Catalonia	Spain	Catalonia	San Fernando	c. July, 1803	June 6, 1806 Monterey	34 years 6 months		Dec. 16, 1840	Santa Barbara	San Jose, San Francisco Solano, San Diego, San Luis Rey, and San Buenaventura
FUSTER, VICENTE	1742	Alcaniz	Aragon	Spain	Aragon	San Fernando	1770	Aug. 30, 1773 S. Diego	27 years 1½ months		Oct. 21, 1800	San Juan Capistrano	San Diego, San Gabriel, San Juan Capistrano, and Purisima
GARCES, FRANCISCO HERMENEGILDO	Apr. 12, 1738	Morata del Conde	Aragon	Spain	Aragon	Queretaro	1766	Fall of 1780 Ft. Yuma	c. 1		July 17, 1781	Ft. Yuma	Concepcion
GARCIA, DIEGO	1744	Araal	Andalusia	Spain	Los Angeles	San Fernando	c. 1786	1787	c. 10	Fall of 1797			San Francisco, Soledad, and San Antonio
GARCIA, JOSE	Before 1775		Cantabria	Spain	Cantabria	San Fernando		Aug., 1800 Monterey	8 years 3 months	Nov., 1808			San Luis Rey and San Diego
GARCIA DIEGO Y MORENO, FRANCISCO	Sept. 17, 1785	Lagos	Jalisco	Mexico		Zacatecas		Jan. 15, 1833 Monterey and Dec. 10, 1841 S. Diego	7 years 2½ months	Nov. 17, 1835	Apr. 30, 1846	Santa Barbara	Santa Clara and Santa Barbara

FOLIO 5

Name	Date of Birth	Place of Birth	Province-Diocese	Country	Franciscan Province Membership	College	Arrival in America	Arrival in California	Years of Service in California	Date of Departure	Date of Death	Place of Death	Missions Served in California
GARCIA RIOBO, JUAN ANTONIO*	1740	Malpica	Galicia	Spain	Galicia	San Fernando	1770	June 2, 1782 S. Francisco	4 years 5 months	c. Nov. 7, 1786			San Carlos, San Diego, and San Gabriel
GIL Y TABOADA, LUIS	May 1, 1773	Santa Fe	Guanajuato	Mexico	Michoacan	San Fernando		Aug. 9, 1801	32 years c. 2 mo.		Dec. 15, 1833	Santa Margarita	San Francisco, San Jose, Santa Ines, Santa Barbara, Purisima, San Rafael, Santa Cruz, and San Luis Obispo
GILI, BARTOLOME	Feb. 16, 1759	Arta	Majorca	Spain	Majorca	San Fernando	Early in 1788	1791	c. 3 yrs. 6 months	Aug. 11, 1794			San Antonio, Soledad San Luis Obispo, and San Diego
GIRIBET, MIGUEL	June 1, 1756	Agramont	Catalonia	Spain	Catalonia	San Fernando	c. Feb., 1785	c. Aug., 1785	14 years c. 5 mo.	Jan. 16, 1800	Aug. 13, 1804	Agramont	San Francisco and San Luis Obispo
GOMEZ, FRANCISCO	1729	Castillo de Laya	Burgos	Spain	Concepcion	San Fernando	Late 1759	Apr. 11, 1769		July 21, 1771			San Diego
GONZALEZ, FRANCISCO	Before 1774			Spain	Santa Elena, Cuba	San Fernando		Apr. 14, 1797 S. Francisco	8 years c. 7 mo.	Nov. 6, 1805			Santa Cruz
GONZALEZ DE IBARRA, FRANCISCO**	1782	Viana	Navarre	Spain	Burgos	San Fernando	1819	Aug., 1820 Monterey	c. 22 years		1842	San Luis Rey	San Fernando, San Luis Rey, and San Diego
GONZALEZ RUBIO, JOSE MARIA DE JESUS	June 6, 1804	Guadalajara	Jalisco	Mexico	College of Zapopan	Zacatecas		Jan. 15, 1833 Monterey	42 years c. 9 mo.		Nov. 2, 1875	Santa Barbara	San Jose and Santa Barbara
GUTIERREZ, JOSE MARIA	1801			Mexico		Zacatecas		Jan. 15, 1833 Monterey	11 years 10 months	Nov., 1844	June 29, 1850	La Quemada, Mexico	San Francisco Solano, San Francisco, and San Antonio
GUTIERREZ, ROMUALDO	c. 1782	Tequisquiapan		Mexico		San Fernando		Aug. 15, 1804	2 years 3 months	Nov., 1806	Sept. 11, 1845		Santa Ines and San Buenaventura
HORRA, ANTONIO DE LA CONCEPCION	1767	San Martin de Rubuales	Osma	Spain	Concepcion	San Fernando	June 26, 1795	Apr. 17, 1797 S. Francisco	c. 6 mo.	1797			San Miguel
IBANEZ, FLORENCIO	Oct. 26, 1740	Tarazona	Aragon	Spain	Aragon	San Fernando	Apr., 1770	Aug. 9, 1801 Monterey	17 years 3 months		Nov. 26, 1818	Soledad	San Antonio and Soledad

* Also known simply as Riobo
** Also known simply as Ibarra

286

Name	Date of Birth	Place of Birth	Province-Diocese	Country	Franciscan Province Membership	College	Arrival in America	Arrival in California	Years of Service in California	Date of Departure	Date of Death	Place of Death	Missions Served in California
ITURRATE, DOMINGO SANTIAGO	1770	Lugiano	Calahorra	Spain	Cantabria	San Fernando	1795	Aug. 22, 1800	9 years 2 months	Oct., 1809	c. 1815		San Juan Bautista
JAYME, ANTONIO	Jan., 1757	Palma	Majorca	Spain	Majorca	San Fernando	c. July, 1794	Aug. 24, 1795	31 years 2 months		Dec. 1, 1829	Santa Barbara	San Carlos, Soledad, and Santa Barbara
JAYME, LUIS	Oct. 18, 1740	San Juan	Majorca	Spain	Majorca	San Fernando	1770	Mar. 12, 1771 S. Diego	4 years 7 months		Nov. 5, 1775	San Diego	San Diego
JIMENO, ANTONIO		Mexico City	Mexico	Mexico		San Fernando		Sept., 1827	31 years 4 months	Jan., 1859	Dec. 25, 1876	Mexico	Santa Cruz and Santa Barbara
JIMENO, JOSE JOAQUIN	Nov. 30, 1804	Mexico City	Mexico	Mexico		San Fernando		Sept., 1827 S. Diego	28 years 6 months		Mar. 14, 1856	Santa Barbara	San Luis Rey, San Luis Obispo, Santa Cruz, Santa Ines, San Gabriel, and Santa Barbara
JUNCOSA, DOMINGO	1740	Cornudella	Catalonia	Spain	Catalonia	San Fernando		Mar. 12, 1771 S. Diego	3 years 3 months	June 8, 1774			San Carlos, San Luis Obispo, and San Antonio
LANDAETA, MARTIN DE	1760	Cortezubi	Vizcaya	Spain	Cantabria	San Fernando	c. 1786	1791	c. 7	1798	Nov. 3, 1809	San Fernando	San Francisco and San Fernando
LASUEN, FERMIN FRANCISCO DE	June 7, 1736	Vitoria	Cantabria	Spain	Cantabria	San Fernando	1759-1760	Aug. 30, 1773 S. Diego	29 years 10 months		June 26, 1803	San Carlos	San Gabriel, Monterey, San Juan Capistrano, San Diego, San Luis Obispo, and San Carlos
LAZARO, NICOLAS	Before 1782	Burgos		Spain	Burgos	San Fernando	1804	Aug. 31, 1805 Monterey	c. 2		Aug. 18, 1807	San Diego	San Fernando and San Diego
LOPEZ, BALDOMERO	1761	Puente	Valladolid	Spain	Concepcion	San Fernando	1786	1791	c. 5	Summer, 1796			Santa Cruz
LOPEZ, JACINTO	1769	Toro	Zamora	Spain	Castile	San Fernando	1793	July 28, 1799 Monterey	2 years 2 months	Oct. 8, 1801			San Antonio and San Juan Bautista
LOPEZ, JULIAN	1761	Carbonero	Segovia	Spain	Concepcion	San Fernando	June 26, 1795	Apr. 14, 1797 S. Francisco	c. 3 months		July 15-16, 1797	San Carlos	San Carlos
MARINER, JUAN	Sept. 24, 1743	Vilaplana	Catalonia	Spain	Catalonia	San Fernando	Early in 1785	1785 Monterey	c. 14		Jan. 29, 1800	San Diego	San Diego
MARQUINEZ, MARCELINO	May, 1779	Trevino	Vizcaya	Spain	Cantabria	San Fernando	1804	July 28, 1810 S. Francisco	7 years 7 months	Mar. 12, 1818			San Luis Obispo and Santa Cruz

Name	Date of Birth	Place of Birth	Province-Diocese	Country	Franciscan Province Membership	College	Arrival in America	Arrival in California	Years of Service in California	Date of Departure	Date of Death	Place of Death	Missions Served in California
MARTIARENA, JOSE MANUEL	1754	Renteria	Guipuzcoa	Spain	Cantabria	San Fernando	c. 1788	1794	c. 11	1805			San Antonio, Soledad, San Juan Bautista, and San Francisco
MARTIN, FERNANDO	May 26, 1770	Robledillo	Ciudad Rodrigo	Spain	Estremadura	San Fernando	June, 1810	July 6, 1811 S. Diego	27 years 3 months		Oct. 19, 1838	San Diego	San Diego
MARTIN, JUAN	Jan. 12, 1770	Villastor	Aragon	Spain	Aragon	San Fernando	c. Sept., 1793	Early in 1794	30 years, several months		Aug. 29, 1824	San Miguel	San Gabriel, Purisima, and San Miguel
MARTINEZ, LUIS ANTONIO	Jan. 17, 1771	Briebes	Oviedo	Spain	Castile	San Fernando	1795	May 8, 1798 Santa Barbara	31 years 11 months	Mar. 30, 1830	1832	Madrid	San Luis Obispo
MARTINEZ, PEDRO ADRIANO	c. 1770		Galicia	Spain	Galicia	San Fernando	1797	Apr. 14, 1797	7 years c. 3 months	After July 1, 1804			Santa Clara, San Juan Bautista, and San Miguel
MARTINEZ DE ARENAZA, PASCUAL•	c. 1762		Alava	Spain	Cantabria	San Fernando	1785	c. 1787	10	Oct., 1797	Before May 14, 1799	Mexico City	San Carlos
MERELO, LORENZO	1756			Haiti?	Santa Cruz	San Fernando		July 28, 1798 Monterey	3 years 2 months	Oct. 8, 1801	Dec. 4, 1801	At sea	San Francisco and San Antonio
MERINO, AGUSTIN	1769	Briones	Calahorra	Spain	Cantabria	San Fernando	1795	Apr. 14, 1797 S. Francisco	2 years c. 8 months	Jan., 1800			San Jose
MIGUEL, JOSE DE	1761	Zarbitu	Navarre	Spain	Cantabria	San Fernando	c. 1786	Aug. 2, 1790 Monterey & Aug., 1800	20	c. end of 1798	June 1, 1813	San Fernando	Santa Barbara, San Luis Obispo, and San Gabriel
MORENO, JOSEPH MATIAS	1744	Almorza	Osma	Spain	Burgos	Queretaro	c. 1770	1780	c. 1		July 17, 1781	Bicuner	San Pedro y San Pablo de Bicuner
MORENO, JUAN	Jan. 27, 1799	Montenegro	Old Castile	Spain	Santo Evangelio, Mexico	San Fernando		1827	18 years and some months		Dec. 27, 1845	Santa Ines	Santa Barbara, Santa Cruz, San Juan Bautista, San Miguel, and Santa Ines
MORENO, RAFAEL DE JESUS	1795			Mexico		Zacatecas		Jan. 15, 1833 Monterey	6 years 5 months		June 8, 1839	San Jose	Santa Clara, San Rafael, and San Jose
MUGARTEGUI, PABLO JOSEPH	c. Oct. 13, 1736	Marquina	Calahorra	Spain	Cantabria	San Fernando	1770	Mar. 13, 1774 S. Diego	15 years and some months	1789			San Diego, San Antonio, San Luis Obispo, and San Juan Capistrano

• Also known simply as Arenaza

Name	Date of Birth	Place of Birth	Province-Diocese	Country	Franciscan Province Membership	College	Arrival in America	Arrival in California	Years of Service in California	Date of Departure	Date of Death	Place of Death	Missions Served in California
MUNOZ, PEDRO	June 19, 1773	Puerto de Banos	Estremadura	Spain	Estremadura	San Fernando	Aug, 1803	Aug. 14, 1804 S. Francisco	13 years and some months	Mar. 12, 1818	c. May 18, 1818	Tepic	San Miguel and San Fernando
MURGUIA, JOSE	Dec. 10, 1715	Domayguia	Alava	Spain	Cantabria	San Fernando		Aug. 30, 1773 S. Diego	10 years 8 months		May 11, 1784	Santa Clara	San Luis Obispo, San Antonio, San Carlos, and Santa Clara
MURO, MIGUEL	Before 1791			Mexico		Zacatecas		Dec. 10, 1841 S. Diego	3 years and some months	1845	June 20, 1848	Zacatecas	San Jose and San Francisco
NOBOA, DIEGO	1742	Compostela	Galicia	Spain	Galicia	San Fernando	1770	June 2, 1783 S. Francisco	11 years 2 months	Aug. 11, 1794	c. 1798		San Carlos and Santa Clara
NORIEGA, MATIAS DE SANTA CATALINA	1736	Andinas	Oviedo	Spain		San Fernando		Sept. 15, 1779 S. Francisco	c. 9	1789	c. 1798		San Francisco and San Carlos
NUEZ, JOAQUIN PASCUAL	Feb. 20, 1785	Luco	Aragon	Spain	Aragon	San Fernando	c. June, 1810	July 6, 1812 S. Diego	9 years c. 6 months		Dec. 30, 1821	San Gabriel	San Fernando and San Gabriel
OLBES, RAMON	Feb. 8, 1786	Ateca	Aragon	Spain	Aragon	San Fernando	c. June, 1810	July 6, 1812 S. Diego	9 years 4 months	Nov. 15, 1821			Santa Ines, Santa Barbara, San Luis Rey, and Santa Cruz
OLIVA, VICENTE PASCUAL	July 3, 1780	Martin del Rio	Aragon	Spain	Aragon	San Fernando	c. June, 1810	Aug. 4, 1813 Monterey	34 years 5 months		Jan. 2, 1848	San Juan Capistrano	San Fernando, San Francisco, San Miguel, San Diego, San Juan Capistrano, and San Luis Rey
ORAMAS, CRISTOBAL	Before 1759	Icod	Tenerife	Spain		San Fernando		1786	8 years and some months	c. Oct., 1794			Santa Barbara, Purisima, and San Gabriel
ORDAZ, BLAS	1792	Corvero del Rio Alamo	Burgos	Spain		San Fernando	1819	Aug., 1820 Monterey	30 years c. 2 months		c. Nov. 11, 1850	San Gabriel	San Carlos, San Francisco, San Miguel, Purisima, Santa Ines, San Buenaventura, San Fernando, San Gabriel, and San Juan Capistrano
PALOU, FRANCISCO	Jan. 22, 1723	Palma	Majorca	Spain	Majorca	San Fernando	Oct. 1749 S. Juan, P. R.	Aug. 30, 1773 S. Diego	12 years 2 months	Nov. 13, 1785	Apr. 6, 1789	Queretaro	San Carlos and San Francisco
PANELLA, JOSE	Feb. 11, 1761	Barcelona	Catalonia	Spain	Catalonia	San Fernando		Apr. 14, 1797 S. Francisco	6 years 5 months	Oct. 4, 1803			San Diego and San Luis Rey
PANTO, JOSE PEDRO	1778	Balberde del Fresno	Estremadura	Spain	Estremadura	San Fernando	Aug, 1803	July 28, 1810 S. Francisco	1 year 11 months		June 30, 1812	San Diego	San Diego

Name	Date of Birth	Place of Birth	Province-Diocese	Country	Franciscan Province Membership	College	Arrival in America	Arrival in California	Years of Service in California	Date of Departure	Date of Death	Place of Death	Missions Served in California
PARRON, FERNANDO	c. 1728	Arroyo del Puerco	Estrema-dura	Spain	Estrema-dura	San Fernando	c. 1759	Apr. 29, 1769 S. Diego	c. 2	1771			San Diego
PATERNA, ANTONIO	1721	Seville	Andalusia	Spain	Andalusia	San Fernando	1750	Mar. 12, 1771 S. Diego	21 years 11 months		Feb. 13, 1793	Santa Barbara	San Gabriel, San Luis Obispo, and Santa Barbara
PAYERAS, MARIANO	Oct. 10, 1769	Inca	Majorca	Spain	Majorca	San Fernando	1793	June 18, 1796 S. Francisco	26 years 10 months		Apr. 28, 1823	Purisima	San Diego, San Carlos, Soledad, and Purisima
PENA SARAVIA, TOMAS DE LA	1743	Brizuela	Burgos	Spain	Cantabria	San Fernando	1770	May, 1772 S. Diego	22 years 3 months	Aug. 12, 1794	Early in 1806	Mexico City	San Diego, San Luis Obispo, San Carlos, and Santa Clara
PEREZ BERNARDINO DE JESUS				Mexico		Zacatecas		Jan. 15, 1833 Monterey	2 years 10 months	Nov. 17, 1835		Tepozot-lan	Santa Clara
PEYRI, ANTONIO	Jan. 8, 1769	Porrera	Catalonia	Spain	Catalonia	San Fernando	July 26, 1795	June 18, 1796 S. Francisco	35 years 7 months	Jan. 17, 1832			San Luis Obispo and San Luis Rey
PIERAS, MIGUEL	1741	Palma	Majorca	Spain	Majorca	San Fernando	1770	Mar. 12, 1771 S. Diego	23 years 5 months	Late in 1794	Apr. 14, 1795	Mexico City	San Antonio
PRESTAMERO, JUAN	1736	Labastida	Calahorra	Spain	Cantabria	San Fernando	c. 1759-1770	Aug. 30, 1773 S. Diego	10 months	July 7, 1774			San Luis Obispo
PUJOL, FRANCISCO	Mar. 7, 1762	Alos	Urgel	Spain		San Fernando	c. 1793	Apr. 14, 1797 S. Francisco	3 years 11 months		Mar. 15, 1801	San Antonio	San Carlos and San Antonio
QUIJAS, LORENZO DE LA CONCEPCION				Ecuador (?)		Zacatecas		Jan. 15, 1833 Monterey	11 years and some months	Early in 1844			San Francisco Solano, San Rafael, and San Jose
QUINTANA, ANDRES	Nov. 27, 1777	Antonorra	Calahorra	Spain	Cantabria	San Fernando	1804	Aug. 31, 1805 Monterey	7 years 1½ months		Oct. 12, 1812	Santa Cruz	Santa Cruz
RIPOLL, ANTONIO	Mar. 27, 1785	Palma	Majorca	Spain	Majorca	San Fernando	July, 1810	July 7, 1812 S. Diego	15 years 7 months	Jan. 23, 1828			Purisima and Santa Barbara
RODRIGUEZ, ANTONIO CATARINO	1777	San Luis Potosi		Mexico	Zacatecas	San Fernando		June 22, 1809 Monterey	15 years 5 months		Nov. 25, 1824	San Luis Obispo	Santa Cruz, San Luis Obispo, and Purisima

290

Name	Date of Birth	Place of Birth	Province-Diocese	Country	Franciscan Province Membership	College	Arrival in America	Arrival in California	Years of Service in California	Date of Departure	Date of Death	Place of Death	Missions Served in California
RUBI, MARIANO	Mar. 26, 1756	Lluch-mayor	Majorca	Spain	Majorca	San Fernando	c. 1786	Aug. 2, 1790 Monterey	c. 3	Early in 1793			San Antonio and Soledad
SAINZ DE LUCIO, JUAN	1771	Guadareya	Burgos	Spain	Cantabria	San Fernando	Aug., 1803	June 6, 1806 Monterey	10 years c. 5 months	Nov., 1816			San Francisco, San Juan Bautista, and San Carlos
SALAZAR, ISIDRO ALONSO	c. 1758		Cantabria	Spain	Cantabria	San Fernando		1791	c. 4	Sept. 14, 1795			Santa Cruz
SANCHEZ, FRANCISCO	Aug., 1813	Leon	Guana-juato	Mexico		Zacatecas		Dec. 11, 1841 S. Diego	42 years 4 months		Apr. 17, 1884	Santa Barbara	Santa Barbara, Santa Ines, San Gabriel, and San Buenaventura
SANCHEZ, JOSE BERNARDO	Sept. 7, 1778	Roble-dillo	Ciudad Rodrigo	Spain	Estrema-dura	San Fernando	July, 1803	Aug. 14, 1804 S. Francisco	28 years 5 months		c. Jan. 15, 1833	San Gabriel	San Gabriel, San Diego, and Purisima
SANCHEZ, MIGUEL FRANCISCO	1738	Baguera	Aragon	Spain	Aragon	San Fernando	1770	Sept. 26, 1774 S. Diego	28 years 4 months		Jan. 27, 1803	San Gabriel	San Gabriel and Santa Clara
SANCHO, JUAN BAUTISTA	Dec. 1, 1772	Arta	Majorca	Spain	Majorca	San Fernando	Aug., 1802	Aug. 4, 1804 Monterey	25 years 6 months		Feb. 8, 1830	San Antonio	San Antonio
SANTA MARIA, VICENTE DE	1742	Haras	Calahorra	Spain	Burgos	San Fernando	1769	June 27, 1775 Monterey & June 3, 1776	30 years 1 month		July 16, 1806	San Buena-ventura	San Diego, San Francisco, and San Buenaventura
SANTIAGO, NORBERTO DE	c. 1760	Samiano	Leon	Spain	Cantabria	San Fernando	1785	Fall, 1786 S. Francisco	24	Late in 1810	c. 1818		San Francisco and San Juan Capistrano
SARRIA, VICENTE FRANCISCO DE	Nov., 1767	San Esteban de Echebarri	Vizcaya	Spain	Cantabria	San Fernando	1804	June 22, 1809 Monterey	25 years 11 months		May 24, 1835	Soledad	San Carlos and Soledad
SENAN, JOSE FRANCISCO DE PAULA	Mar. 31, 1760	Barcelona	Catalonia	Spain	Catalonia	San Fernando	c. Sept., 1784	Oct. 10, 1787 Monterey and May 8, 1798 S. Barbara	33 years 2 months	Sept. 14, 1795	Aug. 24 1823	San Buena-ventura	San Carlos and San Buenaventura

FOLIO 11

Name	Date of Birth	Place of Birth	Province-Diocese	Country	Franciscan Province Membership	College	Arrival in America	Arrival in California	Years of Service in California	Date of Departure	Date of Death	Place of Death	Missions Served in California
SERRA, JUNIPERO	Nov. 24, 1713	Petra	Majorca	Spain	Majorca	San Fernando	Oct. 1749 S. Juan, P.R.	July 1, 1769 S. Diego	15 years 2 months		Aug. 28, 1784	San Carlos	San Diego and San Carlos
SITJAR, BUENAVENTURA	Dec. 9, 1739	Porreras	Majorca	Spain	Majorca	San Fernando	1770	Apr. 14, 1771 S. Diego	37 years 4 months		Sept. 3, 1808	San Antonio	San Antonio and San Miguel
SOLA, FAUSTINO	c.1760	Mondragon (?)	Vizcaya	Spain	Cantabria	San Fernando		1786	c. 4	c. Apr., 1790	1820		San Luis Obispo and San Francisco
SOMERA, ANGEL*	Before 1743	Maravatio	Michoacan	Mexico		San Fernando		Mar. 12, 1771 S. Diego	c.1½	Late in 1772			San Gabriel
SUAREZ DEL REAL, ANTONIO DE LA CONCEPCION	1804			Mexico		Zacatecas		Jan. 15, 1833 Monterey	12 years c. 2 months	Late in 1845	June 3, 1850	Zacatecas	Santa Cruz, San Francisco, and San Carlos
SUAREZ DEL REAL, JOSE MARIA DEL REFUGIO	c.1804			Mexico		Zacatecas		Jan. 15, 1833 Monterey	c.18	1851			San Carlos and Santa Clara
SUNER, FRANCISCO	1764	Olat	Catalonia	Spain	Catalonia	San Fernando	c. July, 1804	Aug.13, 1808 Monterey	c. 22 years 6 months		Jan. 17, 1831	San Buenaventura	San Carlos, San Juan Capistrano, San Luis Rey, Santa Barbara, and San Buenaventura
TAPIS, ESTEVAN	c. 1756	Coloma de Farnes	Catalonia	Spain	Catalonia	San Fernando	1786	Aug. 2, 1790 Monterey	35 years 3 months		Nov. 3, 1825	San Juan Bautista	San Carlos, San Luis Obispo, Santa Barbara, San Juan Bautista, Santa Ines, and Purisima
TORRENT, HILARIO	c.1740	San Hilario	Catalonia	Spain	Catalonia	San Fernando	c. 1786	1786	12 years some months	Nov. 8, 1798	Before May 14, 1799	Mexico City	San Diego
URIA, FRANCISCO XAVIER DE LA CONCEPCION	1770	Ayzarna	Pamplona	Spain	Cantabria	San Fernando	June 26, 1796	Apr.14, 1797 S. Francisco Aug. 13, 1808	35		Nov. 5, 1834	Santa Barbara	Santa Barbara, Purisima, San Fernando, Santa Cruz, Santa Ines, Soledad, and San Buenaventura
URIA, JOSE ANTONIO	1769	Azcoitia	Pamplona	Spain	Cantabria	San Fernando	1796	July 28, 1799 Monterey	13 years c. 4 months	Late in 1812	1815	Mexico City	San Jose, San Fernando, and San Juan Capistrano
URRESTI, JOSE ANTONIO	1775	Manaria	Calahorra	Spain	Cantabria	San Fernando	Aug. 1802	Aug. 15, 1804 Monterey	c.7½		Jan. 4, 1812	San Fernando	San Gabriel and San Fernando
USON, RAMON	1737	Caspe	Aragon	Spain	Aragon	San Fernando	Nov., 1770	Nov., 1772 S. Diego	1 year c. 8 months	July 7, 1774			San Gabriel, San Luis Obispo, and San Antonio

* Also known as Fernandez Somera y Balbuena

292

FOLIO 12

Name	Date of Birth	Place of Birth	Province-Diocese	Country	Franciscan Province Membership	College	Arrival in America	Arrival in California	Years of Service in California	Date of Departure	Date of Death	Place of Death	Missions Served in California
VASQUEZ DEL MERCADO, JESUS MARIA	c. 1808			Mexico		Zacatecas		Jan. 15, 1833 Monterey	11 years and some months	1844			San Rafael, San Antonio, Santa Clara, and Soledad
VIADER, JOSE	Aug. 27, 1765	Gallines	Catalonia	Spain	Catalonia	San Fernando	June 26, 1795	June 18, 1796 S. Francisco	37 years and some months	Fall of 1833			Santa Clara
VINALS, JOSE	Aug. 14, 1759	Barcelona	Catalonia	Spain	Catalonia	San Fernando		May 8, 1798 S. Barbara	c. 6	1804			San Carlos
VITORIA, MARCOS ANTONIO*	1760	Vitoria	Calahorra	Spain	Cantabria	San Fernando	Aug. 1803	Aug. 31, 1805 S. Francisco	30 years 11 months		July 25, 1836	Santa Ines	Santa Barbara, San Buenaventura, San Fernando, Purisima, and Santa Ines
VIZCAINO, JUAN**	1728	Fromista	Palencia	Spain	Concepcion (Old Castile)	San Fernando	Dec. 8, 1749	Apr. 11, 1769 S. Diego	10 months	Feb. 11, 1770			San Diego
ZALVIDEA, JOSE MARIA	Mar. 2, 1780	Bilbao	Vizcaya	Spain	Cantabria	San Fernando	1804	Aug. 31, 1805 S. Francisco	40 years c. 5 months		Early in 1846	San Luis Rey	San Fernando, San Gabriel, San Juan Capistrano, and San Luis Rey

* Also known as Saizar de Vitoria y Odriozola, Marcos Antonio
** Also known as Gonzalez Vizcaino

293

Alférez: an ensign in the Spanish army.

Apostolic college: a Franciscan institution introduced into the New World in 1683 at Santa Cruz de Querétaro. San Fernando College, daughter of Santa Cruz, which sent most of the missionaries to California, was founded in 1734. These colleges were independent of Franciscan provincial rule. Their purpose was to receive and train an elite band of missionaries for the Indian missions and for the regeneration of Christians in civilized areas. Recruits for these apostolic colleges were obtained chiefly in Spain, but a number from various parts of America also entered them. The governing body of such a college comprised a guardian, a vicar, and counselors.

Apostolic visitation: a canonical inspection made within a diocese, religious province, or community by a person delegated thereto by Rome.

Asistencia: a sub-mission having resident, converted Indians, but no resident missionary. It was attended by a missionary from the nearest mission.

Canonical tour (*or* visitation): a formal visit to inspect places and to interview persons within canonical jurisdiction as prescribed by canon law for religious orders.

Chapter: in religious orders an official assembly appointed or elected to consider at the time of canonical visitation appointments and changes of personnel, matters of business, and the spiritual and temporal concerns of the members of a province or apostolic college.

College: *See* Apostolic college.

Commissary (*or* commissioner): a general name for an ecclesiastic appointed to carry out certain functions or duties such as that of commissary prefect, commissary general, commissary of the Holy Office, etc.

Commissary General of the Indies: a Franciscan residing in Madrid responsible for dealing with the royal court and with the Council of the Indies in all matters of personnel and administration relative to Franciscan activity in the Indies. The office was instituted in 1572.

Commissary of the Holy Office of the Inquisition: a priest, diocesan, or member of a religious order appointed by the Holy Office in Mexico City to guard the Catholic faith and morals within a given territory.

Commissary prefect: an office created for the administration of the Indies by the commissary general in Madrid, which eventually operated in California in 1812. This official relieved the president of the missions of some of his offices and duties. The office had general supervision over the missionaries of the mission district and dealt with the territorial government on mission matters.

Conciliar seminary *(seminario conciliar):* a diocesan seminary under the jurisdiction of a bishop.

Confessor: a priest authorized to hear confessions or administer the sacrament of Penance. When so authorized, he is said to "receive faculties" for that office. These faculties are given by a bishop for hearing confessions of the people of a diocese or by a provincial for hearing the confessions of members of the order to which he belongs.

Counselor: an elected adviser to a provincial within a Franciscan province or to a guardian in an apostolic college.

Custos: a vice-provincial in the Franciscan order who substituted for the provincial when the latter was absent or unable to perform the duties of his office.

Definitory: the body of rulers in a Franciscan province comprising a provincial, vice-provincial, and counselors. *See* Discretory.

Diputación: the elected assembly which met at Monterey during the Mexican regime in California.

Disaffiliation: the legal action by means of which one could be separated from the jurisdiction of a province or apostolic college.

Discretory *(discretorio):* an elected body of counselors who together with the guardian of an apostolic college conducted its business and religious affairs. In a province, a discretory served in the local friary. *See also* Definitory.

Ecclesiastical judge: an ecclesiastic with judicial powers, appointed by a bishop.

Ecclesiastical Synod: *See* Synod.

Encyclical letter (*or* circular letter): an official document sent to his subjects by a bishop or religious superior. The documents may deal with a variety of matters: faith, morals, liturgy, general Christian welfare, etc. Today the word is reserved almost exclusively for a papal document sent to the entire Catholic world.

Faculties: canonical powers, i.e., to preach and to hear confessions, given to priests by ecclesiastical superiors, bishops, or provincials.

Fanega: a dry measure of weight the equivalent of about 1.6 bushels.

Friar (from the Latin *frater* 'brother' and the Spanish *fraile*): a member of a religious order dedicated to serve outside his religious house in the ministry of the people, as distinct from a monk, who remains inside a monastery. This differentiation, in which the concept of stability applies to monks and mobility to friars, dates from the thirteenth century.

Friary: a religious house where friars live.

Gente de razón (literally people with reason): a term used by the Spaniards in the Indies to designate non-Indians.

Guardian: the elected superior in an apostolic college, serving usually for three years. In a province he was the elected superior in the more important religious houses but served under the jurisdiction of the provincial. *See also* Provincial.

Habit: the distinctive garb worn by members of a religious community or order. A person entering a religious order is clothed with the habit and is said to "receive the habit."

Hospice: a friary admitting guest friars en route to mission fields, chiefly located at Cádiz in Spain and Vera Cruz and Tepic in Mexico.

League: a standard Spanish measure of distance, 5,000 varas or 2.6 miles.

Minor orders: grades or ranks of ecclesiastical origin through which advance is made to the priesthood. In the Latin or Western Church these minor orders are porter, reader, exorcist, and acolyte.

Moralist: a student of moral theology or Christian ethics, preparing for priesthood.

296

Novitiate: a religious house where novices are received to be trained in the spirit and purpose of the order before taking vows therein.

Obedience: a formal document from a Franciscan superior to his subject, ordering a change of residence, commissioning him to perform a certain type of work, or to carry out a mission, by virtue of his vow of obedience — a term used in most religious orders.

Preacher: a priest who has received the faculties to preach. *See* Faculties.

President of the Missions: the chief religious official in the mission territory appointed by the rulers of the apostolic college of which he was a member. He was considered the field commander of the guardian and discretory of the apostolic college. From 1812 until the end of the mission period, his powers were somewhat curtailed by those of the commissary prefect. During that period, however, as representative of the bishop of Sonora, he outranked the commissary prefect. *See* Commissary prefect.

Procurator: a friar appointed to take care of business matters for a province, apostolic college, friary, or other institution. The procurator of San Fernando College purchased supplies for the California missions.

Profession: the act whereby a novice formally becomes a member of an order — takes his vows, promises to observe the constitutions, and to labor in the order according to the will of his superiors — referred to as "making one's profession."

Province: a geographical unit of the Franciscan order. *See also* Provincial.

Provincial: the chief official in a province of the Franciscan order, elected thereto in a chapter held at the end of a canonical visitation and conducted by a visitor-general from another area. The usual length of service was three years.

Rancheria: an Indian village.

Religious: a member of a religious order or congregation.

Synod (*or* council): an ecclesiastical assembly called together under hierarchical authority for the purpose of discussing and deciding matters of discipline and liturgy for the territory. A synod may be diocesan, metropolitan, national or universal.

Temporalities: nonreligious administration, as distinguished from spiritualities or spiritual administration, i.e., the feeding, clothing, and housing of the Indians; the development of agriculture and animal husbandry; the teaching of trades and skills in the arts; any form of economic, social, and cultural development.

Tonsure: a ceremony by means of which a layman enters the ecclesiastical state.

Triennial chapter: a convocation of appointed and elected friars under the jurisdiction of a visitor-general, in a province or apostolic college, at the end of a canonical visitation, for the purpose of appointing personnel, handling business matters, reforming abuses, and taking steps to strengthen the religious life of its members.

Vara: a measure of length equaling 2 feet, 9 inches.

Viaticum: Holy Communion given to the dying.

Vicar: the second in command at an apostolic college acting in the name of the guardian when the latter was absent or unable to function.

Vicar forane: a dean or an ecclesiastical official, appointed by a bishop, with limited jurisdiction over a portion of a diocese.

Vicar-General: a priest deputized to assist the bishop with ordinary jurisdiction of the entire diocese.

Vice-commissary prefect (vicar): a substitute for a commissary prefect when the latter is absent or unable to perform the duties of office.

Visita: See Asistencia.

Visitor-General: a friar appointed by the general of the order to conduct a formal visitation or inspection of a province or apostolic college and its personnel and to hold a canonical chapter. In the Hispanic period such designations were made by the commissary general of a large geographical area which included a number of provinces and colleges as in Mexico and Peru.

BIBLIOGRAPHY

It is not the purpose of this bibliography to list every document concerning the 142 missionaries described in the foregoing biographies but rather to point out the archives in which such original material may be obtained, the special sections of such archives that treat of strict biographical material, calendars and catalogs listing such material, and printed works and articles describing individual missionaries. Any other method would lead to a book as large as if not larger than this volume itself. As matters stand, even this general coverage serves to show how widely scattered the basic material is.

Large Depositories of Documents

Archdiocesan Archives, San Francisco, California.
Archivo de Indias, Seville, Spain.
Archivo General de la Nación, Mexico, D.F., Mexico.
Archives of the Propagation of the Faith, Rome, Italy.
Bancroft Library, Berkeley, California.
Biblioteca del Museo Nacional, Mexico, D.F., Mexico.
Biblioteca Nacional, Mexico, D.F., Mexico.
De la Guerra Papers, SBMA.
Franciscan Curia Archives, Rome, Italy.
Santa Barbara Mission Archives, Santa Barbara, California.
Santa Cruz de Querétaro Archives, Celaya, Mexico.
Registers of the Sierra Gorda missions and the Lower California missions (few in number and incomplete) and those of the twenty-one missions of Upper California scattered in various places either at the several missions or in the archives of the chanceries in which the missions are located.

Particular Documents Relating to Biographical Material

Libro de Decretos de el Colegio de el Señor San Fernando de Mexico (1734-1858). Archivo General de la Nación, Mexico, D.F.
List of religious belonging to San Fernando College, Mexico City, September 9, 1772. Biblioteca del Museo Nacional, Mexico, D.F.
Listas de Misioneros en California. Santa Barbara Mission Archives.
Diaries of Missionaries. Santa Barbara Mission Archives.
Missión de Sn. Franco. para el Collegio de Sn. Fernando de Mexico [Cádiz], Año de 1749. No. 5546, Contratación, Segunda serie. Archivo de Indias.
Santa Barbara Mission Archives. Biographical *Informe* by V. F. de Sarría, Carmelo, [Calif.], November 5, 1817. Biographical *Informe* by Mariano Payeras, Soledad, [Calif.], December 31, 1820.
Volumes in the Archivo General de la Nación, Mexico, D.F., with detailed biographical materials, principally *reseñas:*
  Bienes Nacionales, Legajo 1008.
  Californias. Vols. XLI, XLVIII, LI, LIX, LXI.
  Clero Regular. Vols. LV, CCXIII.
  Historia. Vol. LXIII.
  Marina. Vol. XXXV.
  Misiones. Vols. IV, VIII, IX, XV, XIX, XX.
  Provincias Internas. Vol. V.

Bolton, Herbert E. *Guide to Materials for the History of the United States in the Principal Archives of Mexico.* Washington, D.C., 1913.

Chapman, Charles E. *Catalogue of Materials in the Archivo General de Indias for the History of the Pacific Coast and the American Southwest.* Berkeley, 1919.

Geiger, Maynard, O.F.M. *Calendar of Documents in the Santa Barbara Mission Archives.* Washington, D.C., 1947. There is a one-hundred-page typewritten supplement to this containing a list of documents obtained since 1947.

Arricivita, Juan Domingo, O.F.M. *Crónica Seráfica y Apostólica del Colegio de Propaganda Fide de la Santa Cruz de Querétaro.* Mexico, 1792.

Arroyo de la Cuesta, Felipe, O.F.M. *Vocabulary and Phrase Book of the Mutsun Language of Mission San Juan Bautista,* ed. J. G. Shea. New York, 1861.

Bancroft, H. H. *History of California.* 7 vols. San Francisco, 1886-1890.

Bolton, Herbert E. *Anza's California Expeditions.* 5 vols. Berkeley, 1930.

————. *Fray Juan Crespí Missionary Explorer ... 1769-1774.* Berkeley, 1927.

Boscana, Gerónimo. *A New Original Version of Boscana's Historical Account of the San Juan Capistrano Indians of Southern California,* tr. John P. Harrington. *Smithsonian Miscellaneous Collections,* XCII, No. 4. Washington, D.C., 1934.

Chapman, C. E. *A History of California. The Spanish Period.* New York, 1921. Useful for a contrasting study of Junípero Serra and Fermín Francisco de Lasuén.

Colegio de San Fernando 1735-1897. No. 3. Mexico.

Cutter, Donald C. *Malaspina in California.* [San Francisco, 1960]. Deals with Lasuén and Tomás de la Peña with regard to particular incidents.

Dakin, Susanna Bryant. *A Scotch Paisano. Life of Hugo Reid in California.* Berkeley, 1939. Contains material on Tomás Esténaga, José Bernardo Sánchez, and José María Zalvidea of Mission San Gabriel.

Da Silva, Owen, O.F.M. *Mission Music of California.* Santa Barbara, 1941. Material on the padre musicians of California with emphasis on Narciso Durán.

Davis, Carlyle, and William Alderson. *The True Story of "Ramona."* New York, [cop. 1914]. Data on Francisco Sánchez.

Davis, William Heath. *Seventy-Five Years in California.* San Francisco, 1929. Data on Friars Miguel Muro, Vásquez del Mercado and José María de Jesús González Rubio.

Duflot de Mofras, Eugène. *Exploration du Territoire de L'Oregon des Californies et de la Mer Vermeille.* 2 vols. Paris, 1844. Accounts of various padres he met while visiting the missions.

Duhaut-Cilly, Auguste. *Voyage Autour du Monde.* Paris, 1834. Its California aspects were translated by Charles Franklin Carter. *See* Articles.

Durán, Narciso. *Expedition on the Sacramento and San Joaquin Rivers in 1817,* tr. C. E. Chapman. *Publications of the Academy of Pacific Coast History,* II, No. 5. Berkeley, 1911.

Engelhardt, Zephyrin, O.F.M. *The Franciscans in Arizona.* Harbor Springs, Mich., 1899.

―――. *The Franciscans in California.* Harbor Springs, Mich., 1897.

―――. *The Holy Man of Santa Clara or Life, Virtues and Miracles of Fr. Magin Catalá, O.F.M.* San Francisco, 1909.

―――. . . . *Mission La Concepcion Purisima.* Santa Barbara, 1932. Biographies of Francisco Arroíta, Mariano Payeras, and a list of the missionaries who functioned there between 1797 and 1844.

―――. . . . *Mission Nuestra Senora de la Soledad.* Santa Barbara, 1929. Biographies of Mariano Rubí, Bartolomé Gilí, Florencio Ibáñez, Vicente Francisco de Sarría, and a list of missionaries who functioned at Soledad between 1791 and 1840.

―――. . . . *Mission San Carlos Borromeo.* Santa Barbara, 1934. Data on Junípero Serra, Juan Crespí, Francisco Palóu, Julián López, Fermín Francisco de Lasuén, resident presidents, and a list of missionaries who labored there between 1770 and 1846.

―――. . . . *Mission San Diego.* San Francisco, 1920. Biographies of Francisco Gómez, Juan Vizcaíno, Luís Jayme, Juan Figuer, Juan Antonio García Riobó, Juan Mariner, Hilario Torrent, José Panella, Nicolás Lázaro, José Pedro Panto, Fernando Martín, together with a list of all the missionaries who ministered there between 1769 and 1846.

―――. . . . *Mission San Juan Bautista.* Santa Barbara, 1931. Biographies of Andrés Dulanto, Estevan Tapis, and Felipe Arroyo de la Cuesta, together with a list of missionaries at the mission between 1797 and 1854.

―――. . . . *Mission San Luis Obispo.* Santa Barbara, 1933. Biographies of Juan Prestamero, José Cavaller, Domingo Juncosa, Antonio Rodríguez, Luís Martínez, Luís Gil y Taboada, and a list of missionaries who labored there between 1772 and 1841.

―――. . . . *Mission Santa Ines, Virgen y Martir.* Santa Barbara, 1932. Biographies of José Calzada, Marcos Antonio de Vitoria, Felipe Arroyo de la Cuesta, Ramón Abella, Juan Moreno, and a list of missionaries who labored there between 1804 and 1850.

―――. *The Missions and Missionaries of California.* 4 vols. and index. San Francisco, 1908-1915.

―――. . . . *San Antonio de Padua, the Mission in the Sierras.* Santa Barbara, 1929. Biographies of Miguel Pieras, Francisco Pujol, Buenaventura Sitjar, Juan Bautista Sancho, and a list of missionaries who officiated at the mission between 1771 and 1840.

―――. . . . *San Buenaventura, the Mission by the Sea.* Santa Barbara, 1930. Biographies of Vicente de Santa María, José Señán, José Altimira, Francisco Suñer, Francisco Xavier Uría, Buenaventura Fortuny, and a list of missionaries who officiated at the mission between 1782 and 1853.

―――. . . . *San Fernando Rey.* Chicago, 1927. Biographies of José Antonio Uría, Martín de Landaeta, José Antonio Urrestí, José de Miguel, Pedro Múñoz, Pedro Cabot, Tomás Esténaga, and a list of missionaries who officiated at the mission between 1797 and 1847.

―――. *San Francisco or Mission Dolores.* Chicago, 1924. Biographies of Francisco Palóu, Pedro Benito Cambón, Diego García, Juan Sainz de Lucio, José María Fernández, José de la Cruz Espí, Antonio Dantí, and a list of the missionaries who officiated there between 1776 and 1845.

―――. *San Gabriel Mission.* San Gabriel, 1927. Biographies of Ángel Somera, Pedro de San José Estevan, Cristóbal Oramas, Isidro Barcenilla, Miguel Sánchez, Antonio Cruzado, Francisco Dumetz, José de Miguel, Román Francisco Fernández de Ulibarri, Joaquín Pascual Nuez, Gerónimo Boscana,

José Bernardo Sánchez, Tomás Esténaga, Blas Ordaz, and a list of missionaries who labored at San Gabriel between 1771 and 1852.

———. *San Juan Capistrano Mission.* Los Angeles, 1922. Biographies of Gregorio Amurrió, Pablo Mugártegui, Vicente Fuster, José Faura, Juan José Norberto de Santiago, José Barona, Vicente Pascual Oliva, and a list of missionaries who served at the mission between 1775 and 1850.

———. *...San Luis Rey Mission.* San Francisco, 1921. Biographies of José García, Domingo Carranza, Jayme Escudé, Antonio Peyrí, Francisco González de Ibarra, José María Zalvidea, and a list of all the missionaries who officiated at San Luis Rey between 1798 and 1846.

———. *San Miguel, Arcangel.* Santa Barbara, 1929. Biographies of Pedro Adriano Martínez, Juan Martín, Marcelino Ciprés, Juan Cabot, and a list of missionaries who labored at San Miguel between 1797 and 1841.

———. *...Santa Barbara Mission.* San Francisco, 1923. Biographies of Antonio Paterna, Andrés Dulanto, Juan Lope Cortés, Antonio Jayme, Antonio Ripoll, Francisco Xavier Uría, Buenaventura Fortuny, Francisco García Diego y Moreno, Narciso Durán, José Joaquín Jimeno, Antonio Jimeno, José María de Jesús González Rubio, and Francisco Sánchez, together with a complete list of the missionaries who officiated there between 1782 and 1884.

Font Obrador, Bartolomé. *El Padre Boscana Historiador de California.* Palma, 1966.

Garcés, Francisco Tomás Hermenegildo. *On the Trail of a Spanish Pioneer,* tr. and ed. Elliott Coues. 2 vols. New York, 1900.

Geiger, Maynard, O.F.M. *The Life and Times of Fray Junípero Serra.* 2 vols. Washington, D.C., 1959. The bibliography, pp. 405-484, has valuable biographical material.

———. *Mission Santa Barbara (1782-1965).* Santa Barbara, 1965.

Habig, Marion Alphonse, O.F.M. *The Alamo Chain of Missions.* Chicago, 1968.

Ibáñez, Florencio, O.F.M. *Los Pastores< The Shepherds> ...,* tr. María López de Lowther. Hollywood, Calif., [195-?]. This book also contains a facsimile of Ibáñez' original Spanish.

Janssens, Victor Eugene August. *The Life and Adventures in California of Don Agustín Janssens, 1834-1856,* ed. W. Ellison and F. Price. San Marino, Calif., 1953.

Landaeta, Martín de. *Noticias acerca del Puerto de San Francisco (Alta California),* ed. J. C. Valadéz. Mexico, 1949.

Langsdorff, Georg H. von. *Langsdorff's Narrative of the Rezanov Voyage to Nueva California in 1806,* ed. Thomas C. Russell. San Francisco, 1927.

Lasuén, Fermín Francisco de. *Writings ...,* tr. Finbar Kenneally, O.F.M. 2 vols. Washington, D.C., 1965. Contains abundant material on the friars who labored in California under Lasuén between 1785 and 1803, particularly with regard to changes in personnel, personal characteristics, physical and mental handicaps.

Lamadrid Jiménez, Lázaro, O.F.M. *El Alavés Fray Fermín Francisco de Lasuén (1736-1803) Fundador de Misiones en California.* 2 vols. Alava, 1963.

McCarthy, Francis. *The History of Mission San Jose, California, 1797-1835.* Fresno, Calif., 1958.

Omaechevarria, Ignacio, O.F.M. *Fray Pablo de Mugártegui en su Marco Social y Misionero.* Bilbao, 1959.

Ord, Angustias de la Guerra. *Occurrences in Hispanic California,* tr. Francis Price and W. H. Ellison. Washington, D.C., 1956. This author treats of thirty-eight of the California missionaries, many of whom she personally knew and was contemporary to between 1815 and the end of the Mexican period. She characterized a number of their personalities.

Palacio y Basave, Luis del Refugio de. *Historia Breve . . . de Zapopán.* Guadalajara, 1925.

Palóu, Francisco, O.F.M. *Historical Memoirs of New California,* tr. and ed. Herbert E. Bolton. 4 vols. Berkeley, 1926.

————. *Palóu's Life of Fray Junípero Serra,* tr. and ed. Maynard J. Geiger, O.F.M. Washington, D.C., 1945. The notes in particular (pp. 309-497) contain many biographical references.

————. *Relación histórica de la Vida y Apostólicas Tareas del Venerable Padre Fray Junípero Serra.* Mexico, 1787.

Pattie, James O. *The Personal Narrative of. . . .* Philadelphia, 1962.

Priestley, Herbert Ingram. *Franciscan Explorations in California,* ed. L. A. Fisher. Glendale, 1946.

Robinson, Alfred. *Life in California.* San Francisco, 1891. Robinson, related by marriage to the De la Guerra family, was a merchant who traveled through the California mission territory a number of times. He described twenty of the California missionaries with whom he had mercantile and social relations, starting in 1829.

Salazar, Buenaventura, O.F.M. *Misioneros de California.* Bilbao, 1935.

Sanahuja, Pedro, O.F.M. *Historia de la Seráfica Provincia de Cataluña.* Barcelona, 1959.

————. *Vida del P. Magín Catalá.* Barcelona, 1924.

Señán, José Francisco de Paula. *The Letters of . . . ,* tr. P. A. Nathan and L. B. Simpson. San Francisco, 1962.

————. *The Ventureño Confesionario,* ed. Madison S. Beeler. Berkeley, 1967. (University of California Publications in Linguistics, XLVII.)

Serra, Junípero, O.F.M. *Writings,* ed. Antonine Tibesar, O.F.M. 4 vols. Washington, D.C., 1955, 1966. Contains valuable information on the friars who labored under Serra between 1769 and 1784.

Sitjar, Buenaventura. *Vocabulario de la Lengua de los Naturales de la Mision de San Antonio, Alta California,* ed. J. G. Shea. New York, 1861. (Shea's Library of American Linguistics.) Concerns the linguistic efforts of Sitjar.

Sotomayor, J. F. *Historia del Apostólico Colegio de Nuestra Señora de Guadalupe de Zacatecas.* Zacatecas, 1874.

Spearman, Arthur D., S. J. *The Five Franciscan Churches of Mission Santa Clara.* Palo Alto, 1963.

Thompson, Joseph, O.F.M. *El Gran Capitan, José de la Guerra.* Los Angeles, 1961.

Torchiana, H. A. *Story of the Mission Santa Cruz.* San Francisco, 1933.

Vancouver, George. *Vancouver in California,* ed. Marguerite Eyer Wilbur. 3 vols. in 1. Los Angeles, 1954. ("Early California Travel Series," Nos. 9, 10, and 22.)

Weber, Francis J. *A Biographical Sketch of the Right Reverend Francisco García Diego y Moreno, First Bishop of the Californias, 1785-1846.* Los Angeles, 1961.

————. *Documents of California Catholic History.* Los Angeles, 1965.

White, Michael C. *California All the Way Back to 1828.* . . . , ed. Glen Dawson. Los Angeles, 1956. Has material on Zalvidea, José Bernardo Sánchez, Miguel Sánchez, and Durán.

ARTICLES

Abad, Antolín, O.F.M., ed. "Registro de los franciscanos Misioneros del Puerto de Santa María (1803-1868)." *Archivo Ibero-Americano,* CIV (Madrid, 1966), 297-364.

El Clamor Público, Los Angeles, Calif., February 9, 1856. Eyewitness account of the "benevolent kidnapping" of Fray José María de Jesús González Rubio.

Duhaut-Cilly, Auguste. "Duhaut-Cilly's Account of California in the Years 1827-1828," tr. Charles Franklin Carter. *California Historical Society Quarterly,* VIII, Nos. 2-4 (1929), 130-166, 214-250, 306-336.

Geiger, Maynard, O.F.M. "The Apostolic College of Our Lady of Sorrows, Santa Barbara, California (1853-1885)." *Provincial Annals* (Santa Barbara, 1948-57), II, No. 2-XIX, No. 3. Deals with biographical material of José María de Jesús González Rubio, Francisco Sánchez, J. J. Jimeno, and A. Jimeno.

———. "Biographical Data on the California Missionaries (1769-1848)." *The California Historical Society Quarterly,* XLIV, No. 4 (1965), 291-309.

———. "Dates of Palóu's Death and Lasuén's Birth Determined." *The California Historical Society Quarterly,* XXVIII, No. 1 (1949), 19-22.

———. "The Franciscan 'Mission' to San Fernando College, Mexico, 1749." *The Americas,* V, No. 1 (1948), 48-60. Biographical data on thirty-three Franciscans who came to Mexico in 1749-1750, a number of whom later served the missions in California.

———. "Important California Missionary Dates Determined." *The Americas,* IV, No. 3 (1948), 287-293.

———. "Important Dates on Fathers Palóu and Lasuén Found." *Provincial Annals,* VIII, No. 2 (Santa Barbara, 1946), 29-30.

———. "The Internal Organization and Activities of San Fernando College, Mexico (1734-1858)." *The Americas,* VI, No. 1 (1949), 3-31. Contains biographical data on 114 friars belonging to San Fernando College in 1772 and on others between 1734 and 1858, including the offices they held in Mexico.

———. "Junípero Serra, O.F.M., in the Light of Chronology and Geography (1713-1784)." *The Americas,* VI, No. 3 (1950), 291-333.

———. "The Mallorcan Contribution to Franciscan California." *The Americas,* IV, No. 2 (1947), 141-150. Treats of the sixteen Mallorcan missionaries who served in California.

———. "The Scholastic Career and Preaching Apostolate of Fray Junípero Serra, O.F.M., S.T.D. (1730-1749)." *The Americas,* IV, No. 1 (1947), 65-82.

———. "Where Is Serra Buried?" *Provincial Annals* (Santa Barbara, 1960-64), XXIII, No. 2-XXVI, No. 1.

Guest, Florian, O.F.M. "The Indian Policy under Fermín Francisco de Lasuén, California's Second Father President." *The California Historical Society Quarterly,* XLVI (1966), 195-224.

Pazos, Manuel, O.F.M. "El V. P. Fr. Juan Antonio Joaquín de Barreneche, martirizado por los indios Yumas del Río Colorado el 19 de julio de 1781." *Archivo Ibero-Americano,* N.S., IV (Madrid, 1941), 455-473.

Pérez, Eulalia. "Keeper of the Keys. The Recollections of Senora Eulalia Perez . . . ," tr. Nellie Van de Grift Sanchez. *Touring Topics,* XXI, No. 1 (Los Angeles, 1929), 24-27, 52.